Physical Activity and Sport
for the
Secondary School Student

Neil J. Dougherty IV, Editor
Rutgers University

Sponsored by the
National Association for
Sport and Physical Education

an association of the

American Alliance for Health, Physical Education,
Recreation and Dance

The American Alliance for Health, Physical Education, Recreation and Dance is an educational organization designed to support, encourage, and provide assistance to member groups and their personnel nation-wide as they initiate, develop, and conduct programs in health, leisure, and movement-related activities. The Alliance seeks to:

- Encourage, guide, and support professional growth and development in health, leisure, and movement-related programs based on individual needs, interests, and capabilities.

- Communicate the importance of health, leisure, and movement-related activities as they contribute to human well-being.

- Encourage and facilitate research which will enrich health, leisure, and movement-related activities and to disseminate the findings to professionals and the public.

- Develop and evaluate standards and guidelines for personnel and programs in health, leisure, and movement-related activities.

- Coordinate and administer a planned program of professional, public, and government relations that will improve education in areas of health, leisure, and movement-related activities.

- To conduct other activities for the public benefit.

Foreword

Physical education and sports, like other educational programs, have been undergoing continual revision. In response to developments in the field, the Middle and Secondary School Physical Education Council, a structure of the National Association for Sport and Physical Education, has updated and completely revised the popular book, *Physical Education and Sport for the Secondary School Student.*

The earlier editions and now the fourth edition have been the culmination of efforts of many concerned professionals who saw a need to provide the secondary school teachers and students with a comprehensive and authoritative textbook on contemporary physical activities and sports concepts. This fourth edition carries a new title, *Physical Activity and Sport for the Secondary School Student.* The book is designed to provide the student with an overview of sports, information on skill and technique acquisition, safety, scoring, rules and etiquette, strategies, equipment, and related terminology. In addition, several new chapters have been included to keep pace with the trends in present-day program offerings.

It is the intention of the National Association for Sport and Physical Education that this book will assist the student and physical education teacher in selecting and developing a well-balanced program of activities which today's youth can value throughout their lifetime.

This book should be used in conjunction with an awareness and understanding of the definition of "The Physically Educated Student" and *Outcomes of Quality Physical Education Programs.* This brochure and booklet are available from the American Alliance for Health, Physical Education, Recreation and Dance. These materials provide the framework on which teachers develop physical education programs that will enhance the ability of all students to pursue active lifestyles throughout their lives.

JUDY YOUNG, Executive Director
National Association for
Sport and Physical Education

Contents

**Physical Activity and Sport
for the Secondary School Student
Editorial Committee**

Neil J. Dougherty IV
Rutgers University
New Brunswick, NJ

Patricia Barry
Montgomery County Public Schools
Rockville, MD

Diana Bonanno
Rutgers University
New Brunswick, NJ

CHAPTER 1

Health Fitness

RUSSELL R. PATE
University of South Carolina
Columbia, SC

INTRODUCTION

A basic characteristic of all animal life is the capacity for independent movement. Though styles of movement vary greatly within the animal kingdom, the motivations for movement are essentially the same in animals ranging from the one-celled protozoa to the higher order mammals. All animals, regardless of size and structural complexity, must move through their environment to find food, seek shelter, and to escape or defend against enemies. It is no exaggeration to say that, for animals, movement is the basis of life.

The human being, *Homo Sapiens*, is a perfect example of an animal species whose survival has depended on the ability to move effectively. Through most of their two million years on earth, humans have lived as hunters and gatherers. The food supply, consisting mainly of wild animals, and naturally grown vegetables, was secured through the use of physical abilities such as endurance, strength, and speed. For early humans, a new physical fitness test was presented daily and the prize was a valuable one—survival!

Today, machines do much of the physical labor which humans used to do by hand. Indeed, the typical American of today is employed in a job which presents little or no physical challenge. Most Americans use automobiles for transportation, employ numerous "labor-saving devices" in their occupations, and even use machines to reduce the physical effort of leisure time activities. Thus, modern people, if they choose, can lead a life almost totally devoid of vigorous physical activity. Some authorities have suggested, partly in jest, that the species name should be changed to *Homo Sedentarius*!

The many technological advances of the past century have resulted in an enhanced standard of living for most Americans. However, oddly enough, the life span of the typical American has increased only marginally since 1900. As indicated in Table 1, in 1900 the typical adult at age 20 could expect to live for another 42.8 years, while in 1986 the average 20-year-old was expected to live another 56.2 years. It cannot be denied that numerous medical breakthroughs have occurred since 1900. However, most of these advances have contributed to treatment and prevention of infectious diseases such as smallpox, pneumonia, and tuberculosis. To date, medical science has not been successful in preventing chronic diseases such as coronary heart disease, stroke, and cancer. Today most Americans die, not from the infectious diseases which killed their grandparents and great-grandparents, but from chronic diseases and accidents (see Table 2). It is perhaps ironic that modern technology, which has contributed so much to our standard of living, has apparently brought with it a series of health risks for which science has yet to provide solutions.

Table 1. Life expectancy of Americans: 1900–1986

Remaining Life Expectancy in Years

Year	At birth	At 20 years	At 65 years
1900	47.3	42.8	11.9
1950	68.2	51.3	13.0
1960	69.7	52.4	14.3
1976	72.8	54.6	16.0
1986	74.8	56.2	16.8

Source: U.S. Bureau of the Census, *Statistical Abstract of the United States: 1990* (110th edition). Washington, D.C., 1990.

Table 2. Leading causes of death in 1990 and 1987 (deaths per 100,000 population)

	1900	1987		1900	1987
1.	Pneumonia and influenza (202)	Diseases of heart (312)	6.	Kidney diseases (89)	Pneumonia and influenza (28)
2.	Tuberculosis (194)	Cancer (196)	7.	Accidents (72)	Diabetes (16)
3.	Intestinal diseases (143)	Stroke (62)	8.	Cancer (64)	Suicide (13)
4.	Diseases of the heart (137)	Accidents (39)	9.	Senility (50)	Chronic liver disease and cirrhosis of liver (11)
5.	Intracranial lesions (107)	Chronic obstructive pulmonary diseases (32)	10.	Diphtheria (40)	Kidney diseases (9)

Source: National Center for Health Statistics. *Prevention profile. Health, United States, 1989.* Hyattsville, Maryland: Public Health Service 1990.

Mounting evidence suggests that an inactive lifestyle, made possible by modern technology, is a direct contributor to many chronic diseases. Indeed, health professionals have coined a new term, hypokinesis, to describe a style of living characterized by lack of physical exercise. The so-called hypokinetic diseases are those which occur more frequently in sedentary persons than in persons who maintain high levels of physical activity. Often listed among the hypokinetic diseases are coronary heart disease, obesity, diabetes, high blood pressure, and low back pain. Clearly, industrialization and modern technology have left Americans vulnerable to a deadly set of health risks. The health challenge of the last decade of the 20th century is to conquer these diseases of affluence. Thus, the purposes of this chapter are: to discuss the relationship between exercise habits and health; to describe the specific components of physical fitness which, if maintained at a high level, can help prevent hypokinetic diseases and enhance the quality of life.

CONCEPTS OF HEALTH AND FITNESS

DEFINITIONS OF HEALTH

Twentieth century Americans are fortunate to live in a society which provides them with a considerable degree of security. The great affluence of today's society has liberated them from the day-to-day struggle for survival and has permitted them to strive for higher levels of human existence. Today it is common to ponder over the "quality of life."

Certainly, good health maintenance is an essential component of a high quality of life. In the absence of good health, it is impossible to enjoy the other benefits of an economically and culturally wealthy society. Since health is such a key aspect of the quality of life, it is not surprising that modern America has made a massive investment in health care and health promotion. America's health consciousness is evident at every turn.

In 1988, for instance Americans spent $539.9 billion on health care, an increase of 10.4% from the previous year. This figure represents 11.1% of the gross national product (total output of goods and services).

Diseases—Treatment and Prevention

While 20th century Americans may be paying more for health services than any previous society, their basic approach to health care is neither unique nor new. Most organized health activities have been and continue to be disease-oriented. Persons have considered themselves healthy if they have not suffered from the symptoms of some ailment or illness. Indeed, health has often been defined as a state of being free from disease or pain.

Traditionally, most professional health care has been designed to provide treatment for existing disease conditions. The earliest physicians spent most of their time attempting to cure or reduce the symptoms of illnesses, the causes of which were virtually unknown. Today, a much greater understanding of the causes of disease is had and treatment procedures have become highly sophisticated. Still, most health care professionals are primarily trained to help sick people become well again.

Nobody can argue with the need to provide health care for the sick and disabled. However, the inadequacies of a health care system which deals narrowly with treatment of disease while overlooking the benefits of disease *prevention* are being rapidly recognized. Among the weaknesses of a treatment-oriented health system are: no adequate treatments exist for many diseases (for example, no emergency care facilities can help a person who experiences a sudden lethal heart attack); many diseases, even if treated, leave permanent disabilities; most diseases involve painful or irritating symptoms which reduce the afflicted person's functional capacity; cost of medical treatment can be massive.

Today, health planners are beginning to place greater emphasis on prevention of disease. A prevention-oriented approach to health maintenance has the potential to minimize the above-mentioned problems. Since 1900 notable successes with the infectious diseases have been recognized, many of which now can be prevented through inoculations. However, there is yet to be success in preventing the chronic diseases which are now the most common causes of death. Since the chronic diseases are often caused by societal and personal lifestyle characteristics (e.g., cigarette smoking, sedentary living, industrial pollution), prevention of these diseases will depend on changing human behavior. Some of those changes, undoubtedly, will be difficult to achieve. However, such changes are possible, and they are necessary if further significant improvement in the health of the population is to be achieved.

Wellness

Relatively new to the field of public health is the concept of wellness. Wellness might be defined as a state of physical, mental, emotional, and spiritual health consistent with optimal human function. The wellness philosophy is based on the assumption that improvement of health variables, above the level needed to avoid disease, enhances quality of life. The wellness trend is an important one in contemporary America and suggests that the traditional definition of health, i.e., absence of disease, is no longer adequate. Thus, a more current and comprehensive definition of health might be a state of body, mind, and spirit characterized by absence of illness *and* by a level of vigor which permits fulfillment of human potential.

DEFINITIONS OF PHYSICAL FITNESS

The term physical fitness is familiar to almost everyone. Surveys indicate that the typical American appreciates physical fitness, considers exercise to be a good health habit, and understands that one's physical fitness is related to his/her exercise habits. *Nonetheless, many Americans fail to exercise regularly enough to maintain adequate physical fitness and many others use exercise improperly and consequently fail to achieve the potential benefits of good physical fitness.* These deficiencies suggest that many persons do not have a clear understanding of what physical fitness is and how it can be attained. To correct this problem it is important to develop a clear definition of physical fitness.

Over the years, many definitions of physical fitness have been proposed. One widely accepted definition suggests that physical fitness is the ability to perform daily tasks with vigor and alertness, without undue fatigue, and with ample energy to enjoy leisure-time pursuits and to meet unforeseen emergencies. It is important to note that this definition indicates that fitness is something which pertains to everyday lives. Physical fitness is not to be equated simply with performance on certain physical fitness tests. Rather, the ultimate test of physical fitness is the ability to meet, efficiently and effectively, the physical demands of daily life. Also, this definition of physical fitness implies that fitness is a matter of concern for everyone. Since

Table 3. Definitions of physical fitness components.

Agility—Speed in changing direction or in changing body positions.
Balance—Maintenance of a stable body position.
Body Composition—Fatness, ratio of fat weight to total body weight.
Cardiorespiratory Endurance—Ability to sustain moderate intensity, whole body activity for extended time periods.
Flexibility—Range of motion in a joint or series of joints.
Muscular Endurance—Ability to perform repeated, high intensity muscle contraction.
Muscular Strength—Maximum force applied with a single muscle contraction.
Power—Maximum rate of force generation and work performance.

everybody encounters physical demands, everybody needs to maintain an adequate level of physical fitness.

In studying physical abilities, researchers have identified several components of physical fitness. These components, which are listed and defined in Table 3, combine to determine an individual's overall physical performance capacity. As depicted in Diagram 1, all of the physical fitness components can be important in the realm of athletics; however, only a few of the fitness components are known to be related to health. These latter components contribute to health-related physical fitness which is a state characterized by: ability to perform daily tasks with vigor and without undue fatigue; demonstration of physical traits

Athletic Fitness
{
Agility
Power
Cardiorespiratory Endurance
Muscular Strength/Endurance
Body Composition
Flexibility
Speed
Balance
}
Health-Related Physical Fitness

Diagram 1. Components of athletic fitness and health-related physical fitness.

associated with minimal risk of developing hypokinetic disease. The following sections of this chapter provide a discussion of the health-related fitness components which should be of concern to everyone.

RELATIONSHIPS BETWEEN PHYSICAL FITNESS AND HEALTH

Throughout much of recorded history, humans have recognized physical fitness as a key component of a healthy lifestyle. The ancient Greeks were perhaps the first to actively promote exercise as a contributor to good health. Their philosophy, embodied in the Latin phrase *mens sano in corpore sane* (a sound mind in a sound body), has survived through the ages and today provides a philosophical basis for many health fitness programs. Today it is clear that regular exercise can contribute to good health by reducing the risk of developing certain diseases and by improving the body's ability to function, which in turn contributes to wellness and the quality of life. Developing a clear understanding of the values of physical fitness requires consideration of how health can be affected by regular exercise.

EXERCISE AND DISEASE PREVENTION

Evidence indicates that individuals who exercise properly are less likely than inactive persons to develop three specific health problems: coronary heart disease; obesity; low back pain. All of these diseases are widespread in modern America and have become more prominent as our population has become more inactive.

Coronary Heart Disease
Diseases of the cardiovascular system, i.e., the heart and blood vessels, are responsible for roughly one-half of all deaths in the United States each year. Most of these cardiovascular disease deaths are due to a disease process called atherosclerosis. Atherosclerosis involves the buildup of fatty deposits, called plaque, on the inner wall of the arteries. Arteries are blood vessels which carry oxygenated blood to all the body's tissues. If these vessels become clogged with plaque, blood flow and oxygen delivery to vital tissues can be impaired or completely shut off. If the

arteries affected by atherosclerosis are those which carry blood to the heart muscle the result can be coronary heart disease and, eventually, a heart attack.

The causes of coronary heart disease are not fully understood. However, several coronary heart disease risk factors have been identified. These risk factors are characteristics which, if present, tend to increase a person's chances of developing the disease. The primary and secondary coronary heart disease risk factors are listed in Table 4. It is important to note that physical inactivity is now considered to be a risk factor for coronary heart disease.

Table 4. Coronary heart disease risk factors.

Primary Risk Factors

Elevated Serum Cholesterol
High Blood Pressure
Cigarette Smoking

Secondary Risk Factors

Obesity
Physical Inactivity
Psychological Stress
Diabetes

It is well-established that physically active persons are less likely than sedentary persons to develop heart disease. This inverse relationship between physical activity and heart disease was first identified by researchers who found that persons who held physically active jobs were less likely to develop heart disease than those who had sedentary occupations. It has since been determined that those who regularly engage in leisure-time physical activity are also at lower risk for the development of heart disease. Even when other heart disease risk factors such as smoking, blood pressure, cholesterol levels, and family history are taken into account, the association between regular physical activity and a lowered heart disease risk remains. (See Table 5.)

The mechanisms behind this relationship are not fully understood. However, many studies have shown that an increase in physical activity produces beneficial changes in cardiovascular health compo-

Table 5. Coronary heart disease risk factors in high and low fit adult men.*

Risk Factor	Low Fit	High Fit
Cholesterol (mg%)	237	217
Diastolic Blood Pressure (mm Hg)	86	80
Serum Glucose (mg%)	112	102
Triglycerides (mg%)	179	87
% Body Fat	29	18

*Cooper, K. H., Pollock, M. L., Martin, R. P., et al. "Physical Fitness Levels vs. Selected Coronary Risk Factors. *JAMA* 236:166-9."

nents. Table 6 outlines the type of changes that are typically seen in previously sedentary individuals after 12 or more weeks of exercise training. The level of exercise intensity required to produce these changes has not been precisely identified but it appears that even low-intensity exercise, when performed regularly, can have a dramatic effect on cardiovascular health. A recent study that examined the relationship between cardiovascular fitness and premature death from cardiovascular disease found that persons of only average fitness had a much lower risk than the least-fit persons. Thus, it appears that even a modest dose of regular physical activity provides a significant health benefit.

Obesity

Excessive body fatness, or obesity, is extremely common in the American popu-

Table 6. Effects of exercise training which may reduce coronary heart disease risk

Increased levels of high density lipoprotein cholesterol (HDL-C, the "good" cholesterol)
Improved ability to transport oxygen through body
Improved efficiency of heart function
Improved tolerance to stress
Increased capacity to break down blood clots
Improved glucose tolerance
Improved body composition
—decrease in fat weight
—increase in lean weight
Decreased arterial blood pressure

lation and is a major cause of ill health. Obese persons are much more likely than persons of normal body fatness to develop diseases such as diabetes and high blood pressure. Also, obesity itself has been established as a risk factor for coronary heart disease.

Obesity is the result of excessive storage of fat in the body's tissues. This storage of fat occurs whenever an individual consumes more calories in food than are expended during daily activities. Obesity can result from overeating and other poor dietary practices. In addition, however, obesity is often caused by physical inactivity.

Obesity is rarely observed in individuals who are very physically active. Persons who continue to exercise regularly throughout adulthood tend to stay in caloric balance and to avoid the gradual addition of body fat which can lead to obesity. An increase in physical activity almost always causes a reduction in body fatness in persons who are moderately or severely obese.

Low Back Pain

One of the most common ailments observed in adult Americans is low back pain. Chronic pain in the low back region can be caused by numerous factors including traumatic injury and genetic malformation of the spine. However, very frequently low back pain results from a condition called lordosis which develops gradually over several years. Lordosis, sometimes referred to as "sway back," is an exaggerated curvature in the lower spine (see Figure 1), frequently developing from lack of proper exercise.

Lordosis and the low back pain it causes are related to two fitness deficiencies: weakness in the abdominal muscles; tightness (shortening) of the low back and hamstring

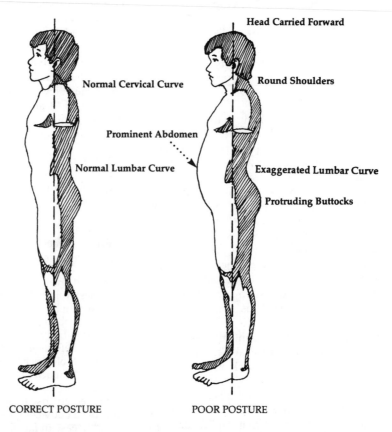

CORRECT POSTURE POOR POSTURE

Figure 1. Lordosis, shown on the right, can contribute to low back pain.

muscles (see Figure 1). Weakness of the abdominal muscles makes the organs of the abdominal cavity protrude and pull forward on the spine. Tightness in the muscles of the low back and hamstring areas tends to tip the hip bone forward, thereby exaggerating the curvature of the lower spine. Lordosis, if it becomes sufficiently extreme, can cause pressure on spinal nerves as they leave the spinal cord. This pressure causes pain which may become chronic and debilitating.

Regular exercisers have reduced risk of developing low back pain since they tend to maintain good strength in the abdominal muscles and adequate flexibility in the low back region. Exercise routines are often prescribed by physicians for persons suffering from low back pain. Exercise cannot prevent or cure all cases of low back pain, but evidence suggests that the incidence of this problem would be lower if everybody exercised properly and regularly.

EXERCISE AND WELLNESS

The disease prevention benefits of regular exercise are highly significant. Most regular exercisers, however, report that the primary benefit of physical activity is simply "feeling better." Many exercisers agree that physical activity makes them feel more alert, relaxed, and vigorous. Persons who improve their physical fitness usually find that they are less fatigued by their daily tasks and are able to participate more comfortably in strenuous activities.

These beneficial effects of exercise are generally attributed to the increase in physical working capacity known to result from training. A person's physical working capacity is closely related to his/her ability to use oxygen for the production of energy in the muscle tissues. A person's ability to consume oxygen is limited by the functional capacity of his/her body's cardiorespiratory system, i.e., strength of heart, elasticity of vessels. Endurance exercise training improves the fitness of the cardiorespiratory system and, thus, the body's ability to use oxygen. These effects make it easier for the physically fit person to perform those activities requiring sustained exertion.

Regular exercise may also carry significant psychological benefits. Many persons find that vigorous exercise helps them relax and to cope with the stresses of a busy life. Some psychologists even use exercise as a means for treating depression and other psychological disorders. The psychological effects of exercise are believed to combine with its physical effects to produce the feeling of well-being which most exercisers experience.

COMPONENTS OF HEALTH-RELATED PHYSICAL FITNESS

The contributions physical fitness can make toward the prevention of disease and promotion of health are highly significant. Thus, it is crucial to know how to evaluate one's own fitness and how to maintain and/or develop a good level of health-related fitness. This section will present several simple tests of health-related fitness and will describe the types of exercise known to improve the health fitness components.

CARDIORESPIRATORY ENDURANCE

Cardiorespiratory endurance is a person's ability to exercise for long periods of time. It is related to the fitness of the heart, lungs, and blood vessels, all of which work together to carry oxygen to the muscles. During exercise the active muscles require increased amounts of oxygen for use in energy production. Good cardiorespiratory endurance enables one to perform activities like jogging or swimming without tiring rapidly. Persons who have good cardiorespiratory fitness tend to be less fatigued by daily activities, and quickly recover after strenuous exertion.

Cardiorespiratory endurance can be easily measured with tests of distance running ability. The mile run for time is one of the tests of cardiorespiratory fitness designated by the American Alliance for Health, Physical Education, Recreation and Dance (AAHPERD). To take the test, all that is needed is a track or other accurately measured area, and a clock. Before running the mile the subject should do some distance

Table 7. AAHPERD Health Fitness Standards* for One Mile Walk/Run   (minutes)

Age	5	6	7	8	9	10	11	12	13	14	15	16	17	18
Boys	13:00	12:00	11:00	10:00	10:00	9:30	9:00	9:00	8:00	7:45	7:30	7:30	7:30	7:30
Girls	14:00	13:00	12:00	11:30	11:00	11:00	11:00	11:00	10:30	10:30	10:30	10:30	10:30	10:30

*Health fitness standards are based on performance scores that are associated with health maintenance and disease prevention. Instead of using normative data which compare children to each other, health fitness standards provide age-specific profiles of a physically fit child against which comparisons can be made.

running for practice and should learn the approximate pace of jogging or running he/she can sustain for the entire mile. An even pace is usually best; one should avoid starting the run at a pace which is too fast. Table 7 provides health-related standards against which the subject can compare his/her performance. If his/her score ranks above the standard, he/she has an acceptable level of cardiorespiratory fitness. Regular participation in a cardiorespiratory endurance program will help to maintain this level. Those scoring below the standard should strive to improve by starting a proper cardiorespiratory exercise program. Chapter 2 outlines the various modes of exercise that are appropriate for this type of exercise program.

BODY COMPOSITION

The term body composition refers to the relative proportions of lean tissue and fat tissue in the body. Lean tissues, which constitute most of the body weight, include the bone, muscle, skin, and connective tissues. Fat (or adipose) tissue consists of tiny fat cells distributed throughout the body. In particular, fat cells tend to accumulate under the skin and around the internal organs. Fat tissue usually represents between 10 and 30 percent of the total body weight. A person's body composition is expressed as percent body fat (% fat).

An estimate of an individual's % fat can easily be obtained by measuring the thickness of skinfolds at one or more locations on the body surface. Two commonly used skinfold sites are the back of the arm (triceps skinfold) and at the medial portion of the calf (medial calf skinfold) (see Figures 2 and 3). The thickness of the skinfolds can be easily measured using a device called a skinfold caliper (see Figure 4). The jaws of the caliper should be placed over a double thickness of skin and subcutaneous fat.

The sum of the thicknesses of these two skinfolds is related to the total amount of fat in the body: the thicker the skinfolds, the greater the percent of body fat. Those with skinfold sums above the upper limit of the appropriate range have a greater percentage of body fat than is desirable for health maintenance (see Table 8). These individuals should begin an exercise program designed to optimize fat loss.

Changes in % fat occur with changes in the balance between calories taken in through the diet and calories used through daily exercise and activity. If more calories are ingested in food than are expended with daily activities, fat will be stored in the body. On the other hand, fat is lost when caloric expenditure exceeds caloric intake. Thus, there are three basic methods by which the % body fat can be reduced: diet modification to reduce caloric intake; increased exercise to increase caloric expenditure; a combination of the first two methods.

For many persons the safest and most effective approach to fat loss is to increase caloric expenditure through exercise. Increased exercise can be combined with a moderate reduction of caloric intake to accelerate this rate of fat loss. Some persons

Table 8. AAHPERD Health Fitness Standards for sum of triceps and subscapular skinfolds (mm)

Boys (age 5–18):	12 - 25
Girls (age 5–18):	16 - 36

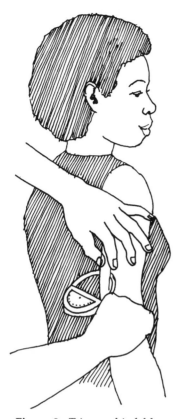

Figure 2. Triceps skinfold.

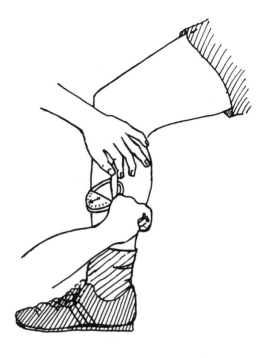

Figure 3. Medial calf skinfold.

can successfully lose fat through dieting alone; however, severe "crash" diets should be avoided. They are often nutritionally unsound, and cannot be maintained on a permanent basis.

When initiating an exercise program to lose body fat, the primary goal should be to burn more calories. This can be accomplished most effectively by participating in activities involving whole-body, moderate-to-high intensity exercise. Activities such as walking, jogging, swimming, and cycling are best. These, of course, are the same aerobic activities recommended for improvement of cardiorespiratory endurance. In general, the guidelines used to design a program for improvement in cardiorespiratory fitness can be used to help reduce body fat. To maximize caloric expenditure fat loss, emphasis should be placed on exercise session duration. Thus, the exercise mode selected should be one that can be sustained for at least 30 minutes.

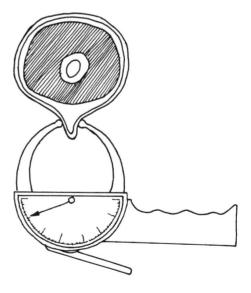

Figure 4. Measurement of skinfold thickness using caliper.

MUSCULAR STRENGTH AND MUSCULAR ENDURANCE

Muscular strength is defined as the greatest force that a muscle can exert in a single, maximal contraction. Strength is highly related to muscle size: the larger the muscle, the greater its ability to generate force. *Muscular endurance* reflects a muscle's ability to perform repeated contractions against a significant resistance. Muscular endurance is related to muscular strength, since when a muscle becomes stronger, its ability to perform repeated contractions usually improves as well. Muscular endurance should not be confused with cardiorespiratory endurance, which is dependent on cardiovascular function, not muscular strength.

Of particular concern in health-related physical fitness is the strength and endurance of the abdominal muscles. The abdominal muscles run between the lower border of the rib cage and the front of the pelvic bone. These muscles serve to flex the spine, as when performing a sit-up. The abdominal muscles also help to hold the organs of the abdominal cavity in place. If the abdominal muscles become weak, the abdominal contents can fall forward and contribute to lordosis, previously mentioned. Maintenance of good strength in the abdominal region is important for the prevention of low back pain.

An accepted method for measuring abdominal strength involves performance of sit-ups. The specific test recommended by the American Alliance for Health, Physical Education, Recreation and Dance is a timed sit-up test in which the participant performs as many sit-ups as possible in one minute. For test purposes, the sit-up should be done with knees bent and arms folded across the chest. A partner should hold the participant's feet and count the number of sit-ups completed. Table 9 provides standards for the sit-up test. Those subjects scoring below the sex- and age-appropriate standard should begin a program to improve abdominal muscular strength and endurance.

It is also important that adequate strength be maintained in the muscles of the arms and the upper trunk. Often, in daily activities, heavy objects need to be carried. If the arm and trunk muscles are weak, ability to lift and carry objects at work or at home can be impaired. Such impairment contributes to accidents and injuries, particularly among the elderly in whom muscular strength tends to be low.

Muscular strength and muscular endurance are best improved by exercises which significantly overload the active muscle groups. Overload occurs when a muscle is forced to work against a greater resistance than normal. Strength improvement is specific to the muscles which are actively overloaded; to improve strength in several muscle groups, several specific resistance exercises are needed.

An effective way to develop good muscular strength and muscular endurance is to practice calisthenic exercises which overload the abdominal and upper body muscles. Figure 5 presents a series of exercises to improve abdominal muscle strength. Figure 6 shows strengthening exercises for the arms and upper body. As a general guideline, 15–20 repetitions of a particular exercise will ensure maintenance of adequate muscular strength and endurance in the exercised muscle groups. Strengthening exercises should be performed at least two to three times per week.

When beginning a strength-building exercise program, the subject should start with exercises that can be properly performed at least five to six times before encountering fatigue. As strength improves and the subject performs 15–20 repetitions with more or less ease, he/she should pro-

Table 9. AAHPERD Health Fitness Standards for sit-ups (number of sit-ups)

Age	5	6	7	8	9	10	11	12	13	14	15	16	17	18
Boys	20	20	24	26	30	34	36	38	40	40	42	44	44	44
Girls	20	20	24	26	28	30	33	33	33	35	35	35	35	35

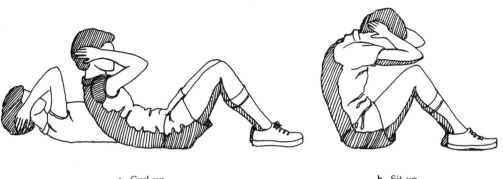

a. Curl-up.   b. Sit-up.

c. Leg raise prone.

d. Side leg raise.

e. Isometric sit-up.

Figure 5. Exercises to strengthen the
abdominal and lower trunk region.

a. Push-up.

b. Modified push-up.

c. Pull-up.

d. Parallel bar dip.

e. Back extension.

Figure 6. Exercises to strengthen the upper
body.

gress to a more difficult exercise. An example would be starting with 5–6 repetitions of the curl-up and, over a number of weeks, progressing to 15–20 repetitions of the full sit-up.

Another approach to strength improvement is weight-training, the use of barbells, i.e., free weights, or supported weights, e.g., Universal Gym, Nautilus, to overload selected muscle groups. Weight-training has become a popular activity and is an effective way to maintain good muscular strength and endurance. Expensive weight-training systems are not necessary for maintenance of good health-related physical fitness. A more detailed discussion of weight-training is presented in Chapter 24 of this publication.

FLEXIBILITY

Flexibility has been defined as the maximum range of motion possible in a joint or series of joints. Joint flexibility can determine a person's ability to perform bodily movements with ease and efficiency. Poor flexibility, which is common in our society, may make one liable to muscle-joint injuries, or may make certain movements impossible.

Joint flexibility is determined by the elasticity of the muscles and connective tissues which cross the joints. Each joint is held together by ligaments, tendons, and joint capsules, all of which are composed of elastic connective tissues. The muscles also include many layers of connective tissues. If these various connective tissues in the muscles and joint tissues are maintained in a stretchable state, good joint flexibility will be maintained. However, if the muscle and joint connective tissues lose their elasticity, the result will be poor joint flexibility. Flexibility is highly specific to each joint; the same person might be very flexible in the shoulder joints, yet quite inflexible in the hip region.

Flexibility is considered a health-related fitness component because lack of flexibility can contribute to low back pain. Poor flexibility in the lower back and in the hamstring muscles can be a cause of lordosis and the pain it causes. Thus, maintenance of good low back/hamstring flexibility is an important goal of lifetime fitness programs.

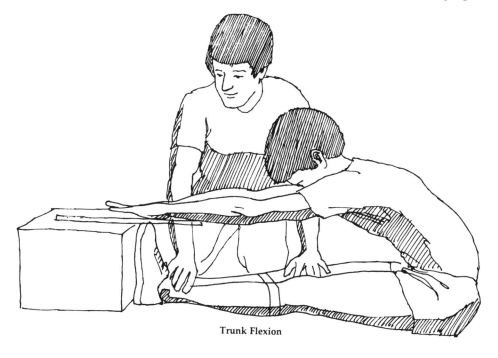

Trunk Flexion

Figure 7. Sit-and-reach test.

Low back/hamstring flexibility can be evaluated easily using the sit-and-reach test (see Figure 7). This test involves reaching as far forward as possible while seated in the straight leg position. Using the apparatus depicted in Figure 7, distance reached can be scored to the nearest centimeter. AAHPERD scoring tables for the sit-and-reach test are adjusted so that a score of 23 centimeters corresponds to toe level. Table 10 provides standards to determine one's rating for low back/hamstring flexibility.

Table 10. AAHPERD Health Fitness Standards for sit and reach (cm)

Boys (age 5–18):	25
Girls (age 5–18):	25

Flexibility in the low back/hamstring region can best be improved by using static stretching exercises, involving prolonged maintenance of a stretched position. As a general guideline, a static stretch should be of sufficient intensity to cause moderate discomfort (but no more) in the stretched muscle. *Excessive, painful stretching may damage muscle or joint tissues and should be avoided.* A static stretch should be sustained for 10–30 seconds. Several examples of static stretching exercises are depicted in Figure 8. These exercises, employed three or more times per week, will develop and maintain a good level of low back/hamstring flexibility in most persons.

FITNESS AND THE HEALTHY LIFESTYLE

This chapter has discussed the contribution regular exercise can make to overall health. Major emphasis has been placed on the four components of health-related physical fitness, why they are important, and how each can be improved.

In concluding this chapter it is important to emphasize that one's health status is determined largely by his or her personal habits and decisions. Recent studies have demonstrated clearly that several of the time-honored "good health habits" do in fact make a difference to long-term health.

One study of 4,000 Californians found that future health status could be predicted on the basis of five health habits: abstention from smoking, moderate alcohol consumption, regular exercise, sleep for 7-8 hours per day, and maintenance of normal body weight. Persons who had all these habits were significantly healthier than those persons having few or none of them. Two of these, regular exercise and maintenance of proper body weight, are directly related to habits of regular physical activity.

In conclusion, the healthy lifestyle is there for the taking. By selecting proper health habits, including regular exercise, much can be done to reduce disease risks and to enhance the quality of life. It is often said that "knowledge is power," but knowledge is powerful only if it forms the basis for action. The knowledge gained by reading this chapter will be useful only if it is applied through carefully planned and executed units of instruction. Now is the time to go to work. Reading about exercise will not help you improve—exercising will!

TERMINOLOGY

Aerobic Energy Production. A chemical process by which oxygen, transported from the atmosphere, is used by the cells of the body to produce energy needed for biological work, e.g., muscle contraction.

Atherosclerosis. A disease process by which fatty plaque is deposited on the inner walls of the arteries; may lead to coronary heart disease.

Body Composition. The percentage of the body weight which is fat (% fat).

Cardiorespiratory Endurance. Ability to sustain moderate intensity, whole-body activity for extended time periods.

Chronic Disease. A disease which develops over long periods of time; often caused by lifestyle and health habits.

Coronary Heart Disease. Impairment of blood flow and oxygen delivery to the heart muscle, caused by atherosclerosis in coronary arteries.

Coronary Heart Disease Risk Factor. A personal characteristic or habit associated with increased risk of developing coronary heart disease.

Flexibility. Maximum range of motion possible in a joint or series of joints.

Hypokinetic Disease. A disease associated with sedentary living, i.e., lack of regular exercise.

a. Bend and reach.

b. Upper back stretcher.

c. Hip flexor stretch.

d. Sit-and-reach.

Figure 8. Static stretching exercises.

Infectious Disease. A disease caused by a germ, bacteria, or other disease-producing agent; can often be communicated between individuals.

Lordosis. An excessive curvative of the lumbar region of the spine.

Muscular Endurance. Ability to perform repeated high intensity muscle contractions.

Muscular Strength. Maximum force which can be applied with a single muscle contraction.

Obesity. Excessive body fatness.

Overload. A level of exercise intensity or resistance which exceeds that to which a person is already adapted.

Physical Working Capacity. Maximum rate at which a person can perform physical exercise; heavily dependent upon the individual's capacity for aerobic energy expenditure.

Static Stretching. Method for improvement of flexibility which involves maintenance of a stretched position for 10–30 seconds.

REFERENCES

AAHPERD. *Physical Best*. Reston, VA: American Alliance for Health, Physical Education, Recreation and Dance, 1988.

American College of Sports Medicine. *Guidelines for Exercise Testing and Prescription*, 4th ed. Philadephia: Lea and Febiger, 1991.

American College of Sports Medicine. *Resource Manual for Guidelines for Exercise Testing and Prescription*. Philadephia: Lea and Febiger, 1988.

Blair, S.N., Kohl, H.W., Paffenbarger, R.S., Clark, D.G., Cooper, K.H., and Gibbons, L.W. Physical fitness and all-cause mortality: A prospective study of healthy men and women. *JAMA* 262: 2395–2401, 1989.

Corbin, C.B., and Lindsey, R. *The Ultimate Fitness Book: Physical Fitness Forever*. Champaign, IL: Leisure Press, 1984.

Fitnessgram User's Manual. Dallas, TX: Institute for Aerobics Research, 1987.

Getchell, B. *The Fitness Book*. Carmel, IN: Benchmark Press, 1987.

Jackson, A.S., and Ross, R.M. *Understanding Exercise for Health and Fitness*. Houston: MacJ-R Publishing Company, 1986.

Nieman, D.C. *The Sports Medicine Fitness Course*. Palo Alto, CA: Bull Publishing Company, 1986.

Prentice, W.E., and Bucher, C.A. *Fitness for College and Life*, 2nd ed. St. Louis, MO: Times Mirror/Mosby College Publishing, 1988.

Sharkey, B.J. *Physiology of Fitness*, 3rd ed. Champaign, IL: Human Kinetics Publishers, 1990.

Williams, M.H. *Lifetime Physical Fitness: A Personal Choice*. Dubuque, IA: Wm. C. Brown Co., 1985.

CHAPTER 2

Aerobic Fitness

RUSSELL R. PATE
and
DAVID BRANCH
University of South Carolina
Columbia, SC

INTRODUCTION

As was discussed in Chapter 1, physical fitness can be defined as *the ability to perform daily tasks with vigor and alertness, without undue fatigue, and with ample energy to enjoy leisure-time pursuits and to meet unforeseen emergencies.* Overall physical fitness consists of several components, one of which is aerobic (or cardiorespiratory) fitness. Because of its broad impact on both day-to-day function and prevention of disease, aerobic fitness is considered by many exercise physiologists, physicians, and public health specialists to be the most important of the various fitness components. This chapter provides a discussion of the importance of aerobic fitness and summarizes the recommended procedures for a sound aerobic fitness program. In addition, this chapter includes brief discussions of several of the most widely used forms of aerobic exercise.

CHARACTERISTICS OF AEROBIC FITNESS

The word "aerobic" refers to a physiological or biochemical process that requires the presence or utilization of oxygen. *Aerobic exercise* is a form of physical activity in which the energy expended by the active muscles is provided through a lengthy series of chemical reactions collectively known as *aerobic metabolism.* Aerobic metabolism occurs in the muscle cells and it is within these cells that oxygen is utilized during exercise. Because very little oxygen can be stored in the muscle cells, oxygen must be constantly transported from the atmosphere to the muscles by the body's cardiorespiratory system (i.e., heart, lungs, blood, and blood vessels). Consequently one's ability to perform aerobic exercise is dependent on the functional capacity of the cardiorespiratory system and the ability of the muscle cells to use oxygen in aerobic metabolism.

Aerobic fitness is a term that refers to the ability to perform aerobic exercise. Such exercise, being related to transportation and utilization of oxygen, involves sustained elevation of the body's rate of oxygen consumption (VO_2). Exercise intensities that might be described as "light," "moderate," or even "vigorous" are considered aerobic if they can be sustained for prolonged periods. Very high intensity exercise, such as that described as "very vigorous" or "exhaustive," is not considered aerobic because it cannot be sustained for a prolonged period and requires some use of *anaerobic metabolism* (which does not involve oxygen consumption). Because aerobic fitness depends, in part, on the functional capacity of the cardiorespiratory system, the terms "aerobic fitness" and "cardiorespiratory endurance" are often used interchangeably.

A person with good aerobic fitness is able to perform moderate to vigorous intensity exercise for prolonged periods without experiencing excessive fatigue. Such a person tends not to be fatigued by normal day-to-day activities such as occupational and household tasks. Also, such persons are able to enjoyably participate in vigorous leisure time activities. Overall, persons with good aerobic fitness are well prepared to meet the physical demands of life. Furthermore, those who are physically fit are at

Table 1. Sample Physical Activity Readiness Questionnaire (PAR-Q)
Adapted from PAR-Q Validation Report, British Columbia Department of Health, June 1975.

For most people, physical activity should not pose any problem or hazard. The PAR-Q (Physical Activity Readiness Questionnaire) has been designed to identify the small number of adults for whom physical activity might be inappropriate or those who should have medical advice concerning the type of activity most suitable for them. In the interest of your safety in participation in aerobic activity, please supply the following information concerning yourself. This information will be held in the strictest confidence. Thank you.

NAME _____ AGE _____ SEX _____

1. Has your physician ever said you have heart trouble? ☐ yes
   ☐ no

2. Do you frequently suffer from chest pains? ☐ yes
   ☐ no

3. Do you often feel faint or have dizzy spells? ☐ yes
   ☐ no

4. Has a physician ever told you that you have a bone or joint problem such as arthritis that has been aggravated by exercise, or might be made worse with exercise? ☐ yes
   ☐ no

5. Is there a good physical reason not mentioned here why you should not follow an activity program?
   ☐ yes
   ☐ no

   If so, please list _____

6. Are you taking ANY prescribed or over-the-counter medication(s)? ☐ yes
   ☐ no

   If so, please list _____

7. Please take this opportunity to comment on any other information (medical, physical, orthopaedic, etc.) concerning your overall health and medical history relative to physical activity.

Table 2. Medical conditions, seen in some children and youth, that require physician clearance before participation in vigorous exercise.

Cardiac Abnormalities
Hypertrophic Cardiomyopathy
Marfan Syndrome
Coronary Artery Anomalies
Aortic Stenosis

Musculoskeletal Disorders
Skeletal Deformities
History of Traumatic or
Overuse Injuries

Convulsive Disorders
(e.g., epilepsy)

Thermoregulatory Abnormalities
History of Heat Illness

Metabolic Disorders
Diabetes Mellitus
Hypoglycemia

reduced risk for development of many of the chronic diseases that plague contemporary American society. Physically active and fit persons are considered less likely than their sedentary, unfit counterparts to develop diseases such as coronary heart disease, obesity, high blood pressure, and cancer. The relationship between health and fitness was discussed in more detail in Chapter 1.

PRINCIPLES OF IMPROVING AEROBIC FITNESS

SCREENING OF BEGINNING EXERCISERS

Aerobic exercise, if used in a reasonable and progressive fashion, is safe for almost everyone. However, there is a small percentage of the population for whom vigorous exercise may increase risk of a cardiovascular or metabolic incident. Accordingly, it is recommended that beginning exercisers be screened for the presence of conditions that could place them at risk during vigorous exercise.

Table 1 presents the Physical Activity Readiness Questionnaire (PAR-Q). This instrument has been widely used as a means of identifying persons who should be evaluated by a physician prior to initiating an exercise program. For a more detailed discussion of health screening for beginning exercisers the reader is referred to the American College of Sports Medicine's *Guidelines for Exercise Testing and Prescription* (1991).

It should be noted that the typical school-age young person is at very low risk of experiencing a significant health problem during exercise. Therefore, it is not generally seen as necessary for teenagers to complete an extensive screening protocol prior to participation in physical education classes. Nonetheless, some do have health problems that could limit their exercise tolerance or, in rare instances, preclude their participation in vigorous exercise. Table 2 lists a number of medical conditions, sometimes seen in young people, that would require physician clearance for participation in vigorous activity programs.

COMPONENTS OF AN EFFECTIVE AEROBIC FITNESS PROGRAM

Cardiorespiratory endurance can best be improved by regular participation in aerobic exercise. As noted above, aerobic activities are those which increase the body's rate of aerobic metabolism for long periods of time. They also cause a sustained increase in heart rate. Table 3 lists several of the most popular aerobic activities. In designing an exercise program one should select an activity or set of activities which he/she enjoys and participates in regularly. Many people combine the aerobic activities of Table 3 into an overall program which is practical and enjoyable, such as playing racquetball once per week and jogging twice per week.

Table 3. Modes of aerobic exercise.

Aerobic dance
Basketball
Cycling
Handball/Racquetball
Ice skating
Jogging/Running
Roller-blading
Rowing
Swimming
Walking/Hiking

Having selected an aerobic activity, it is important that the activity be used properly. Following are some guidelines that will help to design a successful aerobic fitness program:

1. **Frequency of exercise.** Aerobic exercise should be engaged in three or more times per week. When first beginning an exercise program, it is usually best to exercise every other day. As fitness improves, frequency of training may be increased to five or six sessions per week.

2. **Duration of exercise.** Aerobic exercise should be sustained for at least 20–30 minutes per session. In starting a program it is often wise to exercise intermittently for 15–20 minutes. However, within a few weeks most persons are able to sustain 30 minutes of continuous, aerobic exercise.

3. **Intensity of exercise.** To produce improvement of cardiorespiratory endurance, aerobic exercise must be used with sufficient intensity. However, it is important to note that only a moderate intensity of exercise is required. This intensity will cause the heart rate and breathing rate to increase, and will often bring about sweating. An easy way to establish a proper exercise intensity is to check the heart rate. This can be done by feeling the pulse in the wrist or neck (see Figure 1). The procedure outlined in Table 4 should be used to determine the training heart rate range.

When beginning a training program it is necessary to experiment to determine the intensity of exercise that will elicit the selected training heart rate. As shown in Figure 2, heart rate tends to increase as exercise intensity increases. By checking his/her heart rate at several exercise intensities, the subject will find the intensity corresponding to the desired training heart rate.

Table 4. Computation of a heart rate range for aerobic exercise training

STEP 1
Measure resting heart rate.

STEP 2
Estimate individual maximum heart rate:
$HR_{max} = 220 - age$ (years)

STEP 3
Compute lower limit for training heart rate range.
$(HR_{max} - resting\ heart\ rate) \times .40 + resting\ heart\ rate$

STEP 4
Compute upper limit for training heart rate range.
$(HR_{max} - resting\ heart\ rate) \times .80 + resting\ heart\ rate$

Example
A 40 year old man with a predicted HR_{max} of 180 and a resting heart rate of 60 would have a training heart rate range (based on 40% and 80% of HR reserve) of 108–156 beats/min.

Lower limit $.40 \times (180-60) + 60 = 108$

Upper limit $.80 \times (180-60) + 60 = 156$

Heart rate is expressed as beats per minute.

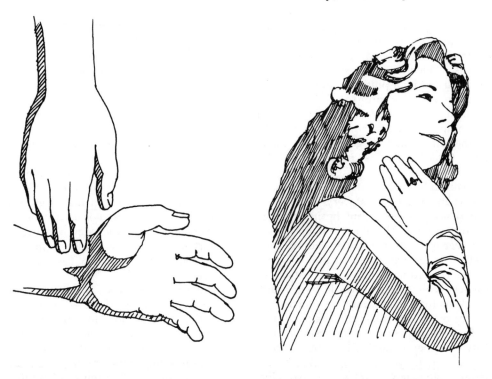

Figure 1. Heart rate, as monitored by palpation of the radial artery (at the wrist) or carotid artery (at the neck), can be a useful guide to exercise intensity.

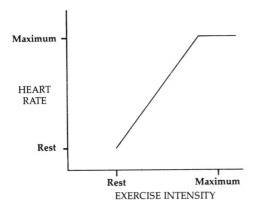

Figure 2. Relationship between heart rate and exercise intensity.

Having identified the appropriate intensity, the goal should be to sustain that intensity for 30 minutes. However, few beginners are able to accomplish this and should instead use intermittent exercise in which recovery periods alternate with exercise periods. For example, a beginning jogger might alternate 3 minutes of jogging with 2 minutes of walking for a total of 20 minutes.

4. **Warm-up and cool-down.** Each training session should begin with light calisthenic exercises and/or some other form of low intensity exercise. This allows the body to gradually adjust to the demands of aerobic exercise. Likewise, each session should finish with a gradual cool-down. Usually five minutes of walking or light calisthenics is sufficient. Such activity allows the body to gradually return to the resting state. Also, during the cool-down phase, static stretching exercises may be performed to promote maintenance of good joint flexibility.

5. **Progression.** An important principle of aerobic fitness programming is embodied in the word "progression." Available evidence indicates that long-term adherence to exercise can be promoted by starting with light to moderate exercise and building gradually to a more demanding program. Also, risk of orthopedic injuries (e.g., "shin splints," tendinitis) can be reduced by increasing the overall dose of exercise in a gradual manner.

Table 5 summarizes the current recommendations for each of the components of an aerobic fitness program.

ADAPTATIONS TO AEROBIC EXERCISE TRAINING

Regular participation in aerobic exercise causes physiological adaptations that are often collectively referred to as a "training effect." These physiological adaptations carry important benefits in terms of both aerobic fitness and health. Aerobic exercise training improves aerobic fitness by increasing the individual's capacity for very vigorous exercise *and* by reducing the stress or fatigue associated with performance of a standard level of moderate exercise. For example, after a jogging program, the participant can be expected to run at a faster pace before experiencing exhaustion *and* can be expected to experience less fatigue when running at a set pace (e.g., 10 minute mile pace).

These improvements in aerobic fitness are known to be due to physiological adaptations in both the trained skeletal muscles and the cardiorespiratory system. With aerobic training the cardiovascular system

Table 5. Components of an aerobic fitness program.

Component	Recommended Dose
Mode	Rhythmic, large muscle group activities, e.g., walking, jogging/running, cycling, swimming, rowing, aerobic dance
Intensity (I)	40–80% of Maximal Oxygen Consumption (VO_2max) 55–90% of HR_{max}
Duration (D)	15:00–60:00 per session
Frequency (F)	3–5 days per week
Progression	Initial Phase (3–4 weeks)—Low intensity and duration
	Improvement Phase (5–16 weeks)—Moderate intensity, duration, and frequency
	Maintenance Phase (Long-term)—Moderate to high intensity, duration, and frequency

adapts so that the heart becomes a more powerful and efficient pump. A key adaptation is an increase in the heart's stroke volume, that is, the volume of blood pumped by the heart with each beat. This increase in stroke volume results in an increase in the maximal volume of blood pumped per minute by the heart during exhaustive exercise (i.e., maximal cardiac output). Also, this change in stroke volume is associated with a decrease in heart rate during rest and standard submaximal exercise.

The muscles as well as the cardiorespiratory system adapt to aerobic exercise training. The cells in the muscles that are active in training (e.g., leg muscles with bicycling) adapt to training by increasing their capacity for oxygen use in aerobic metabolism. As a result, the trained muscles are able to use oxygen at a higher rate during exhaustive exercise. Also, during submaximal exercise, the trained muscles are less prone to production of fatigue-causing substances like lactic acid. The overall effect of these adaptations is a markedly improved capacity for sustained performance of moderate to vigorous exercise.

INJURY PREVENTION

Exercise is a stressor to the body and the novice exerciser is at increased risk for the development of certain muscle, bone, and joint injuries. Fortunately, injury risk can be minimized by adherence to the exercise prescription guidelines described above. In addition, prevention and precaution are also important. The following are common causes of injury:

1. **Being misinformed.** The exerciser should know how to properly use any piece of exercise equipment. Gimmicks or regimens that are advertised as "shortcut" ways to aerobic fitness are usually unrealistic and unsafe.
2. **Overuse.** Many novice exercisers begin a program of exercise with the best of intentions, but become injured by trying to do too much too soon. Moderate levels of exercise used in accordance with the procedures outlined in Table 5 will result in an enjoyable program with a minimal risk of injury. A key to injury

prevention is proper progression in the exercise program. Many injuries can be avoided by starting with an easy program and gradually increasing the dose of exercise.
3. **Competing with another individual.** The novice exerciser should always remember to "listen to his/her body" for signs of overexertion. It is a mistake to attempt to compete with a person who is more physically fit.

ENVIRONMENTAL CONCERNS

One should be aware of the dangers of exercising in extreme environmental conditions. *Hypothermia* is a condition in which the loss of body heat exceeds body heat production. This condition is a particular concern in very cold temperatures, but it can develop in temperatures as mild as 40 degrees F, especially if one is wet. Hypothermia can be fatal if the individual is unable to move to a warm, dry environment. Frostbite of the extremities is another cold related danger. Precautions against these dangers include:

1. Dress in layers.
2. Cover the extremities, especially the head, feet, and hands.
3. Avoid getting wet.
4. Avoid exercising alone in very cold conditions.

Hyperthermia, on the other hand, involves storage of excess heat in the body. It can cause *heat cramps, heat exhaustion,* and *heat stroke,* heat related illnesses of increasing seriousness. During days of high temperature and/or humidity, the body's *thermoregulatory* ability (ability to maintain its core temperature) is impaired. This is especially true on days of high humidity due to limitations in the rate at which sweat will evaporate from the body surface. Outdoor exercise should be limited to either the early morning or the evening during days of high heat and/or humidity. Preventive actions include drinking plenty of fluids, wearing light colored and porous clothing, adequate acclimation, and indoor exercise. Recommended treatments range from rehydration (for heat exhaustion) to prompt medical attention (for heat stroke).

MODES OF AEROBIC EXERCISE

As was noted above, many specific modes of activity can be used in a program that is designed to enhance aerobic fitness. The activities listed in Table 3 can be used as aerobic exercises because they involve prolonged elevations of the rate of aerobic metabolism. In selecting a particular activity or set of activities, a key is to pick activities that are accessible and enjoyable to the individual. Furthermore, it is important that the selected activities be used in a safe and effective manner. Following are brief discussions of several of the primary aerobic exercise activities: jogging, walking, aerobic dance, and swimming. For each activity, recommendations for safe and enjoyable exercise are provided.

JOGGING

Jogging is a familiar activity that requires minimal skill. Jogging, defined as *slow running,* is similar to running in that both feet leave the ground during each stride. In other words, both running and jogging have a "flight phase."

There are many different individual styles of jogging, all of which have the following principles in common:

1. In jogging, as the foot comes forward to strike the ground, the heel should make contact first. Often, this is difficult to see with the naked eye and it may appear that the foot is flat. One should avoid "running on the toes," that is, hitting the ground first with the ball of the foot, which can cause soreness and lower leg injury.
2. The jogger should maintain an erect posture, avoiding excessive leaning backward or forward. The muscles of the trunk and neck should be as relaxed as possible.
3. The arms should be kept at a low carriage and should be permitted to move freely and to travel slightly across the front of the body. The arms, hands, and fingers should remain as relaxed as possible.
4. In jogging, only moderate knee lift is required. This is in contrast to the high knee lift demonstrated by sprint runners, which is too excessive for long duration, low to moderate intensity running.
5. The jogger should breathe in a relaxed, natural manner. Most joggers will quickly arrive at a natural running stride to breathing pattern. A common pattern is two strides, inhale, two strides, exhale. At any rate, the jogger does not need to consciously regulate breathing. One should breathe through both the nose and the mouth.

Advantages of Jogging

Jogging enjoys widespread popularity. Approximately 30 million Americans jog regularly. There are several benefits of jogging, including the following:

1. **Jogging is an easy skill.** Nearly everyone can jog because running is one of the fundamental movement patterns that is learned during childhood.
2. **Jogging is relatively inexpensive.** The only expense associated with jogging is the cost of proper running shoes. While running shoes are not cheap, proper shoes are necessary to protect against orthopaedic injury. One does not need to purchase expensive equipment or club memberships to enjoy jogging.
3. **Jogging is an individual activity.** While it is fun to jog with a partner or group, a lone individual can enjoy this activity. This means that one can jog whenever it is personally convenient without having to worry about coordinating schedules with a friend. This is a major advantage that jogging has over many other activities.
4. **Jogging requires no special facilities.** One can enjoy jogging virtually anywhere: home, school, work. The only facilities needed are a place to change clothes and a facility to shower after jogging. With proper dress, jogging can be done outside year-round in most parts of the United States. Thus, no special tracks, gymnasia, machines, or courts are needed.

Tips for the Beginning Jogger

It is important for the beginning jogger to realize that exercise is a stressor to which the body must become accustomed. If exercise is applied gradually, most persons can rapidly adapt to it. However, if exercise is applied too rapidly, injury, illness, perceived lack of improvement, and/or attrition may result. It is important for the beginning jogger to realize that perseverance and self-discipline are essential ingredients for success. If the attainment of fitness was an effortless process, *all* Americans would be fit. Such is certainly not the case. A certain amount of discomfort, and possibly discouragement, may be encountered in the initial phase of a conditioning program.

Table 6, a suggested beginning jogging program, illustrates an important point that merits reinforcement. It is important to begin *gradually*, with some *walking* in the early weeks. This strategy will greatly reduce the incidence of injury while the individual becomes accustomed to the new stress of exercise. *Peer support* is valuable, especially early in the program, in order to instill activity as an opportunity for enjoyable social interaction.

Table 7 is a suggested program for the younger and/or more aerobically advanced individual.

Proper Jogging Footwear

Proper footwear is an *essential investment.* Good running shoes have the following characteristics:

1. A moderately elevated heel consisting of material with good shock-absorbing

Table 6. Suggested jogging program for older and/or previously sedentary beginners. Frequency of exercise is three days per week on nonconsecutive days.

Week	Activity	Duration (min)	Intensity (%HR reserve)
1	Walk	15:00	55–65
2	Walk	20:00	55–65
3	Walk	20:00	55–65
4	Walk/Jog	20:00	60–70
5	Walk/Jog	25:00	60–70
6	Walk/Jog	25:00	60–70
7	Walk/Jog	25:00–30:00	65–75
8	Walk/Jog	25:00–30:00	65–75
9	Jog	30:00	65–75
10	Jog	30:00	70–80
11	Jog	30:00	70–80
12	Jog	30:00	70–80

Table 7. Suggested jogging program for younger and/or previously moderately active beginners. Frequency of exercise is three or more days per week.

Week	Activity	Duration (min)	Intensity (%HR reserve)
1	Walk/Jog	20:00	60–70
2	Walk	25:00	60–70
3	Walk	25:00	60–70
4	Walk/Jog	25:00	65–75
5	Walk/Jog	30:00	65–75
6	Walk/Jog	30:00	65–75
7	Walk/Jog	30:00–35:00	70–80
8	Walk/Jog	30:00–35:00	70–80
9	Jog	30:00–35:00	70–80
10	Jog	35:00+	75–85
11	Jog	35:00+	75–85
12	Jog	35:00+	75–85

qualities, i.e., the jogger should be able to compress, with the fingers, the sole portion of the heel.

2. The heel should be well padded and should fit so that little or no slippage of the foot occurs during running.
3. The toe portion of the shoe should be deep enough to avoid rubbing the toenails and should fit so that the toes do not contact the front of the shoe during running.
4. An arch support should be included and should be aligned comfortably with the arch of the foot.
5. The outer sole of the shoe should be made of a very sturdy rubber material which will withstand many miles of jogging. Most joggers find that the heel portion of the outer sole wears first and this area should be reinforced to give longer wear.
6. The front part of the shoe should be snug so that very little lateral foot movement occurs.

There are literally hundreds of jogging shoes in the marketplace today. No one shoe will meet the needs of all joggers. The beginning jogger should secure the assistance of an *experienced, knowledgeable retailer* in deciding on the right shoe.

WALKING

Walking is an activity that is enjoying widespread popularity in the United States. Walking has most of the same advantages as jogging. When one walks, in contrast to jogging, one foot is always in contact with the ground; hence there is no "flight phase" as in jogging. As a result, walking appeals to many people due to the lower risk of orthopaedic injury. In addition, walking is an activity that can be performed indoors, a big advantage in the hot summer months. Walking provides a wonderful opportunity for peer support. Many malls have walking clubs, providing an opportunity for social interaction and a way to exercise comfortably when the weather is inclement.

Tips for Beginners

Table 8 provides a sample aerobic program for the old and/or low fitness walkers to young and/or highly fit walkers. As in jogging, the key to success is *gradual progression*.

Table 8. Suggested walking programs for low, moderate, and high initial levels of fitness.

	Low Mileage Intensity		Pace	Moderate Mileage Intensity		Pace	High Mileage Intensity		Pace
Initial Phase (3 days per week; 10:00 warm-up; 10:00 cool-down)									
Week 1	1.5	40%	24:00	2.0	50%	20:00	3.0	60%	17:00
Week 2	1.5	40%	24:00	2.0	50%	20:00	3.0	60%	17:00
Week 3	1.5	40%	24:00	2.0	50%	20:00	3.0	60%	17:00
Week 4	1.5	40%	24:00	2.0	50%	20:00	3.0	60%	17:00
Improvement Phase (3–4 days per week; 10:00 warm-up; 10:00 cool-down)									
Week 5	2.0	40%	24:00	2.5	50%	20:00	3.5	60%	17:00
Week 6	2.0	40%	24:00	2.5	50%	20:00	3.5	60%	17:00
Week 7	2.0	40%	24:00	2.5	50%	20:00	3.5	60%	17:00
Week 8	2.0	40%	24:00	2.5	50%	20:00	3.5	60%	17:00
Week 9	2.5	40%	23:00	3.0	50%	19:00	4.0	60%	16:00
Week 10	2.75	40%	22:00	3.25	50%	19:00	4.0	60%	16:00
Week 11	2.75	40%	22:00	3.25	50%	19:00	4.0	60%	16:00
Week 12	2.75	40%	22:00	3.25	50%	19:00	4.0	60%	16:00
Week 13	3.0	40%	22:00	3.5	50%	18:00	4.5	60%	15:00
Week 14	3.0	40%	22:00	3.5	50%	18:00	4.5	60%	15:00
Week 15	3.0	40%	21:00	3.5	50%	18:00	4.5	60%	14:00

Selection of a Good Walking Shoe

As with jogging shoes, the purchase of proper walking shoes is an essential investment against injury. The following features are found in a good walking shoe:

1. The walking shoe should be light weight.
2. The walking shoe should be made of durable material. Shoes constructed of leather and/or leather with mesh generally prove to be durable. In addition, a leather with mesh construction allows for shoe ventilation.
3. The walking shoe should have an adequate heel cushion. Shoes with a thick Vibram or durable rubber outersole and a well cushioned, slightly elevated heel provide protection against injury.
4. The walking shoe should provide protection against excessive pronation. Pronation is the inward "roll" that occurs after the heel strikes the ground. An excessive amount of pronation can lead to injury.
5. The walking shoe should allow for a comfortable "roll" or "transfer" of body weight from the heel to the ball of the foot during the footstrike.
6. The walking shoe should be slightly stiff. The walking shoe should be stiffer than a jogging shoe to provide for optimal heel to ball of foot transfer of body weight.
7. The walking shoe should have a well supported arch as well as ample room at the toe box.

As with selection of jogging shoes, the reader is advised to seek the advice of an *experienced, knowledgeable retailer* before purchasing walking shoes.

AEROBIC DANCE

It has been estimated that over 20 million Americans participate in aerobic dance. This relatively new form of aerobic activity clearly enjoys widespread popularity. There are several different forms of aerobic dance, set to the accompaniment of ballet, jazz, pop, modern, disco, and folk music.

In addition, aerobic dance can be performed in the water or as "low impact" aerobics (analogous to walking, with which one foot is constantly in contact with the floor). "High impact" aerobics (analogous to jogging), includes the "flight phase." Studies have documented the physiological benefits of aerobic dance training, including increases in VO_{2max} and decreases in resting heart rate and heart rate at standard submaximal workloads, perceived exertion, skinfold measurements, and serum cholesterol.

Aerobic Dance Shoes

As in walking and jogging, proper footwear is an *essential* investment. Following are some tips concerning selection of a proper aerobic dance shoe.

1. As in a jogging shoe, the outer sole should be flexible and durable.
2. The midsole and inner sole must be constructed of material that is a good shock absorber.
3. The toe area should provide for plenty of room.
4. Especially in high impact aerobic dance, the forefoot must absorb a lot of the impact. Therefore, this area of the shoe must be well cushioned. In addition, this area of the shoe must be flexible in order to prevent lower leg stiffness.
5. The shoe should have a good arch support as well as a solid, firm heel counter to give good support and stability in these areas.
6. Many aerobic dance shoes are of the "high top" variety. If the exerciser has weak ankles, he/she may wish to consider such a style.
7. The shoe should be *comfortable*. The exerciser should not purchase a pair of shoes that are not comfortable after 10 minutes of in-store wear.
8. As with walking and jogging shoes, the prospective buyer should seek the advice of a retailer with experience and knowledge in fitting an aerobic dance shoe to his/her foot.

SWIMMING

Swimming for aerobic fitness offers several advantages over walking, running, and aerobic dance. First, swimming is a nonweight bearing form of exercise involving less stress to the bones and joints than weight bearing activities. The high humidity in the air above the water provides an advantage to exercisers with certain respiratory ailments. Also, the usually cool temperature of the water promotes temperature regulation by rapidly conducting heat away from the exercising body.

Disadvantages of swimming as an aerobic activity include the necessity for a pool facility, which can be expensive. Swimming requires a greater degree of skill than many other modes of aerobic activity. Also, there is some evidence that swimming does not cause as great a change in body composition (i.e., loss of body fat) as does running, walking, and cycling when used for similar amounts of time.

Many swimmers feel that gains in aerobic fitness can best be accomplished by swimming in "sets." However, lap swimming will satisfy the components for aerobic exercise that are described in Table 5. Several sample sessions are described in Table 9. All sessions should begin with an appropriate warm-up consisting of wall swimming and stroke drills. Sets can be of any dis-

tance or intensity depending on the skill and fitness levels of the swimmer.

Information about swimming skills is presented in Chapter 18.

REFERENCES

American College of Sports Medicine. *Guidelines for Exercise Testing and Prescription*, 4th ed. Philadelphia, PA: Lea & Febiger, 1991.

American College of Sports Medicine. *Resource Manual for Guidelines for Exercise Testing and Prescription*. Philadelphia, PA: Lea & Febiger, 1988.

Blair, S. *Living with Exercise*. Dallas, TX: American Health Publishing Company, 1991.

Garrick, J.G., and Requa, R.K. Aerobic dance: A review. *Sports Medicine* 6:169–179, 1988.

Jackson, A., and Ross, R. *Understanding Exercise for Health and Fitness*. Houston, TX: MacJ-R Publishing Company, 1986.

Kravitz, L. *Anybody's Guide to Total Fitness*. Dubuque, IA: Kendall/Hunt Publishing Company, 1986.

Nieman, D. *The Sports Medicine Fitness Course*. Palo Alto, CA: Bull Publishing Company, 1986.

Rippe, J.M., and Ward, A. *The Rockport Walking Program*. New York: Prentice-Hall, 1989.

Sharkey, B.J. *Physiology of Fitness*, 3rd ed. Champaign, IL: Human Kinetics Publishers, 1990.

Table 9. Examples of several swimming sessions

Warm-up 2 minutes each: Bobbing with breathing
  Flutter kick on back (on the wall)
  Flutter kick on stomach (on the wall)
  Rhythmic breathing on the wall

Beginning training session: (1 minute rest between each)
  1 × 25 yard freestyle
  1 minute bobbing with breathing
  1 × 25 yard freestyle
  1 minute rhythmic breathing on wall
  1 × 25 yard elementary backstroke

  (add more distance and/or other sets as fitness improves)

Beginning training session: Lap swimming according to components described in Table 5

Intermediate training session: Pyramid 100 yard walk/swim—Rest
  200 yard walk/swim—Rest
  300 yard walk/swim—Rest
  400 yard walk/swim—Rest
  300 yard walk/swim—Rest
  200 yard walk/swim—Rest
  100 yard walk/swim

Intermediate training session: Interval session 12 × 100 yards

Cool-down: 1 minute rhythmic breathing on wall
  2–3 minutes flutter kicking on stomach
  2–3 minutes flutter kicking on back

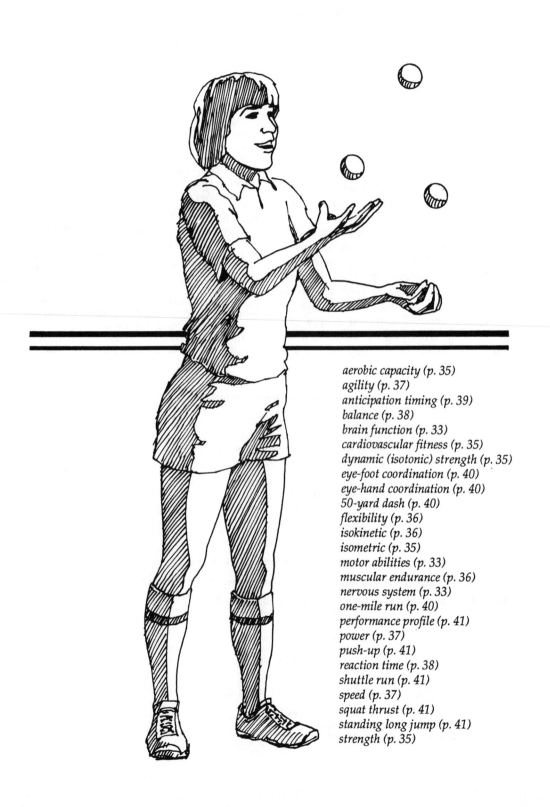

CHAPTER 3

Motor Skill Development and Evaluation

JERRY R. THOMAS
Arizona State University
Tempe, AZ
and
JACK K. NELSON
University of Idaho
Moscow, ID

INTRODUCTION

As individuals mature from childhood through adolescence to adulthood, their ability to perform the motor skills associated with various sports and physical activities improves. This increase in performance is due to a number of factors. First, as people grow they become bigger and stronger. Thus, they can run faster, throw and kick farther, jump higher. Second, regular participation increases the efficiency of one's heart and circulatory, respiratory, and muscular systems, enabling better performance in many sport skills. Finally as children get older, they have performed more sports skills (due to past experiences). These experiences with a variety of skills increase their ability to learn new skills in new situations. All of these factors taken together are responsible for motor skill development and result in increased levels of motor performance with increased age.

By high school most students can perform a variety of everyday motor skills and many specific sports skills. Each of us can probably catch and throw a softball, do the standing broad jump, dribble and shoot a basketball, as well as many other sports skills. Individual interest in sports revolves around one or more of the following questions:

- What type of sport would I enjoy participating in on a lifetime basis?
- How do I choose sports which best pro-

vide the health benefits of regular exercise?
- Since my skill level is very good in several areas, how do I select a varsity sport in which I may excel?
- Can I learn certain sports that I can participate in with my family and/or friends?

In this chapter we hope to demonstrate how sports skills develop, how people learn these skills, and how to evaluate and select sports that will best suit individual needs. We will also discuss the basic motor abilities that are essential in sports performance and ways in which these abilities can be measured. A few simple tests of some of these abilities will be described so that students can be tested and develop performance profiles. Students, based on their own abilities and interests, will be better able to select a sport or sports in which to participate, either recreationally or as an athlete, with some information as to their chances for success and enjoyment.

We believe regular participation in sports and physical activity provides many benefits on a lifetime basis such as:

- increased cardiovascular and respiratory efficiency;
- higher levels of muscular endurance;
- skillful movements in sports;
- positive mental health;
- fun and enjoyment;
- opportunities to socialize with family and friends.

MOTOR SKILL DEVELOPMENT

A *motor skill* is the coordinated muscular activity necessary to accomplish a task. The task may involve large muscles and a great deal of movement such as running, jumping, and turning handsprings, or it may involve the small muscles of the body and relatively little movement such as in typing, sewing, and talking. Many activities involve both large and small muscle tasks. *Motor abilities*, on the other hand, are more general in nature and help us develop motor skills. They include such things as strength, muscular endurance, cardiovascular endurance, power, speed, balance, flexibility, agility, and reaction time. The relation between motor skills and motor abilities can be seen in the long jump. Motor abilities such as power and speed play an important role in the development of the long jump as a motor skill.

Let us turn our attention to several factors that directly affect students' ability to learn and perform motor skills.

Age changes in motor performance. The performance of fundamental skills (running, jumping, throwing, catching, strik-

ing, and kicking) increases in a rather consistent fashion for both boys and girls during the elementary school years. Diagram 1 illustrates that performance for these skills increases at each age level for boys and girls up to 11 years. While the average performance of the boys is slightly better than the girls, there is much overlap between the sexes with girls' performance frequently exceeding that of the boys. Most people believe that the motor performance differences between boys and girls before age 11 are due to different cultural expectations for males and females. Girls may not be expected to learn and perform the skills as well.

Beginning at about 11 or 12 years of age, the boys' performance on many tasks goes up rapidly while the performance of girls begins to stabilize. This is due to both physical and cultural (home and community influence) factors. When a boy reaches puberty, large quantities of the hormone testosterone are present in his body. Testosterone promotes muscular development and the strengthening of bones as well as the secondary sex characteristics of whiskers, a deeper voice, and genital development.

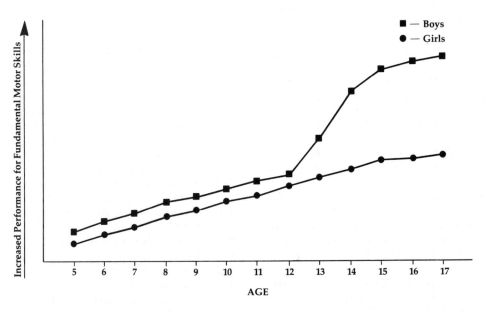

Diagram 1. Age and gender differences in performance of fundamental motor skills (estimated curve).

While small amounts of testosterone are present in girls, it does not lead to excessive muscular development. The muscular development in boys improves motor performance where the rapid application of strength (called power) is important. Thus, skills like running, jumping, throwing, etc., show rapid gains during this time of development.

Girls' performance in many tasks begins to level off at about 11 or 12 years of age. As girls reach puberty and start to develop secondary sex characteristics (e.g., breasts, broader hips), their bodies begin to have a higher percentage of fat. This in combination with the lack of hormone-related muscle development tends to keep girls' performance on power tasks substantially below that of boys after puberty. Nevertheless, cultural factors are basically responsible for the leveling of performance. Many girls no longer participate and practice motor skills or specific sports skills. If societal norms increase the number of girls who participate in sport and exercise on a regular basis after puberty, performance should increase.

Factors that influence skill development. A number of items influence the normal development and learning of motor skills. Physical fitness tends to vary only slightly among younger children but can play a substantial role beginning at about the fourth grade. Children who cannot run for very long or are weak, will find many skills difficult to perform. A child who becomes tired after 2–3 minutes of running, for instance, no matter how skillful in soccer, will not be a very successful player. In this instance cardiovascular endurance keeps him/her from effectively demonstrating the skills. Children and adolescents should look carefully at the sports that interest them. Does physical fitness level restrict success? After completing this chapter, students will be in a much better position to answer this question and take action based upon their response.

Motor abilities are also important in learning sports skills. Most people believe motor abilities such as hand-eye coordination and balance are inherited. Some people have more ability than others. Success

in sports is directly related to motor abilities. While coordination may be improved in specific sports skills (hitting the baseball, for example) by continued practice, if your eye-hand coordination is not good, you would probably do better to pick a sport in which hand-eye coordination is not so important (swimming, for example).

We've talked a good bit about developing *fundamental motor skills*, like throwing, running, jumping, etc. Once the skills are developed during elementary school, they can be applied to specific sports. Even though a student has a good overhand throwing motion, it takes practice to apply this motion to efficiently throw a baseball or football. Students should spend much of their practice time in the correct performance of the specific skills for the sport(s) selected. This continued practice, called overlearning, allows performance of the skill in an automatic way without having to think about the parts of the movement. This overlearning of the correct movement in a variety of situations is what we strive for in sport and what practice is all about.

How people learn skills. When learning a new motor skill or practicing one already known, both the nervous and muscular systems are involved. Suppose a student is learning to hit a tennis ball with a forehand stroke. Think about all the things involved. First the tennis racket is like a 2½ foot extension of the arm. He/she must learn to grip it properly, swing it through a correct arc, turn the racket face at the correct angle, apply the proper amount of force to the swing, watch the tennis ball coming, decide where to hit the ball on the other side of the net, and then execute all of these individual acts with correct timing. How could anyone think all sport skills are physical? *The brain and nervous systems are the key factors in controlling movements.*

We frequently refer to the brain's function as an information processing system with three major components. The first is called a sensory store where incoming information is held very briefly; in the case of the tennis forehand the eyes send signals to the brain about the oncoming ball. In addition, the muscles and joints send signals to brain about the position of various body parts, arms, legs, trunk, etc. Much of this information is taken from sensory store and used by the second component called working memory. Working memory is where everything happens. We integrate all of these incoming signals to make sense of them.

The third component is called the knowledge base and is where information is kept for long periods of time. For instance, you have a plan to control your arms, feet, and trunk for performing the forehand stroke in tennis. This plan has been built up from all the times the stroke was done before. People who have learned this stroke correctly and practiced it numerous times have a very good plan that they can use without thinking about it. However, when a person is just learning this stroke, the plan is being developed and probably has many errors. When hitting a tennis ball, the plan must be adjusted for all of the signals received from the senses, for example, how fast the tennis ball is coming, the player's position on the court, and where the ball is to be hit. This all happens in working memory.

Once the plan is taken from the knowledge base and adjusted in working memory for all the current signals from the senses, then the plan is set into operation, and the stroke is performed. The results of this stroke can be observed and corrections made in the plan if need be, so that performance will be better next time.

Information processing systems work like this to control all motor skills. Two things are important to remember:

1. For slow movements or movements that take a long time, your plan can be corrected for errors along the way. However, if the movement is very rapid, the plan is quickly completed and corrections can only be made for the next time you attempt the skill. For example, when you are going to catch a fly ball in softball, you make adjustments as the ball is coming toward you. You can continue to make these adjustments until just before the ball arrives at your glove. But when you are hitting a ball thrown very fast, you don't have time to make any more adjustments in your plan once the bat swing is begun. That's why a curve will fool you when you are expecting a straight ball.

2. The basic objective of learning nearly all motor skills is to make them as automatic as possible. This means you don't have to think about the parts of the skill itself but can concentrate on other aspects of the situation. In the case of the forehand stroke in tennis, the stroke itself should be automatic so that you can think about your position on the court and where you want to hit the tennis ball. You must practice a skill many times in all the specific situations it will be used to obtain the automatic control of the movement.

To summarize, the most important factor in learning and performing a movement is to develop a good plan. A good movement plan comes from correct instruction, effective information about the outcome of each try at the skill, and sufficient practice to make the plan automatically occur when needed.

One of the most important considerations when learning a new skill is being able to determine when mistakes are made in the movement. Results of mistakes can be frequently seen; for example, the volleyball is hit into the net or out-of-bounds. But what if the plan for the movement was incorrect? Your physical education teacher should help you analyze errors in movements, but you should also learn to analyze your own errors. Sometimes you will be practicing or playing at times other than in physical education class and there will be no teacher to give error information. Try to be aware of where body parts are as the skill is performed so that you can feel if something is wrong. Remember how it felt to do the skill correctly and try to make the next movement in the correct way.

This ability to self-analyze and self-correct is very important and will speed up learning of the skill. But remember, everyone's style is a little different, so the same approaches may not work for everyone. Differences in style do not mean poor form, just that body type as well as other considerations may suggest slightly different techniques. The main thing is not to get discouraged; continue to seek good instruction and practice. Skills will improve so you can have fun when playing and receive the positive health benefits, both physical and mental, of regular exercise.

EVALUATING SKILLS

The remainder of this chapter is designed to aid in evaluating skills to determine the sport(s) in which you are likely to be most successful. Of course, none of the techniques we are suggesting are foolproof. But we believe if these procedures are used appropriately, students can find a sport or physical activity in which they can be successful, have fun, and get regular exercise on a lifetime basis.

PHYSICAL FITNESS COMPONENTS

Cardiovascular fitness involves the proper functioning of the heart, lungs, and blood vessels. It is the ability to adjust to, and recover from, the stress of exercise. Examples of individuals having very high degrees of cardiovascular fitness are marathon runners, long-distance track runners and swimmers, and cross-country skiers.

The term *aerobic capacity* is used in connection with cardiovascular fitness. It refers to the maximum amount of oxygen one can consume per minute. In other words, the ability to vigorously exercise for a prolonged period of time is determined by the body's ability to deliver oxygen to the active muscles and organs. Although cardiovascular fitness (and aerobic capacity) can be improved through exercise, the aerobic capacity is largely determined by heredity. This is why some people are just naturally better suited for distance running than others. The saying that "great runners are born, not made" arises from this fact.

Cardiovascular fitness can be measured in several ways. The most accurate measurement is done in a laboratory in which an individual runs on a treadmill while the air that is breathed out is analyzed for oxygen and carbon dioxide content. The maximum amount of oxygen that can be taken in per minute is thus determined (aerobic capacity). Since this way of measuring cardiovascular fitness requires expensive

equipment, other methods are more commonly used, such as step tests and distance runs. In the step tests, a person steps up and down on a bench at a specific rhythm for several minutes. The pulse rate is then counted immediately afterward.

Distance runs are most frequently used in testing for cardiovascular fitness. A general recommendation is that a distance run should involve at least five minutes of running. Consequently the most common distance runs are the 1-mile, 1½-mile, 2-mile, the 9-minute run, and the 12-minute run. A person who has a higher degree of cardiovascular fitness will be able to run a certain distance, such as a mile, in a shorter time or cover more distance in a set time period, such as 12 minutes, than a less fit individual.

Strength is a very important aspect of physical fitness. Simply stated, it is the ability to exert force. Strength is a necessary component in most sports and is also an important element in carrying out one's daily activities effectively and efficiently. It can be demonstrated in various ways. Force exerted during movement, such as lifting a barbell, is *dynamic (isotonic)* strength. *Isometric* strength is force exerted against an immovable object, such as pushing or pulling against a bar that is bolted to the wall.

Dynamic, or isotonic, strength has been measured mostly by the use of barbells and weights. A 1 RM means one repetition maximum, which is the greatest amount of weight a person can lift one time. Strength-training with weights utilizes multiple RMs. For example, a person utilizing an 8 RM set would select a weight that he or she could only lift 8 times. As the individual grows stronger the number of times the weight can be lifted (repetitions) increases. When the person can lift it 12 times, more weight is added so that the maximum number of repetitions drops to 8 again. This is the basis for progressive resistance weight-training. A major advantage of weight-lifting is that measurement, i.e., knowledge of results, is automatic.

Isometric strength-training is used to supplement dynamic training. For example, we are not equally strong through the entire range of a movement. In other words, a heavier weight can be held better at hip level than when it's held at shoulder level because of mechanical leverage. In lifting weights, one can only lift as much as can be handled at the weakest point. Therefore if one concentrates at that "sticking point" by maximum isometric contraction, strength can be improved at that specific place, and thus more weight can be lifted throughout the entire range of the movement.

Isometric strength-training is also done in home exercise programs through pushing and pulling against doorways, walls, and other immovable objects.

In *isokinetic* strength-training, an individual applies maximum exertion throughout a full range of motion. An example would be if you pushed as hard as you could on a car as it was being raised on a hydraulic lift in a service station. No matter how hard you push, the steady movement of the car would not be affected. Some machines are now used in strength-training that automatically adjust so as to provide variable resistance that equals the force being applied throughout the range of motion. This type of training supposedly combines the advantages of both isotonic and isometric training.

Muscular endurance is repeating a movement that requires less than a maximum effort. One typically thinks of exercises such as sit-ups and push-ups as representing muscular endurance activities. There are many daily tasks that involve muscular endurance. Raking leaves, hammering nails, painting, shoveling, and scrubbing floors are but a few examples of such tasks.

Muscular endurance is related to cardiovascular endurance and also to strength, but they are not the same abilities. For example, a person may have high cardiovascular endurance and be able to run many miles but can do very few push-ups, or a person may be able to lift a very heavy weight but cannot do many sit-ups. Obviously there are a number of factors that influence the relationship between muscular endurance and strength and cardiovascular fitness.

Although muscular endurance seems to be a rather simple clear-cut concept, the measurement of it is not. For example, push-ups supposedly measure muscular endurance of the arms and shoulders. Yet if a person isn't strong enough to push his/ her body weight up more than one or two times, we can't really say that the person has no endurance. The same can be said about pull-ups, sit-ups, parallel bar dips, etc. Because of the involvement of strength, these test items are often referred to as measures of strength and endurance. Nevertheless, an exercise cannot be considered as endurance unless it is submaximal (requires less than your greatest effort). In other words, it has to be done repeatedly.

Flexibility is another part of physical fitness—the ability to move the body and its parts through a wide range of motion. It is important in one's mobility in sport, in the avoidance of injuries, and in posture.

When a person gets "out of shape," one of the first things noticed is reduced flexibility. This is because our muscles shorten when we do not regularly move and stretch. A person with reduced flexibility is more likely to suffer a "pull" or strain when he/she moves suddenly or beyond the normal range of motion. For this reason, teachers/coaches usually include a number of stretching exercises as part of any training program.

Flexibility is quite specific to the individual parts of the body. For example, an individual who is very flexible in the trunk and hips, as evidenced by being able to bend over with the knees straight and touch the hands to the floor with ease, may be very "tight" in the shoulders, or vice versa. Also, there is what is called dynamic flexibility, in which mobility is demonstrated rapidly, and static flexibility, which is a slow steady stretching movement. In most sports, dynamic flexibility is more important than static flexibility.

Flexibility has been measured in a number of ways. One of the most common tests is the sit-and-reach in which the student sits on the floor with feet braced and, keeping the knees straight, reaches forward as far as possible. There are several other simple measures of flexibility that require only a rule or tape measure. For example, trunk (and neck) flexibility can be measured by having the person to be tested lie face down with the hands behind the head. Someone holds the hips down on the mat while the person arches back as far as possible and holds this position momentarily while the tester measures from the mat to the chin. A measurement for shoulder flexibility is done with the person lying face down, arms stretched out in front, holding a stick, such as a yardstick, in both hands. Then, with the chin touching mat, the person raises the arms as high as possible off the mat. The distance from the mat to the stick is used as an indication of shoulder flexibility.

Flexibility of specific joints such as the ankle, knee, elbow, etc., is sometimes assessed by physiotherapists and athletic trainers using a protractor-type device called a *goniometer*. This is often done to measure the patient's progress in regaining range of motion in a joint following inactivity due to injury, such as having been in a cast. There are also more accurate and expensive instruments available for measuring flexibility in laboratory research.

MOTOR FITNESS COMPONENTS

Power is unquestionably one of the most important elements in athletics. Power is the ability to exert maximum force in the shortest period of time. The explosive charge of the football player, the great thrust of the shot putter, the long drive off the tee in golf, the mighty swing of the baseball bat, and the knockout punch in boxing illustrate power in sports. In fact, most of the popular team and individual sports are predominantly "power-oriented."

Evidence of natural power, explosiveness, force, etc., is one of the first things a coach looks for in new players in many sports. Preseason workouts and inseason practice drills focus heavily on power development.

The measurement of power is not an easy task. Power is comprised of both strength and speed, but it is the coordinated combination of the two abilities that actually constitutes power performance. In other words a person may be tremendously strong and yet not be as powerful as a person of lesser strength. Furthermore, increased strength will generally improve power but certainly not in direct proportion.

The standing broad jump and the vertical jump have often been used as power measurements. Less frequently, tests of such skills as the medicine ball throw, shot put, stair climb, and rope pull have also been utilized as power tests. Nearly all of these tests are quite easy to give and are accurate measures. However, as with most tests, they are specific to the part of the body that is primarily involved. For example, the standing broad jump primarily measures the power of the legs, while the rope pull or seated medicine ball throw tests the power of the arms and shoulders.

Speed is another important aspect of a number of sports. Speed of movement is largely innate, which means that it is hereditary. One is either fast or not. Speed of movement, such as running, can be improved to a small degree by the practice of proper starting techniques and perhaps the development of better mechanics of movement.

Generally, speed is measured by some short run such as the 50-yard dash, the 100-meter run, etc. In football, the 40-yard dash has gained widespread popularity as the measure of speed for that sport, although probably a much shorter distance such as 5 yards would be considerably more appropriate if it could be measured accurately.

Agility is the ability to change direction rapidly with a high degree of accuracy. A runner in football who is able to dodge, start, and stop quickly and skillfully change direction displays outstanding agility. In fact, some individuals without great straightaway running speed are still very effective because of their ability to shift their body weight and change direction quickly and accurately.

Agility does not have to involve running. It can also be shown by rapid changes in body position, such as in gymnastics, diving, and wrestling.

Running tests of agility, commonly given in practice drills in athletics, relate quite highly to power. This is understandable because of the explosiveness that is required in many agility drills that call for rapid starts and acceleration. Obviously there are many different kinds of agility, such as zigzag runs, shuttle runs, squat-thrusts, and back pedaling, that are part of the conditioning and practice drills in athletics. A good teacher or coach will use agility drills (and tests) that involve the types of movements necessary for that particular sport.

Balance is the ability to maintain one's equilibrium. It is an important element in carrying out our daily activities effectively and efficiently. Balance is an important part of the body movements required in many sports as well.

There are different kinds of balance. One kind is called *dynamic balance,* which is the ability to maintain proper body position while moving. Most sports require this kind of balance, but in many different ways. Obviously ice skating, roller skating, skiing, and all forms of dance are excellent examples of activities which demand dynamic balance. Any sport which involves agility and running, such as football, soccer, basketball, baseball, etc. also involves dynamic balance.

Static balance is the type of balance in which a stationary position must be maintained for a certain period of time. All of the events in gymnastics require static balance. Often in sports, static balance immediately follows movement such as when the basketball player leaps high to grab a rebound or pass and must land and keep from traveling, when the gymnast who turns a flip must land and maintain balance on the beam, and in bowling, shot putting, discus, and javelin throwing where the performer must suddenly stop after release and maintain balance to keep from going over the foul line.

Another form of balancing ability involves balancing an object either when moving, such as trying to avoid spilling coffee while carrying a cup across a room, or when stationary, such as balancing the cup on your knee while seated. This kind of balance is not too prevalent in sports, yet it points out again the great amount of specificity of performance.

Because of the extreme amount of specificity, tests of balance are rarely included as a part of fitness tests. One could, however, measure certain kinds of balance by such tasks as walking on a beam, by standing on the ball of one foot as long as possible, and by tumbling stunts such as headstands and handstands.

Reaction time is a critical part of athletic performance. Reaction time is the time it takes a person to react or move after a stimulus has been given. The stimulus could be any number of things such as the starting gun in a race, the snap count in football, the movement of an opponent, the crack of the bat in baseball, etc. Success in many sports depends on one's ability to *recognize* the correct stimulus and to react accordingly.

Although the definition is very simple, reaction time is quite complex. Many things influence reaction time. For example, the type of stimulus (whether a sound, a sight, or a touch) makes a difference in how quickly one will react. The intensity of the stimulus, that is, whether a *loud* sound or a *bright* light, will affect reaction. The movement or series of movements one has to perform after reacting greatly influences the speed of reaction. A person can react much faster if all that is required is to step on the car brake when the signal light turns yellow. On the other hand, if an individual has to perform a complicated or delicate maneuver, the reaction time will usually be considerably slower. An important point here is that practice and skill attainment in the required movement, or task, will greatly improve the speed of reaction. This is the reason why student pilots practice emergency procedures over and over until the procedures become virtually automatic, so that when an emergency occurs the pilot can react instantly without having to pause and think of the sequence of steps.

A very similar situation is present in sports. Through countless hours of practice, the athlete develops more and more skill (called expertise) in the various aspects of the sport, thus decreasing the need to think about what has to be done, which in turn enables a faster response.

The measurement of reaction time in the research laboratory is done with electrical timers, which permit measurement of response to different kinds and intensities of stimuli and simple and complex responses. A very simple measure of reaction can be accomplished using a yardstick. In this method, one utilizes the law of constant acceleration of free falling bodies (gravity) and merely converts distance to time.

The tester holds the yardstick at the top and lets it hang between the person's thumb and index finger. The upper surface of the thumb should be aligned with the 4-inch mark. The person being tested looks at the 8-inch mark and is told to react by catching the stick when it starts to fall. The tester says "ready" and drops the stick, varying the time between "ready" and the release. The distance the stick falls before it can be caught is changed to time by the formula:

$$\text{time (seconds)} = \sqrt{\frac{\text{(distance in inches)}}{6(32)}}$$

For example, if the stick drops 6 inches, the time that elapsed before the subject could react and pinch the fingers would be .18 seconds.

$$\sqrt{\frac{6 \text{ inches}}{6(32)}} \quad 0.18 \text{ seconds or } 180 \text{ msec}$$

Anticipation timing involves the prediction of when an object such as a ball, an opponent, a shuttlecock, etc. is going to arrive at a particular point. The outfielder in baseball must determine where the fly ball is going to land (and when) to move under it in time to make the catch. The tennis player constantly has to make decisions as to where and when to move and the footwork required to enable him/her to be in position (not too close to the ball, not too far away) to return the opponent's shot.

This is quite complex. There is much that is unknown about this kind of decision-making. Teachers/coaches constantly stress "keeping your eye on the ball." Yet, in many instances, we are simply not able to keep our eye on the ball and make the necessary movement. For example, to watch a pitched baseball all the way to contact with the bat is impossible. Consequently, we must decide whether we are going to swing and, if so, start the swing sometime before the ball arrives and hope that we have correctly judged where the ball is going to be and the exact instant when it will be over the plate. The faster one's reaction time, the more time one has before beginning the swing. Moreover, the speed with which one can whip the bat around can also be advantageous.

The more one practices and the more experience one has in a sport, the more "clues" one picks up that help in anticipation timing. In tennis, for example, such things as where the opponent is looking, the placement of the feet, body movements, the swing of the racket (its trajectory and speed), and the sound of the ball as it is struck give information that will influence one's prediction as to the flight of the ball. Naturally a player is sometimes badly fooled by some of these clues. A good player often tries to take advantage of the use of clues by deliberately looking in another direction and trying to disguise the force and path of the swing.

The saying "keep your eye on the ball" is good advice even if it is not always possible. Undoubtedly as a result, the performer concentrates more on the moment of contact, maybe even creating an illusion of seeing the bat or racket strike the ball.

OTHER MOTOR ABILITIES

Skillful performance as is seen in athletics, dance, crafts, and many daily activities requires coordination of different parts of the body during movement. Since there are different kinds of movement, it follows that there are different kinds of coordination. Some tasks primarily involve the coordination of the hand and arm in conjunction with vision such as in shooting a basketball, pitching in baseball, passing a football, and bowling. These skills require *eye-hand coordination*.

A number of sports involve skillful movements of the feet and legs in which *eye-foot coordination* is necessary. Place kicking and punting in football and dribbling with the feet in soccer are examples of the need for this type of coordination.

The term *general or total body coordination*, is sometimes used to refer to the simultaneous movements required of the total body as in a gymnastics routine, catching a pass in football, dribbling and shooting a lay-up in basketball, throwing the javelin, pole vaulting, high jumping and hurdling in track, and on and on. One thing to bear in mind is the specificity of performance and, consequently, the specificity of coordination. We are prone to generalize too much and assume that because someone demonstrates good coordination in a sport that he/she will also be good in another or all sports. While there may be some similarities in movement patterns and basic skills in several different sports, success in one sport does not guarantee success in another.

HOW TO PREDICT SPORT SUCCESS

Obviously, it is impossible to predict success in sports with any degree of certainty. There are simply too many factors involved. Instead, one can try to narrow the range of probabilities in accordance with one's abilities and characteristics.

It might be easier to rule out sports for which one is obviously not suited. For instance, a person who is tall and/or heavy should not dream of becoming a jockey. By the same token, an individual who is small and slow will probably be unsuccessful in football. Hence, genetics (heredity) does place limitations with regard to the chances of success in a number of sports. We should hasten to add, however, that there is always the exception. High levels of drive, ambition, and perseverance have been known to make up for limitations in size and natural abilities.

In the following section, some basic physical performance tests are described.

All of them can be done with very little equipment, and the directions are simple. You have probably performed these tests at one time or another in your physical education classes.

These tests represent measures of motor fitness that are basic to athletic performance. Naturally, they should not be taken too seriously. In other words, just because a student is below average on a test does not necessarily mean that he/she is hopelessly weak in that area. These tests should be thought of as mere indicators of abilities in certain areas. Remember, the various abilities such as speed, power, agility, and endurance that are involved in a sport are quite specific in the way in which they are utilized. Nevertheless, a profile can be constructed on these different kinds of abilities that may aid in predicting whether students are better suited for some sports than others.

TESTING MOTOR PERFORMANCE

One-mile run (cardiovascular endurance). It is best if a 440-yard track is available for this test, but the mile run can be done practically anywhere that the correct distance can be laid off. The only equipment necessary is a stopwatch or any wristwatch that can indicate the elapsed time to the nearest second. When ready, the tester starts the watch (note the exact time to the second) as students start to run. Read times off the stopwatch as students cross the finish line (or note the time to the exact second on a wristwatch). Note: it is important to have students practice distance running for awhile to get into some kind of shape as well as to establish the best pace. Attempting to get a realistic measure of ability to run a mile if one has not been practicing is a waste of time.

50-yard dash (running speed). Measure off exactly 50 yards, preferably on a running track. A stopwatch is needed to record the time to the nearest tenth of a second. The watch should be started as soon as the student starts to move and stopped at the exact instant that he/she crosses the finish line. Take at least two trials and use the best score.

Standing long jump (explosive power). All that is needed for this test is a yardstick or tape measure and a flat surface to jump on. Students stand with the feet comfortably apart, toes just behind a starting line. The student swings the arms back and bends the knees, then springs forward as far as possible swinging the arms forward. Have someone spot the student's exact heel placement in the event that he/she moves after landing. The measurement is taken from the starting line to the heel nearest the starting line. In other words, if a student lands with one foot slightly ahead of the other, the heel of the trailing foot is used as the point of landing. Take three trials and use the longest jump measured in feet and inches as the score.

Push-up (muscular strength and endurance). No equipment is necessary for this test. Students lie down with the chest on the floor and hands about shoulder width apart, then push up to a straight arm support and return keeping the body straight throughout. The total number of repetitions without rest is the score.

Bent knee push-up (muscular strength and endurance). The only difference in the bent knee push-up is that the weight is supported by the hands and knees rather than the hands and feet. The starting position is thus modified to the extent that the knees are bent while lying face down. As students push to a straight arm support, the body must be kept straight from shoulders to knees.

Shuttle run (running agility). You need a good smooth running surface such as a gymnasium floor with 2 lines (Line A and Line B) 30 feet apart. The starting position is on the hands and knees with the hands just behind the starting line (Line A). A starter gives the commands, "get set, go!" On the command "go," the student scrambles to his/her feet and sprints to the other line (Line B). He/she touches a hand to the floor just beyond that line and turns around and races back to the starting line (Line A). He/she touches the floor again just over the starting line and races back to the other line (Line B). Once more he/she touches a hand to the floor just beyond that line and then sprints back across the starting line (Line

A). (Hence, he/she runs between the lines 4 times and touches a hand to the floor 3 times.) The timer starts the watch on the command "go" and stops the watch as the student's chest crosses the finish line. The score is to the nearest tenth of a second. Take three trials and use the fastest time as the score.

Squat-thrust (body movement agility). A timer with a stopwatch should help the student take this test. The student starts in a standing position. When ready, he/she (1) moves to a squat position with hands on the floor, (2) thrusts the legs backward to a push-up position with weight resting on the hands and feet, (3) returns to the squat position, and (4) rises to a standing position. Each of the four parts of the squat-thrust counts one point. In other words, one complete squat-thrust is worth four points. The score is the number of points acquired within 10 seconds. The timer starts the watch on the command "go" and stops the watch at the end of 10 seconds, at which point, he/she yells "stop!" Three trials are performed and the best score is recorded.

DEVELOPING PERFORMANCE PROFILES

In Table 1 are some standards of performance in the tests described above based on many scores from boys and girls approximately 15 years of age. Students can plot their own profile according to how they scored in each of the tests.

Sample Profile. A 15-year-old boy who is 5'6" tall and weighs 130 pounds had the following scores: mile (7:48), 50-yard dash (6.9), standing broad jump (8'0"), push-ups (55), shuttle run (10.1), and squat-thrusts (32) (see Diagram 2). In this example, the boy demonstrated excellent explosive power, muscular strength and endurance, and body movement agility. His cardiovascular endurance, running speed, and running agility were fair to average. With the boy's size, he probably would not excel in a sport such as football or perhaps basketball or baseball. He also would probably be at a disadvantage in track and field. On the other hand, he may be admirably suited for

Table 1. Standards of performance on motor skills tests.

Standards for Fifteen Year-old Boys

	Excellent	Good	Average	Fair	Poor
1. Cardiovascular Endurance (1-mile run)	6 min. & under	6:10-6:40	6:50-7:20	7:30-8:10	8:25 & over
2. Running Speed (50-yard Dash)	6.2 sec. & under	6.4-6.7	6.8-7.0	7.1-7.3	7.5 & over
3. Explosive Power (Standing Broad Jump)	7'9'' & over	7'6''-7'1''	7'0''-6'6''	6'5''-6'1''	5'10'' & under
4. Strength and Endurance (Push-ups)	48 & over	45-38	37-32	31-28	25 & under
5. Agility-Running (Shuttle Run)	9.4 sec. & under	9.5-9.9	10.0-10.3	10.4-10.8	11.0 & over
6. Agility-Body Movement (Squat-thrust)	32 & over	31-28	27-16	15-12	10 & under

Standards for Fifteen Year-old Girls

	Excellent	Good	Average	Fair	Poor
1. Cardiovascular Endurance (1-mile Run)	7:10 min. & under	8:20-9:15	9:20-10:30	10:45-12:15	12:30 & over
2. Running Speed (50-yard dash)	7.3 sec. & under	7.5-7.9	8.0-8.3	8.4-9.0	9.1 & over
3. Explosive Power (Standing Broad Jump)	6'3'' & over	6'1''-5'7''	5'6''-5'1''	5'0''-4'7''	4'6'' & under
4. Strength and Endurance (Bent Knee Push-ups)	31 & over	30-25	24-13	12-7	6 & under
5. Agility-Running (Shuttle Run)	10.3 sec. & under	10.5-11.0	11.1-11.6	11.7-12.4	12.5 & over
6. Agility-Body Movement (Squat-thrust)	30 & over	29-26	25-14	13-10	9 & under

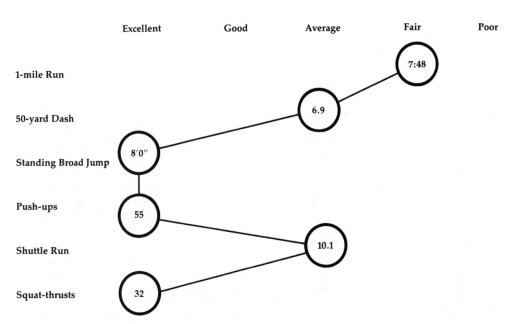

Diagram 2. Sample profile of 15-year-old boy on six motor performance tests.

sports such as gymnastics or wrestling in which his strength, muscular endurance, explosive power, and body movement agility would be helpful.

This is merely a very limited example of how motor fitness abilities, with respect to possible sports participation, might be rated. There are, of course, many other sports in which the boy's abilities may or may not be well-suited. Remember also, that one's desire and determination can play a very important role in whether or not a person will be successful in any sport.

In this chapter we have tried to describe some of the processes that are involved in developing motor skills and some of the abilities that are necessary for success in sports, dance, and other activities. By testing some of these important physical abilities, students should be better equipped to decide for what sport(s) they might be best suited.

Regardless of the chosen sport and for what purpose (recreation, fitness, or varsity competition) it is selected, it will take lots and lots of practice before students will be highly skilled. In addition, as they become more skilled, they will get more enjoyment out of playing the sport. People usually will not play a sport for fun if they are very poor performers unless they can see that they are improving. For example, tennis isn't much fun if the ball is constantly hit into the net or out-of-bounds. The ball has to be kept in play. But students should not become discouraged right away. Improvement comes with practice, and with improvement comes enjoyment and satisfaction.

PRACTICE REGULARLY

Evaluate progress so that students can chart improvement. In tennis, for example, count the number of times the ball can be hit against the wall and the number of times the ball is served into each service court. If this is regularly done, improvement is obvious. The same kind of self-testing can be done in any sport.

Also, remember that by improving motor abilities such as strength, endurance, flexibility, etc., skill performance can be improved. For example, fatigue can slow reactions and speed of movement, and thus the student cannot get into the proper position quickly, which means they cannot make a good play. By improving stamina students will find that they can play at a higher skill level for a longer time.

So get in shape, listen to your teacher or coach, and practice, practice, practice. You will find that the joy of effort, the thrill of the challenge, and pride of accomplishment will carry over and enhance all aspects of your life.

REFERENCES

Corbin, C.B., & Lindsey, R. *Concepts of physical fitness* (7th ed.). Dubuque, IA: Wm. C. Brown, 1990.

Johnson, B.L., & Nelson, J.K. *Practical measurements for evaluation in physical education* (4th ed.). New York: Macmillan, 1987.

Pangrazi, R.P., & Darst, P.W. *Dynamic physical education for secondary school students* (2nd ed.). New York: Macmillan, 1987.

Payne, V.G., & Isaacs, L.D. *Human motor development* (2nd ed.). Mountain View, CA: Mayfield Publishing, 1991.

Seefeldt, V. (Ed.). *Physical activity & well-being.* Reston, VA: AAHPERD, 1986.

CHAPTER 4

Archery

CLAIRE CHAMBERLAIN
University of Lowell
Lowell, MA

Archery is a sport for all ages. It requires concentration and focus on detail. Once the basic, gross motor skills are mastered, it is a matter of fine-tuning the many details that lead to success. Much as golf is you-against-par, archery is you-against-the-target.

Once basic skills are mastered, there are a variety of competitive levels and activities from the beginning archer to the advanced. "Games" may be adapted for the school or camp setting, while more advanced shooting activities from target archery to archery golf may be found at local, state, or district levels. Expert shooters, of course, find opportunities at the national, international, and Olympic levels.

For target archery, the technique remains the same even if the equipment becomes more sophisticated and the competition increases.

More important than shooting technique, however, is the constant observation of safety procedures—not only for the participants but also for the liability involved for the supervisors. (For specifics on safety, see the chapter on archery in *Principles of Safety in Physical Education and Sport*, AAHPERD.)

SKILLS AND TECHNIQUES

Before shooting, be sure to check the equipment for safety. In addition, understand your responsibilities for your personal safety and for that of other shooters. Mandatory equipment is an arm guard for bow arm.

EYE DOMINANCE TEST

To determine eye dominance, the student should place his/her hands together, making a circle, at arm's length away from the face. Sight an object through the hole. Use both eyes to see at first. Without moving the hands, close the left eye. Can the object still be seen? If it cannot, it indicates left-eye dominance. Still not moving the hands, open the left eye and close the right. Can the object still be seen? If it cannot, or if it has shifted, the student is right-eye dominant.

Results. Right-handed people who are right-eye dominant will shoot with their right eye open and left closed. Left-handed people who are left-eye dominant will shoot with their left eye open and right closed. Those who are "opposite," i.e., right-handed people with left eye dominance (or left-handed people with right eye dominance), need to shoot and to aim with both eyes open.

This is an essential factor in successful shooting. Using the incorrect eye or eyes will lead to inconsistent and inaccurate shooting.

SEVEN STAGES OF SHOOTING

There are, basically, seven stages of shooting. Each stage is an important building block to successful shooting and needs to be mastered before one can assume there might be a problem with the point of aim (POA).

Before beginning, make certain bows are braced (strung) well and that the loops at either end of the string are well-attached in the bow's notches. Remember to check to see it is not strung inside out and to make sure the bow is right-side up. The "fat" part of the grip is "up" on fiberglass bows. With wooden bows and a carved grip, the arrow rest should be "up."

The following directions are written as they would be given to a right-handed shooter.

1. Stance

Straddle the shooting line with your left side to the target. If you are directly opposite the target, use a square stance. To the extreme right or left, choose either an open or closed stance.

Your weight should be evenly distributed and comfortable. Knees easy. Shoulders back. Head level. Hips straight ahead. Hold your bow in your left hand comfortably so that the bow is parallel to the floor and the string is between your inner arm and body.

2. Nock

To nock the arrow (i.e., to place the plastic nock into the string) locate the cock feather. The arrow has three feathers: two hen feathers alike in color and one odd-colored feather, the cock feather. Keep the tip (metal point) pointed down and in control as you nock the arrow.

With your bow at your side, and with your arm hanging down, use your right hand to move the arrow up, over the bow so the cock feather is up, pointing to the ceiling, and place the arrow on top of the bow. Insert the nock gently, but firmly, into the string, opposite the arrow rest. The arrow should be on the arrow rest and nocked at a 90° angle to the bow. This is an important detail to ensure consistent shooting. An arrow nocked too low will fly high, and the archer runs the risk of a feather cut on the bow hand. An arrow nocked too high will fly low.

As a final check, once the bow is upright, the arrow should be on the left side of the bow for a right-handed shooter, with the cock feather pointing left.

Note: At first, beginning archers should practice the remaining stages *without* an arrow. There are many details to consider, and it is wise to coordinate the gross motor movements first. Once they feel comfortable after several tries, only then add the arrow. Remember, once the bow is loaded with an arrow, the archer now has a loaded weapon in his/her hands, which should be respected as such.

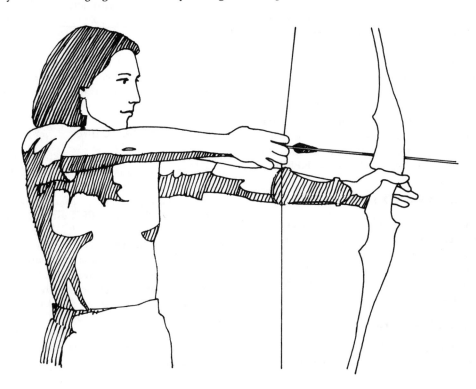

Figure 1.

3. Draw (practice first without an arrow)

The easiest method to use when drawing back the bow is to lift the bow into the upright position. The left hand (bowhand) should grip the bow gently. The pressure is in the V of the palm, as the main action is to push the bow. The fingers are gently closed around the grip, simply to get them out of the way.

Many beginners have a weak grip, with the hand position having slipped from the strong V to the weak thumb. Make certain you are not pushing with the thumb. If you do, you might lose control of the bow.

Perform the following series of directions:

Maintain a firm left wrist . . . not stiff, just firm.

Place three fingers of your right hand on the bowstring, directly opposite the arrow rest. Use the index, middle, and ring fingers, just in front of the first joint. Putting "too much finger" on the string results in a sloppy release. The index finger goes above the arrow, the other two below.

With the bow upright, and your left arm extended toward the target, pull your right arm straight back to the wall behind you. The muscles between your shoulder blades should be doing most of the work. Your right elbow and forearm are parallel to the floor, at shoulder level.

The three fingers will act like hooks on the string. As you pull back, keep the fingers parallel to the floor. If you allow the string fingers to slant downward, you will put undue pressure eventually against an arrow (a prime beginner's error), and the arrow will flip-flop away from the bow.

The left elbow is important. The left arm should be firm, not stiff, with the elbow slightly rotated to the left, away from the path of the bowstring.

Adjust the elbow slightly away from that path without moving the shoulder or wrist. If left in the way, the inside of the elbow can be struck by the string, and the resulting black and blue mark is called a "bow bite."

The draw motion, then, is a smooth pull action on the string from an extended left bow arm position.

Figure 2.

Figure 3.

4. Anchor (practice at first without an arrow)

The archer must anchor the string hand to the *same* place each time. Notice on your relaxed right hand the natural V between your thumb and index finger. That V is what must be placed on the right side of the face with the thumb right under the jaw-bone. Once the string is drawn, it literally touches the tip of your nose and the thumb is placed under the jawbone.

The string is brought to the nose, not the head to the string. The head remains upright and the string should bisect the nose and lips.

The archer wants to come back to the same anchor each time to allow consistent power with each arrow. If the string is not pulled back far enough, power is lessened, and the arrow will fly low. If one overdraws (goes beyond the proper anchor point) one risks pulling the arrow back beyond the bow and shooting one's own hand or having the arrow hit the belly (inside) of the bow and shatter in one's eyes. Both instances can be avoided easily. If the anchor is correct, the arrow will extend beyond the bow at least one inch. If it does not, get longer arrows immediately.

5. Aim (practice without an arrow at first)

The eyes are above the level of the imaginary arrow. Using the dominant eye, the shooter should look down the shaft of the arrow and look at the metal tip. (The tip should be at least 1" beyond the bow. If it is not, relax the draw and check the anchor point. If that is correct, get longer arrows.)

The head should remain stationary. Moving the head during the draw-aim-release sequence is a common beginner's error.

The tip of the arrow should be aimed at the target. The aim can be adjusted by moving the bow arm right, left, up, or down. This is known as "instinctive shooting." Once this is mastered, one can move to bow sights or ground markers.

Where to aim comes with practice and is dependent upon distance from the target and bow poundage. Keep in mind, when arrows leave the bow, they tend to fly up initially and come down with distance, loss of power, and gravity. The farther away one is from the target with a light-weight bow, the higher he/she will need to aim. The closer one is, the lower the aim. At short range a shooter may need to aim at the ground in front of the target in order to get the gold.

6. Release

The string should roll off the three fingers smoothly and evenly in a good release.

Although repeatedly releasing the string from full draw without an arrow can hurt the bows, it may be important for beginners to try *once* without an arrow. They need to experience the act of opening the string fingers, keeping the string hand anchored, and feel the action of the string and possible "chatter" (vibration) from the bow. Beginners sometimes concentrate so much and are so nervous that they honestly forget to open their hooked fingers to release the string. They then wonder why the arrow didn't go anywhere or why it simply fell to the floor, or ground, in front of them.

Sometimes, too, they merely move their fingers up/down the string rather than letting go of the string altogether.

If the arrow does fall to the floor (ground), make sure you know how to retrieve that arrow: Do *not* bend forward across or step across the shooting line to pick it up. Reach with the bow to pull it back safely across the line first. If the shooter cannot reach it with the bow, it is considered shot. If the archer attempts to step forward across the line, he/she may be shot by a neighboring archer!

The teacher should conduct practice retrieving an arrow by having the class stand in full draw without an arrow. Cry out the warning cry of "Hold your arrows!" Have them relax their draw, point their imaginary arrows down to the floor and then pretend they had an arrow fall from the bow in front of the shooting line. Failure to instill this basic safety rule early could result in a serious accident later.

In class, should it actually happen, and someone forgets and steps in front of the line, the power to call "Hold your arrows" must be given to everyone in class. All must share the responsibility for safety. Ask the offenders to leave the line of shooting until the next end (next group of six arrows to be shot).

7. Follow-through

The archer should simply "pose for a picture" after the string has been released. Some beginners tend to drop one or both hands upon release in a collapsed motion. This can adversely affect the point of aim (POA).

Now, practice with an arrow

HINTS FOR THE BEGINNER

Many beginners use their left index finger on the arrow to help steady it when nocking the arrow. This is fine until they begin to draw the string back. That index finger must go back under the arrow in the proper grip position. If not, the arrow will be released between their index and middle fingers, and they will get a terrific feather cut.

Before you release an arrow for the first time, check your left bow arm elbow to make sure it is out of the way.

Emphasize not moving your anchor to underdraw or to overdraw your arrow.

When students are finished shooting their six arrows, they should step back away from the shooting line. No arrows may be retrieved until Lady Paramount or the Field Captain (woman or man in charge of an archery event) gives the signal for all archers to retrieve.

Control arrow tips. They should be pointed only toward the floor or toward the target.

Arrows on beginners' bows may flip-flop to the side. Generally, there are two reasons for this problem. One is that there is too much pressure being exerted against the arrow by the string hand. Those fingers are *next* to the arrow, not squeezing it. Second, check to see if the fingers are slanted downward in the full draw position. This produces too much pressure as well. The fingers should be straight-back hooks.

Students must remember to aim the tip of the arrow and to remember where they aimed. If they missed high, go back to the original place and lower the bow arm downward. Many things can contribute to a poor result. If all skills in the seven stages of shooting are correct, then look to adjusting the POA. The aim analysis chart is shown in Figure 4.

Beginners need to learn to behave safely, concentrate on details, and analyze errors. Figure 5 provides a summary of the skills necessary for safe, accurate shooting.

If beginners start to shake in full draw, it may be that the bow weight is too heavy for them or they are remaining in full draw position too long. They should be using their shoulder blade muscles to pull back.

RETRIEVING ARROWS

Once shooters have finished, they step back away from the shooting line. In that way, Lady Paramount or the Field Captain can, in one glance, determine if that end is complete. (An "end" is a series of six arrows shot.)

Lady Paramount or the Field Captain gives the signal to retrieve arrows. Some beginners, after they have shot their first end, may try to retrieve their arrows immediately and start across the shooting line while others are still shooting. The teacher should cry out "Hold your arrows!" immediately!

Arrows must be carefully removed from the target. To do this the archers should place a finger on either side of the arrow, with the hand flat against the target. This helps protect the target and target face. With the other hand, gently, but firmly, twist and pull the arrow out. Archers must be sure to check behind first so that no one is standing directly behind the arrow being retrieved.

Retrieve arrows from the center of the target first, then move to arrows progressively further away from the gold. Establish this pattern now, as when you begin to score, one scores in order, from high to low.

For those arrows that are buried up to the fletching (feathers) it is best to pull them through the back side of the target in order to preserve the feathers.

For arrows on the ground, check to see that they have not been hit by other arrows. Look for pinprick holes which, if deep

Figure 4. Aim analysis chart

(Written for the right-handed shooter)

ARROWS GO HIGH
1. Anchoring while mouth is open or teeth not closed
2. Releasing before arrow point comes down to POA
3. Forefinger to bow hand up so arrow rides high
4. POA placed too high or sight placed too low
5. Bow arm thrown up at instant of release
6. Longer draw and follow-through
7. More extension in bow arm
8. Releasing below chin
9. Arrow nocked low

ARROWS GO LEFT
1. Hunching left shoulder
2. Squeezing arrow nock
3. Hitting left arm, shoulder, sleeve, pocket, or wrist on release
4. Gripping bow with fingers pressing on right side of bow
5. Flinching with left arm
6. Pulling bow string with fingers in draw instead of with upper arm, shoulder, and back muscles
7. Releasing while string is away from face
8. POA lined up to left of Gold or bowsight not far enough out
9. Wind blowing arrow to left
10. Top of bow tilting to left

Extremely Left: Sighting with wrong eye

GOOD FORM SENDS ARROWS HERE

ARROWS GO RIGHT
1. Plucking string to right on release
2. Throwing bow hand to right
3. Throwing bow arm to right
4. Wind blowing arrow to right
5. POA lined up to right of Gold or bowstring pulled out too far
6. Top of bow tilted to right

Extremely Right: Left-handed archer sighting with wrong eye

ARROWS GO LOW
1. Creeping
2. A head-on wind
3. Dropping left arm on release
4. Not being up to POA on release
5. POA placed too low; or sight placed too high
6. Not bringing arrow to full draw before release
7. "Lazy" third finger—not keeping draw in center of hand
8. Right elbow dropping, breaking alignment at wrist (i.e., only wrist and hand pull)

Figure 5. Archery performance skills listing*

(For right-handed, right-eye dominant shooters)

 1. Checks all equipment thoroughly for safety
 2. Bow braced (strung) correctly—not scratching the floor—loops secured
 3. <u>Stance:</u>   Straddling shooting line
                  Left shoulder toward target
                  Feet shoulder width apart
                  Weight evenly distributed
                  Knees "easy"
                  Upright posture
 4. Bow is right-side up
                  Bow is strung correctly—not inside out
 5. <u>Nock:</u>   Cock feather is up
                  Arrow at 90° angle from grip
 6. <u>Draw:</u>   Left hand holding bow between thumb and forefinger (V shape)
                  Left index finger is away from arrow
                  Hand not too high on the grip
                  Right hand: "Girl/Boy Scout" fingers on the string (only 3)
                  Three fingers are hooks on the string and LIGHTLY next to arrow
                  Left elbow turned slightly out of path of string
                  Arrow tip is at least one inch beyond bow
 7. <u>Anchor:</u>   Right thumb V against jawbone—firmly
                  String against lips and bisecting nose
                  Head facing target and upright—not tilted
                  Arrow tip is at least one inch beyond bow
 8. <u>Aim:</u>   Left eye closed
                  Right eye looking down the)
                       shaft of arrow to tip)   "Instinctive
                  Tip of arrow aimed at target)   method of
                  Left hand grip has not slipped   aiming"
                  Right elbow pointed to back wall
 9. <u>Release:</u>   Right hand stays anchored
                  Fingers open easily to release string; string ROLLS off
10. <u>Follow-through:</u> Maintains entire position until arrow hits or misses
11. Places bow on floor to mark position and steps back from shooting line when finished
12. Retrieves arrows well; protects target face
13. Checks arrows after each end to check for safety
14. Knows target value for scoring
15. Replaces equipment properly
16. Observes all safety rules
17. Knows the following terms: Lady Paramount/Field Captain; "Hold your arrow!";
                  Hanging arrow; Creeping; Flinching; Pinching; POA; Bounce-off
18. Knows how to safely retrieve arrow that has fallen in front of the shooting line
19. Helps others in observing proper procedure, shooting style, safety, and care
               of equipment

*Underlined items indicate the seven stages of shooting

enough, have destroyed the integrity of that arrow. These should be discarded.

For lost arrows in grass, the archers should walk slowly and move their legs and feet, sweeping the ground gently in front of them. Generally, if arrows get buried they can be felt by your foot. When found, carefully remove the arrows and wipe off any dirt or moisture before shooting them again. Dirt and moisture can weigh down the arrow and adversely affect its flight.

When retrieving arrows the archers must keep all tips down and in control. Archers should either place them immediately into the quiver, or hold them tips down and separately so that the feathers are not jammed against each other.

There must be no horseplay or running while carrying arrows. As a courtesy, all archers at the same target should stay and help to locate any missing arrows before returning to the shooting line.

If one is shooting alone, the bow is carried to the target and placed against the target when looking for lost arrows. This will indicate to others who come that someone is there, looking for arrows, and they will not begin to shoot.

After the arrows have been retrieved, shooters return to the shooting line, resume their stance, and do not touch an arrow to shoot until Lady Paramount or the Field Captain announces "You may shoot" or "Fire at will." This is a fundamental safety rule.

SCORING

When scoresheets are used, record scores from high to low, with one exception. "Bounce-offs" are arrows which hit the legally-scoring part of the target, but, in fact, bounce off. They may bounce off for many reasons. Two main reasons are that the tip may be dull or the arrow hit an unusually hard, tightly-packed part of the target matt.

Bounce-offs are recorded first and count as 7 points. Circle that 7 on the scoresheet to indicate it is a bounce-off. Then record the remaining arrows from high to low.

Arrows which split two scoring areas will be recorded as the higher of the two

scores. If there is any question, this determination is made by Lady Paramount or Field Captain.

For school or camps, the targets are scored by color: gold = 9, red = 7, blue = 5, black = 3, white = 1. For more advanced classes, these colors can be split from this "5-point score" to a "10 point score." The target faces generally are divided by black lines in the center of each color so that you could now score: gold = 9 or 10, red = 7 or 8, blue = 5 or 6, black = 3 or 4, white = 1 or 2.

Arrows that hit the "apron" or "skirt" (the part of the target outside the outermost part of the white circle) = 0.

For arrows that miss or hit the apron, record 0 on the scoresheet.

If, for any reason, someone has less than six arrows to shoot during an end, record a dash (−) on the scoresheet to differentiate between an arrow not shot and one that was shot but got a 0.

The total for each end is recorded. At the end of that day's round (a series of ends shot) record the total for the day.

To help improve, it is interesting to calculate each day the average per end shot (divide the total by the number of ends), the average per arrow (divide total by the number of arrows), and the total number of golds. Do this for each shooter and for the group as a whole.

EQUIPMENT

When ordering equipment for the first time, it is advisable for the teacher to talk with the manufacturer about the age, height, and strength of the group. Equipment needs vary based on these factors. Youngsters, for example, need lighter poundage in the bows and shorter arrows.

The teacher needs to ask about bows, arrows, quivers, strings, bow wax, arm guards, fingertabs, target matts, target stands, target faces, and arrow glue. Fiberglass bows are economical and can last a long time. Wooden arrows for beginners are fine as well. A class needs a variety of arrow lengths, as this is dependent on draw length and the bow weight. When shooters choose an arrow length, it must be such

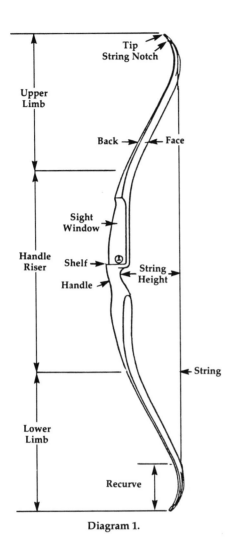

Diagram 1.

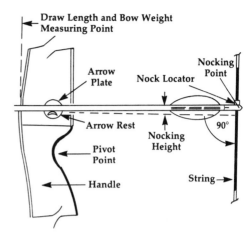

Diagram 2.

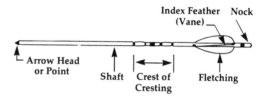

Diagram 3.

GENERAL SAFETY

that when they are in full draw the arrow extends beyond the bow at least one inch.

Storage of equipment is important too. Make sure there is plenty of room in a cool, dry place so that equipment will not dry out. The manufacturer can provide hints and then the school maintenance department can adapt an area for the class.

Always check the equipment each time before the day's shooting. Look for any possible damage to the bow, the string, or the arrows. When in doubt, replace the string or discard damaged bows and arrows.

Diagrams 1, 2, and 3 illustrate the various components of the bow and arrow.

1. Everyone on a shooting range shares the responsibility for individual and group safety. The warning cry of "Hold your arrows!" should be taught. Anyone can call this out should anything be amiss, from someone leaning forward of the shooting line to retrieve a dropped arrow to a dog wandering onto the range. Shooting ceases instantaneously. If shooters are in full draw, they relax to beginning stance immediately until the situation is rectified, and Lady Paramount or the Field Captain gives permission to resume shooting. Practice this fundamental safety provision.

2. No one commences shooting or retrieves arrows without permission from Lady Paramount or the Field Captain.

3. Shooters should wear comfortable clothing: no bunched sleeves to interfere with the bow string, no objects in breast pockets, no dangling earrings or

necklaces. Long hair should be secured.

4. The archery range should be well marked to forewarn visitors from wandering in or around the area.

5. Emergency procedures should be established and well-posted. Know emergency telephone numbers. Know the location of the nearest telephone and keep handy any change needed.

6. Keep bandaids handy for minor feather cuts.

7. Allow no horseplay or running on the archery range.

8. Be strict with all archery safety rules: remember, archers are handling loaded weapons. This fact must be made known *and* appreciated.

9. Keep unused tackle locked up.

10. No more than four archers per target shooting at once.

11. Make sure the area behind the targets has an archery curtain if inside, or wide, open space and/or upgrade, if outside.

TERMINOLOGY

Bounce-off. An arrow which fails to pierce a scoring part of the target and bounces off.

Bow. A device made of a piece of flexible material that is used to propel an arrow. A bow-string connects the two ends.

Bow Sight. A mechanical device placed on the bow with which the archer can aim directly at the target.

Bow Square. A device, usually shaped in a T, used to measure string height and nocking height.

Cant. To tip or hold the bow to the right or left of vertical while at full draw. The reference to right or left is determined by the position of the upper limb.

Creep. To allow the arrow to slowly move forward before the release; to not maintain full draw before release.

Draw Weight. The weight, measured in pounds, used to bring the bow to full draw. The weight of the bow drawn to the standard draw length.

End. A set number of arrows that are shot before going to the target to score and retrieve them.

Field Archery. An archery round in which the archer shoots from a variety of distances in woods and fields.

Field Captain. Man in charge of an archery event.

Fletching. The feather, plastic vanes, or other devices that are attached to the arrow shaft to stabilize the flight of the arrow.

Flinching. Moving or jerking the string hand backwards when releasing the string. Can cause overdrawing the arrow and/or erratic flight.

Handle. That part of the handle riser where the hand is in contact with the bow.

Hanging Arrow. An arrow which fails to pierce fully the target and literally hangs down. Can become a target itself unless fixed immediately.

Index Fletching. The fletching that is set at a right angle to the slot in the nock.

Kisser Button. An indicator or protrusion, usually constructed from plastic, placed on the bow strings so that it touches the lips or teeth while the archer is at full draw.

Lady Paramount. Woman in charge of an archery event.

Laminated Bow. A bow made of several layers (usually two layers of fiberglass and hardwood core) of different material glued together.

Let Down. Returning from full draw to the undrawn position with control without releasing the string.

Nock. To place an arrow on the bow string. The attachment on the rear end of the arrow which is placed on the bow string and holds the arrow on the string.

Nocking Point. The area of the bow string covered by the nock.

Peek. To move the head or bow arm in order to watch either the arrow in flight or where it hits the target.

Pinching. Too much finger pressure by the string hand against the arrow, causing the arrow to flip flop against the bow.

POA. Point of aim.

Pressure Point. The spot on the arrow plate or rest against which the arrow lies and presses when the bow string is released.

Quiver. A device used to hold arrows.

Spine. The stiffness or amount an arrow bends, determined by hanging a two-pound weight from the center of the arrow and measuring the amount of the bend.

Square Stance. The position of the feet in which an imaginary straight line would touch the toes of both feet and extend to the center of the target.

Stabilizer. A piece consisting of a weight which is extended at a distance by a relatively lighter rod, mounted on the handle riser. Any weight attached to the handle riser to minimize torque.

Standard Draw Length. When the bow string is drawn back to 26¼" from the nocking point to the pivot point, and then adding 1¾"; not to be confused with the manufacturer's true draw length (nocking point to pivot point) or the archer's draw length (arrow length required by each archer).

Torque. An undesirable twisting of the bow by the bow hand or of the bow string by the string hand.

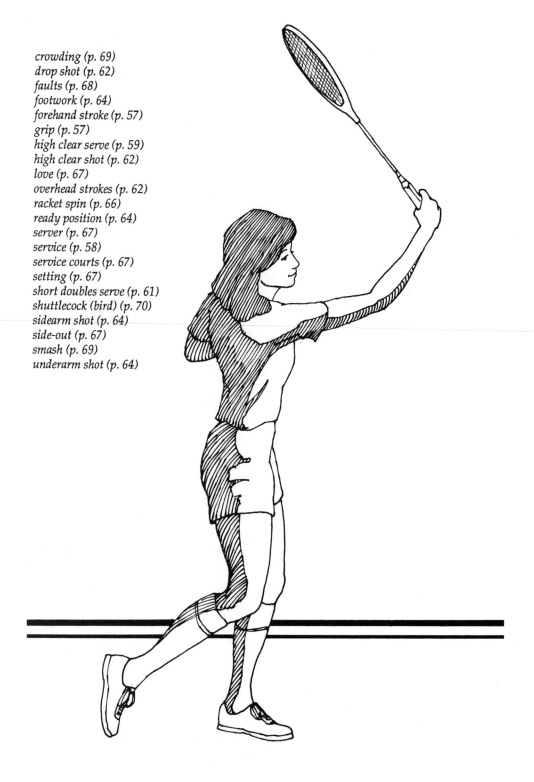

CHAPTER 5

Badminton

MARY L. REMLEY
Indiana University
Bloomington, IN

INTRODUCTION

Badminton is a sport that can be successfully played and enjoyed by anyone, young or old, male or female, after a brief practice period. It may be played as a backyard game for fun and relaxation or as a highly competitive, fast-moving contest requiring great speed, agility, and finesse as well as good hand-eye coordination and quick judgment. Skill levels range from the beginner to the advanced player who is interested in worldwide competition.

Because the indoor shuttlecock (bird) is very light and slows down rapidly with certain stroke actions, the pace and flight of the bird make the contest one of strategy as well as one of precise execution of fundamentals. Players may find that court knowledge, placement of the shuttle, and position anticipation are as important in winning matches as powerful shots and physical prowess. Badminton is remarkably deceptive, and the highly competitive game requires quickness of reflex, mind, and movement.

Although organized badminton is comparatively young in the United States and the American Badminton Association was founded only in 1936, the sport has a long history. It was played in England in the seventeenth century, and evidence suggests it was played in China even earlier. In the late 1800s the game was played in India where it was called *poona* and probably introduced by British army officers. The name, badminton, however, was derived from Badminton, the country estate of the Duke of Beaufort in Gloucestershire, England when it was played there by a group of army officers home on leave from India. Until 1901 when the present court

dimensions and shape were established, most courts were in the shape of an hourglass. Modern courts are well lighted and feature hardwood floors with well-marked boundaries. The game is especially well suited for physical education classes as it can be adapted to a wide range of skill levels and offers opportunities for both same gender or mixed gender play within the same class structure.

SKILLS AND TECHNIQUES

GRIP AND STROKING ACTION

The important consideration in gripping the racket is that it should permit the player to develop great racket head speed and yet make contact with the bird squarely so that it can be sent to the desired spot on the court. The stroking action is usually one of rotating the forearm in combination with wrist action so that the racket head moves quickly.

The forehand stroke is used most frequently, and a correct grip is demonstrated by placing the palm of the dominant hand flat against the strings of the racket. Then slide the hand down the racket, keeping the face of the racket and the palm in the same relative position, until the end of the handle is almost even with the edge of the hand. The handle should lie diagonally across the palm of the hand. The fingers and thumb close around the handle in a natural but slanted manner, much like shaking hands. Each finger is spread slightly with the index finger spread as far as possible while still having it wrapped around the handle. This should make a gap about finger width between the index and middle finger.

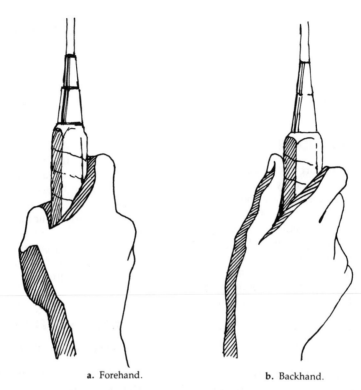

a. Forehand.   b. Backhand.

Figure 1. Note that the thumb closes around the grip in the forehand;
in the backhand it is extended down the back of the handle.

The backhand grip is taken by placing the thumb directly in back of the handle instead of at an angle. This position gives the player a stronger grip since the thumb acts as a lever and adds control and power in helping accelerate the racket head to hit the bird (see Figure 1). For both forehand and backhand strokes the handle should be gripped loosely with fingers and thumb in order to allow free and supple movement of the hand and wrist.

SERVICE

The contest and each point is started by having the player (or side in doubles) who has won the last rally serve the bird with an underhand motion. At the point of contact the racket head must be lower than the server's serving hand, and the bird must be below the server's waistline. The server generally hits the bird high to the back of the opposite court; low, just over the net, to the front of the receiving court; or quickly straight at the player who is receiving the serve (the receiver). Typically, more long serves are used in singles and more short serves in doubles because of the size of the court and the requirements necessary to cover the court. The service court is long and narrow in singles and short and broad in doubles (see Diagram 9).

The high shot is called the high clear serve because it is intended to be hit high enough so that it will be out of reach of the receiver and come down vertically on the back boundary line. The short shot is called the short serve, and it is intended to barely clear the net to drop near the short serve line so that the receiver will have to hit the bird up in the air to return the serve. The server will then have the option of hitting the bird down rapidly (smash), hitting the bird down slowly (drop shot), or hitting a high clear shot to the back of the opponent's court.

High Clear Serve

The high clear serve is hit with a powerful underhand action attempting to hit the bird "out" so that it goes deep into the court as well as high. Height is necessary to give the server time to prepare for a return and also to give the bird a vertical descent in the backcourt, making it harder to return. It is against the rules to "step into" the serve; therefore, the server cannot move his/her feet until the shuttlecock is struck. A weight shift from the back foot forward is helpful, however, to add power to the shot. Beginners may find it helpful to stand a little sideways and almost hit the shuttle out of the hand. More experienced players will probably face the opponent more directly and hit the bird after dropping it. Dropping the bird also allows the server to disguise the type of serve until the last moment.

The server should place the nondominant foot in a comfortable forward stride position and start with the racket arm extended backward with the weight primarily on the back foot. The wrist should be cocked with the racket held about waist height. As the bird is dropped, the weight is shifted forward, the racket head swings forward, the wrist is uncocked, and the forearm is rapidly rotated inward. The follow-through should be high and extend over the opposite shoulder, actually pulling the entire body into a square position (the ready position) so that movement may be made in any direction. Height and depth of the bird flight should be emphasized (see Figure 2 on the following page for the high clear serve sequence).

The Poole Long Serve Test can be used to evaluate high clear serving ability. The court is marked with four 1- or 2-inch lines, 16 inches apart as shown in Diagram 1. The first is drawn parallel to the court lines and 2 inches in back of the back boundary line. The shots landing in the various zones are scored 5-4-3-2-1 if the serve is hit legally and goes over the extended arm and racket of a player who stands 11 feet from the net in the 15-inch marked square (see Diagram 1).

Shots hitting the line are considered to be in the highest point zone. The best 10 out of 12 serves are scored with 50 a perfect score. A rope or extra net hung across the court 11 feet from the net and 9 feet high may be substituted for the player, although the opponent standing in the court makes the test seem more gamelike. The test can be shortened to the best six out of eight trials with similar results for most students. The Poole test provides a good practice drill, and maintaining a record of practice scores may be useful in motivating players to practice their serving skills.

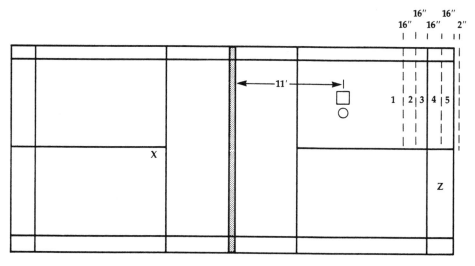

Diagram 1. Court markings for the Poole Long Serve Test.

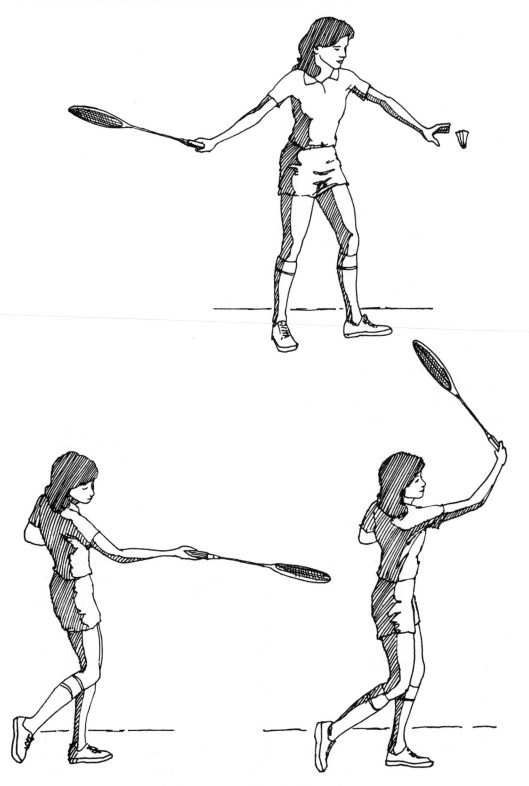

Figure 2. Sequence of the high clear serve.

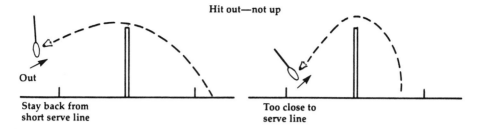

Hit out—not up

Out

Stay back from
short serve line

Too close to
serve line

Diagram 2. Short serve paths (out and low to the net rather than up and down—short of service line).

Short Doubles Serve

Since the length of the service court is shorter for doubles than singles, and the basic strategy in doubles is to hit the bird downward whenever possible, the short, low serve is generally used. This serve forces the receiver to hit the bird up so that the serving team can take the offensive. The starting position is similar to that taken for the high clear serve; however, some players shorten the backswing in order to contact the bird quickly, before the receiver can recognize it and, therefore, prepare for the short shot (rules prevent the receiver from moving until the bird is hit by the server). The shuttle is contacted higher and "guided" over the net rather than being "struck" with great force.

The stroke has a flat sweeping motion that is made without uncocking the wrist—almost pushing the bird over. The bird should reach its highest point on the server's side of the net, be on a downward path as it crosses the net, and is usually directed toward the front center corner of the court (see Diagram 2). Only change-ups or sur-prise attempts are made to the side corners because the receiver has better angles on the return from the outside and can put the server off-balance immediately.

A modified version of the French Short Serve Test may be used for evaluating the short serve. The test is designed to evaluate the placement accuracy of a low short serve that would be difficult to smash. A rope is stretched 14 inches above the net and fastened to the net standards. One- or 2-inch wide markings are placed as shown in Diagram 3. The first arc is placed 12 inches from the center corner, and subsequent lines are 6 inches apart. A prepared target marked on oilcloth or cardboard makes the test easy to administer and convenient to use in practice since it can simply be placed on the court, then removed when no longer in use. The point values are 5-4-3-2-1 and shots on the line are given the highest point value. The best 10 out of 12 trials are totaled for the score, and six out of eight may be used for most students. The server stands 2-3 feet from the short serve line and near the center line in the proper service court.

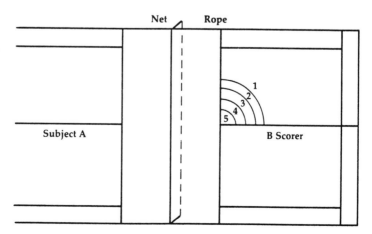

Net   Rope

Subject A

B Scorer

Diagram 3. Court markings for the French Short Serve Test.

Drive Serve

The drive serve is a quick "change-up" action usually sent directly at the receiver or, if possible, past the receiver. The shot is disguised until the last instant and then performed with the racket head down in a "flick" type action. The bird should just miss the top of the net.

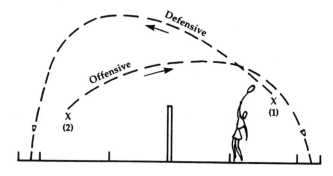

Diagram 5. Defensive clear (1) and offensive clear (2).

OVERHEAD STROKES

The overhead strokes are divided into forehand and backhand motion with the desired bird flight being the deciding factor in the type of action. For the high clear, the bird is contacted as high as possible and in front of the body. This makes it easier to hit the bird "out and up" and to get it to the back baseline where it should come down at a steep angle (see Diagram 4). At times a player will find it advantageous to hit an offensive clear shot. This shot takes less time to get to the court since it is hit just out of the reach of the opponent, trying to get the bird down behind the opponent (see Diagram 5). An action stance is taken that will place most of the weight on the foot on the racket side with the opposite foot well forward. The position and action is very much like throwing a ball a long distance. In preparation, the racket head drops low behind the back and the forward action is

initiated with the elbow high. Just before contact is made with the bird, the elbow is straightened, the forearm is rotated, the wrist uncocked, and the whole arm fully extended to reach up at the bird. High racket head speed is important as weight is transferred from the back foot to the front, and the grip is tightened as contact is made. To hit the bird downward (an offensive smash) the racket face contacts the bird slightly over the top, and wrist action builds speed as the bird is hit forcibly downward (see Figure 3).

For the drop shot, the action should appear the same to the opponent, but the forearm rotation and wrist action are held back until after the bird is hit, and only the arm moves rapidly to disguise the action. The bird is hit flat and at the top of the net, dropping quickly to the floor once it is over the net. Contacting the bird in front of the body is a key concept for all basic overhead shots.

The Poole Forehand and Backhand Clear Tests may be used to evaluate the player's overhead clear performance. The court is marked as shown in Diagram 6. A 15- by 15-inch square is drawn 11 feet from the net to show the "opponent" where to stand for the test and to establish if the clear is high enough so that it would not be an easy "kill" shot. Another 15- by 15-inch square is marked at the intersection of the doubles long serve line and the centerline on the other side of the net, as shown. The person taking the test must keep one foot in this square until the bird is hit. The point values are 2-4-3-2-1 as shown with shots on the

Diagram 4. Arc of clear or serve.

a. Correct arm and wrist alignment. Bird is directed downward.

b. Poor alignment. Wrist is ahead of the racket. The flight of the bird is too horizontal.

Figure 3. Arm and racket angles in smash.

lines given the higher values. The player taking the test places a bird with feathers (or plastic) down on the forehand side of the racket, tosses the bird in the air, and then hits a high clear forehand or backhand shot depending upon the test. Tossing the bird in this manner takes some practice for beginners. The test consists of the points gained from the best 10 of 12 trials; six of eight shots will usually give similar results.

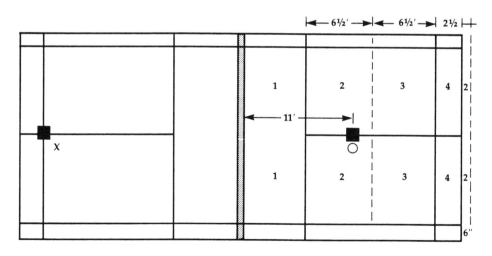

Diagram 6. Court markings for the Poole Forehand and Backhand Clear Tests.

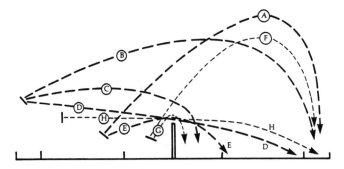

Diagram 7. Trajectory of the different strokes.

A. Singles.
B. Clear.
C. Drop.
D. Smash.

E. Doubles (low) score.
F. Net clear.
G. Net (hairpin) drop.
H. Drives.

SIDEARM AND UNDERARM SHOTS

Like the overhead shots, the racket head speed, direction of the action, the angle of the racket face, and a clean contact in the center of the racket face are all important to a good execution of the sidearm and underhand shots. The bird flight desired is the determining factor in the manner in which the bird is hit. These shots are used when the flight of the bird is lower than that necessary for the overhead shots. The type of action required is the same as for the overhead shots, except that the bird is contacted from a low position in front of the body or to the side of the body (see Diagram 7 for trajectory lines of the different strokes).

FOOTWORK IN GENERAL

The purpose of working on footwork is to enable the player to get in position to hit the bird effectively. The ready position is an important part of footwork; in order to start quickly the body should be balanced with knees bent and weight on the balls of the feet. The position is usually taken 2 to 3 feet behind the short service line, near the center line, but a little to the "nonracket" side (see Diagram 8). This location helps protect the backhand side of the court and also facilitates moving to the front corners of the court. A high clear shot is necessary for the opponent to get the bird to the back corners thus giving the player more time to move to the corners. The racket is normally held about waist high with the head up and square to the net just to the backhand side of the face (see Figure 4).

A good drill for footwork practice is for two players to rally trying to hit the bird to the four corners—no "kill" shots. After each hit, the player should return to the ready position.

Figure 4. Ready position.

Footwork to the left front court (underhand clear or net shot).

1. Take a small "get ready" step backward with the left foot. This movement gets the player into a delicate balance position that helps to move the whole body quickly. The right shoulder moves forward and the left shoulder back as weight is shifted to the left foot.
2. The second step is a cross-over step with the right foot in the direction the player wants to move. The backswing is taken near the end of this step.
3. The next step with the left foot is adjusted depending upon the bird location.
4. The last step before the bird is hit is always with the foot on the racket side— the right in this case. Shift the weight to this foot, stretch, hit the bird, step up close to the right foot with the left, and start the return to the ready position by almost falling backward at the start and then taking small quick steps to get back.

Footwork to the right front court (underhand clear or net shot).

1. The first step is taken with the left foot, again to put the player in delicate balance and to give direction to the movement.
2. Then step with the right foot toward the target as the backswing is taken.
3. Adjusting the left foot stride for the bird position, take the last right foot step

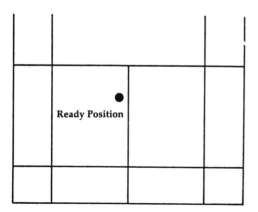

Diagram 8. Court location for ready position.

with a body and leg stretching action and hit the bird with most of the weight on the racket-side foot.
4. In the follow-through from the shot, bring the left foot up near the right and again, in a nearly falling action with the body lowered, return to the ready position with small quick steps.

Footwork to the left (backhand return of smash or drive).

1. The left foot moves back in a small "jab" step to get the player on delicate balance; the right shoulder is turned so the back is toward the net, and the weight is shifted to the left.
2. The second step is a cross-over step with the right foot toward the bird location as the backswing is taken. The weight is then shifted to the right foot, and the arm and body stretched toward the bird.
3. After the shot, the left foot moves to a position next to the right and the body falls backward to the ready position by taking short quick steps.

Footwork to the right (to smash a return or hit a drive or drop shot).

1. Pivot to the right on the balls of the feet, shifting the weight to the right and turning the left shoulder toward the net.
2. Take a short step to the right with the right foot.
3. Take a short step with the left to get on balance and set up for the hit.
4. The last step is with the right foot (always the racket foot) adjusting the length to the bird position.
5. After hitting, push off the right foot and return to the ready position by taking small quick steps.

Footwork to the back left (for deep backhand).

1. Pivot to the left on the balls of the feet and shift weight to the left.
2. Take a small step forward and left with the right foot to give a small base lined up in the direction of progress and push off right foot to start movement back.
3. Rotate the body hard to the left and step backward with the left foot.
4. Step toward the anticipated bird position with a long right stride.

5. Take a medium step with the left foot and combine this motion with the backswing in adjusting to the bird position.
6. The last step is with the racket foot (the right if right-handed) in a stretch toward the bird.
7. Step toward the racket foot with a small step with the left; shift the weight toward the ready position and return to it with small quick steps.

Footwork to the back right (for overhead forehand strokes).
1. The left foot steps forward to set up the line of movement, but the weight remains primarily on the right foot for a pivot on the ball of the right foot.
2. Push quickly with the left leg and step down the line of movement with the right, rotating the body to face the sideline.
3. Step with the left foot to a spot close to the right toe with the weight heavy on the right.
4. The last step is made with the racket foot (the right) in adjusting to the bird location and preparing for the hit.
5. Lean toward the ready position on the follow-through and return to the base position with short quick steps.

In summary, all footwork is designed to move the player quickly into position to make the desired shot and return to the ready position. Wide stances are stable but time-consuming. Narrow positions are unstable but permit the player to move quickly if he/she can have the center of gravity headed in the right direction.

SAFETY

Most injuries in badminton are due to lack of warm-up followed by fast quick movements and consequent pulled leg muscles or due to players overextending themselves during competition. A hundred or more smash shots in a one-day doubles tournament, for example, may result in injury to the elbow or shoulder joint. Players should be aware that they should warm up completely before a match and then not play in extended tournaments without being in good physical shape. They should

remember to pace themselves in this sport, which requires fast, quick movements.

Occasionally in doubles, two players who are not regular partners will both go for the same shot and either hit the other player or his/her racket. Voice signals such as "I've got it!" should be used when there is any question about both players going after the bird. A typical example occurs when the player in the backcourt is coming up to hit the bird hanging over the partner who is in the front court.

RULES

STARTING THE GAME

A racket spin or a coin toss is used to determine who gets the choice of courts or to serve or receive at the beginning of a match. If the racket spin is used, some mark is identified which is only on one surface of the racket and the opponent is asked to name that mark or the other (M or W, for example, on the end of the handle of a Wilson racket). The player then places the head of the racket on the floor and spins it as it is turned loose to fall to the floor. The side that is up determines who gets the choice of court preference or to serve or receive. The other side gets the alternate choice. In singles it is generally wise to choose to serve, since points are made only by the serving side. In doubles, the choice is often to receive because the first server has only "one hand down." As players develop skill, however, the choice, even in doubles, may well be to serve, since a winning rally puts the team on the scoreboard.

The side winning the serve starts the contest with a serve from the right-hand court (as players face the net). The server must serve so that the bird would land in the right-hand receiver's court (as the receivers face the net). The rally continues until one player fails to return the bird to the playing area. In singles, if the server commits an error, the serve and scoring opportunity goes to the other side, no point. If the receiver commits an error, a point is scored by the server, and he/she serves again, this time from the left service court to the left receiver's court.

The server should announce the score each time before the next serve is made, giving the server's score first. "Love" means no score; "side-out" means the serve goes to the opponent. In doubles, "hands down" is used to indicate the serving options remaining on the side. With no hands down, both players on the side have a chance to serve; with one hand down, the partner who has not yet served has a chance to do so; with two hands down, side-out is called and the service goes to the other side.

The side taking the first serve in doubles starts with one hand down, as though a fault had already been made in that serving turn. When the serve is lost, side-out is called and service goes to the other side. After the first person serves, however, each side gets two hands down before side-out. When one side earns the serve in doubles, the player who has the right court serving or receiving responsibility serves first. This player continues to serve, alternating service courts until the serving team makes a fault or an error. The serving and receiving court locations for players in doubles are determined according to the players' responsibility or court position at the beginning of the game. The player who started in the right court on the first point should always be there for serving or receiving when the team score is even (0, 2, 4, 6, etc.). When the team's score is odd, the players should be in the opposite court to that from which they began the game. On the serve, the player who is in the receiving court must return the bird; after the serve either player may return the bird.

After the first serve in singles, the person winning the serve serves according to the score (from the right side if his/her score is even and from the left side if the score is odd).

SCORING

Badminton scores are made when a player is serving and the opponent fails to return a serve or a following shot during a rally. If the server commits an error (faults) on the serve in singles or is not able to return a shot after the serve, the side is out (loses the serve). In doubles, except on the first serve at the beginning of the game, the first error (fault) on the side is one hand down, the second is side out.

The point total required to win a game is 11 in women's singles and 15 in men's singles or any doubles match. In women's singles, if the score is tied at 9, the player who first reached 9 has the option of "setting" the game to 3 or playing to 11. If the game was not set at 9 and the score is tied at 10, the player who first reached 10 has the option of "setting" the game to 2 points. If the score is tied at 13 in men's singles or any doubles game, the side first reaching 13 has the option of "setting" to 5; if the score was not set at 13 and the score is tied at 14, the side first reaching 14 has the option of setting at 3. After the game has been set, score is called "love-all" and the side which first reaches 5, 3, or 2 (depending on the "set") wins the game. In handicap games, setting is not permitted. A match is two out of three games.

THE COURT

The court in badminton is 20 feet wide and 44 feet long. One and one-half inch lines divide the court into specific areas for the service conditions and playing conditions of the game (see Diagram 9). The posts shall be 5'1" from the floor and placed on the side boundaries of the court. The net shall be 5'0" at the center with a 3-inch white tape at the top. The outside lines mark the boundary area for doubles play; the singles court does not include the alley areas on either side of the court.

The service courts are bounded by the short serve line and centerline in singles and doubles. The doubles service court is shortened by not including the back alley while the singles court is narrowed by not including the side alley (an easy reminder is "doubles service, short and fat; singles, long and thin"). Serves are made on a diagonal path—right service court to right receiving court. After the service in doubles, the entire court including the space behind the long service line is used for play. Birds landing on the line are always good.

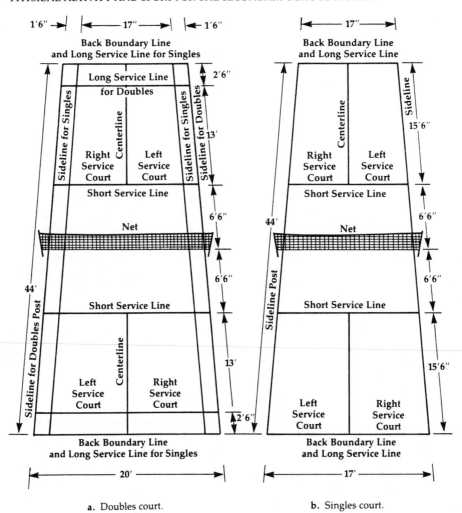

a. Doubles court.

b. Singles court.

Diagram 9.

FAULTS

Faults are violations of the rules that result in points for the serving side or loss of serve; for example:

1. Both the server and the receiver must stand within the proper service court when the serve is delivered, and neither can move his/her feet until the bird is struck.
2. On the serve the bird must be contacted below the server's waist and the server's racket head must be lower than the server's hand.
3. No preliminary feints or movements can be made by the server or the receiver prior to the server striking the bird.
4. If the bird touches the top of the net and continues to the correct court, the bird is legally in play.
5. The shuttlecock can be hit over the net only with the racket, and it can be contacted only once on each side of the net.
6. If the shuttlecock is not returned to the proper area, it is a fault unless it is touched by an opponent or his/her racket before it touches the court.
7. A player or his/her racket may not touch the net, reach over the net before the bird crosses over it, or cross under the net while the bird is in play. Follow-through over the net with the racket after a stroke near the net is legal, however, as long as the net is not touched.

8. The shuttlecock must be contacted cleanly. If it is hit twice, comes to rest on the racket briefly, or is "slung" off the racket, this is a fault. The bird may be hit with any part of the racket.

STRATEGY

BIRD FLIGHT STRATEGY

Badminton players should learn to try to force the opponent to hit the bird up in the air so it can be returned with an offensive hit down toward the court. If the bird comes across the net low and fast, shots may be returned just over the net in a drop shot action so the original player will again have to hit the bird up and, therefore, be on the defensive. Since neither player wants to be on the defensive, a common return for a drop shot is to return a drop shot just over the net in a "hairpin"-like action. When a player overplays a position, the opponent should try to get the bird down toward the court and behind the receiver. This often forces a weak return, thus setting up a kill shot (smash) to win the rally.

SINGLES STRATEGY

Singles is basically a game of patience and court position, maneuvering the opponent around the court with a series of drops and clears until he/she makes a mistake. If the bird is smashed too early, for example, from the back alley when playing a high clear, an experienced opponent can frequently drop the bird back to the front court, forcing a weak upward hit. He/she is then ready for a smash to win the rally. Smashing too often will also soon tire a player. Varying shot velocity and placement while trying to unbalance the opponent and searching for weaknesses are better strategic tactics.

The most difficult shot for most players to return is deep to the backhand side, especially if the player is leaning forward to cover net shots. This, in effect, is what it means to "get the bird down behind the opponent." The basic serve in singles is high and deep to the back alley near the center of the court so the opponent does not have sharp angles to use for the return. This also pro-vides time for the server to respond to the bird when it is returned to his/her court.

DOUBLES STRATEGY

The basic serve in doubles is short, low, and just over the net to the center corners. This serve gives the opponent only angles that must pass the server in "ready position" and also forces the opponent to hit the bird in an upward trajectory. Because most serves are short, the receiver will often crowd the line, and if the bird is hit too high, the receiver looks for a quick smash. To counter this "crowding" action, the server should occasionally serve a low, fast, clear shot to get the bird down behind the receiver; serve a drive serve at the receiver to force an error or a weak return; or play a serve to the outside alley corner to catch the receiver off-balance. These alternatives should not be overused, however, because they give the receiver good angles back to the server's court, especially if the shot is not perfect. Any imbalance of the receiver from the server's shot is nullified in doubles by the partner who can simply cover a little more court on the next shot. In doubles all players should look for the chance to hit the bird downward and go on the offensive.

A team may use one of three basic formations, sides, up-and-back, and combination. For up-and-back, the basic court coverage is for the server and receiver to play short and cover the short shots; partners play back for the long shots. If one player is not as strong as the other, the team may decide to have the weaker player always play the net position. The greatest advantage of this formation is the ability to attack effectively.

The simplest court position is a side-by-side position in which each player is responsible for his/her half of the court. The player on the forehand side should usually take shots down the middle unless he/she is out of position or is clearly the weaker player. Side-by-side strategy is easy to learn and leaves little doubt about where each team member should play. Smart opponents, however, will play only to the weaker player. Attacking effectively is also more difficult when this formation is used.

Most skilled doubles teams play some combination of formations depending on the position of the bird at the time and the anticipated shot from the opponents. For example, when the shuttle is up in the air and the team is on the attack, an up-and-back formation is used; when the shuttle must be hit up by the team, a side-by-side formation is used in order to be in the best defensive position. To be effective, the combination formation requires extremely good teamwork as well as advanced skills.

SUGGESTED LEARNING HINTS

SERVE

1. Start all serves from the same position.
2. Begin serve with wrist cocked, racket back.
3. Drop, don't toss the bird.
4. Keep both feet on the floor until the bird is hit.
5. For long serves, lead with the wrist; snap racket forward at point of contact; follow through high.
6. For short serves, use no wrist snap; guide the bird over the net; follow through toward top of net.

OVERHEAD STROKES

1. Move quickly to get "behind" the bird.
2. "Track" the bird with the nonracket hand (extend arm toward bird as it approaches).
3. Contact the bird as high as possible.
4. Fully extend arm and racket to meet the bird.
5. Contact the bird in front of the body.
6. For clears, "throw" the racket head at the bird; use a powerful wrist snap; contact the bird with the racket face flat.
7. For drop shots, slow the racket at contact; angle the racket face downward.
8. For smashes, get the racket over the shuttle; use a powerful wrist snap; follow through toward the floor.

GENERAL HINTS

1. Return to "ready position" after each stroke.
2. Watch the bird at all times.
3. For birds near boundary lines, look from flying shuttle to boundary lines, back to shuttle.

4. Anticipate the shuttle flight, get to position *before* the shuttle.
5. Use a loose grip on the racket handle.
6. Practice placing the bird—hit away from the opponent.
7. Hit the bird against a wall to develop wrist snap and strength.
8. "Talk" to the doubles partner; call for questionable shots—"I've got it!"
9. Practice court courtesy:
   Know the rules and use them.
   Announce the score before serving.
   Determine if opponent is ready to receive serve.
   Use clears and drives, not drops or smashes for warm-up.
   Retrieve birds from adjoining courts only after a rally ends.
   Call carry or slung shots immediately— before the opponent attempts a return.
   Call line shots in/out immediately.
   Ask to replay a line shot only when its landing point is truly unknown.

EQUIPMENT

RACKETS

Selecting a racket is a matter of personal choice, but the key factor is balance. While heavier rackets may give a little more "slugging" power, they lack speed in handling. Frames may be made of wood, fiberglass, or metal and are generally strung with nylon, which can be strung tighter than gut and usually lasts longer. Wooden rackets should be stored in a press. For instructional purposes consideration must be given to durability and cost; however, the cheapest rackets are rarely the best "bargain." Buying in a mid-range cost from a reputable dealer should provide a racket of durable quality that may be used by students of all levels. Poor equipment makes learning more difficult, and it needs to be replaced too frequently.

SHUTTLECOCKS

The shuttlecock or bird as it is commonly called is usually nylon with a rubber tip or goose feathers with a kid-covered cork tip. Because of expense, the latter is used primarily for tournament play. The range of weights available is from 73 to 85 grams with the heavier bird flying farther and used in colder temperatures (the warmer the room, the faster the shuttle will fly). The correct bird is determined by the players at the beginning of the game. The bird is struck with a full underhand stroke from just in front of the back boundary line and is deemed correct when it lands not less than 1' and not more than 2'6" short of the other back boundary line. The nylon shuttle can last 10-15 games, while a shuttle of goose feathers may be useless after a few rallies or a game. Feather birds must also be kept moist to prevent breakage.

TERMINOLOGY

Alley. The 18-inch extension on each side of the singles court used only in doubles play.

Back Alley. The area, 30 inches in depth, between the back boundary line and long service line in doubles. The area is used in both singles and doubles play, except for the serve in doubles.

Baseline. The back boundary line of the court on both ends. This line is also the back boundary for the singles serve. For doubles service only, the long service line is 30 inches nearer the net than this baseline.

Base Position. The position approximately in the center of the court to which a player attempts to return after making each shot.

Bird. Another word for shuttlecock. The common structure is nylon, and for most tournament play, of goose feathers.

Block. Placing the racket in front of the bird to make it drop to the opponent's court. Very little stroke movement is made in this shot.

Carry. Holding the bird on the racket during a stroke; carry is an illegal hit or fault.

Cross-court. A stroke hit diagonally from one side of the court to the other.

Double Hit. Hitting the bird twice on the same shot. This is an illegal hit or fault.

Drive. A hard flat shot, usually passing a player close to the net or a shot right at an opponent.

Drop Shot. A bird which just clears the net and immediately starts to fall in the opponent's court.

Fault. A violation of the rules.

Foot Fault. A violation of the rules in which the feet of the server or receiver are not in the position required by the rules. This could be either an illegal position outside the serving/receiving court by the server/receiver or movement of the feet on the serve.

Game Point. The point which, if won by the server, wins the game.

Hairpin Net Shot. A stroke made from below and close to the net, just clearing the net to fall sharply downward on the opposite side.

Inning. The time during which a player or team is serving.

Kill Shot. A fast downward return which usually cannot be returned.

Let. A legitimate interruption of play such as interference from outside the court that allows an exchange or rally to be replayed.

Love. A term used to indicate no score.

Match. The best 2 out of 3 games.

Match Point. The point which, if won by the server, wins the match.

Obstruction. A fault called when a player hinders or interferes with an opponent who is making a shot. It may occur, for example, when a player has made a weak shot then yells or waves the racket to disconcert the opponent.

Overhead. A stroke played from above head height.

Rally. The exchange of strokes when a shuttle is in play.

Ready Position. The basic position taken by a player just before the opponent strikes the shuttle. Knees are slightly bent, and the racket is held in front of the body about chest high.

Receiver. The player in the proper court scheduled to receive the service.

Round-the-head Shot. A forehand stroke made on the backhand side of the body. It is usually an overhead stroke, either a clear, drop, or smash.

Second Service. Term used in doubles play to indicate that one person has lost the service and is "down"; the partner retains the serve.

Setting. Way of extending the game by increasing the number of points required to win a tied game. Player who first reaches the tied score has the option of setting.

Server. The player who delivers the service.

Service Court. The area into which the service must be delivered.

Short Service Line. The line 6½' from the net over which serves must cross to be legal.

Shuttlecock. The official name for the shuttle or bird.

Side-by-side Formation. A doubles formation in which players play on one-half of the court and cover the territory on that side.

Side-in. The side whose turn it is to serve.

Side-out. Term used when the serving side loses the serve and becomes the receiving side.

Smash. A hard overhead stroke hit downward with great force. It is the chief attacking stroke in badminton.

Underhand. A stroke made when the shuttle is contacted below the level of the shoulders and the racket is below the hand. It is used to serve or to hit a bird that has dropped below net height.

Wood Shot. A shot in which the bird is hit with the frame of the racket rather than the strings. The shot is legal.

CHAPTER 6

Basketball

JAMES E. BRYANT
San Jose State University
San Jose, CA

INTRODUCTION

Basketball is an American game designed by James A. Naismith in 1891 to accommodate football players in their off-season conditioning and recreation program. It has evolved in the past 100 years from a slow moving, low scoring game with rudimentary skills to a fast paced, high scoring, acrobatic form of entertainment. It is a city game played in the 1990s by individuals of all ages and sizes on asphalt playgrounds and gymnasiums throughout the United States. It is an international game played at a competitive level in Australia, Barbados, Brazil, China, Germany, Italy, Russia, Yugoslavia, and nearly every other country in the world. In the United States, competitive basketball games at the high school and collegiate level are highly structured events sponsored by individual high school activities associations and NCAA and NAIA collegiate organizations. The game at the international level and the professional game are institutionalized so that the very fiber of American society is touched by the game. Implications related to economics, politics, religion, and social stratification are clearly part of the game in the decade of the 1990s, and the cultural impact has been dramatic.

Perhaps one of the most dramatic changes in basketball in recent years has been the tremendous increase in participation among girls and women, who now play basketball at all academic grade levels and in the international arena. A second visible change has occurred related to skill level of participants. Youngsters in elementary school play extensive organized schedules through youth sport programs, and in unorganized playground experiences children have watched, learned, improvised, and developed skills of the game far beyond those of just 10 years ago.

The game today is an individual game blended into a team concept. It is a stylistic, truly aesthetic game played aggressively with a need for stamina and endurance coupled with strength and balance. It is a game measured not only in points scored by a team to determine a winner, but in the style and appearance of acrobatic moves that enhance individualized performance.

Basketball is part of the secondary school physical education curriculum. It is found in various forms of extramural participation including interscholastic athletics and in intramural programs. The skills and strategies associated with the game are of great importance in any course planning for basketball, but it is also important to not lose sight of the tremendous American character related to the game. The skills and strategies and the character of the game should be enhanced in an instructional situation in secondary schools, and that enhancement should provide students with increased opportunities for an appreciation and understanding of the game along with the joy of increased ability to play at the secondary school level and beyond.

SKILLS AND TECHNIQUES

Six basic techniques are associated with basketball: dribbling, passing, receiving, shooting, rebounding, and defense.

DRIBBLING

Dribbling is an individual skill. Used effectively it contributes to overall basketball success. Dribbling enables the player to advance the ball the length of the court. It should be used to penetrate a defense in order to set up a pass, to maintain control of the offense, and to beat a defensive player one-on-one. Dribbling contributes to the concept that basketball is a game of one-on-one, two-on-two, and three-on-three play. If the game were truly five-on-five there would be considerably less usage of the dribble than presently exists.

There are two basic forms of dribbling: high dribble for speed, typically with a lot of floor in front of a player, and a low dribble, usually used in the half court game and designed to protect the ball. The fundamental skills of dribbling include a cross over dribble and a drop step dribble. The "styling" that occurs with the dribble usually includes behind the back and between the legs dribbling. The game is so advanced that the "styling" dribble moves become fundamental for the talented player and learning at this level should not be discouraged if a student attempts to develop these dribbling skills.

Fundamentally, the dribble should be executed with the head up looking for teammates and the basket. The ball should always be protected with the nondribbling arm flexed to block off the opponent. In a confined area the body should be in a flexed position. The ball is dribbled primarily with the fingers of the hand applying a pushing action along with "touch" to the ball.

Points to remember when dribbling the ball are:
- use both the dominant and nondominant hands interchangeably
- penetrate a defense and pass off the dribble
- keep the ball slightly out in front, but protected
- dribble, stop and pivot
- change pace and direction with the dribble
- use both the "cross over" and "drop step" to advance the ball
- look for an open player to pass to and look for the open shot off the dribble

Figure 1. Proper dribbling position.

Figure 2. High dribble.

PASSING

Passing a ball is critical to basketball success. Combined with the dribble a pass becomes extremely effective in two-on-two situations. In three-on-three, four-on-four, and five-on-five situations the pass is basic to success. In miss-match situations (e.g., three-on-one fast break) the skill of passing is specific to success in order to score. The pass is also instrumental in any form of a slow-down offense designed to protect a lead or change the tempo of a game. The pass is what makes basketball a team game.

There are many types of passes. The most basic passes are two hand chest and bounce passes, the two hand overhead pass, and the baseball pass. Passes that are more individualized or relate to the "styling" and "flow" of the game include shovel pass off the dribble and behind the back. These stylistic passes become fundamental for the advanced player, and those students who work at developing advanced skill should be encouraged to develop these passes.

The chest pass is the most basic of all passes. It is used deceptively in that a player can put the ball on the floor to dribble, begin a jump shot, or pass the ball from the starting position of the pass. The pass should be executed by holding the ball directly in front of the body, chest high, with the fingers on the side of the ball and thumbs in back (parallel to each other). The elbows are close, but not against the body. As the pass is executed the arms are extended forward with one leg stepping in the direction of the receiver. As the weight is transferred forward and the arms are extended, there is a snap of the wrist ending with palms of the hands positioned outward.

The bounce pass is similar to the chest pass in execution, but the target is the floor two-thirds distance from the passer to the receiver. This pass should be used judiciously since it is a slower pass than the chest pass, thus easier to intercept if anticipated by the defensive player.

The overhead pass is most often used to "feed" the big player under the basket or as

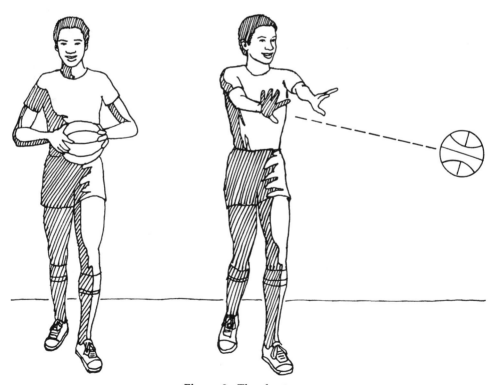

Figure 3. The chest pass.

Figure 4. The bounce pass.

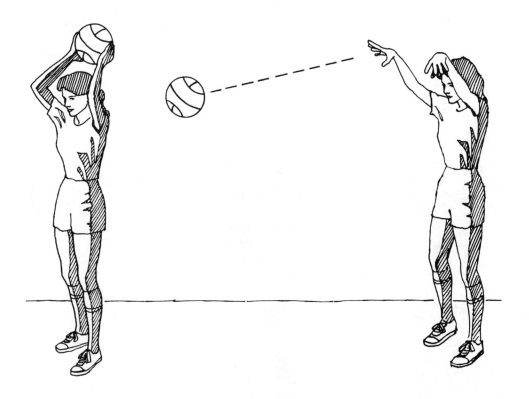

Figure 5. The overhead pass.

an outlet pass following a rebound. When executing the overhead pass the hands are on each side of the ball and toward the back with widespread fingers. The thumbs should be pointed toward each other. The ball is held above the head, and the pass is initiated by a short step toward the passing target. As the weight is transferred forward arms are extended, and the wrists snap as the ball is released. The follow-through is completed with the arms forward and thumbs and palms down.

The baseball pass is executed just as a baseball might be thrown. The problem with this pass in basketball is that the basketball is much larger than a baseball, consequently more difficult to control. Baseball passes are often thrown with the additional use of the nondominant hand supporting the ball cradled in the passing hand. The pass is executed off the shoulder with the dominant hand throwing the ball and the nondominant hand keeping the ball from falling out of the hand until the pass is released.

Fundamentally, passes have to be timed to meet the receiver's movement. The offensive player's head has to be up looking for an open player.

Points to remember when passing the ball are:
- emphasize correct form
- execute passes while moving and while the receiver is moving
- the target is nearly always the chest of the receiver
- avoid telegraphing passes by the positioning of the passer's head and eyes
- control the ball with the fingers
- snapping of the wrist at release imparts spin on the ball and enables the receiver to have a better chance of catching the ball
- after fundamentals are developed encourage development of passing off the dribble and behind the back skills

Figure 6. Baseball pass.

RECEIVING

Catching the ball effectively and then doing something with the ball after catching it are continuations of the pass. The receiving player must "see" the ball and track the ball through the pass. The receiver should work at developing "soft" hands, which means "giving" with the pass so that the fingers, hands, wrists, and arms absorb the impact of the ball off the pass. It is also critical that a receiver meet the pass. That is, the receiver must physically step to the ball and meet it. Then there is an absorption of the force of the ball by the fingers, hands, wrist, and arms as they give with impact of the ball. Passes should be caught with both hands if at all possible.

Once a pass is received the options for the player in possession are to shoot, pass, or put the ball on the floor to dribble. These options need to be practiced as a continuation of the skill development of receiving the pass. To stand and hold the ball after a pass is a negative reaction in the game of basketball.

Points to remember when receiving a pass are:
- when possible try to catch the pass with two hands
- meet the pass by stepping toward the flight of the ball
- catch the ball with the fingers and absorb the force in the hands, wrist, and arms
- permit the arms to give with the force of the pass
- see the ball from release to receipt of the pass
- react after catching the ball by continuing the offensive effort

SHOOTING

Shooting a basketball has become extremely sophisticated. The fundamentals of shooting must be developed in order to establish a foundation that leads to a high skill level. Basic to the shooting game are the lay-up, free throw, and jump shot.

Figure 7. Receiving a pass.

Lay-up

The lay-up is considered to be the most fundamentally important shot in the sense that it is the shot taken closest to the basket with the highest degree of potential accuracy. The lay-up should be developed using both the dominant and nondominant hands. The backboard is a key target area. The ball should be directed to the rectangular area of the backboard from a side approach. The ball should be placed softly on the backboard at about a foot and a half above the rim and within the rectangle section nearest the shooter. The shooter should explode upward in a jumping action with the body and arms extended. The palm of the hand should face the backboard at release of the ball, and the ball should be released at the height of the jump. The jump requires a one foot take off, and the synchronization of arm and leg should be in opposition, with the take off foot opposite that of the shooting hand (i.e., right shooting hand, left take off jumping foot). Once the fundamental lay-up is developed there are countless variations of the lay-up that defy fundamental structure including reverse lay-ups, front rim approach, "wrong foot" jump, and, of course, the dunk.

Points to remember when shooting a lay-up include:

- look at the rectangular area of the backboard as the target
- place the ball softly off the backboard
- shoot left-handed off the left side of the basket and right-handed off the right side of the basket
- transfer horizontal movement when approaching the basket to an explosive vertical jump to lay the ball against the backboard
- start the jump with the ball positioned at about waist level and extend the body and arms
- protect the ball from the defense with the nonshooting arm from the beginning of the jump to release of the ball

a. Lay up with a soft touch.   **b.** Take off on the foot opposite the shooting hand.

Figure 8. The lay-up.

Free throw

The free throw is perhaps the easiest shot to execute since the defense may not attack the shooter. Shooting a free throw accurately requires confidence, concentration, and consistency.

Several stances can be assumed when beginning a free throw, but it is important to consistently use only one. The most comfortable position is to place the feet approximately shoulder width apart and the foot of the dominant shooting hand slightly in front of the other foot. There is a fluid relaxed motion used when shooting a free throw that begins with the bending of the legs at the beginning of the shot followed by a full extension of those legs at release and follow-through. The ball is shot with the fingers and the heel of the hand in contact with the ball. The ball should be positioned at waist to shoulder level with elbows into the body at the beginning of the shot, and as the full motion reaches extension the ball moves upward to a release point at about forehead level. At the release of the ball the forearm extends from the elbow with a break at the wrist best

described as a "goose neck." This goose neck position provides the back spin to the ball that gives it direction plus the shooting "touch." The target for the shooter should be the front of the rim. The concentration associated with this shot requires focusing on the front of the rim and attempting to reach and drop the ball just beyond the target. In order to accomplish this effort the ball is shot with an arch that clears the rim, and the final follow-through includes the center of the gravity of the shooter moving forward with the weight balanced on the balls of the feet.

Reminders to reinforce the free throw shooting technique include:

- relax and concentrate
- shoot the ball with spread fingers and the heel of the hand
- be consistent by using the same stance and motion on each shot
- be fluid and natural by bending and extending legs from beginning of the shot to release of the ball
- complete the shot by extending the arm and forming a goose neck with the wrist
- shoot with an arch

Figure 9. Free throw shooting.

Jump Shot

The jump shot is the most difficult. There are two basic types: the continuous and the delayed. The continuous jump shot is an extension of the free throw, while the delayed jump shot may be described as a jump with release of the ball at the peak of the jump.

To understand the continuous jump shot, imagine the free throw shot with a jump and the release of the ball occurring on the way up to the peak of the jump. This is a fluid, rhythmical shot taken by a player shooting from a distance from the basket. Shooting on the rise prior to the peak of the jump permits the shooter to use the body to assist in projecting the ball to the basket.

Reminders for the continuous jump shot technique include:

- imagine the free throw form with a jump added
- release the shot on the way up to the peak of the jump
- extend the arm on the follow-through and complete the shot with a goose neck
- be fluid and rhythmical throughout the total shot

The delayed jump shot is executed differently in the sense that the jump is executed within a three foot radius (going up and coming down in the same space), and the ball is released at the peak of the jump (before the body begins to return to the floor). Leg bend to extension and arm extension with a goose neck follow-through are significant parts of the shot. Shooting with an arch, using the front rim as the target area, and controlling the ball with the fingers and heel of the hand with the elbows in to the body are consistent with the free throw.

One specific aspect of the jump shot that needs to be emphasized is the rotation of

Figure 10. Delayed jump shot.

the body on its long axis. As the shooter faces the basket and then goes up to the peak of the jump there is a natural rotation of the body on the long axis that permits the alignment of the joints of the shooting side of the body (i.e., shoulder, elbow, wrist, hip, knee, and ankle) ending with the shooting side partially facing the basket at the completion of the shot. This alignment permits the body to work in rhythm with application of force. This rotation occurs with the free throw and the continuous jump shot as well as the delayed jump shot.

The delayed jump shot technique is different from the continuous jump shot in the following ways:

- the shot is released at the peak of the jump
- the jump is taken within a three foot radius
- the player is expected to jump

REBOUNDING

There are two basic rebounding situations: defensive and offensive. Both of these situations require timing and positioning. In addition, rebounding requires a mental toughness and aggressiveness to avoid intimidation when playing under the basket. Rebounding does not require tremendous jumping ability, but it does require anticipation, timing, and a sense of where other people are on the court. The act of rebounding occurs following an attempted field goal and off the free throw lane following a free throw. It is a team effort, particularly when rebounding from a defensive position.

The defensive rebound requires a blocking out technique. Typically, a defensive player is positioned between the basket and the offensive player. When a shot is taken the defensive player must either cross step or drop step and position in between the offensive player and the basket. A wide, strong base of support with legs shoulder width apart and partially bent, hips lowered, elbows wide with arms generally parallel to the floor, and the body braced to absorb contact from the offensive player characterizes the blocking out position.

There is enough contact with the offensive player to "feel" the player and the player's attempt at moving to the ball. The block out is sustained until the defensive player anticipates the need to move to the ball to gain possession (i.e., release the block out and go to the ball as it comes off the backboard/rim area).

Gaining possession is completed by good timing. The rebounder jumps into the ball and gains control at the highest point of the jump. The legs and elbows are spread wide with the buttocks extended to provide rebound room. The ball should be caught with hands on both sides of the ball or with one hand on top and the other on the bottom of the ball. The landing should maintain the wide base, and the ball should be positioned at the chest level with elbows firmly fixed outward to protect the ball.

The offensive rebound requires that the offensive player "fights" around the block out with deceptive movement in order to get into a position to gain possession of the ball. The same technique for gaining position is consistent with an offensive and defensive rebound whether rebounding from a missed field goal or missed free throw.

Techniques to remember regarding a rebound are:

- block out when on defense and sustain contact with the offensive player until it is time to gain possession of the ball
- maintain a wide base in the block out position and when going up after the ball
- maintain the wide base and protect the ball at chest level with elbows out when coming down with the ball following the rebound
- anticipate where the ball will carom off the backboard/rim and move to that area
- the shooter has the best feel for where the ball is going and should be positioned to follow the shot
- the offensive players should be deceptive in their movement to "fight" around being blocked out
- it is not how high a player jumps, but the anticipation of where the ball will bounce

DEFENSE

There are numerous team defenses that players are required to play. The individual team defensive position, however, is very consistent. One-on-one on the perimeter of the court a defensive player defends against a player by positioning between the basket and the offensive player. If a defensive player is defending under the basket then the player plays between the basket and the offensive player, sides the player, or fronts the player.

Perimeter one-on-one play requires that the player establish a low center of gravity with legs bent with a shoulder-width base. The head is up and the back is upright. It is important for the defensive player to slide or shuffle with the movement of the offensive player with hands positioned low and palms up. It is also acceptable to defend with one hand extended up and one positioned low. The slide is the most critical part of individual defense. If an offensive player moves to the defensive player's right side the right foot of the defensive player drops and slides in that direction. When the offensive player changes directions to move toward the defensive player's left side the player keeps the right foot positioned, but drop steps with the left and begins to slide on the left side. The key to perimeter defense is to give ground grudgingly and to never cross the feet.

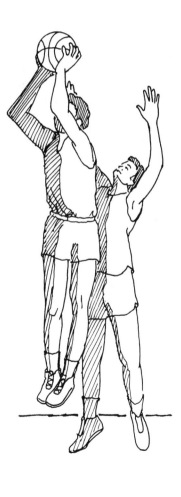

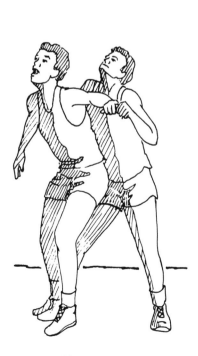

Figure 11. Rebounding sequence (block out).

Figure 12. Perimeter defense.

Defending under the basket typically requires either a side or a front position. In both cases the idea is to deny the offensive player access to the ball. Part of the denial is to position defensively in an upright position with hands held high when fronting the offensive player, and one hand held in front of the offensive player and one behind if siding the offensive player. Once the ball is controlled by the offensive player underneath the basket it is imperative that the perimeter defensive position be reestablished by the defensive player.

Reminders of perimeter defensive techniques include:

- staying low with a shoulder-width base
- sliding with the movement of the offensive player
- denying the offensive player a straight line to move
- avoiding crossing the feet
- keeping hands active and aggressive with both down or one extended up and one down
- denying the offensive player the ball under the basket

a. Fronting   b. Siding   c. Behind

Figure 13. Defending under the basket.

STRATEGY

Strategy is associated with various offensive and defensive sets. Offensively there are numerous pattern offenses, free lance offenses, offenses against zones, and fast-break offenses. Defensive situations include various defenses. Examples are: player-to-player defenses with variations of sagging, switching, and pressure; zones described as 1-3-1, 2-3, 1-2-2, 2-1-2, 3-2; and presses that are both zone and player-to-player.

Pattern offenses are described in many terms. Examples are the "passing game," "triangle," and "shuffle." Patterns are often set up in a 1-3-1 configuration with the point guard initiating the offense.

Most patterns may be too complicated for a class situation, but free-lance offenses are not. Free-lance offenses permit freedom of expression and both individual and team concept opportunities. There are rules to follow that protect the integrity of the offense. These rules include:

- maintain floor balance with at least two players on any one side at one time
- if you pass you cut
- there always has to be a "back player" for defensive purposes
- dribbling is limited and passing is encouraged
- if a player drives to the basket teammates should look for a pass

Offenses against zones are similar to pattern offenses, but simple rules can make attacking a zone defense easier. Again, rules are used to increase effectiveness against zones:

- if the zone has two players out front (e.g., 2-1-2 zone) the offense should balance the court with only one player out front (e.g., 1-3-1 offensive set). If confronting a one player defensive front (e.g., 1-2-2) balance the court with two offensive players out front
- pass around the perimeter to "move" the zone
- split seams in the zone and then pass outside for the shot (i.e., one player drives between two players in the zone until they are forced to cover the offensive player, which creates a passing lane to an open teammate)

- keep moving and cutting
- pass instead of dribble

The fastbreak offense requires practice off a rebound, a stolen ball, and a free throw. The basic premise of a fastbreak offense is to: (1) make an outlet pass, (2) fill three lanes on the break, and (3) complete the break with the middle player stopping at the free throw line and culminating the break by either shooting or passing to a teammate in a wide lane for a lay up. Fast break play is one of the most exciting and fun things to do in basketball and should be encouraged.

Player-to-player defenses are the base for all defenses. Whether the defense is a sagging, switching, or pressure defense there are specific team rules to follow:

- the defensive player tries to maintain position between opponent and basket
- never let an offensive player drive the baseline
- always keep a hand up when a player shoots
- when defending under the basket attempt to at least assume a side position
- help out from the weak side
- talk on defense

Zone defenses are played with player-to-player rules on an individual basis since player-to-player is the foundation for all defenses. The differences most observable between a player-to-player and zone are:

- keep hands up throughout the zone
- the defensive player is defending against an offensive player who enters the defensive player's zone
- the zone must attempt to maintain form and not collapse against a perimeter passing effort
- weak side play help is critical underneath the basket

There are several types of presses, classified as trapping, half court, three quarter court, full court, player-to-player, 3-1-1 zone, 2-1-2 zone, 1-2-2 zone, 1-3-1 zone, and many other combinations. The basic premise of any press is to apply pressure to force an offensive error. This is accomplished by double teaming a dribbler, forcing long passes, and forcing the offense to dribble or pass in a direction they don't want to go.

GAME SITUATIONS

There are countless game situations related to basketball. A major concept to remember with basketball is that the game is basically a one-on-one, two-on-two, and three-on-three game. Seldom does the game involve all five players at one specific time. As a result, the game can be played full court with five against five in a formal playing situation or it can be played half court with less than five against five. There are also a variety of games that can be played when drills are used that simply add incentive to a learning situation. In addition, there are countless shooting games including variations of Horse, free throw challenges, and jump shot challenges.

RULES

The rules of the game of basketball are extensive and should be reviewed in detail.

Rules vary depending on the level of play (i.e., junior high school/middle school, high school, college, professional, international). Even court dimension size is different depending on level of play.

Typically, the basketball court is 50' × 94' in high school, but a junior high school/middle school court might be of a smaller configuration.

Basketballs also vary in size. The basketball circumference for boys/men is approximately 30" while a girls/women's ball is slightly smaller.

The game is, of course, played by five players but the terms for positions also vary. Traditionally there have been two forwards, two guards, and a center. In the modern game, positions are often described as point guard, off guard, wings, etc.

With these variations, rules for specific levels of play should be reviewed directly from an official rule book.

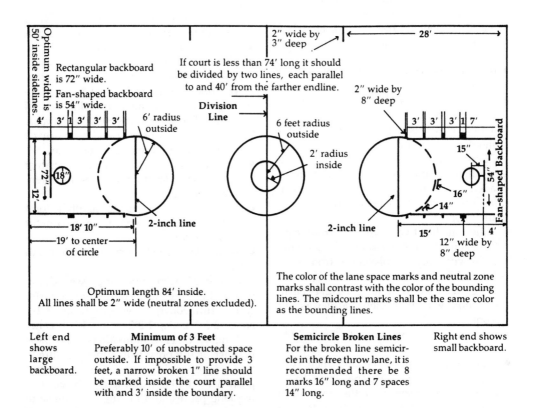

Diagram 1. Regulation basketball court.

EQUIPMENT

One of the great aspects of basketball is the limited need for equipment. One basketball can meet the needs of ten people playing the game. Obviously, one basketball is not enough for a teaching situation, which theoretically requires a basketball for every student. Additional equipment for the player includes basketball shoes and wearing apparel (shorts and shirt). It is important to emphasize basketball shoes as a required piece of equipment and a safety feature. Features that should be recommended when selecting a basketball shoe are:

- a high collar on the top of the shoe
- a Y band, which is a leather strap around the ankle
- a heel counter
- a full air mid sole for shock absorption
- a wide base sole

Two additional pieces of equipment have merit for a player. One is the use of mouth guards to protect against permanent damage of teeth, and a second is protective eye wear to avoid eye injuries, including detached retinas and scratches.

Instructional equipment is also helpful. Cones for setting up drills and establishing teaching stations need to be available. Video tape and television monitors to transmit insight to skill and team play, and to provide visual feedback to individual student skill development and play are extremely helpful. There are also countless teaching aids, including written materials for students that will add to the students' learning and enjoyment of the game.

SAFETY

It is critical to be aware of safety in basketball. The reader should refer to the AAHPERD publication *Principles of Safety in Physical Education and Sport* for a complete breakdown of safety and basketball; a brief listing of safety factors appears below:

- quality supervision of participation of students
- quality planning on the part of an instructor of a class
- quality instruction providing accurate information to students by the instructor
- use of personal safety equipment (i.e., shoes, mouth guard, protective eye wear)
- buffer zones between teaching stations and playing areas
- padded mats behind all baskets
- padding on backboards
- breakaway rims
- clean floors
- elimination of all obstacles on the floor

SKILL EXERCISES

Exercises are designed to encourage skill development. There are countless exercises that can be established depending on student readiness, maturation level, and ability. The exercises presented below are representative of skill exercises within the various individual skill areas.

Dribbling Exercises

1. Dribble in a restricted area while changing speeds and directions.
2. Set up obstacles (cones, chairs, etc.) and dribble through them.
3. Dribble in a one-on-one situation with the defensive player in a passive role.
4. Dribble in a one-on-one situation with the defensive player in an assertive role.
5. Play dribble tag with five to six players in a confined area.

Passing and Receiving Exercises

1. Pass the ball from a stationary position and then extend to a moving down court situation—concentrate on meeting the pass and giving with the force of the pass as a receiver.
2. Pass to chest high targets on a wall.
3. Establish a four corner passing/receiving routine with corners numbered 1, 2, 3, and 4. Corners numbered 1 and 3 are opposite corners as are 2 and 4. Number 1 passes to 3, 3 passes to 4, 4 passes to 2, and 2 passes to 1. The procees is repeated. The passer goes to the corner where the pass is directed.

Shooting Exercises

1. Shoot lay ups with two lines, one formed to the right and one to the left. Players

alternately dribble and shoot. This exercise can be expanded to one line passing and one shooting with further creative lay up possibilities that combine lay ups, passing, and dribbling.
2. Start in close shooting either free throws or jump shots five feet from the basket and progress back to increasing distances.

Rebounding Exercises
1. Stand in front of the backboard (or wall) and self toss the ball to the surface. Time the jump and rebound the ball with body wide, elbows out. Expand the exercise by including an outlet pass to a partner.
2. Work with another player and block out trying to hold the block for at least two seconds before releasing and rebounding the ball as tossed off the backboard or a wall.

Defensive Exercises
1. Work with three players (an offensive pivot player, a passer, and the defensive player). Practice siding and fronting the offensive player while the passer tries to pass the ball in to the offensive player. The offensive player plays passively and then more assertively as the defensive player develops skill.
2. Play defense against a dribbler; first sliding with the dribbler in a passive form and then working in a more assertive form to pressure the offensive player.
3. Work with three players (a defensive player in the middle and two passers 15' apart). The defensive player plays defensive against the passer and once the pass is made turns and defends against the other passer. (This exercise can also be used as a passing exercise.)

SELF-TESTING OF SKILLS

Self-testing activities can be challenging to students if practical. These activities tend to have goals associated with them and they need to be designed to address student readiness and maturation. Examples of some self-testing activities are listed below.

Passing and Receiving
1. Pass (using the different passes) to a wall target at varying heights and keep track of the number of accurate passes within a time frame.

Shooting
1. Shoot 25 free throws each day with an increasing target success rate goal. Final goal is 20 out of 25.
2. Make as many lay ups in succession under the basket in a 60 second time frame as possible.
3. Set up five spots on the floor at varying distances and angles. Angles should include baseline, top of the key, and 45 degree angle. Shoot 25 shots from each spot with final goal of 50 percent from each spot.

Rebounding
1. Stand in the middle of the "key" (the dotted area of the free throw lane), and rebound balls off the basket as tossed there by a partner. The goal is to rebound each ball before it strikes the floor.
2. Jump and touch the rim or net repeatedly six times. Rest 10 seconds and then repeat. Do this ten times.

Defense
1. Face the offensive player on the baseline and prohibit the drive on the baseline. Keep track of the success rate.
2. Front and side the pivot player when being fed by a partner. Keep track of the times the pivot player is denied the ball on the feed.

TERMINOLOGY

Changing Directions. To dart quickly from left to right and vice versa.

Follow-through. The continuation of the body movement after a skill is executed.

Feed. The act of passing a ball to a player in a position to score.

Flow. Being in rhythm with the game and emotion of play. Often associated with instinctive, nonthinking play.

Goose Neck. The descriptive position of the forearm, wrist, and hand on the follow-through of a free throw or jump shot.

High Dribble. Dribble used for speed in an open court area.

Low Dribble. Dribble used for protection of the ball in a congested area.

Outlet Pass. The pass following a rebound to initiate a fast break or start of the offensive attack.

Pivot. The act of turning by lifting one foot off the floor and turning on the ball of the other foot to face in a different direction.

Rotation. The backspin imparted on the ball as it is released.

Styling. The aesthetic part of the game usually associated with individual moves with the end product usually representative of how good a player looks as opposed to the outcome of the move that results in scoring or continuation of a successfull play.

Take-off Foot. The foot opposite the shooting hand used to push off the floor when executing a lay up.

Top of the Key. The position on the floor at the top of the free throw circle just a little over 19' from the basket.

Touch. The feel of the ball.

REFERENCES

Atkins, K., & Raines, R. *Winning basketball drills.* West Nyack, NY: Parker, 1985.

Bryant, J. E. Basketball. In N.J. Dougherty, IV (Ed.) *Principles of safety in physical education and sport.* Washington, DC: AAHPERD.

Harkins, H.L. *Modern basketball team techniques.* West Nyack, NJ: Parker, 1985.

Isaacs, N. D., & Motta, D. *Basketball: The keys to excellence.* New York: Winner's Circle Books, 1988.

Lahodny, J. *Drills for winning basketball.* West Nyack, NJ: Parker, 1986.

CHAPTER 7

Bowling

ETHEL M. HALE
Hillsborough County Schools
Tampa, FL
and
BILL RALSTON
Florida Lanes
Tampa, FL

INTRODUCTION

Spare students the everyday physical education activity; put them in a better *frame* of mind; *strike* out in a new direction. Including bowling in the physical education program will add a new dimension to a curriculum.

A lifetime sport, bowling is an activity that can be enjoyed by people of any age, size, or level of physical development. Being an indoor activity, bowling is not a seasonal sport. It can be played year round.

Physical education is charged with the unique responsibility of developing motor skills, and bowling provides an excellent opportunity to develop skillful movers. Becoming a skilled bowler requires that the student demonstrate an understanding of the need to put together a sequence of movements. The conditions under which bowling skills are performed remain constant, providing an opportunity for students to refine their skills based upon their individual developmental level.

HISTORY

Bowling may be one of the oldest non-combative sports. Egyptian children used small round stones to knock over sticks or tall stones in a form of bowling about seven thousand years ago. The Italian game of Bocci, bowling a ball at a target ball on the grass, dates back to 50 B.C. Early Polynesians in the Pacific had a game which resembled bowling as they used flat stones to knock over other stones or sticks; their lane was 67 feet long (the same distance from the foul line to the head pin in our present ten-pin game).

Around 1100 A.D. the king of England outlawed bowling-on-the-green as the men were bowling-on-the-green too much and they were not practicing archery. During the 1500s Martin Luther standardized the rules for the popular game of nine-pins. Bowling was brought to this country by settlers from Holland in the 1600s. Many cities had places for bowling-on-the-green. Bowling soon became an indoor activity. Shortly thereafter an enterprising man added the tenth pin, rearranged the placement of the pins, changed the width of the lane, and devised the present ten-pin game.

In 1895, in an attempt to standardize the game, the American Bowling Congress (ABC) was founded. This organization still governs all aspects of the game. The Women's International Bowling Congress (WIBC) was organized in 1916 and governs women's bowling. The American Junior Bowling Congress (AJBC) was established to deal with the concerns of young bowlers. Youth bowling has grown at an incredible rate, with organized bowling for children from age three through college age bowlers. To deal with this increased interest the AJBC became the Young American Bowling Alliance (YABA) in 1982.

The interest in bowling has continued to grow at all levels. Bowling has become the largest participation sport in the United States with more than 70,000,000 bowlers.

BOWLING LANES

The ideal atmosphere for teaching bowling skills is a bowling center with regulation bowling lanes (see Diagram 1). In many cases traveling to the center is not feasible. There are now a variety of alternatives.

A variety of bowling equipment is available through physical education equipment catalogs. Much of this equipment has been modified to meet the needs of the physical education class. There are directions available for marking the gymnasium floor. For outdoor bowling there is a set of scaled down carpeted lanes, complete with markings, which can be used to simulate bowling conditions. By using the local bowling center as a resource, a variety of other approaches can also be explored.

EQUIPMENT

The equipment required to participate in bowling at a bowling center is a bowling ball and bowling shoes. Bowling centers have this equipment available. Bowling balls are furnished at no cost and bowling shoes may be rented. It is recommended that individuals who bowl on a regular basis acquire their own equipment.

A good rule of thumb for selecting the proper weight bowling ball is to select one which is one-tenth of the person's body weight. The ball should be one which the bowler can control, not too heavy and at the same time not too light. Bowling shoes are necessary as they allow the bowlers to slide as they release the bowling ball.

It is not necessary to dress in a particular way to bowl. However, one should select clothing which is loose and allows freedom of movement.

SKILLS AND TECHNIQUES

While bowling is a game of individual style, it is necessary to develop that style based on sound technique. Beginning with an understanding of the starting position and the proper stance, the student can then develop a four-step approach which includes a rhythmic sequence of steps and ball movement.

All instructions in this chapter are designed for the right-handed bowler. It will be necessary for the left-handed bowler to make the appropriate adjustments.

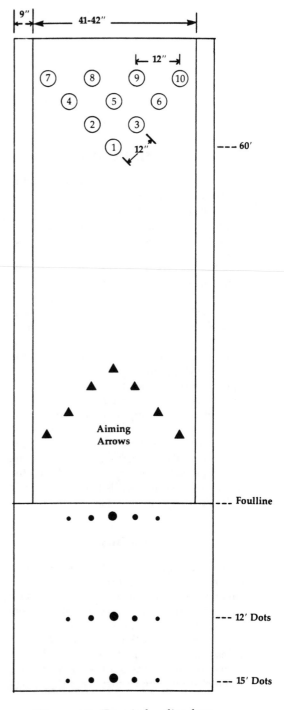

Diagram 1. Ten-pin bowling lane.

STARTING POSITION

To determine the correct starting position for the four-step approach, the bowler should stand with his/her heels at the foul line and back to the pins. Take four and a half normal walking steps back from the foul line toward the two rows of dots on the approach.

This distance is a beginning point. The bowler must now determine where to stand on the approach. Using the dots on the lane as a reference point, it is recommended that the bowler place the inside edge of the left foot on the board which covers the middle dot.

THE STARTING STANCE

A number of components make up the proper stance. To look at these components one should look at the body from the waist down and the waist up. Another significant area to be considered is ball position. It has been said that bowling is a game of straight lines and right angles. The bowler's starting stance must be correct if he/she is to be able to line up squarely to the pins, travel toward the target and deliver the ball.

Foot position provides the foundation of the stance. The bowler's feet should be comfortably close together and parallel with the left foot slightly forward. Place the right toe even with the left arch. In assuming a starting stance the bowler should flex his/her knees. By doing so, two thirds of the bowler's body weight is placed on the left or non-starting foot.

As part of the stance, the bowler should bend slightly at the waist. It is essential that the bowler keep his/her shoulders square to the target. As demonstrated in Figure 1, a perpendicular line can be drawn from the bowler's toe through the knee up to the shoulder. By keeping this line, the bowler remains in a balanced position.

The last element of the starting stance is ball position. The ball should be held using the suitcase grip. Also known as the handshake grip, it is characterized by holding the ball with the thumb at 10 o'clock and fingers at 4 o'clock position. The ball is held at waist height in front of the right hip. The left hand should be used to steady the ball while the right hand supports the majority of the ball weight. In this conventional grip the thumb and fingers are placed all the way into the ball.

The wrist and forearm should form a straight line. Firm and straight are the key points in holding the ball. Do not cup the ball or bend the wrist.

THE 4-STEP APPROACH

The 4-step approach is the most basic of all approaches. It is the most commonly used approach because the time needed to swing the ball correlates closely to the time required to take four steps. It is essential that the bowler have sound footwork, as sound footwork allows the bowler to move to the foul line to deliver the ball while maintaining good balance.

The sequence of foot movements and ball movements are rhythmic in nature. It must be understood that the weight of the bowling ball creates momentum as the footwork takes the bowler closer to the foul line. Because of this momentum each step taken

Figure 1. Starting stance.

a.   b.   c.

d.   e.

Figure 2. The 4-step approach (side view).

gets longer and faster. The path of the steps taken should follow an imaginary line drawn between the bowler and the target he/she wishes to hit.

Having assumed the proper starting stance, with the ball held at waist height in front of the right hip, the bowler is now ready to begin the 4-step approach.

Step 1: The first step (right foot for right-handed bowlers, left foot for left-handed bowlers) should be a short and slow one. Simultaneously, the ball is pushed out and begins its downward swing (Figure 2, a). Synchronization is crucial in the first step and push-away of the ball if the bowler is to deliver the ball at the foul line in balance.

Step 2: The second step is a little longer and a little faster. The ball is now in its backward swing and at the end of the second step is above the right calf (Figure 2, b).

Step 3: As the momentum builds, the ball continues its backward arc. At its highest point the ball will reach approximately head or neck level. The right foot continues its step as the ball reaches the top of its backswing (Figure 2, c)

Step 4: In this final step the left foot slides forward to the foul line. The ball will be moving down and forward to the point of release. The ball is released at ankle level. At the point of release the thumb will come out of the ball first and a split second later the fingers will come out (Figure 2, d). This release will put a natural sideways rotation on the ball creating a controllable hook on the ball. Although as a beginning bowler it might seem that a ball which hooks would appear to be an advanced skill, this is not the case. It is in the best interest of the bowler to develop a natural swing and release. The resulting hook can be dealt with by understanding and using the target arrows on the lane.

Just as in any skill progression, the follow-through is an important part of the 4-step approach. Even though the ball was released at the bottom of the arm swing, the follow-through is a continuation of the rhythmic sequence of the approach (Figure 2, e). The path, rotation of the ball, and the ability to control the ball are affected by the arm swing and follow-through. The arm which released the ball should continue its forward movement, in an arc or pendulum style, so that the arm does not cross the midline of the body. The proper arm swing and follow-through permits the ball to be released by the hand from the ten and four, thumb and finger positions. This release imparts the proper rotation on the ball.

It will be helpful to the student to use imagery prior to putting the 4-step approach into practice. By visualizing the foot and ball position in each step the bowler can see where he/she is at each point of the approach. This imagery will also allow the student to visualize the increase in the tempo of the footwork and ball movement.

TARGET

In our discussion of the starting position and 4-step approach much attention was given to the importance of keeping the shoulders square to the target. It is now time to discuss which target can be used. There are two common targets for bowlers, the pins and the target arrows which appear on the lanes.

For the bowler who is a pin bowler, the target is self-explanatory. Pin bowling is quite difficult as the target is 60 to 63 feet away from the point of release. Pin bowlers need to look at the pin or pins as the ball is being released. Using the pin or pins as a

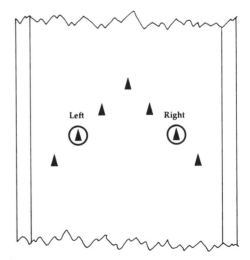

Diagram 2. Target arrows for the right- and left-handed bowler.

target requires that the bowler has control and understands the rotation and curve of the ball.

While some bowlers aim at the pins, it is more common to see the bowler use the target arrows on the lane as the target. Called spot (arrow) bowling, the bowler keeps his/her eye on the target arrow until the ball is released. These small dart shaped marks are 12 to 15 feet beyond the foul line. On the first ball it is recommended that the right-handed player aim for the second arrow from the right and the left-handed player aim for the second arrow from the left (Diagram 2).

Spot bowling is easier, in that the target is 12 to 15 feet from the foul line as opposed to 60 to 63 feet away for pin bowling. The ball moves straight down the lane before

curving prior to impact with the pins (Diagram 3).

In spot bowling the bowler does not have to make allowances for the curve in the same way as the pin bowler. The ball will pass over the target arrow after leaving the bowler's hand. The pin bowler must have control of the ball and allow for the curve of the ball which will take place. There is a large degree of difficulty controlling the roll for that 60 to 63 foot distance.

SPARES

Obviously strikes are the ultimate goal of the bowler, but most players do not get many strikes. Because of this, the ability of the bowler to make spares becomes very

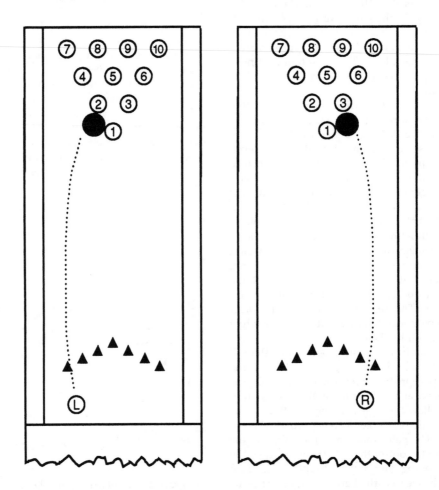

Diagram 3. Ball paths for the left-handed and right-handed bowler.

important. The more accurately spares are made, the more controlled the player has become and in turn the easier it will become to make strikes.

Attempts at spares become necessary when pins are left after the first ball has been delivered. There are certain spare leaves that almost defy being made: the object in this case is to knock over as many pins as possible.

If the bowler has not made a strike on the first ball, it will be necessary to attempt a spare. The number of pins remaining can be as few as one or as many as ten. The 4-step approach and the delivery remain the same. The adjustment is made in either the starting point of the bowler or the target arrow to be used. To determine the starting position it is necessary to identify the key pin. The pin **closest** to the bowler is the key pin. The key pin must be the first pin hit. Diagram 4 identifies the key pin positions.

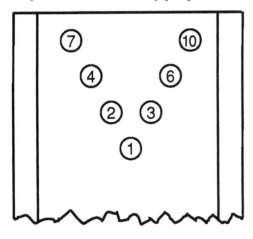

Diagram 4. Key pin positions.

All adjustments for spare conversion are made to the starting position for a strike. Using the head pin (1) as a reference point, move 3 boards to the right for each pin to the left of the head pin. Your target is now between the second and third arrow from the right side of the lane. For pins remaining to the right of the head pin move 4 boards to the left for each pin to the right of the head pin. The target for these pins is between the second and third arrow from the left side of the lane.

Bowling is a game involving straight lines and angles. Attempting spares is a perfect example of the need for an understanding of angles. By moving the appropriate number of boards in either direction the bowler has the most lane to work with.

While this seems to be an oversimplification of spares, it is impossible to explain each spare individually. For the beginning bowler the concepts to remember are: (1) don't alter the armswing, (2) move the appropriate number of boards to the left or right so as to give the bowler as much room as possible for spare conversion, and (3) alter the target arrow.

ETIQUETTE

Bowling has some unwritten customs or rules of etiquette. Those which are most common are listed below.

1. Be ready to bowl when it is your turn. Once your ball has hit the pins, leave the lane.
2. Do not talk to or bother a player who is ready to bowl.
3. Wait for your turn. Let the bowler on your right bowl first.
4. Use your own ball.
5. Stay on your approach.
6. Do not foul.
7. Don't bowl until the pins are ready.
8. Keep food and beverages behind the settees.
9. Do not put liquids, powder, or foreign substances on your bowling shoes.
10. Always exhibit good sportsmanship.
11. Return rental shoes and bowling balls to proper place.

SCORING

Bowling has a unique scoring system. At first glance it seems quite difficult. Once the basic concepts of scoring are understood the student will become comfortable with it. In recent years computerized scoring has become common in bowling centers. This trend does not negate the need to learn how to score.

A total of ten frames make up a single game, with each player receiving a maximum of two deliveries per frame, except for the tenth or final frame.

1. A strike (X) counts as 10 plus the number of pins knocked down on the next 2 rolls (these rolls come in the next frame). In the tenth frame the 2 extra rolls come immediately and are only given for the first strike.
2. A spare (/) counts as 10 plus a bonus of the number of pins knocked down on the next roll (this roll comes in the next frame). In the tenth frame the extra roll comes immediately.
3. In frames where all of the pins are not knocked down by the first two rolls the score for that frame is the total number of pins knocked down by the first and second roll.
4. In bowling, scoring is cumulative. The score of each frame is added to the score of the previous frame.
5. If the bowler goes beyond the foul line while delivering the ball, he/she receives a zero (0) for that roll.

Diagram 5 serves as an example of a properly scored game. One can use this frame-by-frame explanation to see how the score was arrived at.

Frame 1—7 pins were knocked down with the first ball, 3 pins with the second. This counts as a spare (/). The frame total is 15 (10 for the spare + 5 for the first ball of the second frame).

Frame 2—5 pins were knocked down on the first ball plus 3 on the second. The frame score is 5 + 3 = 8. The cumulative score is 15 (frame 1) + 8 (frame 2) = 23.

Frame 3—9 pins with the first ball, 1 pin with the second ball counts as a spare (/). Score in this frame is 10 for the spare + 0 (for a foul line violation on the first ball of the 4th frame) = 10. The total score at the end of the third frame is 23 + 10 = 33.

Frame 4—0 pins (a foul line violation) for the first ball plus 6 with the second for a total of 6. The cumulative score is 33 + 6 = 39.

Frame 5—The total for the frame is 5 (5 for the first ball, 0 with the second). The total to this point is 39 + 5 = 44.

Frame 6—A strike on the first ball. Score for the frame is 28 (10 for the strike in the 6th frame + 10 for a 7th frame strike + 8 for the first ball of the 8th frame). The cumulative score is 44 + 28 = 72.

Frame 7—STRIKE! The score for this frame is 20 [10 for the strike + 10 for spare (8 + 2) in the 8th frame]. Cumulative score is 72 + 20 = 92.

Frame 8—8 pins with the first ball and 2 pins on the second ball for a spare. (The circle around the 8 in the 8th frame denotes a split in the remaining pins). The frame score is 20 (10 for the spare + 10 for a 9th frame strike). The total score at the end of the 8th frame is 92 + 20 = 112.

Frame 9—Strike with the first ball. Score in the frame is 30 (three consecutive strikes equals 10 + 10 + 10). The cumulative total is 112 + 30 = 142.

Frame 10—Three consecutive strikes. Score for the frame is 30 (10 + 10 + 10). Bonus balls are allowed only for the first strike. The final score is 142 + 30 = 172.

In bowling a perfect score is 300. While the perfect game is the ultimate, 300 is a rare score. Since scoring is cumulative in bowling, the bowler should take advantage of the opportunity to score extra pins on strikes and spares. These extra pins are the ones which help to add up to large score.

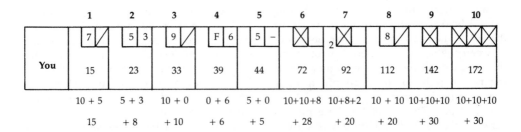

Diagram 5. How to score the game.

TERMINOLOGY

Approach—The area of the lane on which the bowler takes his/her steps prior to delivering the ball at the foul line.

Arrows—A series of seven triangular darts, 12 to 15 feet beyond the foul line. Used in aiming at targets.

Automatic Scoring—Computers which keep score automatically.

Backup Ball—Ball that curves to the right for the right-handed bowler, or to the left for the left-handed bowler.

Blow (also miss, open error)—Failing to get a strike or a spare in a frame.

Bonus—The number of additional pins scored after getting a strike or a spare.

Channel Ball—Rolling the ball into the shallow 9-inch wide trough on either side of the bowling lane.

Cherry (also chop)—Knocking down at least the front pin or pins during a spare attempt and leaving adjacent or rear pins standing.

Convert—The ability to make a spare.

Count (pin count)—Failure to get at least 9 pins in a frame or 9 pins on the first ball following a spare or multiple strikes.

Curve—A ball that is rolled toward the outside of the lane which then curves back toward the center of the lane.

Dead Ball—A ball rolled on the wrong lane or out of turn; also a delivered ball that causes little or no pin action.

Dead Mark—Last ball spare or strike in the tenth frame; no bonus is allowed on a dead mark.

Delivery—Rolling the ball.

Double (also called a chicken)—Two consecutive strikes in a game.

Dutchman or Dutch 200—Alternating strikes and spares in a game.

Fast Lanes—Term used when the ball does not curve due to lane conditions.

Foul—Touching or going over the foul line when delivering the ball. It is also a foul to touch anything beyond the foul line even if the foul light does not go on. A foul counts as a ball rolled but a zero is received for that ball.

Foul Line—The line separating the approach and the lane.

Frame—A game consists of ten frames per player; either one ball (strike) or two balls are rolled per frame, except in the tenth frame, an extra ball is received if the player gets a spare, and two balls if the player gets a strike on the first ball.

Handicap—A score adjustment based on the difference between team or individual averages. Usually 75%, 80%, or 90% of the difference is used.

Hook—A ball rolled so that the ball takes a straight path and then takes a sharp turn (hook) at the end.

Kingpin—Name given to the "5" pin.

Lane—Name given to the wooden or synthetic surface that extends from the foul line to the end of the pin deck.

League Bowling—Bowling in a regularly scheduled league format, usually done by teams.

Mark—A strike or a spare.

Nose Hit—When the ball hits the number 1 pin squarely.

Perfect Game—A score of 300. Twelve consecutive strikes in a game.

Pin—The regulation pin is 15 inches tall and usually weighs a minimum of 3 pounds 6 ounces.

Pin Bowler—Player who looks at the pins when releasing the ball.

Pin Deck—The area where the pins are spotted. The pin deck is 41-42" wide.

Pin Spots—Spots on the pin deck. Pins are placed 12 inches apart, center-to-center, forming a 36-inch triangle.

Pit—Area at the end of the pin deck into which the pins fall.

Pocket—The 1-3 pins for the right-handed bowler and 1-2 for the left-handed bowler.

Return—The track on which the ball returns to the bowler.

Series—Usually three games, such as in a league session.

Span—Distance between the thumb hole and the finger holes on a bowling ball. There are three basic spans: conventional; semi-fingertip; and fingertip grips.

Spare—Knocking down all 10 pins with two balls in a frame. A spare counts as 10 plus the number of pins knocked down with the next ball. There are 1,023 different spare combinations.

Split—When an intermediate pin is missing in any series of pins, providing the head pin is not standing after delivering the first ball in a frame.

Spot Bowler—A player who uses the target arrows rather than looking at the pins when releasing the ball.

Strike—Knocking down all 10 pins with the first ball in a frame except in the tenth frame where the bowler may have three chances for strikes. A strike counts 10 plus the number of pins knocked down on the next two balls.

REFERENCES

American Junior Bowling Congress. *Rules and Regulations.* Greendale, WI, current year.

Borden, Fred, and Elias, Jay. *Beyond the Beginner.* Greendale, WI: Young American Bowling Alliance, 1990.

Showers, Norman E. *Bowling,* 3rd ed. Glenview, IL: Scott, Foresman and Company, 1981.

Young American Bowling Alliance. *In-School Program: Resource Manual.* Greendale, WI.

CHAPTER 8

Dance

LYNNE FITZGERALD
Morehead State University
Morehead, KY

INTRODUCTION

Movement is basic to life itself. As we journey through life we experience a broad range of feelings and emotions: love, pain, joy, anger, and satisfaction. These are spontaneously revealed through changes in the shape, posture, energy level, and movement of the body. Dance evolves from the conscious desire or the intention to share our experience, using the body and movement as the medium of expression. The dancer develops forms that give shape and meaning to movement so the intention is communicated. Forms of frameworks are used to organize the elements of dance, such as space, time, and energy, so that dance takes on a character that is revealed in meaningful movement patterns performed by individuals or groups of dancers.

Throughout history many dance forms have evolved in order to reflect the essence of a culture. People throughout the world have created dances to express their religious and spiritual experience, to celebrate life events such as birth, death, and marriage, and to capture the tales and human struggles which document their heritage. More recently, dance forms have been designed to frame the creative and expressive needs of the artist, further expanding the nature and function of dance to provide personal meaning.

The diverse roles fulfilled by dance throughout history make it difficult to define; therefore scholars and educators tend to think about and describe dance in terms of categories or from labels, such as folk, square, social, ethnic, jazz, tap, modern, and ballet. Each of these forms of dance has a set of characteristics that articulates its uniqueness.

Teachers of dance use these labels to communicate the types of dance to be included in the dance or physical education curriculum. The potential for dance to contribute to student learning is broad in scope, restricted only by the physical education teacher's interest, perception, and preparation.

This chapter provides students with information clarifying the (1) educational goals of dance, (2) movement skills basic to dance, (3) background, role, and characteristics of the following dance forms: ballet, modern, social, folk, and square, (4) safety guidelines, and (5) equipment needs.

EDUCATIONAL GOALS

The educational goals of dance reflect the assumption that dance has the potential to contribute to the development of all aspects of student learning: physical, mental, emotional, and sociocultural. Goals are accomplished through student participation in a variety of well constructed dance classes.

1. Students will expand their movement/dance skill and vocabulary through participation in dance activities. The more varied the dance program the greater the opportunity for learning new skills that will support student participation in dance through life.

2. Students will develop increased fitness (strength, flexibility, agility, power, and coordination) through participation in carefully constructed learning experiences in conjunction with related performance activities.

3. Students will develop an understanding and appreciation of self and others as well as social interaction skills, when opportunities for independent and

group creativity, expression, and performance are built into the dance program.

4. Students will develop a variety of cognitive skills when opportunities for recall, problem-solving, dance making, and observation are included in the dance program.

5. Students will develop an appreciation of the history of American and international cultures through the study of and participation in a variety of ethnic, folk, square, and social dance forms.

MOVEMENT SKILLS

Dancing involves moving in and through space and there are two types of movement skills that establish a solid foundation to prepare students for successful participation in traditional dance forms. Movements that occur "in place" are typically referred to as nonlocomotor movement because they are practiced while at least one foot maintains contact with the floor. The body or isolated body part moves around its own axis above a stationary base of support. Locomotor movements travel through space most often using the feet as the source of movement carrying the dancer from one place to another place. Nonlocomotor and locomotor skills are addressed more extensively in the following sections.

NONLOCOMOTOR MOVEMENTS AND SKILLS

Nonlocomotor skills are often learned during the introductory or warm-up phase of a class. These skills can be performed while dancers are lying down, sitting, or standing. Many students find it is easier to focus on movement concepts and warm-up variables when moving the entire body or isolated parts of the body over a stationary base of support.

The following are examples of nonlocomotor movements common to dance: pushing, pulling, bending, stretching, swinging, swaying, spinning, twisting, and turning. Action words are used to describe nonlocomotor movements, and these often trigger mental pictures that students are asked to fulfill through a movement

response. Teachers can make long lists of action words or phrases that can be used to stimulate movement exploration and improvisation. Students can learn to distinguish the unique characteristics of nonlocomotor movements when they focus on such things as timing, force (energy used), and shape of the body.

The nonlocomotor framework is also effective for warm-up activities because students find it is easier to focus on such things as alignment, posture, and technique when they are moving above a stationary base of support. The goal of the warm-up is twofold: first, to prepare the joints to move through a full range of motion and second, to gradually raise the core temperature of the body so students can safely and successfully participate in the large muscle activities that are part of the class.

LOCOMOTOR SKILLS

Learning locomotor skills is important because this prepares students to participate in a variety of dance activities that are constructed by combining and varying the locomotor skills. Descriptions of the basic locomotor skills are presented below.

1. **Walk:** weight transfers from heel to toe, alternating feet (r,l,r,l, etc.), even rhythm.

2. **Run:** weight is carried on the ball of the foot, alternating feet (r,l,r,l, etc.), even rhythm and faster paced than the walk.

3. **Hop:** weight transfers from the heel through the ball of the foot, the body is propelled by springing off and landing on that same foot (r,r,r,r), even rhythm.

4. **Jump:** the body is propelled by springing off one or both feet and landing on both feet, even rhythm.

5. **Leap:** the body springs off one foot and lands on the other foot (l,r,l,r, etc.), even rhythm, larger than a run, and includes a movement of aerial suspension.

Dance steps can be learned by introducing students to variations or combinations of these skills. For example, a walk becomes a:

1. **Shuffle step**, when students are asked to vary the walk by transferring their weight from the ball of the foot to the

heel, alternating feet to an even rhythm, and the tempo is lively.

2. **Two-step**, when students are asked to combine a step, close, step, alternating feet (r,l,r, and l,r,l), with the weight shifting to the support foot on each step. The rhythm is uneven—quick, quick, slow.

3. **Waltz step**, when the stepping pattern is varied. Step 1 moves forward, step 2 moves sideways, and step 3 closes sideways, weight transferring to the stepping foot which alternates. R-forward, l-sideways, r-closes followed by l-forward, r-sideways, l-closes. The rhythm is even and tempo is slow.

4. **Grapevine step**, when the dancers' facing and the direction of the stepping is varied to the side. This four step pattern involves a side step, followed by a rear cross step, followed by a side step, and a front cross step, l,r,l,r (moving left) or r,l,r,l (moving right) with the weight bearing foot alternating. The rhythm is even and tempo variable.

A walk combined with a hop results in the following dance steps:

1. **Schottische step**, involves 3 walking (or running) steps combined with a hop. The weight bearing foot alternates on each walking step (r,l,r) and the hop occurs on the same foot as the last step (r). (r,l,r,r and l,r,l,l). The rhythm is even and the tempo variable.

2. **Polka step**, involves 3 walking steps and a hop. However, the walking steps, though alternating, are step-*close*-step, with a hop on the pick-up beat (hop [on R], l,r,l and hop [on L], r,l,r). The rhythm is uneven with the first two steps being equal, the third step being slower, and the hop is very quick. The tempo is fast.

Each of the locomotor skills and dance steps that have been described can be learned as part of an introductory dance unit or specific steps can be incorporated into the learning process when the step is part of a specific dance introduced for a lesson. The two-step, polka, schottische, and grapevine steps are common to folk dance. The waltz is part of social dance and the shuffle step often has a role in square dance.

DANCE FORMS

Several dance forms are discussed in the pages which follow. The discussion focuses on a brief history, the characteristics of each form, and the role of that form in our society.

BALLET

History reveals that ballet had its beginnings in the courts of Italy in the late 15th century. At this time ballet was performed by amateurs who captured the essence of a ritual or story through movement executed amid a great deal of pageantry. Ballet, as a theater art form performed by trained professionals, emerged in Europe during the Renaissance.

The classical form of ballet combines patterns of dramatic movement, and spectacular technical feats have been combined in an effort to please the spectator. The dance is further enhanced by elaborate stage designs, costumes created to highlight performers' virtuosity, and live orchestral music, which establishes a rich background inspiring the dancers. While dancing, ballet dancers maintain a vertical body while moving from the smallest possible base of support. Their arms move through elegant and yet controlled arm positions intended to enhance or support the important movement of the legs. Traditionally, legs work from a turned out position at the hip and female dancers often execute movement en pointe (on their toes).

The movement vocabulary of the ballet dancer includes five basic foot positions with corresponding arm positions and eight body facings. From these basics the dancer learns to jump, leap (jeté), turn, and bend and to execute five arabesques or poses. Dancers train so that they will be able to fulfill the elements of their dance according to the characteristics of their gender. Male dancers' roles require demonstrations of power, strength, and stability while female roles are shaped to depict delicacy, ease, and elegance. Outstanding female performers are called ballerinas and outstanding male performers are called danseurs.

Figure 1. Ballet.

MODERN DANCE

Modern dance is an American art form that emerged in the 20th century. Modern dance is free of the traditional choreographic structures of ballet. Dances are designed to fulfill the essence of a choreographer's point of view, which is possible because their dancers have fulfilled a rigorous training program and participated in a number of improvisational structures.

Modern dance training systems tend to be named after the dancer/choreographer who developed the technique to be used to prepare their dancers with the skills necessary to fulfill their choreography. Some of the training systems which have stood the test of time are those of Martha Graham, Mary Wigman, Erick Hawkins, Merce Cunningham, and Twyla Tharp.

Technique is learned during the warm-up, which focuses on the development of strength, flexibility, agility, endurance, control, and balance inside the movement framework of a specific person's dance system. Dancers also learn how energy is used to influence the quality of one's move-

Figure 2. Modern dance.

ment. The ultimate goal is for the dancer to develop the ability to respond efficiently to the movement challenges of a choreographed dance.

Another aspect of modern dance is improvisation. Improvisation is a method used to give students an opportunity to respond to a movement problem, suggestion, or framework presented by the teacher. Creative and spontaneous movement results and these responses often provide rich movement sequences or patterns which can be used in a dance.

The choreographed dance is the ultimate outcome of modern dance. The purpose of the dance is to communicate the choreographer's (dance maker's) intention to the audience. The themes for modern dance are endless; some possibilities include: life experiences (events, rituals, happenings), human nature (emotional renderings, relationships, human experience), chance, and music. Most modern dances are presented on a stage and music/sound, costumes, and props are used to enhance the performance.

Modern dance is exciting because it continues to change and grow with the times. New systems of training and choreographic frameworks continue to emerge, reflecting the experience and philosophy of young artists.

SOCIAL DANCE

Social dance started with the court dances of the Renaissance period in Europe. The ladies and gentlemen of the court were taught dance steps, appropriate dress, and etiquette by the dance master so they could participate in the dance of gala events.

Social dance is a label used to describe coupled/partner dances performed for recreational or competitive purposes. Each dance includes a specific foot pattern and variations, which might incorporate glides, turns, dips, and/or swing steps. There is also a more or less formalized relationship to a partner. In this partnership the male dancer is responsible for leading his female partner through the dance. When leading, he might use his right hand to signal

Figure 3. Ballroom dance.

changes to his female partner so she is prepared to follow his lead into the next step sequence or variation. Social dances evolve and are performed to music that establishes the rhythm, tempo, and atmosphere appropriate for a specific dance.

Social dance which is performed in formal settings (proms, dinner dances, military balls) has often been called ballroom dance. Some of the more traditional forms of ballroom dance in America include the Waltz, Tango, Samba, Rumba, Cha Cha, and Jitterbug. Social dance forms that are performed in less formal settings (school dances, discotheques, and parties) are called popular dance. Popular dances continue to change in light of music fads that catch the heart of the public.

In the 1920s, when ragtime, jazz, and the big band music were popular, the Charleston, the Jitterbug, and the Boogie emerged. In the 1960s and 1970s the Twist, the Swim, the Chicken, and the Hustle were developed in response to the popular rock and roll music. The Moon Walk, the Electric

Figure 4. Popular dance.

appropriately challenging and satisfying experience for all.

Country music is common to square dance and the fiddle has traditionally been recognized as the favorite musical instrument because it creates a lively and rhythmical background for dancing. A variety of instruments have, however, been recorded to create authentic sound for teaching and practice purposes.

Dancers can have a positive learning experience through square dance when they are familiar with the dance skills, hand positions, and figures or movement patterns common to this form of dance.

The Square

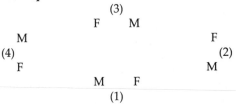

Clarifiers:

1. Couples are numbered 1, 2, 3, and 4 in a counterclockwise fashion. The starting positions are commonly referred to as the "home" position.
2. Couples 1 and 3 are the lead couples.
3. Couples 2 and 4 are the side couples.
4. Corner lady is the lady to the left of each man.

It is important to develop an understanding of one's position and related role in the square. To promote this understanding, the teacher can present an introductory series of cues focusing on maneuvers so performers can try these out. An example of a "practice call" is presented below:

"1 and 3 go forward and back,
2 and 4 go forward and back.
All join hands and circle left,
reverse circle right,
go back home.
Heads go into the middle.
Join hands, circle once around
and go back home.
Sides circle to the left
in the middle of the ring,
once around, go back home.
Everybody swing."

Slide, and the Achy Breaky Heart have emerged in response to the hard rock music enjoyed in discotheques throughout the country.

Many Americans enjoy participating in social dance, be it in formal or informal settings. Dance studios are available for people who want to develop or expand their ability to participate in this cultural experience.

SQUARE DANCE

American square dance is a product of our country, and it reflects a blend of European and regional contra dances, quadrilles, and sets. Square dance has a rich, country flavor and yet its popularity extends from rural to metropolitan areas. People come together at recreation centers and clubs to share the square dance experience.

A unique feature of square dance is the caller, who functions as a leader. The caller is responsible for establishing the frameworks of each dance by informing the dancers in the square the specific skills and movement patterns to be executed. Therefore, the caller is responsible for creating an

Figure 5. Square dance, promenade position.

Basic Square Dance Skills

Once students understand their position and role in relation to the other dancers in the square, they are ready to learn square dance skills. *Dance A While* (Harris, Pittman, & Waller) describes 50 basic movements that should be understood if students are to be prepared to successfully execute a wide variety of square dances. A practical approach to teaching these skills is to introduce those dance patterns that are part of a specific dance or dances. This approach allows students to use specific skills immediately, increasing the meaning of practice.

Eight of the most basic square dance movements are explained below, presented in the progressive order recommended by Harris et al.

1. **Shuffle:** a walking step, weight transfers from ball of the foot to the heel, alternating feet, r,l,r,l. Even rhythm, lively tempo.
2. **Honors** (bow to your partner): partners turn slightly to face each other while shifting the weight to the outside foot and pointing the inside foot toward partner. Can include a call to honor your corner.
3. **Do-sa-do:** partners face, pass each other right shoulder to right shoulder, move around each other back to back, and return to original position facing partner.
4. **Promenade:** partners move around the circle in the promenade (skating) position. Partners are side by side, lady on the right, hands are joined right hand on top.
5. **Twirl:** partners face and take right hands. The man lifts his right hand turning the lady under his own right arm once around clockwise.
6. **Waist swing:** partners face, lady places hands on man's shoulders, man places hands on lady's waist, they execute the shuffle step while turning clockwise.
7. **Allemande left:** corners take a left forearm grasp and turn each other once around and go back home.
8. **Grand right and left:** partners face each other holding right hands. They move forward, pulling by partner with the right, meet and pull past the next person with the left, and so on, the lady traveling clockwise, the man counterclockwise until each one meets the original partner.

Figure 6. Folk dance, Ukranian girls dance.

FOLK DANCE

The cultural heritage of people throughout the world has been captured and revealed in a variety of art forms that have stood the test of time. Folk dance is unique because movement has been organized and presented to communicate the ethnic tradition of a region or country. These dances have been passed on from one generation to the next through participation in rituals, festivals, and celebrations. Today people all over the world participate in folk dance as a way to recapture their ethnic roots or to enjoy a rich international cultural experience.

The scope and depth of learning through participation in folk dance will reflect the number of factors the teacher decides to focus on during instruction. Student performance will be enriched when they understand the role of a folk dance in relation to its cultural roots.

Basic Folk Dance Skills

Several dance steps are common among folk dances, including the (1) shuffle, (2) polka, (3) schottische, (4) waltz, and (5) grapevine steps. Each of these has been described in the locomotor skill section of this chapter. For further performance information, refer to the specific folk dance cues articulated on record jackets or in folk dance literature.

SAFETY GUIDELINES

Though severe injuries are not common to dance, muscle strains and sprains, shin splints, and foot callouses do occur. Safe practice will reduce the risk of dance injuries and therefore enhance the dancers' experience. Be sure:

1. That the dance floor is not slippery or sticky and is free of obstructions.

2. That record or tape players are in good working order and review operation procedures.
3. That appropriate clothing and footwear are worn.
4. To warm-up, ensuring physical readiness to handle the dance activities that are part of the class.
5. All understand and can execute each dance step and combinations, as these will be performed in the culminating dance activities of the day.
6. Performers are familiar with the music, rhythm, tempo, starting cues, and dance pattern change cues prior to performing a dance. When the tempo of the music is quick or the dance steps and movement patterns are complex, slow the tempo of the music down for practice.

EQUIPMENT

EQUIPMENT

The equipment needed for dance is minimal so school systems with a tight budget can offer a dance program with little investment. Most essential is a facility free of obstructions with a hardwood or tiled floor, free of splinters or chips.

A high quality record player (with a tempo control lever) and/or a tape recorder (with recording and dubbing options), and records, tapes, or compact discs are critical to dance. This equipment is often part of a school's general or music department equipment and therefore available for use by the physical education department for dance. Quality records and/or tapes must be purchaseed so that appropriate dance music can be used to enhance the students' learning and performance experience.

RESOURCE MATERIALS

The information presented in the folk and square dance section of this chapter is presented to provide basic information that can be used to implement a dance program. For additional information about these and other dance forms refer to:

Dance A While (6th ed.), Jane Harris, Anne Pittman and Marlyss Waller, AAHPERD, 1900 Association Dr., Reston, VA 22091.

The Caller-Teacher Manual for the Basic Program. Sets in *Order,* American Square Dance Society, 462 N. Robertson Boulevard, Los Angeles, CA 90048.

The following record companies produce folk and square dance records that include complete performance information:

Folk Dance House, P.O. Box 2305, N. Babylon, NY 11703.

Folkways Records, 907 Sylvania Avenue, Englewood Cliffs, NJ 07632

Hoctor Records, Waldrich, NJ 07463.

REFERENCES

Gilbert, Anne Green. *Creative Dance for All Ages: A Conceptual Approach.* Reston, VA: National Dance Association, AAHPERD, 1992.

Gray, Judith Ann. *Dance Instruction.* Champaign, IL: Human Kinetics Pub., Inc., 1989.

Harris, Jane, Pittman, Anne, & Waller, Marlys. *Dance A While* (6th ed.). Reston, VA: AAHPERD, 1988.

Kennedy, Douglas. *Community Dance Manual: Books 1-7.* Reston, VA: AAHPERD.

Lockhart, Aileen. *Modern Dance: Building and Teaching Lessons.* Madison, WI: Wm. C. Brown, 1982.

Minton, Sandra. *Modern Dance: Body and Mind.* Englewood, CO: Morton Publishing Company, 1984.

Penrod, J., & Plastino, J.G. *The Dancer Prepares: Modern Dance for Beginners.* Mountainview, CA: Mayfield Pub. Co., 1990.

Schild, Myrna M. *Social Dance.* Madison, WI: Wm. C. Brown, Pub., 1985.

Sherbon, Elizabeth. *On the Count of One: The Art, Craft, and Science of Teaching Modern Dance* (4th ed.). Reston, VA: AAHPERD, 1990.

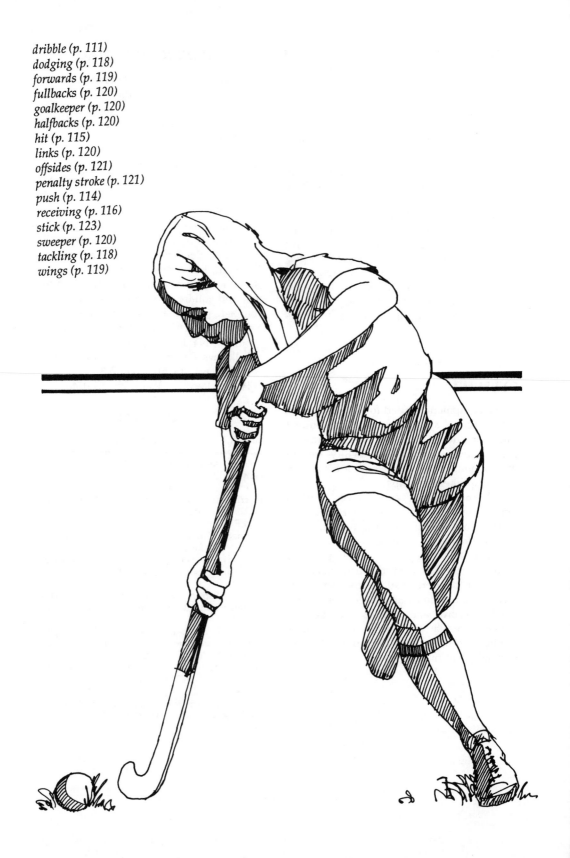

CHAPTER 9

Field Hockey

KATHLEEN T. MARRON
Quince Orchard High School
Gaithersburg, MD

INTRODUCTION

Field hockey is a game played by two teams of no more than 11 players each. The sport promotes the development of speed, endurance, coordination, agility, strength, and teamwork. Basic skills include dribbling, passing, tackling, and dodging. Field hockey is played by men and women of all ages throughout the world. It was one of the first organized team sports for women.

An Englishwoman, Constance Applebee, introduced the game in the United States at the Harvard Summer School in 1901. The sport has continued to grow since that time and is played now in schools, colleges, clubs, and associations throughout the country. The United States Field Hockey Association (USFHA) now governs play for women and the Field Hockey Association of America (FHAA) governs play for men, but a plan to merge these two groups should be completed by January 1993.

Field hockey is a recognized Olympic sport for men and women. Enthusiasm for the sport increased tremendously when the United States women's team won the bronze medal at the 1984 Games in Los Angeles. USFHA programs for young players expanded to include the Junior Program, the Futures Program, and the Olympic Development Camps. National Tournament play expanded to include indoor (March) and outdoor (November) competitions for men, women, high school, and junior players.

SKILLS AND TECHNIQUES

Several basic skills and techniques must be developed by each player. These include the dribble, the push, and the hit or drive, skills that are fundamental to learning how to receive and send the ball to a teammate during game play. Learning the basic skills establishes a foundation for the advanced skills.

This section explains the basic skills. Each explanation includes a breakdown of the skill technique and specific drills for individual improvement.

THE DRIBBLE

The dribble is a technique for moving the ball down the field using a series of taps while maintaining control when running. The basic grip must be learned first in order to perform the dribble correctly.

Lay the stick down with the toe facing away from the body. The flat part of the stick contacts the ground. Reach down with the left hand and grasp the stick 1½ to 2 inches from the end of the stick. The left hand forms a "V" down the rounded side of the stick. Wrap the fingers around the stick with the left thumb pointed toward the ground as it is slightly rotated to the front of the stick. Lift the stick to a vertical position with the toe resting on the ground. Place the right hand on the stick approximately 6 to 8 inches below the left with the palm facing forward. Fingers and thumb are wrapped around the stick. The left elbow should be held away from the side of the body. (See Figure 1.)

The bottom, or right hand, is held loosely when dribbling. The right hand is the "direction hand" on the stick and the left hand is the "power hand." The left turns the stick and provides the power for the dribble. The "dribbling grip" enables the student to use the reverse stick motion during dribbling and dodging situations. The reverse stick motion keeps the ball closer to the stick. This skill is effective when an opponent approaches from the left. The ball can be pulled to the right with the reverse. The toe of the stick points toward the student as it pulls the ball across in front of the body.

The ball is contacted in front and to the right of the body when dribbling. The hands take the basic grip position on the stick and the knees are flexed slightly. The feet point in the direction of the dribble and the body leans slightly forward for balance. The head moves to permit the eyes to watch both the ball and the immediate field of play. Dribbling must be practiced at various speeds for effective play. Only the flat side of the stick can be used to contact the ball.

There are no "left-handed" sticks. This is quite different from the sticks used in ice and street hockey. Students need to understand this difference.

Practice Drills: Dribbling

1. Within a 25 by 30 yard area or a half field setting, take a stick and a ball and experiment with different ways to move the ball on the field while maintaining control. Only the flat side of the stick can be used and the backswing and follow-through cannot come above the waist.

2. This drill practices looking up for an opponent while maintaining control of the ball on the stick. Each player has a stick and a ball. Dribble anywhere within the striking circle without touching anyone else. Look up to see someone approaching in order to change direction to avoid contact. Maintain control of the ball. Work at medium speed in a larger area with students in a physical education class. The teacher can use a whistle to change speed—one whistle for full speed, two short whistles for stop. The stop should be made with the stick on the ball.

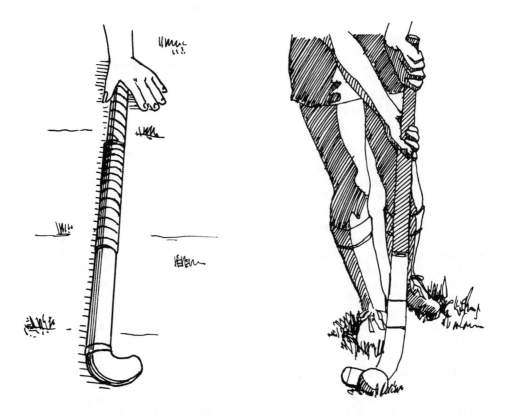

Figure 1. The grip.

3. Take four sticks and lay them perpendicular to each other on the field. This gives the perception of a square and the working distance for this drill. Start at the bottom right corner and dribble around the outside of the square. Move forward, step to the left while pulling the ball to the left, dribble toward the body while stepping backward on the toes, and finish by doing a reverse dribble to the right while stepping right. Variations include asking the students to spell their names or make other geometric patterns on the field. Check for proper grip and flexed knees.

4. To practice the slalom dribble, place 7 to 9 cones alternately 3' apart from each other. Dribble straight toward the cone and go to the left of the first cone and to the right of the second cone. Alternate through to the last cone, turn around, and continue the weave back to the starting point. This drill requires the body to weave while moving and controlling the ball. (See Diagram 1.)

5. Set the triplets drill by having the students form groups of three with two people in a line behind each other and the third person directly across and facing the twosome. There is one ball between three. The side with two players begins the drill. (See Diagram 2.) Player A dribbles toward Player C who is standing 20 yards away. Player C receives the ball and dribbles toward Player B. Player B dribbles toward Player A who has taken C's place in line. Continue as a basic warm-up.

If there is an even number of students, a group of four can be used. Always start the drill with the balls on the same side of the field. A variation has Player A look up as Player C holds up fingers to one side. The dribbler calls out the number of fingers. That number changes often until the player reaches the destination. Player C then does the same thing as Player B holds up fingers for the count. This drill works on maintaining possession while looking up. The zigzag dribble can be practiced in the triplets formation. Dribble forward at a 45 degree angle, moving across the left side

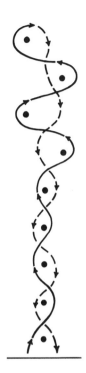

Diagram 1.

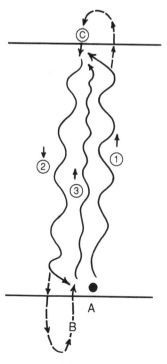

Diagram 2.

Figure 2. The push stroke. Note the position of the hands and the follow through to obtain maximum accuracy.

of the body approximately 3 feet. Now, dribble across the right side at a 45 degree angle moving approximately 3 feet. Continue down the field in this zig-zag pattern.

6. To practice the reverse stick dribble, students begin by standing with feet shoulder width apart. The ball and stick are on the right side of the body in front of the right foot. The knees are flexed and the focus is on the ball. Pull the ball to the left side of the body; the right or bottom hand is loose while the left hand turns the stick. When the ball reaches a point opposite the left foot, the stick is reversed by turning the toe toward the body. Pull the ball toward the right with the stick in this reverse position. The left hand at the top of the stick must do the turning. The right hand remains loose for easy turning. Check the grip to be certain that the fingers remain wrapped around the stick.

THE PUSH

This is the first stroke to be taught. It is quick and easy to execute successfully. The push is very accurate over a short distance as a pass or shot on goal. It is easy for a teammate or partner to receive and control.

The left hand is at the top of the stick and the right hand held slightly below the left, similar to the dribbling position. The stance is sideways with the left shoulder pointing in the direction of the pass. The left wrist and elbow are held away from the body. The feet are astride and pointing in the direction of the pass. The ball is contacted opposite the left foot. The stick rests behind and against the ball. There is no backswing.

The pass is executed by pushing through the ball with the right hand while the left hand is pulling the stick back at the top. This is a push/pull motion. The weight is shifted from right foot to left foot with the body staying low to the ground. This weight transfer helps increase the force of the pass and control its direction along the ground. The follow-through is low in the direction of the pass. (See Figure 2.)

Practice Drills: Push Passing

1. Partners stand 4 yards apart facing each other, each placing the stick on the ground to the left side of the body. Feet are shoulder width apart. One player begins with a ball in the right hand. Step forward with the left foot, remain low to the ground, and roll the ball

toward partner. The partner receives the ball and rolls it back. Follow through to accent the weight transfer from the right to left foot. The ball rolls without bouncing. The right hand finishes toward the partner to emphasize the direction on the follow-through.

2. Place two extra sticks or cones 12 to 18 inches apart between partners. Partners attempt to roll the ball with the hand back and forth between the targets. When the motion feels comfortable, do the same thing while using the sticks. Increase the difficulty by moving the cones or sticks closer together. Emphasize staying low, transfering the weight, keeping the stick in contact with ball, and pushing through the ball with the right hand while the left hand pulls the stick back at the top.

THE HIT

The hit or drive is used to pass the ball over a long distance or send a shot on goal. The position of the hands changes. The left hand is at the top of the stick. The "Vs" made from the forefinger and thumb of both hands are placed on the front of the stick in line with the toe. The back of the left hand faces the direction of the hit. The forefingers of each hand are separated. The backswing brings the left arm straight back with the stick's toe pointing up at waist level. There is a weight transfer with the hips coming through first. The stick comes through as the weight is transfered from the back foot to the front foot. The right hand slides up the stick toward the left hand. The follow-through finishes with the stick pointing in the direction of the hit. The toe points up. The left shoulder points in the direction of the hit.

The right hand provides direction. Emphasize cocking the right wrist to allow the left arm to be pulled across the body on the backswing. Keep the head down and the knees flexed for balance. Topping the ball occurs when the head is not kept down while focusing on the ball. Undercutting occurs when the ball is contacted below its center and it rises dangerously off the stick. Correct both poor techniques immediately to avoid dangerous play.

Another important aspect of the drive is that the right arm should be away from the body when the stick is brought up into the backswing. The wrist must be firm and the

Figure 3. Hitting on the move.

stick gripped firmly at the moment of impact with the ball. The focus must be kept on the ball. The stick must be controlled by the wrists with the swing coming just above the waist on the backswing and follow-through.

Hitting to the right side is more difficult than hitting to the left or straight ahead. The student must overrun the ball and turn to make contact when the ball is opposite the heel of the right foot. The trunk of the body is twisted to allow the right shoulder to be pulled back and the left shoulder turned in the direction of the hit.

Hitting or driving must be practiced while moving to make the skill more gamelike. Practice dribbling, then sliding the bottom hand up the stick and hitting the ball while running. Practice driving left, right, and straight ahead. (See Figure 3.)

Practice Drills: Hitting

1. This is a stationary activity to show the position of the stick as it moves through the backswing, forward motion with contact, and follow-through. Stand without a stick; feet are shoulder width apart. Start with the right arm held straight in front just above waist height. Fingers are together with the thumb facing up and the palm of the hand facing away from the body. Lift the arm through a backswing and then bring the hand down, crossing the body with a straight arm. The thumb points away as the palm is open and perpendicular to the body. The thumb leads upward through the follow-through so that the flat part of the open palm is now facing the left side of the body. The right arm remains straight.

2. To practice the backswing with the weight transfer, arrange partners with one person standing approximately 5 feet behind the other. The person in front has a stick. During the backswing the student slowly brings the stick back as the partner holds the toe of the stick. (Partner catches the stick on the slow backswing.) The back partner attempts to throw the stick forward as the front partner practices moving the hips and controlling the forward swing into the

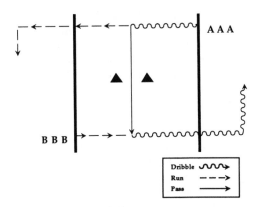

Diagram 3.

follow-through. The student feels the pull through with the left hand leading the stick into contact with the ball on the hit.

3. The back partner catches the stick in the slow backswing and gives resistance at waist level. The front partner attempts to lead with the hips and swing forward with the stick. This action gives resistance and helps with the concept of leading with the hips while swinging forward. A complete transfer of weight is made putting more power into the hit. The hands are together on contact and the left shoulder is pointed in the direction of the hit.

4. Set a target of cones approximately 6 to 8 feet apart between lines A and B. (See Diagram 3.) Player A starts with the ball. The player dribbles forward, hits the ball through the cones, and then runs forward as Player B receives the ball from the left, dribbles forward, and then runs to the end of line A. Students exchange lines. Move both lines to the right and practice passing and receiving from the right as line A again starts with the ball. These are excellent practices for hitting to the left and right and hitting on the move.

RECEIVING THE BALL

Receiving the ball and fielding the ball are interchangeable terms. Watching as the ball comes onto the stick is the key to success. Holding the stick at an angle to the ball helps lessen the deflection of the ball off the stick while receiving. The left hand and the top of the stick must be farther away from the body than the right hand. The right hand is held loosely as the ball makes contact with the stick. This traps the ball close to the stick and allows for immediate play by the receiver.

The stick must be held at right angles to the ground when receiving the ball from straight ahead. The left hand must again be farther away from the body than the right hand to trap the ball. Giving on the reception keeps the deflection at a minimum. A deflection or rebound can give possession to an opponent.

When receiving from the left, allow the ball to come across in front of the left foot and receive it inside the right foot. The dribbling grip is used on the stick.

When receiving from the right, rotate the body in the direction of the oncoming pass. The flat side of the stick faces the ball. The feet and left shoulder point in the direction of the opponent's goal. The left elbow is high and away from the body. The left wrist is held straight. (See Figure 4.)

Some common mistakes to be avoided when receiving the ball include the following:

1. Turning the flat side of the stick away from the direction of the ball.
2. Permitting the left hand and top of the stick to be inclined backwards, away from the ball. This causes an upward deflection.
3. Failure to keep the eyes focused on the ball.

Practice Drills: Receiving

1. Practice with a partner. Have the partner roll or push the ball. The receiver attempts to stop the ball without a deflection.
2. Practice with several balls. Have a partner roll the ball at various speeds to the

Figure 4. Receiving from the right.

right and left side. Stopping the ball on a given spot is the objective. Trap the ball with the stick to eliminate the deflection.
3. Similar to #2: move forward to meet the ball and control it immediately after it makes contact with the stick.

TACKLING

Tackling is a defensive skill used to take the ball away from an opponent. It requires timing, patience, and concentration. Face the opponent whenever possible. The defensive player's feet must be shoulder width apart with the left foot forward, knees bent slightly in a balanced position. The eyes are focused on the ball rather than the opponent. The weight is evenly distributed and the back is flexed forward. Watch the opponent's approach to time the tackle when the ball is off the stick during the dribble. When attempting to tackle, be careful not to create an obstruction by placing the body between an opponent and the ball.

A straight tackle is used when the opponent is approaching from the front. The defender maintains eye contact with the ball while remaining goal side of the opponent (between the opponent and the goal). Physical contact or stick interference is not permitted. When the ball is off the opponent's stick during the dribble, the defender should release the right hand from the stick and reach for the ball.

When tackling the opponent from the left, the approach should be from behind and on the right side of the opponent. The defender should stay even or slightly ahead of the opponent with the ball; time the ball to rebound off the stick during the dribble. Release the right hand and reach across with the stick. There are three tasks to accomplish when making this move: (1) place the stick on the ball so the dribbler will overrun it and the ball becomes trapped by the tackler's stick; (2) pull the ball toward the tackler who is at least a step ahead; and (3) push the ball out to the left side of the dribbler. The objective is to gain possession of the ball.

When tackling the opponent on the right, the defender should be at least one step

ahead to prevent obstruction or stick interference. The defender should run beside the opponent. Remove the left hand as the right hand slides to the top of the stick and jab with the stick. Focus on the ball and push it to the right and out of the opponent's possession.

Practice Drills: Tackling

1. This is a one-on-one situation. Player with the ball starts at the top of the cone area or 10' by 10' square box and attempts to reach the back line with the ball. The defender's objective is to tackle and gain possession and dribble across the front line.
2. This is called the "Cougar drill." Students are on a line with a ball each. One player stands between two lines without a ball. The middle person calls out "Cougar." The students with a ball attempt to dribble to the opposite line 25 yards away. The student in the center attempts to touch the ball. The dribblers who are touched join the center without a ball and now call out "Cougar!" The remaining students attempt to dribble back to the line where they started. This continues until there is one student remaining. This is a good game for a large group. It is fun, allows for conditioning, and enables students to work on tackling and ball control skills.

DODGING

Dodging is a skill used for maintaining possession of the ball. The player tries to elude an opponent. Timing the dodge is very important. If attempted too soon or too late, the defender still has an opportunity to make a successful tackle. There are three basic dodges that each player should be able to execute.

The *pull to the left dodge* begins by approaching the defender straight on. At a distance of approximately 3 feet from the defender, the dribbler should step wide with the left foot while drawing the ball across the body to the left. The step must be wide enough to avoid the outstretched defender's stick. A second tap sends the ball straight ahead to pass the opponent. The right foot steps forward to follow the ball. The dribbler then cuts back behind the opponent to prevent that player from tackling back.

This skill can be visualized by using a stick lay-out to see the pattern of the ball as the dribbler moves through the dodge. The first stick is placed 2 to 3 feet directly in front of the defender. The second is laid perpendicular to the toe of the first one, indicating the step left while pulling the ball to the left. The third is placed perpendicular to the toe of the second and parallel to the first, indicating the tap straight ahead beside the defender. The fourth stick is parallel with the second stick, setting the pattern for pulling the ball straight across directly behind the defender. The fifth is in line with the first stick and parallel to the third stick. This shows the continuous movement down the field.

The *nonstick side dodge* is movement around the left (nonstick) side of the opponent. The dribbler moves straight toward the opponent. The ball is passed to the nonstick side as the dribbler runs opposite to get by on the opponent's stick side. This is sometimes called a "Y" dodge. The player then moves behind the opponent and collects the ball and continues in possession. Cutting directly behind the opponent prevents a tackle back.

Visualize this dodge by taking a stick and laying it toe first in front of the defender. A second stick is placed wide to the nonstick side. A third stick is laid to the stick side, forming a "Y" with the defender between the two sticks. The ball goes to one side while the player moves to the other to regain possession without committing obstruction.

The *reverse stick dodge* takes excellent timing in order to fake the defender. The player approaches the opponent and then makes a reverse stick move by pulling the ball across to the nonstick side of the opponent. A second move sends the ball forward as the player steps forward with the left foot to get by the defender. The player avoids obstruction by keeping the shoulders square to the opponent.

Practice Drills: Dodging

1. Each student has a partner. The defensive player stands straight with stick in front of the body. The offensive player approaches and attempts a "Y" or nonstick side dodge. The defensive player then turns to face the opposite direction. The offensive player attempts a second dodge. Students reverse roles.

2. The same drill becomes an active one-on-one move. The defender attempts to tackle or touch the ball with the stick. This affects the timing and makes this drill more gamelike for both offensive and defensive players.

3. This drill is done in triplets. Two cones are set 2 feet apart and perpendicular to both lines. Player A approaches the cones and executes a dodge and then dribbles straight ahead to pass the ball to Player C. Player C dribbles toward the cones, executes a dodge, and then passes to Player B. Player B repeats the drill and passes the ball to Player A. The drill continues with emphasis on changing speed and direction and on timing the dodge.

THE PLAYERS

Field hockey is played by two teams of 11 players each. Positions include forwards (wings and inside forwards), links, halfbacks, fullbacks, sweepers, and the goalie. The lineups will vary depending on the skills and abilities of the players. Two of the most common lineups are shown in Diagram 4.

The forwards are the attacking or offensive team members. The wings and the inside forwards are responsible for scoring. These players must have good stick skills and they must be able to dribble, pass, receive, and shoot on goal while moving. They must move well with or without the ball, creating spaces and opportunities for good passes. Forwards must have good dodging skills to go one-on-one with the goalie. Using a variety of dodges while constantly moving keeps the defense guessing and off-balance. Good teamwork in passing and interchanging with other forwards is essential.

The links and halfbacks are midfield players. In the 4-2 system the two links form triangles with the inside forward and the wing on each side of the field. These players must have strong defensive and offensive skills. They must play both ends of the field equally well.

The halfbacks, fullbacks, and sweeper must have strong defensive skills. They must have excellent endurance to cover particular areas of the field to mark (closely defend) an opponent who is close to the goal. They must anticipate the action in order to intercept passes or cause the offensive players to misdirect passes and miss dodges or shots on goal.

The sweeper and fullbacks intercept the long through passes and closely defend any offensive player coming into the scoring circle. They must have a long, hard drive for clearing the ball away from the goal, passing it out to a wing or far down the field when possible. Communication is a key to success.

The goalkeeper or goalie thinks only of stopping the shot on goal. Once the shot has been stopped and possession maintained, the goalie clears the ball with a strong kick. The direction of that kick determines where the team now begins an attack on the opposite goal. It is often said that the goalie is the last line of defense and the first line of attack.

The goalie is the only specialist on the team. One-on-one instruction from the teacher/coach is needed. Because this extra time and instruction is needed, the position is often eliminated due to a lack of time and equipment. Do not include this position in a physical education class unless the students can be properly prepared.

The players on the team must work well as a unit, practicing individual skills to create plays and situations for success. Good stick work, conditioning, and a general knowledge of the game will enhance the team play.

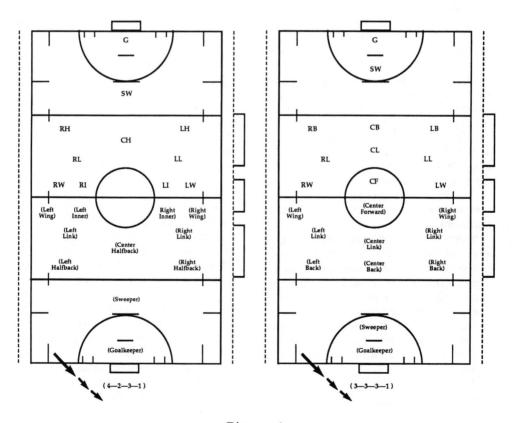

Diagram 4.

THE GAME

The game begins with a pass back from the center of the field on the 50 yard line (similar to soccer). The pass back is used also to restart the game after a goal is scored. All players except the one making the pass back must be on their own side of the field. All opposing players must be at least 5 yards away from the ball. The ball must be played back toward the teammates with any legal stroke. It may not initially cross the center line into the opponent's half of the field. Players are allowed to cross the center line as soon as the ball is passed back. (See Diagram 6.)

A goal is scored when the ball is hit by an offensive player into the goal. The shot on goal must be made from inside the adjacent striking circle. It must pass between the goal posts and under the crossbar. Each goal is worth one point.

Rule violations or fouls include advancing, offsides, obstruction, swinging dangerously at an opponent, using the round side of the stick, unsportsmanlike conduct, unnecessary roughness, stick obstruction, and picking up and throwing the ball. The penalty for fouling outside the striking circle is a free hit for the opposing team. It is taken on the spot where the foul occurred. Fouls by the attack within the circle give the defense possession and a hit out of the circle. Fouls by the defense within the circle result in a set play called the penalty corner.

Whenever the ball goes out of bounds either at the side line or at the end line, the team not putting the ball out of bounds takes possession. The ball is placed on the spot where it went out over the side line and put into play with a drive, push, or flick (not above knee height). If the ball goes over the end line off the attack, the defense brings it 16 yards up the field opposite where the ball crossed the end line, and puts it into play.

There are several set play situations. The long hit is taken from the end line by the attack when the defense unintentionally hits the ball over the end line and a goal is not scored. It is taken on the side where the ball crossed the end line; all players are 5 yards away; any legal stroke may be used.

The penalty corner is taken when the defending team commits a fouls within the striking circle. Five defenders line up behind the end line and the attack takes positions along and outside the top of the striking circle. An attack player hits the ball out from the end line to teammates and play resumes.

The penalty stroke is a stationary shot by an attack player toward the goal with only the goalie providing the defense. It is awarded because the defense commits a flagrant or deliberate foul that keeps a goal from being scored. The shot has no back swing and it is taken on a line 7 yards in front of the goal's center.

Offsides occurs when there are fewer than two opponents between a player without possession and the goal. The player must be within the 25 yard line at the time. The defending team is awarded a free hit if the opponents are caught offsides.

The game is played in two halves of 30 to 35 minutes each. There is a brief 5 to 10 minute intermission. High school teams are allowed a single one minute time out each half. Substitutions are usually unlimited.

Adaptations have been made for indoor play. Only the dribble and push pass are allowed (no backswing). There is no offsides and each team has six players, one of which is a goalie. The hockey stick has a thinner toe area. The indoor game is a good way to stay in condition and improve stick work because of the smooth surface.

TACTICS AND STRATEGIES

Game tactics and strategies are developed through the interaction of individual skills among teammates. Many smaller games occur on the hockey field during game play. It is often said that the team that wins the most little games will win the big game. Players must be alert at all times and proficient in moving with or without the ball. Hockey uses many triangle combinations of players. Defenders maintain a triangle by staying goal side and ball side of the opponent. Offensive players maintain a triangle by positioning for effective flat, through, and back passes.

Drills: Pass ⟶ Run -----▸ Dribble 〰⟶

1. Fill-the-corner: using an imaginary square, pass and move to the empty corner; reverse directions.

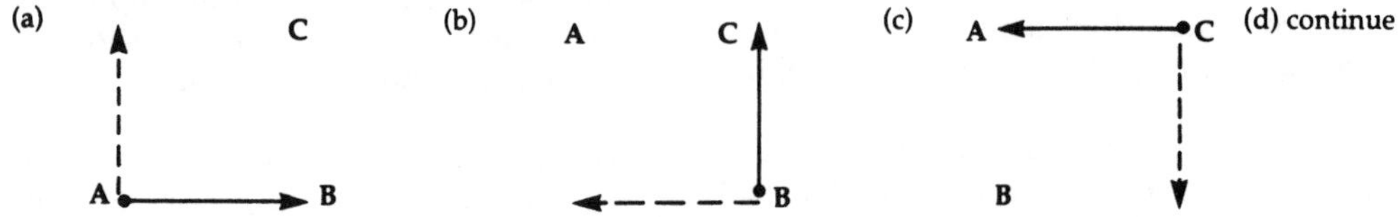

(a)   (b)   (c)   (d) continue

2. Pass-to-empty corner: player moves to meet the pass; passer moves to fill the spot left by the receiver.

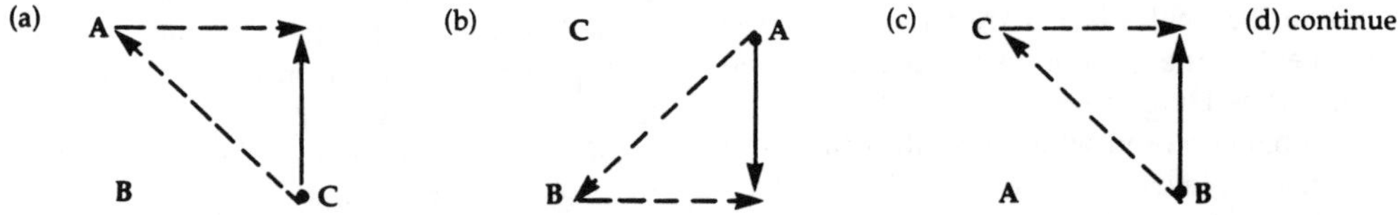

(a)   (b)   (c)   (d) continue

3. Moving triangle: using the length of the field; switch roles each time down the field and use the flat pass to the right; maintain spaces while receiving on the move.

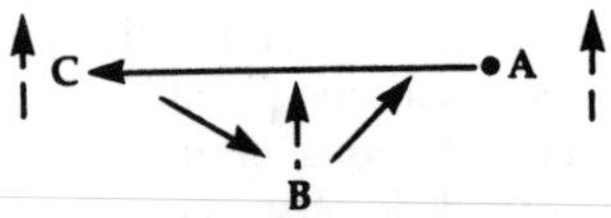

A sends *flat* pass to C
C sends *back* pass to B
B sends *through* pass to A

4. Through pass: maintaining spaces; moving to receive the pass; filling the open position.

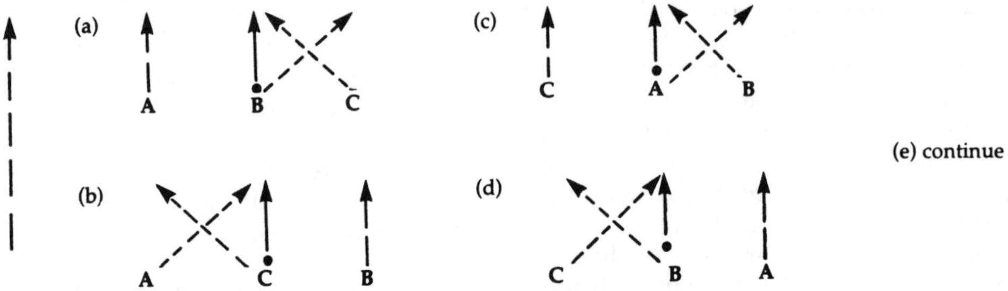

(a)   (c)   (e) continue

(b)   (d)

5. Weave: always follow the pass; receive on the move; use flat passes.

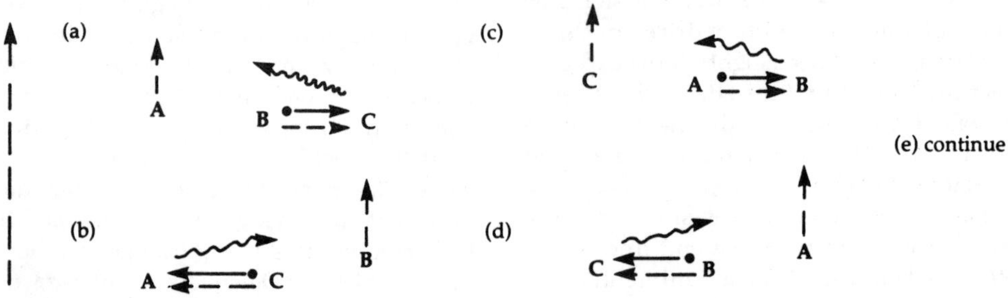

(a)   (c)   (e) continue

(b)   (d)

6. Repeat #5 and add one defender—3 *v* 1; repeat #5 and add two defenders—3 *v* 2.

Diagram 5.

The drills in Diagram 5 are designed for two or three students working together using the triangle concept of team play. Practice games should be kept to 3v3, 4v4, 5v5, or 6v6. Basic concepts developed through these small games will easily carry over into the full field game.

EQUIPMENT

Basic equipment for the game includes a stick, ball, mouth guards, and shin guards. The Indian head style stick has a short, compact toe making it easy to manipulate during reverse stick moves. The English head style stick has a longer, thinner toe which is more difficult to manipulate when controlling the ball close to the body. Most sticks used in high schools are 33-36 inches long and weigh 18-21 ounces. The handle or grip is covered with leather, toweling, or rubber. All sticks are flat on the left side and rounded on the right. There are no "left-handed" sticks in field hockey.

To measure the proper length for a stick, the student stands straight while holding the top of the grip in the left hand. The toe of the stick rests on the ground. The student slowly swings the stick in front of the body. The stick should brush the top of the grass if it is the proper length.

The hockey ball is slightly larger than a baseball. It is constructed of seamless plastic or it has a sewn leather cover. Most hockey balls are white, but they can be colored in contrast to the playing surface.

The hockey goals are rectangular with a wooden or metal frame covered by a string or plastic net. Each goal measures 12' wide by 7' high by 4' deep. The facing on each goal is flat and 2" wide. If boards are used inside the bottom of the goal, they must be 18" high, painted a solid dark color, and flush to the goal posts so as not to decrease the width of the front of the goal. (See Diagram 6.)

The goalkeeper must wear specialized protective equipment. This includes goalie shoes or kickers, a full face mask or helmet with mask, chest protector, gloves, and leg pads. If this equipment is not available for game play during a physical education class, it is suggested that games be played without this position.

Extra protective equipment for field players includes shin guards and mouth guards. Both are required for players during interscholastic games.

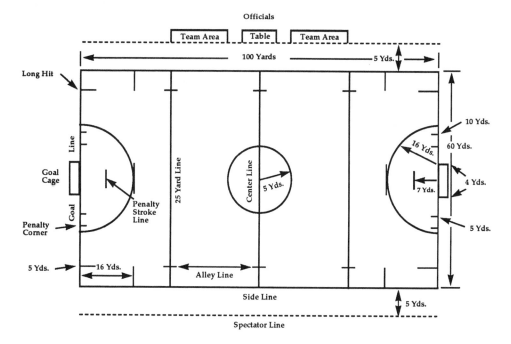

Diagram 6.

TERMINOLOGY

Attack (Offense). Team that has possession of the ball.

Advancing. Foul called for using any part of the body to move the ball or any part of the body except the hand to stop the ball.

Ball Control. Ability to maintain possession of the ball by means of dodging, dribbling, passing, tackling, receiving, intercepting, or scoring a goal.

Circle. Scoring area around each goal.

Cutting. Moving to meet the ball or pass or creating space into which the ball can be hit by a teammate.

Dangerous Use of Stick. Raising any part of the stick above a player's own shoulder in a dangerous or intimidating manner when playing or attempting to play the ball.

Defense. Team that does not have possession of the ball.

Defense Hit. Free hit that is taken after the attacker commits a foul inside the circle.

Diagonal Pass. Pass that travels approximately on a 45 degree angle.

Dodge. Method of avoiding an opponent while maintaining possession of the hockey ball.

Dribble. Series of taps taken to move the ball while maintaining control with the stick.

Drive. Hard, direct pass or shot on goal.

Flick. Stroke in which the ball is lifted to knee level with no backswing, a natural extension of the push pass.

Free Hit. Method of putting the ball in play following an opponent's foul outside the circle.

Goal. Worth one point and is awarded when the ball crosses the goal line between the goal posts and under the crossbar.

Long Hit. Method for an attacker to put the ball in play on the end line from a spot that is 5 yards in from the nearest sideline.

Marking. Defending against a player by staying close, stick to stick, and goalside.

Obstruction. Foul that occurs when a player places any part of the body or stick between the ball and an opponent who is trying to play the ball.

Offside. When the player is ahead of the ball in the opponent's half of the field and there are fewer than two opponents between the 25 yard line to the end line at the time the ball is played.

Open Space. Where there is no defender in the immediate area.

Pass Back. Method used for putting the ball in play at the start of the game, following halftime, and after each goal.

Penalty Corner. Awarded to the attack when the defense commits a foul inside the circle.

Penalty Stroke. Shot on goal taken by an attacker against the goalkeeper from penalty stroke line 7 yards in front of the center of the goal.

Push Pass. The ball is pushed along the ground directly off the stick in which there is no backswing.

Scoop. A legal stroke executed by placing the stick under the ball, using a shoveling motion, to lift it into the air with no backswing.

Side In. Method for putting the ball in play after it has gone out of bounds over the side lines.

Sixteen Yard Hit. Occurs when the ball is hit out of bounds over the end line by the attacking team and no goal is scored.

Square Pass. Also known as the Flat Pass. Type of pass that travels perpendicular to the side line.

Stick Obstruction. Occurs when a player hits, holds, hooks, slashes, or strikes the opponent's stick.

Tackle. Method for taking possession of the hockey ball from an opponent.

Through Pass. Pass that travels straight down the field and is parallel to the side lines.

Transition. Changing of a team's possession and adjustment from offense to defense and vice versa.

Undercutting. Propelling the ball with a hard hit below the center of the ball which causes it to be lifted into the air in a dangerous manner.

Width. Maintaining space on the field which measures side line by side line for both play and players.

REFERENCES

Castelijn, Boudewijn. *USA Field Hockey Coaching Manual,* 2nd ed. Colorado Springs, CO: U.S. Field Hockey Association.

Field Hockey Rule Book. Kansas City, MO: National Federation of State High School Associations, 1991.

Schultz, Bobby. *High School Players' Field Hockey Journal.* Reston, VA: American Alliance for Health, Physical Education, Recreation and Dance, 1990.

CHAPTER 10

Flagball

MARYANN DOMITROVITZ
Pennsylvania State University
University Park, PA

INTRODUCTION

Fascination for football is evidenced by the many programs that exist from the youth league to the professional football conferences. Many individuals cannot participate in organized football programs and are not content in the role of spectator. These men and women are becoming actively involved in some form of recreational football. Recreational leagues range from flag or tag football teams for men and women to programs involving coed flag football competition. Recreational programs in cities, high schools, and colleges have utilized the rules and strategies of regulation football, flag football, and tag football. These modifications allow the game to be safe, enjoyable, and competitive for the participants.

Flagball is an activity that can be included in the physical education curriculum. Basic skills and strategies can be introduced at the elementary level and culminate with the more advanced skills and strategies at the high school level.

A flagball team is composed of eight participants (four men and four women) although the game can be modified to accommodate from six to ten players. The playing field (40 x 100 yards) has four 20-yard zones and 10-yard end zones. Scoring takes place by a touchdown (6 points), conversion (run or kick—1 point), safety (2 points), or field goal (3 points). The ball is advanced by running or passing, although some modifications are stipulated in the rules. Progress of the player in possession of the ball is stopped by pulling off one of the flags attached to a belt worn around the waist.

All the skills and strategies of regulation football minus the contact are utilized, making flagball a fun, challenging, and physically demanding activity.

SKILLS AND TECHNIQUES

OFFENSIVE AND DEFENSIVE STANCE

In the game of flagball, blocking (physical contact) is not permitted in the rules; therefore, the priority is not on physical strength but on quickness. On signal, the responsibility of the offensive lineman/woman is to move quickly and screen for a teammate whether it be for a run or pass play. (A screen is a player maintaining a position, without use of contact, between a defender and the ball carrier. The arms and elbows of the screener must remain in contact with his/her body). The defender must be adept in quickness and control and must attempt to move around the screen and rush the quarterback or ball carrier.

Since the quick, controlled movements when the ball is snapped are essential qualities for both the offensive and defensive lineman/woman, the stance used by each is quite similar. If a three-point stance is used, place the feet shoulder width apart, reach forward and rest one hand on the ground. Raise the posterior so the back is nearly parallel to the ground and rest the free arm on the leg above the knee. To ensure balance, the weight should be equally distributed on the feet and the

Figure 1. Three-point stance.

hand, with the head raised and the focus forward. (See Figure 1.)

A three-point stance is not specified in the rules; therefore, it is acceptable for the lineman/woman to be positioned on the line with the knees flexed and the hands resting on the legs just above the knees. The rule enforced is that the offensive lineman/woman must be motionless prior to the snap. However, this rule does not apply to the defensive lineman/woman.

Points of Emphasis
Three-Point Stance
- Feet parallel, shoulder width
- Knees flexed
- Arm extended forward, hand on ground
- Weight evenly balanced on feet and hand
- Back parallel to ground
- Head raised, focus ahead

Two-Point Stance
- Feet parallel, shoulder width
- Knees flexed
- Hands resting on top of thigh above knee
- Weight evenly balanced on feet
- Back parallel to ground
- Head raised, focus ahead

Offense vs. Defense Drill

How long can you prevent the defense from touching the cone?

How quickly can you outmaneuver the offense and tag the cone?

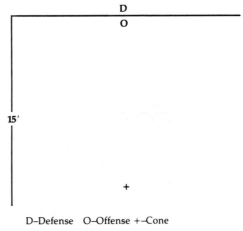

D–Defense   O–Offense   +–Cone

Procedure
1. Designate a spot 15 feet from the cone for the offense and defense.
2. Offense must assume three-point stance.
3. Defense may cross the line when offense moves from three-point stance.
4. Offense may not use contact in attempting to obstruct the defender's movement to the cone.
5. Defense must move around the offense and tag the cone.

CENTERING AND RECEIVING

Before offensive play can take place the ball must be exchanged between the center and the quarterback. This is done either by positioning the quarterback directly behind the center or in a shotgun formation 10 to 15 feet behind the center. Since flagball is primarily a passing game, most teams utilize the shotgun formation in that it gets the ball deep into the backfield and the decision to pass or run is made easier. If the direct exchange is used, the center assumes the three-point stance, focuses forward and grips the ball in the same manner as for the throw (Figure 2). With a secure grip, the ball resting on the ground and the nose of the ball pointing forward, the center sweeps the arm straight back and up between the legs. As the ball is being swept back, the center rotates the ball one-quarter turn so the ball can be placed securely into the hands of the quarterback. It is most important that the swing of the arm and the

Figure 2.
Centering the ball.

rotation of the football be executed simultaneously.

In order that the quarterback may receive the ball, a pocket must be formed by placing the heels of both hands together, spreading the fingers, and placing the throwing hand on top.

Both hands are positioned under the center with the back of the top hand pressed against the buttocks of the center. The quarterback with the knees bent, feet parallel, and shoulder width apart, calls the signal for the exchange. Movement away from the center should not occur until the ball has been exchanged.

If the shotgun is used, the center widens the stance, looks at the target, and eliminating the one-quarter turn, spirals the ball back to the quarterback.

Points of Emphasis

Direct Snap
- Assume three-point stance
- Ball resting on ground, nose pointing downfield
- Grip football same as for throw
- Swing extended arm back and up between legs
- Rotate ball one-quarter turn during swing
- Snap ball into quarterback's hands
- Snapper's palm faces quarterback's hands
- Focus ahead

Long Snap
- Widen stance
- Drop head, look at quarterback's target
- Snap ball directly back to quarterback
- Utilize forceful underhand toss
- Spiral ball to quarterback

Receiving Direct Snap
- Quarterback directly behind snapper
- Feet shoulder width, knees bent
- Heels of hands together, hands and fingers spread
- Rotate hands, throwing hand on top
- Back of top hand pressed against snapper's buttocks

Centering Drill
How successful are you centering the football to the quarterback?

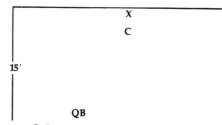

C–Center   QB–Quarterback   X–Ball

Procedure
1. Center is positioned 15 feet from the quarterback.
2. Quarterback counts the number of successful snaps out of 10 attempts.
3. A successful attempt is any ball reaching the quarterback above the waist.

HANDOFF AND PITCHOUT

After receiving the snap, the exchange (handoff) between the quarterback and the backfield player occurs. The backfield player, preparing to receive the ball, raises the arm nearest the quarterback to chest level. This near arm must be parallel to the ground with the open hand facing down. The far arm, also parallel to the ground, is across the waist with the palm up. As the ball is placed in the stomach, quickly close the hands on the football and then put the football into the carrying position prior to running down field.

If the play is designed as a pitchout, the quarterback places the hands under the football and tosses the football underhand to the backfield player. Toss the football so it is received at chest level. The backfield player must concentrate on the football until it is caught in the hands and then tucks it into the body.

Points of Emphasis
Receiving Handoff
- Raise arm closest to quarterback to chest height
- Top arm is parallel to ground, palm down
- Bottom arm is at waist height
- Bottom arm is parallel to top arm, palm up
- Close hands around ball when placed into stomach

GRIP AND PASSING

Prior to passing the football, it must be securely gripped in the throwing hand with the thumb and the index finger comfortably spread. Place the thumb and index finger on the circle of the football with the remaining fingers placed on the laces.

The nonthrowing hand should press the football into the throwing hand and both hands assist in raising the football to ear level (Figure 3). As the football continues to be brought back behind the shoulder, the shoulders and body rotate so the nonthrowing side of the body is facing the direction of the pass. When the nonthrowing hand can no longer remain in contact with the football, it should be extended in the direction of the intended flight of the football. The rear foot (plant foot) bearing the majority of the weight initiates the throw by transferring weight onto the forward foot, which is pointing in the intended direction of the pass. As the weight is being transferred, the hips and shoulders unwind resulting in the chest facing the intended target. The throwing arm, led by the elbow, is whipped forward over the shoulder. As the arm is extended, the wrist and fingers snap downward on the release. This imparts a spiral to the ball. Follow through by extending the throwing arm in the intended direction of the pass and, after releasing the ball, draw the arm downward to the nonthrowing side. The throw is completed with the weight on the forward foot and the passer concentrating on the target of the throw.

Pitchout Drill
How successful are you at pitching the ball to the halfback?

How successful are you at receiving a pitchout?

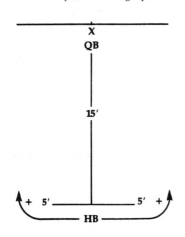

X–Ball   +–Cone
QB–Quarterback   HB–Halfback

Procedure
1. Halfback is positioned 15 feet behind the quarterback.
2. On signal from the quarterback, the halfback cuts left/right.
3. Quarterback pivots and pitches to the halfback.
4. A total of 10 pitchouts, 5 to each side, is attempted.
5. A successful attempt is one that reaches the halfback above the waist.
6. Quarterback counts the number of successful attempts.
7. Halfback counts the number of successful catches.

Figure 3. The grip.

Points of Emphasis
Grip
- Fingers relaxed, comfortably spaced
- Thumb and index finger on circle of football
- Fingers 3, 4, 5 placed on laces

Passing
- Nonthrowing hand presses football in the throwing hand
- Raise football to ear level
- Rotate shoulders and body back
- Football behind shoulder, elbow shoulder height
- Nonthrowing hand pointing in pass direction
- Weight on rear foot
- Transfer weight to front foot
- Whip throwing arm forward and over the shoulder
- Extend throwing arm, snap wrist and fingers on release

CUTTING, RECEIVING, AND CARRYING

Before receiving a pass, the offensive player must maneuver into an open area. This can be accomplished by running a predetermined pass pattern that allows you to free yourself from the defender. The quick change of direction (cut) needed to put yourself into an unguarded position is executed by pushing off the inside of the foot that is on the opposite side of the intended cut. Therefore, if a player wants to cut to the right, the push is off the inside of the left foot. This cut can be made easier by running at a controlled speed, taking short steps, and lowering the body by bending the knees. After the cut has been mastered, a fake, which can be done with the head and/or shoulders, should be incorporated into the movement. Once the cut is made into an open area, turn, face the quarterback, and concentrate on the flight of the football. This concentration must continue until the football rests in the hands of the receiver.

As the pass approaches, extend both arms with the palms facing the football and the thumbs pointing inward. Spread and relax the fingers, and when contact occurs both the arms and fingers give and pull the football into the body. If the pass is thrown below the waist, the fingertips are pointing down and the little fingers are facing inward. Once the football is in the possession of the receiver and before running, put it into the carrying position by spreading and extending the fingers over its point. The football is then tucked into the crook of the elbow and held tightly against the body. (See Figure 4.) Moving downfield, the ball carrier must combine speed, quick cuts, and pivots to prevent removal of a flag. Since contact is not permitted in flag football, utilizing teammates for screening purposes is a strategy that must be incorporated into the offense.

Points of Emphasis
Cutting
- Push off inside of foot, using foot opposite side of intended direction
- To cut right, push off left foot
- To cut left, push off right foot
- Take short steps, bend knees

Receiving the Pass
- Turn and face quarterback
- Extend arms, palms facing football
- Point thumbs inward, spread and relax fingers
- On contact, give with the catch
- Pull football into the body

Carrying the Football
- Spread fingers and cover tip of football
- Tuck opposite end of football into crook of elbow
- Pull arm tightly into body

Passing and Catching Drill

How many passes can you successfully throw?
How many passes can you successfully catch?

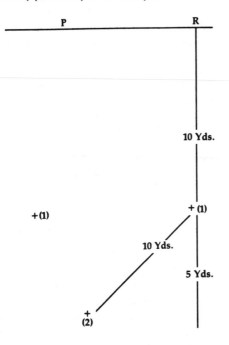

+–Cone   P–Passer   R–Receiver

Procedure
1. On a signal from the passer, the receiver runs toward the first cone, cuts behind the cone, and heads toward the second cone.
2. Passer must throw the football after the receiver passes the first cone but before reaching the second cone.
3. Receiver must be ready to catch the pass after cutting behind the first cone.
4. 10 passes are attempted, 5 from each side.
5. A successful throw is one that reaches the receiver between the waist and top of head.

Figure 4. The carrying position.

PUNTING

When a team fails to advance the designated distance for a first down or score, one of the options available to the offense is punting the football. In flagball, rushing the kicker is not allowed; therefore, complete concentration should be on the execution of the punt. After receiving the football, the punter rotates it so the laces are on top. With hands on either side of the football, extend both arms forward and simultaneously take one short step onto the kicking foot followed by a normal step onto the support foot. As the kicking foot swings forward, drop the football enabling contact to occur on the upswing. Contact, with a firm ankle and the toe pointing down, is made on the instep of the foot at approximately 18" to 24" off the ground. Maximum distance is achieved by a full extension of the kicking leg with the follow-through continuing to shoulder height. When the support foot leaves the ground, extend both arms to the side to ensure balance and control.

Points of Emphasis
Punting
- Grip ball, hands on either side
- Extend arms forward, waist height
- Take two steps, first step is onto kicking foot
- After second step, drop football, swing leg forward
- Firm ankle, point toes down
- Contact ball with instep
- Extend kicking leg in direction of punt
- Follow through with leg to shoulder height

Punting Drill
How far can you punt the football?

P
_____

5 Yd.

10 Yd.

15 Yd.

P–Punter

Procedure
1. Punt the ball from behind the designated line.
2. Measure the best punt out of 5 attempts.
3. Measure the punt from the line to the spot where the ball hits the ground.

PLACE KICK

In most instances, place kicking in flagball (kickoff, field goal) is done without a tee; therefore, the mechanics for the kickoff and field goal attempts are similar. After the holder receives the football the laces are turned forward and it is placed on the ground tilted back slightly. (See Figure 5.)

The kicker, with the head down, approaches the football and focuses on a spot below the center where contact must occur. The support foot, pointing in the direction of the kick, is planted to the side and slightly to the rear of the football. As the kicking leg is brought forward, the knee is bent and the ankle is flexed and firm. The swing of the leg must be forceful with full extension forward and upward using the arms to aid in maintaining balance.

Points of Emphasis
Place Kick
- Kicker focuses on spot for contact
- Plant nonkicking foot to the side and rear of football
- Point nonkicking foot in direction of kick
- Kicking leg is swung forward, knee bent
- Firm and flex ankle
- Swing leg from the hip
- Fully extend leg forward and upward

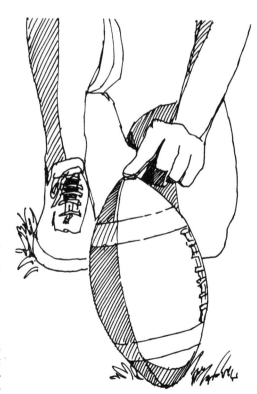

Figure 5. Holding the ball for the place kick.

Field Goal Drill
How many successful field goals can you kick?

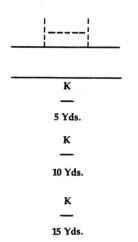

K
—
5 Yds.

K
—
10 Yds.

K
—
15 Yds.

K–Kicker

Procedure
1. Count the number of successful field goals out of 9 attempts.
2. Take 3 attempts at 5 yards, 10 yards, and 15 yards from the goal line.

SAFETY

Due to the game's structure, the outdoor setting, and the variety of weather conditions under which the game is played, numerous injuries occur in flagball. Many of the sprains and strains can be prevented by an adequate amount of time spent warming up prior to participation. Improper techniques of running, throwing, catching, and kicking result in injuries to ankles, fingers, elbows, and shoulders, but injuries can be prevented by proper teaching and coaching.

Too often, more serious injuries occur as a result of collisions due to one or more participants playing in an uncontrolled manner. A player unable to stop, turn, or change direction quickly can be a hazard to other participants; therefore, the no-contact rule must be strictly enforced. The individual supervising or officiating the activity must not allow the participants to confuse flagball with regulation football where the participant has the benefit of protective equipment.

Acceptable playing conditions, adequate warm-up, proper technique, good coaching, and responsible officiating contribute to safe and enjoyable participation in this activity.

FLAGBALL RULES

1. **Team**—Eight players, *four men and four women*, shall constitute a team.
2. **Field**—The playing field shall be 100 yards long and 40 yards wide. There shall be a 10-yard end zone at each end of the field. Goal posts will be placed on the back line of the end zone. The field shall be marked by lines dividing the field into four 20-yard zones. The inbounds line shall be 10 yards from the sidelines. (See Diagram 1.)
3. **Time**—The game shall be played in halves of 20 minutes each. Teams will switch ends of field at half-time only. The rest period shall be five minutes at the half. Each captain may call one time-out (1 minute) each half.
4. **Start of Game**—The team captain winning the coin toss may elect one of the following: kick, receive, or goal to defend during the first half. At the start of the second half, teams will reverse field positions and the team who kicked off at the start of the game will receive.
5. **Kick-off**—The kick-off shall be made from the kicking team's 20 yard line. It must be a place kick and the ball cannot be teed up in any manner. The receiving team must position five players on the mid-field line. The kick must travel 20 yards before becoming a free ball.
6. **Scrimmage Plays**—Prior to start of play, offensive team must come to a "set" position for one second. One player only may be in motion, but cannot be moving toward the scrimmage line. Advancement via the run from behind the line of scrimmage is restricted to females only. There are no advancement restrictions for a male once he has obtained possession of the ball beyond the line of scrimmage.
7. **First Downs**—A team shall be allowed four downs to advance the ball across

each zone line (20 yards apart). Each time a team advances the ball across a line, it is awarded a first down and will be allowed four more downs to make the next zone line. Upon a change of team possession, the line to gain shall be that line immediately down field from the spot where the ball becomes dead.

8. **Detached Flag**—Ball becomes dead when ball carrier's flag becomes detached from the flag belt. The ball carrier cannot use hands or clothing to prevent opponents from pulling flag.

9. **Blocking**—No blocking is permitted. Offensive players may screen for the ball carrier by keeping both arms in contact with their body and moving laterally into the path of an opponent. No contact is permitted.

10. **Passing**—All forward passes must be thrown from a point behind the line of scrimmage. Restrictions on use of forward pass:
    a. During a 4-down series, males are restricted to only one forward pass attempt. If the down in which the pass was attempted is repeated because of a penalty, or if a new series begins, he may again attempt one pass in the series.
    b. Male pass receivers must receive all forward passes beyond the line of scrimmage.
    c. There are no restrictions on female passing or pass-receiving.

11. **Fumbles**—All fumbles may be recovered by either team, but only the offensive team may advance the ball following a recovery.

12. **Dead ball**—The ball becomes dead when:
    a. The ball carrier's flag becomes detached from flag belt (pulled or falls off).
    b. When any part of the ball carrier's body other than hands and feet touch ground.
    c. Following an incomplete forward pass.
    d. Following recovery of a fumble by defensive team.
    e. When ball goes out of bounds.

13. **Kicking**—When the offensive team elects to kick, it must call the play "kick." No player on either team may cross the line of scrimmage until the ball has been kicked. A punt or kick-off may be made by either sex, but advancement of the ball from either of these two techniques is restricted by the following: Male punt or kick-off receiver—cannot advance the ball forward from his point of contact with the ball; but may, however, move backwards or perpendicular to that first point of contact. Advancement is only possible by a female ball carrier.

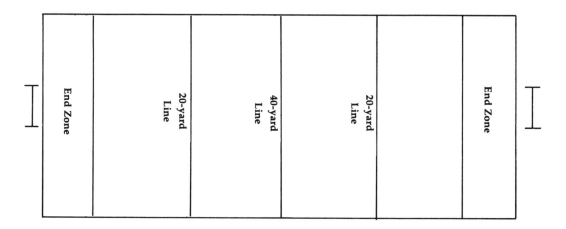

Diagram 1. Playing field.

14. **Scoring**
    - Touchdown—6 points—Try after touchdown—1 point (kick or run).
    - Field Goal—3 points—Team must announce intention to attempt field goal. Neither offensive nor defensive players may cross the scrimmage line until ball has been kicked. The kick must be made from a spot directly behind the point from which ball is centered. The ball shall not be teed up in any manner for placement attempts.
    - Safety—2 points—A safety results when the offensive team is responsible for grounding the ball behind its own goal line.

15. **Substitutions**—Unlimited substitution is permitted.

16. **Equipment**—Plastic or metal spiked and cleated shoes are prohibited. Sneakers or shoes with molded rubber cleats are permitted. Players may not wear any device that might cause injury to other participants. Two flags, attached to the flag belt in a proper manner, shall be worn by all players.

17. **Tie Games**—If teams are tied in score, the team with the most first downs will be declared the winner. If teams are tied in score and first downs, an overtime series of plays will be run. The ball shall be placed on the mid-field line, and one team will start a series of four downs (choice of first offensive series by toss of coin). Team "A" (offense) will attempt to advance ball as far as possible into "B's" territory in four consecutive downs. Team "B" will then take over ball at point where "A's" series ended. The position of the ball at the conclusion of "B's" four downs will determine winner. If ball is in "A's" territory, then "B" is the winner. An interception or recovery of a fumble by opponents will terminate a team's series of downs. The recovering team will start play from the point where the recovery was made, or the interception run-back ends. *No punting or field goal attempts are permitted in the overtime series.*

18. **Penalties**
    - Offside—5 yards.
    - Illegal motion—5 yards.
    - Intentionally grounding ball—Loss of down and 5 yards from spot of pass.
    - Illegal forward pass—Loss of down and 5 yards from spot of pass.
    - Illegal advancement by male—5 yards from line of scrimmage and loss of down. −5 yards from spot of illegal advancement on punt or kick-off.
    - Illegal wearing or protecting of flag—15 yards.
    - Unnecessary roughness—15 yards and disqualification of player.
    - Defensive pass interference—Offensive team ball at point of foul—automatic recorded first down.
    - Offensive pass interference—15 yards and loss of down.

STRATEGY

Offense

Since the game of flagball is primarily a passing game, the offensive strategy should be composed of a variety of passing plays with running options available. (See Diagram 2.)

Basically, the offensive skills most essential for success in advancing the football are throwing, catching, and open field running. A variety of options should be incorporated into the strategy because everyone is eligible to run, throw, and receive the football, except in situations as specified in the rules. The limitation on the number of forward passes that a male quarterback may throw emphasizes the need for skilled quarterbacks. It is also important that the offensive line people are agile and skilled in executing screens preventing the rushing defensive players from getting to the quarterback.

Defense

The defensive strategy in the game of flagball is to pressure the quarterback and prevent the ball from being advanced via the run or pass. This pressure is the responsibility of the defensive linemen/women who must evade the opponent's screen, contain the quarterback, and remove one flag before a pass can be attempted. While the quarterback is being subjected to this pressure, the linebackers and corner backs must remain with their assigned opponent. Usually, person for person coverage is used in flagball. Each defender must constantly maintain a position between the opponent and the goal line. If an opponent does gain possession of the football, a flag must be quickly removed. This can be accomplished by the defender moving toward the opponent, focusing on the waist, reaching out and quickly pulling a flag from the belt. As soon as the flag is removed, the defender immediately raises the flag above the head so that the official and players are aware that play has stopped. See Diagram 3 for several examples of offensive and defensive formations.

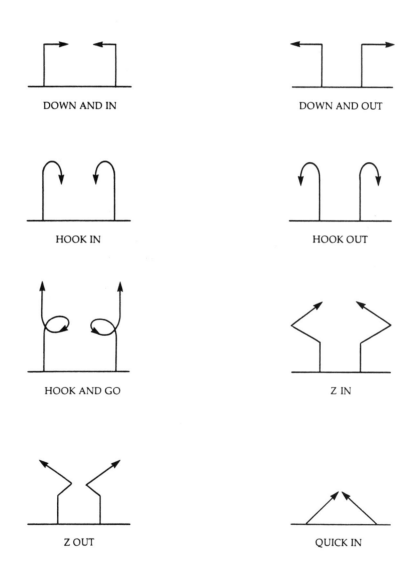

DOWN AND IN

DOWN AND OUT

HOOK IN

HOOK OUT

HOOK AND GO

Z IN

Z OUT

QUICK IN

Diagram 2. Pass patterns.

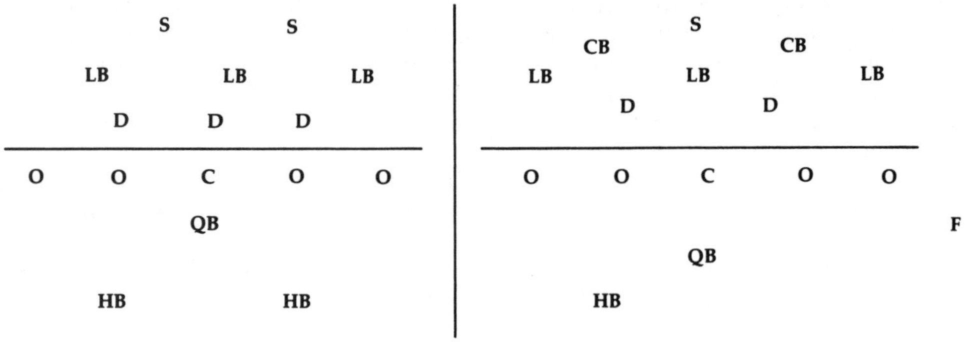

```
        S        S                              S
                                    CB                  CB
   LB        LB        LB      LB        LB          LB
      D     D     D                D           D

   O    O    C    O    O        O    O    C    O    O
        QB                                          F
                                          QB
      HB          HB              HB
```

Offense
C–Center; O–Offensive Line Player; QB–Quarterback; HB–Halfback; F–Flanker

Defense
D–Defensive Line Player; LB–Linebacker; CB–Corner Back; S–Safety

Diagram 3. Examples of offensive and defensive formations

EQUIPMENT

Footballs

The size of the football selected for play is dependent upon the age level participating in the activity. What must be taken into consideration is the fact that the game involves women throwing and catching the football; therefore, the size of the football is of prime consideration. A youth-size football should be considered for the younger participants while an intermediate size is more appropriate on the high school and college level.

A rubber-covered football is more durable for teaching, intramural, and recreational situations, whereas a leather-covered football (which is more expensive) may be more appropriate for competitive situations.

Flags and belts

Consideration must be carefully given to the selection of the type of flags and belts to purchase. Regardless of the type of closure, rings or Velcro, the belt should be easily adjusted as needed by the participants. The most functional attachment of flags to the belt seems to be with Velcro on flags and belt. Although the most common material used in the construction of flags and belt is a flexible plastic, a heavy canvas fabric that seems to be the most durable is also available from some companies.

It should also be pointed out that strips of any durable fabric can be tucked into waistbands of gym shorts or warm-up suits allowing the game of flagball to be introduced without an expensive investment in equipment.

Down marker

Although official down markers are available, a plastic pylon, 36" in height, can also be used. In situations where first downs are determined by crossing into a designated zone, the pylon, with the downs painted around the side is all that is needed.

TERMINOLOGY

Center. The offensive lineman/woman who snaps the football to the quarterback.
Defense. The team that does not have possession of the football.
Fake. A move made by a player for the purpose of deceiving an opponent.
Field Goal. A three-point score when the football is kicked from a place kick over the crossbar and between the uprights.
First Down. The first of four attempts to move the football forward into the next 20-yard zone or end zone.
Forward Pass. A pass thrown from behind the line of scrimmage toward the opponent's goal line.
Handoff. An exchange of the football from the quarterback to a teammate.
Offense. The team that has possession of the football.

Offside. Movement across the established line of scrimmage before the football is snapped.
Safety. An offensive player in possession of the football is downed in own end zone (2 points).
Screen (Block). An offensive player positioning the body between an opponent and the ball carrier.
Scrimmage Line. Imaginary line drawn from forward tip of the football to the sidelines.
Touchdown. An offensive player having possession of the football in opponent's end zone.

REFERENCES

Little, Mildred J., Dowell, Linis J., & Jeter, James M. *Recreational Football.* Dubuque, IA: William C. Brown, Co., 1980.
Windemuth, Timothy. *Flagball for the '90s.* Reston, VA: American Alliance for Health, Physical Education, Recreation and Dance, 1992.

CHAPTER 11

Floor Hockey

GARY R. GRAY
Iowa State University
Ames, IA

INTRODUCTION

Floor hockey is a fast-moving team sport that resembles the game of ice hockey in many ways. There are, however, several differences between the two games, and it is largely because of these differences that participants of all ages can quickly learn to play and enjoy the game of floor hockey. The primary difference, of course, is the fact that floor hockey can be played in a gymnasium of almost any size, provided that there is enough room for the players to move around safely. Floor hockey does not share ice hockey's need for an ice arena or ice skating ability of the players. In addition, the equipment used in floor hockey is somewhat different from that used in ice hockey. Floor hockey is generally played with either a plastic or wood and plastic stick and either a plastic puck or small ball. Another major difference between floor hockey and ice hockey is the fact that floor hockey is **not** a body contact sport.

After basic instruction primarily concerned with control of the stick, the puck, and the body, the players can enjoy participation in the exciting game of floor hockey. Since floor hockey is a novel activity to many individuals, carefully planned instruction must occur not only for students to master the skills necessary to play the game but also so that students can play the game safely. Teachers should plan lessons carefully so that students can master the beginning skills prior to the more advanced skills and prior to playing the game. Carefully planned progressions should be utilized in the instructional unit.

It is very important to master control of the stick prior to competition in floor hockey. It is simply too dangerous to allow a student to play the game when the stick cannot be kept low and away from the bodies of other players. Therefore, teachers must be consistent in calling penalties for rule violations and taking measures to reduce the likelihood of physical injury by the actions of players. Likewise, teachers are encouraged to make modifications when it can be determined that such modifications will increase the likelihood of student success and/or decrease the likelihood of injury.

SKILLS AND TECHNIQUES

Several skills must be learned before a player is able to play the game of floor hockey in a safe and successful manner. They include gripping the stick, stick handling (sometimes referred to as dribbling), passing, and shooting. This section explains the key elements related to each of the basic skills in the game of floor hockey.

THE GRIP

Most players will have a preference regarding whether the right hand or left hand is at the top of the stick. If the right hand is at the top of the stick and the left hand is below it, the player is said to shoot left; if the left hand is at the top of the stick and the right hand is below it, the player is said to shoot right. A player should try both hand positionings before determining which one is preferred. Normally, one will quite simply "feel" better than the other.

The important principle to remember concerning the grip is to be sure that the hands are not placed too closely together. A floor hockey stick is not used as a golf club is used and therefore should not be gripped the same. If the hands are placed together near the top of the stick as they are in holding a golf club, there is a tendency to swing the floor hockey stick in a golf club-like manner. This is extremely dangerous and must be avoided. (See Figure 1.)

The bottom hand should be placed at a comfortable distance down the stick away from the top hand. This distance will vary somewhat depending upon the length of the stick and the size of the player; however, a good guide to use is to place the lower hand somewhere from slightly more than one-third to slightly less than halfway down the stick. This enables the player to maintain good control of the stick by keeping it low while passing and shooting as well as maintaining good control of the puck while stick handling, passing, and shooting.

The top hand should be placed at the extreme top of the stick so as not to leave several inches of stick above the hand. Exposed stick above the top hand not only makes a stick more difficult to control but also creates a danger to other players who might get jabbed with this portion of the stick. If the player cannot maintain his or her grasp at the top of the stick, then the stick is probably too long for that player.

Both hands are placed on the stick in the "handshake" position, that is, with the stick being held across the palms from the base of the index fingers to the heels of the hands below the fifth fingers and between the "V" formed by the index fingers and the thumbs. The fingers should maintain a firm but not rigid grasp of the stick. Likewise, the wrists should be firm but not so rigid that they cannot rotate when passing and shooting. Finally, players should be taught to, whenever possible, keep both hands on the stick to maintain optimum control of the stick.

STICK HANDLING

Stick handling, sometimes referred to as dribbling, is the technique used to move down the floor with possession of the puck. Stick handling is performed best with both hands on the stick in the proper position. The puck is kept directly in front of the body and is pushed down the floor in front of the player's body. Often the player will tap the puck using alternate sides of the stick in an attempt to elude an opponent who might be approaching.

With this maneuver, the stick handler can decide to make a quick move to the right or to the left in an attempt to get by the opponent. While stick handling, it is important to flex the knees comfortably and to bend slightly forward at the waist, but not so much that the player is leaning over. The bottom hand on the stick is almost straight at the elbow while the top hand is bent at approximately 90 degrees at the elbow. With the hands and arms in this position, the puck can be appropriately controlled in front of the body.

It is also important to remember that the best stick handlers are able to advance the puck by keeping the head and eyes up to determine the direction in which they want

Figure 1. The grip.

to proceed. By looking down at the puck excessively, the stick handler is unable to know where approaching defenders are located, where the opponents' goal is located, and where fellow teammates are located in the event a pass might be required. It is also more dangerous to stick handle with the head and eyes down since the likelihood of a collision is increased. Therefore, although most players will need to look down at the puck to some extent to successfully maintain control of it, players should practice keeping the head and eyes up as much as possible. Players should remember that it is possible to look several feet in front of the puck and still see the puck with one's peripheral vision.

Practice Drills: Stick Handling
1. Practice walking down the length of the floor with the puck positioned a stick's length in front of the body. Tap the puck alternately with each side of the stick while walking.
2. Stick handle the puck down the length of the floor while jogging slowly.
3. Stick handle the puck down the floor while varying the speed with which the body moves.
4. Stick handle the puck down the length of the floor without looking directly at the puck. Look down the floor several feet in front of the puck.
5. Stick handle the puck while walking through a maze of plastic cones. As control of the puck increases, the player can increase speed (see Diagram 1).
6. Stick handle the puck through a maze of plastic cones that are spread at irregular distances. As control of the puck increases, the player can increase speed (see Diagram 2).

PASSING

Passing is the skill used to send the puck from one player to another. Actually, the skill of passing consists of two phases: (1) originating the pass by directing the puck to a teammate and (2) completing the pass by receiving the puck from a teammate.

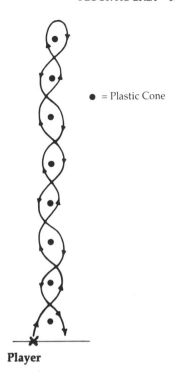

● = Plastic Cone

Player

Diagram 1.

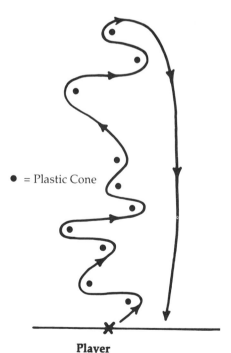

● = Plastic Cone

Player

Diagram 2.

Originating the Pass

The puck can be passed to a teammate from either side of the stick's blade; however, many players will find it easier to control the puck if it is passed from the regular shooting side of the blade. For a left-handed shooter (left hand on the bottom, right hand on top), this is the right side of the blade as one looks down at the stick. For a right-handed shooter, it is the opposite. Players should practice passing the puck from either side of the stick due to the fact that in a game, one cannot always turn to position the body so that the puck can be passed from the favored side of the stick. Furthermore, when teammates are rapidly advancing the puck down the floor against the opponents, there is no time to change body positions. The puck must simply be directed to the teammate from whichever side of the blade is nearer the teammate. In other words, if the pass is to be directed to the left, then this quick action is performed with the left side of the stick; conversely, if the pass is to be directed to a teammate to the right of the player with the puck, then the right side of the stick is preferred.

Generally, the shorter the pass, the greater the accuracy. Players should be encouraged to execute short, quick passes in an attempt to maintain control of the puck. Although longer passes are sometimes in order, these are more difficult to execute and often lead to interceptions by the opponents.

The pass can be initiated by either having the blade of the stick already in contact with the puck or with a short, low backswing of a few inches. Players should be cautioned not to take a long or high backswing, however, since this action, in addition to being dangerous, might result in a puck that is passed so hard it is difficult for the teammate to receive. If the pass is executed from a stationary position, the passer should assume a balanced stance with the feet at least shoulder width apart. The knees should be flexed slightly, and the player should bend forward slightly at the waist.

For beginners, it is easiest to learn passing by positioning the body so that the passer is standing sideways to the target.

However, with calculated control of the stick, the passer should be able to pass the puck to various teammates who are either to the side or somewhere in front of the passer. The adjustment needed is simply executed by altering the position of the body in relation to the puck by either moving the feet or moving the stick, or both.

The puck, as previously mentioned, can be passed using either side of the stick, depending upon the location of the receiver. The important point to remember in order to execute an accurate pass is that the blade of the stick must be pointing in the exact direction of the receiver. This angle can be changed by moving the entire body, by adjusting the position of the feet, or simply by changing the position of the stick by altering the position of the arms. Even the wrists can assist the player in making changes to the direction that the stick is pointing.

The passer should shift the body weight by stepping toward the receiver. If a left-handed passer is passing the puck to the right of the mid-line of the body, the passer should step toward the intended target with the right foot. If the pass is being executed using the backhand side of the stick and passing to the left of the mid-line of the body, then the passer should step toward the receiver with the left foot. A smooth transfer of body weight will enable the passer to execute a more successful pass.

The passer's eyes should move from a position of watching the puck in contact with the stick to a position of focusing on the intended target just prior to the actual execution of the pass. By looking at the target just prior to release of the puck, the passer should increase accuracy. The passer will also be able to determine the appropriate speed to put on the pass by quickly judging the approximate distance to the receiver. After the blade of the stick is directed to the receiver, sending the puck toward the target, the passer should follow through with the stick in a short, low manner toward the target. A properly executed follow-through should also enhance accuracy. The passer should be very careful, of course, not to follow through either high or long or perform any other action with the stick that might cause the stick to strike an opponent.

If the passer initiates a pass while walking or running, all actions are the same except for the synchronization of the actual release of the puck with the shifting of body weight caused by the foot movement of the walk or run. In other words, as the passer, who is walking or running, steps toward the intended receiver to facilitate the transfer of body weight, the release of the puck must occur. This, of course, is more difficult to time exactly if the passer is running quickly down the floor. Players will find that as their skill in passing and stick control increases, the transfer of body weight, especially when executing very short passes, becomes less critical. Experienced players do not need to rely as much on this transfer of body weight for passing accuracy.

Receiving the Pass

In order for a pass to be successfully executed, it must not only be sent toward its intended target but also properly received. Receiving a pass in floor hockey is, in a sense, similar to catching a ball. The player must successfully "catch" the puck with the stick. If this phase of the passing action is performed incorrectly, the puck often bounces off the receiver's stick and into the control of the opponents. Although the ideal position for beginners to be positioned is sideways to the passer, an experienced player can receive the puck from almost any position.

The key factor in successfully receiving a pass is to position the blade of the stick perpendicular to the approaching puck. In this manner, the player is then able to draw the stick back slightly to cushion the puck onto the stick in an attempt to "catch" it. If the receiver's stick is not perpendicular to the approaching puck, then there is a greater tendency for the puck to slide off the blade of the stick. Nevertheless, if the receiver successfully cushions the puck onto the stick, thereby decelerating it, the puck will remain on the stick of the receiver instead of bouncing off.

Practice Drills: Passing

1. Pass the puck against a wall to work on sending the puck in a line perpendicular to the wall. This drill can be modified by increasing the distance between the player and the wall and by varying the speed of the passes.

2. Pass the puck toward a one-foot-wide target on the wall. This drill can be modified by varying the distance between the player and the wall and also by varying the size of the target.

3. Position two players 15 feet apart. The players will pass the puck back and forth. Gradually increase the distance between the players to approximately 30 feet. This drill can be modified by having the receiving player vary the location of his or her stick, which will serve as the target for the pass, and also by varying the speed of the passes.

4. At one end of the gymnasium, form two single file lines of players approximately 15 feet apart and facing toward the opposite end of the gymnasium. Each pair of players will walk the length of the floor passing the puck back and forth between each other. The second pair of players can begin when the first pair is a safe distance down the floor. As the players come back to the ends of the two lines, they should switch lines so that they can practice passing and receiving the puck with the opposite side of their sticks. This drill can be modified by having the players slowly jog instead of walk.

5. Direct two players to move around the gymnasium floor and pass the puck back and forth between each other. The players can practice moving around all portions of the entire playing area, varying the distance and angles between them.

6. With a goalie standing in front of the goal and one defense person standing near the blue line, two players standing approximately 15 feet apart near their own blue line progress down the floor toward the goalie. The two offensive players pass the puck and attempt to elude the one defense person and execute an open shot on goal.

SHOOTING

Shooting is the skill used to direct the puck toward the opponents' net in an attempt to score a goal. The three types of shots in floor hockey are: (1) the wrist shot, (2) the slap shot, and (3) the backhand shot.

The Wrist Shot

The wrist shot enables the shooter to be very accurate in hitting a specific portion of the opponents' goal. It can also be executed when the shooter is being closely guarded or is otherwise surrounded by several players since the player does not take a windup with the stick. When executed properly, it is a good shot to use in a game. (See Figure 2 a and b.)

Preparing to execute a wrist shot is begun by assuming a body position sideways to the goal with the feet slightly wider than shoulder width apart. The left-handed shooter stands with the right side of the body toward the goal. The opposite is true for a right-handed shooter. The wrist shot is initiated by positioning the heel of the stick

directly behind and in contact with the puck. The puck is normally directly in front of the rear foot, but it can be as far forward as the mid-line of the body. The lower hand on the stick is almost straight at the elbow while the top hand is bent at approximately 90 degrees at the elbow. The shooter steps toward the goal with the foot nearer the goal (right foot for a left-handed shooter) at the same time as the stick drags the puck forward and toward the goal. The puck leaves contact with the stick at a position approximately opposite the front foot as the wrists whip forward, imparting considerable velocity to the puck.

The follow-through with the stick is low, short, and toward the target. Players should be reminded to "turn over" the blade of the stick with their wrists after completing the shot so as not to raise the stick up high and possibly hit someone. Players should be cautioned not to intentionally raise the puck to a dangerous level. The puck should be kept either on the floor or low to the floor so as not to strike an opponent or a teammate in the head area. As was described in

a.

b.

Figure 2. Wrist shot.

the passing section, if a wrist shot is initiated from a walk or run, the player must be careful to coordinate the transfer of body weight (i.e., stepping toward the target) with the release of the puck in order to gain maximum velocity.

The Slap Shot

The slap shot enables the shooter to generate more speed on the puck than does the wrist shot but sometimes this comes at the expense of accuracy. Standing sideways to the target, the shooter assumes a stance with the feet at least shoulder width apart, in such a position that the puck is in line with the front foot. The player draws the stick back in preparation to hit the puck. Although beginning players will need to keep the weight on both feet (see Figure 3, a-c), experienced players will be able to place all of the weight on the front foot as the stick is drawn back into a "wind-up" (see Figure 4). It is very important that the stick stay below the waist so as not to cause a hazard to nearby players. The stick is then brought forward forcefully to contact the puck. Follow-through is forward, short, and low so that surrounding players are not hit with the stick. Players should be taught to turn the blade of the stick over to further protect surrounding players.

It is important for the blade of the stick to make contact with the puck perpendicular to the target. If the stick is even a few degrees off perpendicular, the shot will go wide of the net. It is also important to contact the puck exactly at floor level. If the stick comes forward too low, the stick will hit the floor behind the puck and cause a weak shot. If the stick comes forward too high, the stick will hit the top of the puck and also result in a weak shot. It is even possible to miss the puck entirely if care is not taken with the swing.

The shooter should always keep the head down with the eyes on the puck throughout the entire shot. The slap shot can be taken with very little backswing. Even a short backswing can generate sufficient momentum to the puck to produce a good shot. Great care must be taken to ensure that players do not attempt to generate more force to the puck than they can safely con-

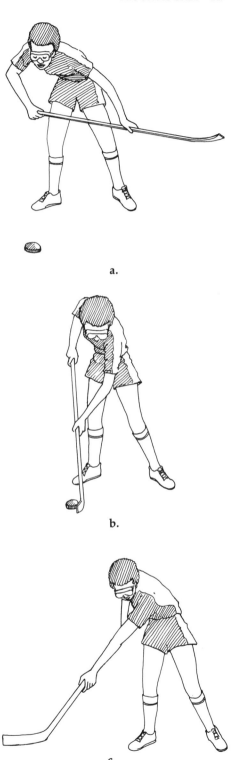

a.

b.

c.

Figure 3. Slap shot.

Figure 4. Wind up for slap shot.

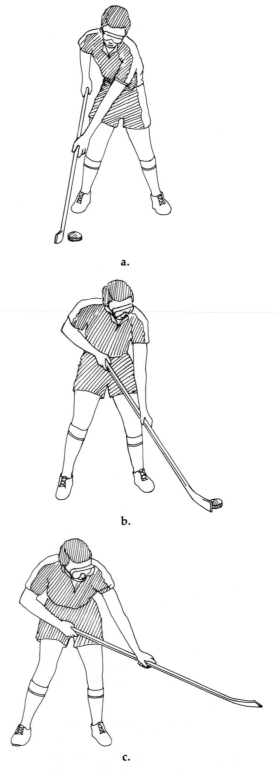

a.

b.

c.

Figure 5. Backhand shot.

trol. A wild swinging stick can be a serious hazard to both opponents and teammates alike. Players should be reminded that the purpose of the backswing, which absolutely must be low for the sake of safety, is to generate an amount of momentum to the puck equal to the amount of control that is needed on the stick as contact with the puck is made and the follow-through is executed. Some players must also be reminded that the slap shot in floor hockey in no way resembles a golf shot.

The Backhand Shot

Essentially, the backhand shot is the reverse of the wrist shot. That is, for a left-handed shooter (right hand at top of stick), the puck is shot from the left side of the stick's blade rather than the right side as it is in the wrist shot. Standing sideways to the target with the feet at least shoulder width apart, the player can grasp the stick either with the regular grip (see Figure 5, a-c) or adjust the lower hand to where it grasps over the stick (see Figure 6). With the overhand grip, it is possible to generate more power from the shot.

The puck is normally contacted with the blade of the stick directly in front of the rear foot (right foot for a left-handed shooter and left foot for a right-handed shooter), but it can be as far forward as the mid-line of the body. As in the wrist shot, the puck is dragged with the stick as the stick develops speed. At a point approximately in front of the foot nearer the goal

Figure 6. Overhand grip.

(front foot), the blade of the stick whips the puck forcefully toward the target. At the same time, the weight is transferred from the back foot to the front foot to facilitate balance and to assist in generating speed on the puck. As in all other shots, the follow-through is forward toward the target but also short and low to minimize the risk of hitting a nearby player with the stick.

Practice Drills: Shooting

1. Standing approximately 15 to 20 feet from a wall, practice shooting the puck against the wall to work on sending the puck in a line perpendicular to the wall. This drill can be done with the wrist shot, the slap shot, and the backhand shot. This drill can be modified by varying the distance between the player and the wall and by varying the speed of the shots.
2. Shoot the puck at a one-foot target on the wall using the wrist shot, the slap shot, and the backhand shot. This drill can be modified by varying the distance between the player and the wall and also by varying the size of the target.
3. Standing at various distances from the goal, practice shooting the puck at the goal using the wrist shot, the slap shot, and the backhand shot. Practice shooting the puck at the corners of the goal. This drill can be modified by placing an obstacle on the floor in front of the goal so that the puck can enter the net only if it is shot into one of the corners.

4. Standing at various distances from the goal, practice shooting the puck at the goal with a goalie standing in front of the goal. This drill can be done using the wrist shot, the slap shot, and the backhand shot.
5. Distribute several pucks one to two feet apart in a line just inside the blue line. Practice shooting the pucks in rapid succession at the goal with a goalie standing in front of the goal. This drill can be modified by distributing the pucks in a line closer to the goal.
6. Standing at various distances from the goal, practice receiving a pass from a teammate and then shooting the puck toward the goal with a goalie standing in front of the goal.

THE PLAYING AREA

The playing area is divided into four sections (see Diagram 3). The center line divides the floor into halves. Within each half, there is a blue line (or any other color of tape that one wishes to use) to identify each team's attacking zone. The distance between each team's blue line and the end of the playing area is approximately one-third of the playing area. Therefore, the distance between the two blue lines is approximately one-third of the playing area. This floor space between the two blue lines, divided evenly by the center line, is known as the neutral zone. These zones are important in determining offside passes.

If there are no floor or wall obstructions, the entire floor space is used as the playing area. This allows the players to execute passes by deflecting the puck off the gymnasium walls to elude opponents. This also maintains an almost continuously moving game by not having play stop when the puck crosses an out of bounds line as in basketball. However, if there are floor or wall obstacles that pose a risk of injury to players, the area near the hazard(s) could be deemed out of bounds, in which case play would stop if players approach the obstacles.

Another strategy would be to place padding around the obstacles to allow play to continue. Still another modification would be to play the game within the basketball lines or other lines already painted on the floor. This would assist in keeping players away from the walls if, perhaps, several obstacles are present. When the puck leaves the playable area by crossing the out of bounds line, play could be restarted by either having a face off or even more quickly by allowing the nonoffending team to either pass the puck back into the playable area or bring the puck back in by means of stick handling.

The goals are placed near each end of the playing area, approximately ten feet out from each end wall. This allows play to occur behind each goal. In small playing areas, it might not be feasible to position the goals away from the end walls. It is often helpful to secure the goals to the floor with tape so that they will be more stable if they are bumped during play.

The goal area is bounded by a goal crease, a taped area on the floor that is to indicate the floor space into which opponents must not enter. The purpose of the goal crease is to allow the goalie adequate freedom of movement near the goal so that he or she will be able to block shots without interference from opponents. The goal crease, although normally a rectangle, can also be arc-shaped. The rectangular goal crease begins one foot to the side of each goal post and runs four feet out from the goal. Of course, the size of the goal crease can be modified by making it larger if more protected space is desired for the goalie.

If the game of floor hockey is played in a very small gymnasium or if two games are being played simultaneously across the width of a gymnasium, the teacher might choose not to use the rule preventing offsides and two line passes since the area of play is rather restricted due to the limited playing area. If the area of play is very limited, care should be taken to determine that the regulation number of six players on the

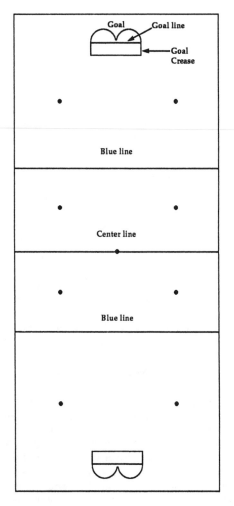

•=face off locations

Diagram 3. The playing area.

floor per team does not cause an overly crowded situation, in which case teams might play with four or five players rather than six. If two games are being played simultaneously on adjoining playing areas, an appropriate buffer zone of several feet in width should be identified and clearly marked on the floor to prevent collisions between players from the adjoining playing areas.

THE PLAYERS

Floor hockey is played between two teams of six players each (see Diagram 4). Each team consists of three forwards, two defense persons, and a goalie. The three forward positions consist of the center and a right and left winger. The defense persons are referred to as right and left defense. Each player has both offensive and defensive responsibilities. Although the three forwards score the majority of a team's goals, they also must play sound defense. When the opponents gain possession of the puck and begin to advance toward the goal, the forwards must quickly run back to assume defensive responsibilities. Hard-working forwards can often break up the opponents' developing plays before they can advance completely into scoring range. Forwards who are slow to move back toward their goal to play defense often find that a shot on goal occurs before they are able to fully participate in the action again. Of course, this will result in many goals since the opposing three forwards will often be challenging only the two defense persons and the goalie.

Similarly, even though the defense persons are known for their defensive responsibilities, they are instrumental in developing and maintaining offensive pressure on the opponents. As the defense persons gain possession of the puck, it is they who begin the next offensive play for their team by passing the puck ahead to their forwards.

The goalie is the player who usually has the last chance to prevent the opponents from scoring. Although not all players will develop an interest in goal tending, some will inevitably be drawn to the position. Some players absolutely crave the challenge

of successfully stopping the opponents' shots on goal. The successful goalie is one who has quick reflexes, can concentrate on the fast-moving action, and has good vision to track a variety of shots. Goal tending will be discussed in more detail in the next section.

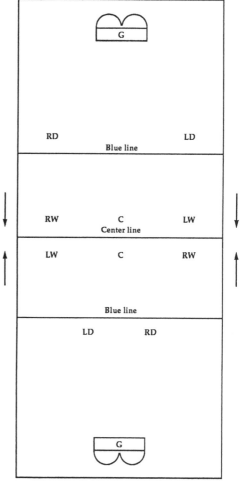

G	= goalie	C	= center
LD	= left defense	LW	= left winger
RD	= right defense	RW	= right winger

Diagram 4. The players at the beginning face-off.

GOAL TENDING

The goalie plays a very important role in the success of a team in floor hockey. The goalie must learn how to effectively use and stop shots with the stick, with the catching glove, and with the body as well as being laterally mobile across the width of the goal. The goalie assumes a stance with the feet at least shoulder width apart and the knees comfortably flexed. The body is bent slightly forward at the waist, the back is relatively straight and upright, and the head is held up. The dominant hand grasps the stick approximately half way down the handle, just above the widened portion of the handle. The other hand holds a catching glove, commonly a baseball or softball glove. The stick is held in front of the body with the blade directly in front of the feet. The catching glove is held up slightly to the side of the body in preparation to catch any high shots.

The goalie should be taught to remain on his or her feet as much as possible in order to maintain maximum mobility near the goal. There may be times when the goalie goes down onto one knee in an attempt to secure a loose puck or a rebound. In any case, goalies should be taught not to sprawl onto the floor or commonly go down to the floor, particularly when the action is very close to the goal crease. A goalie is less mobile and therefore less effective whenever not on the feet. Also, by remaining on one's feet, there is a decreased likelihood that the goalie will be hit in the head area with a stick or puck.

The goalie may hold onto any shot that is stopped, thereby requiring a face-off to restart play. This is commonly done when there are several opponents in close proximity to the goal and when releasing the puck might result in a sudden shot by an opponent. The face-off would be taken in the face-off area corresponding to the direction from which the shot originated, either to the right or left of the goal. When there are no opponents in close proximity to the goal, the goalie usually does not hold onto the puck when a shot is blocked. Instead, the goalie will use the stick to direct the puck to the nearest teammate.

THE GAME

The game of floor hockey begins with all players on their own side of the center line. The referee drops the puck between the sticks of the two centers who are facing each other with their sticks on the floor. This is known as a face-off. The tips of the blades of the two centers' sticks are approximately six to ten inches apart. As the referee drops the puck, both centers attempt to gain possession of the puck by pulling or hitting the puck either back to a winger or to a defense person. An alternate strategy is to hit the puck forward into the opponents' zone and proceed after the puck.

A goal is scored when the puck completely crosses the goal line in the opponents' goal. A puck must be shot into the goal, rather than kicked or hit with the hand or another body part, in order to be considered a legal goal. After the shot, however, the puck may deflect off either an offensive or defensive player or both prior to entering the net. It may not, however, be intentionally directed into the net with the body. Following each goal, play is begun by conducting a face-off at the center of the playing area in the same manner as at the beginning of the game.

When players are moving around the playing area in an attempt to elude opponents and get open to receive a pass, they must be careful not to commit an offside pass violation. An offside pass can occur in two ways. First, it is a violation if a player passes the puck from behind his or her own blue line and it crosses both the blue line and the center line before it is received by the passer's teammate. This is commonly referred to as a "two line pass." Another example of a two line pass that is also illegal is a pass sent from between one's own blue line and the center line across the center line and across the opponent's blue line. The second type of offside pass is one which is initiated from the area between the center line and the opponents' blue line when the pass receiver has both feet across the blue line before the puck crosses the blue line. It is legal, however, for the pass receiver to have one foot across the blue line, as the puck passes the opponents' blue line.

The purpose of ruling these offside passes illegal is to allow the defense persons the opportunity to come up to the opponents' blue line in an attempt to keep the puck in the attacking zone without having to be constantly caught with opponents behind them ready to receive a long, two line pass which could easily result in a breakaway. After a whistle is blown to stop play following an offside pass, a face-off is done from the zone in which the offside pass originated. Of course, instructors could modify the game to allow either or both of the offside pass situations previously described.

SAFETY

In teaching floor hockey in elementary, junior high, and high school settings the possibility of various injuries should be addressed by the teacher. Careful planning is required to minimize the likelihood of injuries. Teachers report that the most common injuries in floor hockey are scrapes, bruises, and/or cuts on the extremities, such as the knees, shins, ankles, feet, hands, wrists, and arms, as the result of being hit by a floor hockey stick. Other injuries identified include those related to being hit by the stick or puck in the head area, including the face, eyes, mouth, and nose. The third category of injuries is related to those caused by collisions between players.

Therefore, the three major safety concerns in the game of floor hockey are related to: (1) control of the body, (2) control of the stick, and (3) control of the puck. This section will address each of these concerns.

Control of the Body

Floor hockey is not a body contact sport. Players should learn to avoid collisions. Body checking, a skill that is common in ice hockey, is simply against the rules in floor hockey. Defensive players should learn to "play the puck" when attempting to secure possession of the puck from the offensive player. The offensive player should not be bumped, pushed, or otherwise interfered with in an unsafe manner. When the defen-

sive player attempts to secure the puck from the offensive player's control, there might be some minor, incidental contact simply due to the closeness of the players. However, this type of contact is in no way meant to physically disrupt the opposing player. Aggressive physical contact is punished with a two-minute penalty, during which time the offending player must sit out and the team must play short handed. If the short-handed team is scored against prior to the expiration of the two-minute penalty, the penalized player may return to the game.

Players should also learn to move around the area of play, with and without the puck, by keeping their heads up rather than down. Simply because a player has possession of the puck does not give that player the right to collide with opponents by charging down the floor with the eyes down on the puck. Players must carefully watch where they run. A parallel can be drawn to the game of basketball where the player with the ball cannot simply collide with a defensive player who might be in his or her pathway. Both players who share the potential to collide must share the responsibility to avoid the collision.

Control of the Stick

Players must learn to control their sticks properly at all times so that improper use of the stick does not cause injuries to other players. The time when use of the stick causes the greatest concern is during shooting. Players must keep their sticks under control during all phases of the shot. This involves taking a short, low backswing, if any, as well as a short, low follow-through after contact with the puck. A long, high follow-through with the stick is a sure way to injure nearby players, both opponents and teammates alike. It is helpful for players to "turn over" the stick blade during follow-through. This prevents the front end of the blade from rising to where it might hit another player.

Under no circumstances should players in floor hockey be allowed to perform "golf shots" where the stick is swung in a very high and dangerous manner. Players who cannot properly execute the shot in floor hockey really should not be playing the game yet. They should devote more time to practice until the shot can be properly executed.

Control of the Puck

Regardless of the exact type of puck used in the game of floor hockey, it is inevitable that it will occasionally rise off the floor, even to a height that could strike a player in the head or upper body. This might occur as the result of a deflection off a stick that is held out to block a shot where the blade of the stick is tilted back in such a position as to cause the puck to rise. Some of these situations are perhaps unavoidable. However, players should learn not to raise the puck purposely to levels that present a potential danger to other players. This can be done by teaching players to perform shots that keep the puck either on the floor or very close to the floor.

More specifically, players should be taught not to tilt the stick blade backward when performing a slap shot, not to use excessive wrist action during the wrist shot, not to "scoop" the puck during the wrist shot and backhand shot, and not to bend the blades of the floor hockey sticks. Each of these actions, if performed, might cause the puck to rise unnecessarily high.

In addition, use of protective eye goggles and protective mouthguards will help in preventing many injuries caused by inadvertent high pucks as well as high sticks. For these same reasons, goalies should wear protective face masks.

EQUIPMENT

Basic equipment items for the game of floor hockey include the stick and puck. Sticks come in various styles, materials, and lengths. Typical floor hockey sticks range from the short, plastic blade sticks with hollow, plastic handles to the longer, wooden handled sticks with plastic blades with various versions in between. It is not recommended to play floor hockey with wooden-blade ice hockey sticks. (Also, it is not recommended to use the type of wooden handle stick that has no blade with which players propel a "doughnut" type

puck by placing the tip of the stick handle inside the "doughnut.") Each major physical education and sport equipment supplier has at least one type of floor hockey stick, and sometimes more from which to choose.

Pucks also come in various types. These range from the plastic, hollow variety to the plastic weighted pucks, with various alternatives in between. Although the weighted pucks tend to stay on the floor better than do some of the hollow pucks, one must consider the potential that these pucks have to cause greater injury to a player when one is hit by the puck. They are, therefore, not recommended.

Some manufacturers produce a special low bounce or "no bounce" type of ball to be used in the game of floor hockey. One consideration in using this device is the fact that it tends to have a true roll, whereas some pucks do not when they roll on edge rather than slide. Additionally, these balls do tend to stay low when they bounce. Another available option is a small, soft, foam ball.

Other equipment includes protective eye guards or goggles to prevent eye injuries caused by the puck or ball and sticks. Protective mouthguards serve to protect the teeth against damage. Players' hands can be protected by wearing leather work-type gloves.

Protective equipment for the goalie includes a face mask to guard against injuries caused by being hit in the face by a puck or ball while trying to stop shots on goal or being hit in the face by a stick in action close to the goal. Other goalie equipment includes a chest protector, a baseball style catching glove, and a protective cup, all used to protect the goalie from shots on goal. The goalie's stick hand can also be protected by wearing a leather work-type glove.

Portable, metal goals can be purchased from various suppliers, or tape can be put on the two end walls in a rectangular fashion to serve as goals. It is often difficult to determine whether a shot actually scored, however, with the goals made of tape on the end walls since some shots will hit the wall very close to the tape and rebound quickly. Portable, metal goals with a cord mesh are preferable.

TACTICS AND STRATEGIES

Although all of the players (particularly beginners) might be tempted to follow the puck around the entire playing area, it is important for each player to play his or her assigned position so that when the puck does enter the player's zone of responsibility, he/she will be there. It takes considerable self-discipline to stay in one's general area of responsibility, particularly when one is new to the game. With experience, however, players learn not only to play their assigned positions but also when to leave their assigned positions to chase a loose puck, when to cover for another player who has left his or her position to secure a loose puck, and when to leave one's position to double team an opponent. Players must know that their teammates will be in their assigned positions so that consistent passing can occur. This section will discuss various tactics and strategies related to playing effective offense and defense.

OFFENSE

When a player secures control of the puck inside his or her own blue line, it is generally advisable to advance the puck either by stick handling or passing the puck out to either side of the playing area. This is particularly important when the player is very close to his or her own goal. It is often more difficult to advance the puck out of one's own end by going up the middle of the floor. Normally, the player will encounter more opponents if this is attempted. As the player with the puck approaches the center line, it is then advisable to stick handle or pass the puck back in toward the middle of the floor. In this manner, the team on offense can attempt a balanced attack as they approach the opponents' blue line. This would involve the three forwards spread evenly across the floor in their assigned positions. If the center happens to move either right or left with the puck, the corresponding winger can switch with the center to maintain a balanced attack.

As the offensive team penetrates the opponents' blue line with the puck, the defense persons on the offensive team should follow the three forwards up the floor. The two defense persons will, if possible, advance up to the opponents' blue line. From this floor position, either defense person will have an opportunity to keep the puck inside the opponents' zone if it appears that the puck might be hit across the blue line by the defensive team. If the defensive team succeeds in hitting or stick handling the puck out of their zone (i.e., across the blue line), the defense person on offense who intercepts control of the puck must wait for all of his or her teammates to vacate the opponents' zone before sending the puck back across the blue line. If all teammates do not cross the blue line with at least one foot before the puck is sent back in, the referee will rule an offside pass and have a face-off outside the blue line.

When the puck goes into either corner of the offensive zone, the corresponding winger should go after the puck. If the winger is successful in gaining control of the puck in the corner, the winger should attempt to pass the puck to in front of the opponents' goal. At this time, the center should be positioned directly in front of the goal post nearer the same corner as the puck. The opposite winger should be positioned directly in front of the opposite goal post. Of course, players can move from these specific positions when it is advantageous to do so to secure a loose puck or to elude the opponents; however being in these general locations will increase the likelihood that the winger with the puck in the corner will be able to execute an effective pass to an open teammate.

DEFENSE

When the offensive team loses control of the puck in the opponents' zone, all of the players must quickly change from an offensive mode to a defensive mode. This includes the three forwards as well as the two defense persons and the goalie. Good defense begins as soon as the attacking team loses control of the puck. It is possible that the team who has just lost control of the puck can regain control of the puck again even before the offensive team can cross their own blue line with the puck.

This can be done by cutting off the main routes out of their own zone—up the right side, up the left side, and up the middle. If these passing lanes are filled by alert defensive players, the defensive team might soon find themselves back on offense again.

Forwards on the defensive team should continue to put pressure on the offensive team as the puck crosses the offensive team's blue line and progresses up across the center line. Defensive pressure should be closely applied as the offensive team approaches the defensive team's blue line since the offensive team is within shooting range. This close pressure is crucial in preventing the offensive team from executing clean, unhindered shots on goal.

When the puck goes into either corner of the defensive zone, the corresponding defense person should quickly follow after the puck in an attempt to beat the offensive winger into the corner. The other defense person guards the other winger in front of the net, while the defensive center guards the offensive center in front of the net. If the defense person is successful in gaining control of the puck in the corner, the defender should attempt to stick handle or pass the puck out of the defensive zone by selecting a route up along the side of the playing area. Care must be taken not to allow the puck to be passed out of the corner to any location near the goal. Often the defender will execute a pass off the wall up to one of the defensive team's forwards who should be inside his or her own blue line.

When the puck goes out to the attacking team's defense persons inside the defensive team's blue line, the defensive team's forwards must apply enough pressure to prevent an unhindered shot from being taken. In this case, the defensive left winger will apply pressure to the offensive right defense person while the defensive right winger will apply pressure to the offensive left defense person.

RULES

1. Teams consist of six players, including the goalie, on the floor at one time. Substitutes may enter the game during any stoppage in play or by "changing on the fly" directly in front of the team's bench area while the puck is in play.

2. A goal is scored when the puck completely crosses the goal line.

3. A player may not enter the opponents' goal crease. If a goal is scored while an opponent is in the goal crease, the goal is not allowed.

4. Body checking, pushing, or other rough play is not allowed. Floor hockey is not a body contact sport. Incidental contact might occur as two opponents attempt to play the puck, but this contact is penalized if it is done in an intentional, aggressive, or dangerous manner. (Penalty: two minutes.)

5. A player may not trip an opponent using the stick, feet, legs, or other body parts. (Penalty: two minutes.)

6. A player may not use the stick to slash at an opponent or the opponent's stick in any action where the player is obviously not playing the puck. (Penalty: two minutes.)

7. A player may not raise the stick above the height of the waist. (Penalty: two minutes.)

8. A player may not hook an opponent with the stick in an attempt to impede the progress of the opponent. (Penalty: two minutes.)

9. A player may not hold an opponent in an attempt to impede the progress of the opponent. (Penalty: two minutes.)

10. A player may be penalized for any action deemed by the referee to be unsportsmanlike or dangerous. (Penalty: two minutes.)

11. A player may not deliberately direct the puck into the goal using the hands, feet, or any other body part. In order to be counted as a legal goal, the puck must be shot with the stick; however, after the shot, the puck may legally deflect off a player, either a teammate or an opponent or both, and go into the goal.

12. When a player is charged with committing a penalty, the player must serve a two-minute penalty by leaving the floor for two minutes of actual playing time. During this time, the player's team

must play with one player fewer than the opponents. If during this two-minute time period, the same team commits another penalty, the offending player must leave the floor for two minutes of actual playing time, and the offending team must play now with two players fewer than the opponents. At no time will one team play with more than two players fewer than the opponents. Therefore, if the same team commits another penalty during the time when they already have two players serving penalties, this third penalty is delayed until the first player's penalty is served.

13. Players may not complete an offside pass. Following an offside pass, play is restarted with a face-off in the zone from which the offside pass originated.

14. Players may use the hands to knock a high flying puck straight down to the floor. They may not attempt to advance the puck with the hands. If this is done, a face-off will result. Only the goalie may grasp the puck with the hands to stop play.

TERMINOLOGY

Backhand Shot. A type of shot, either with or without a backswing, in which the puck is propelled from the opposite side of the stick from which the wrist shot and slap shot are taken (i.e., the nonpreferred side).

Body Checking. An illegal physical action where the player uses the body to bump or push an opponent.

Center. The forward player who is positioned between the two other forwards and who participates in each face-off.

Defense. The team that does not have possession of the puck.

Defense Person. One of the two players who is positioned behind the three forwards and in front of the goalie.

Face-off. The action that begins play at the start of the game and after any other stoppage in play where the referee drops the puck between the sticks of the two centers as the stick blades are positioned with the points of the blades opposite each other and approximately 6" to 10" apart. The two players must allow the puck to drop to the floor before making contact with the puck.

Goal. The mesh covered, metal frame device into which players attempt to score.

Goalie. The player who stands in front of the goal to prevent the opponents from scoring.

High Sticking. An illegal action where the player raises the stick above waist height.

Holding. An illegal action where the player impedes or attempts to impede the progress of an opponent by use of the hands or other body parts.

Hooking. An illegal action where the player impedes or attempts to impede the progress of an opponent by the use of the stick.

Offense. The team that has possession of the puck.

Offside. A player is offside if both feet have crossed the opponents' blue line prior to the puck crossing the blue line. (See also: Two Line Pass.)

Pass. The action with the stick that sends the puck from one player to another.

Score. One point is scored when the puck completely crosses the goal line.

Slap Shot. A type of shot with a backswing in which the puck is propelled by a quick slap with the stick.

Slashing. An illegal action where the player uses the stick to swing at or in the direction of an opponent.

Tripping. An illegal action with the stick or the body that disrupts the feet or legs of an opponent and causes the opponent to fall to the floor.

Two Line Pass. This type of illegal pass from one player to a teammate is one which crosses any two of the three floor lines, which include the center line and the two blue lines. (See also: Offside.)

Winger. The forward players who are positioned to the right and left of the center.

Wrist Shot. A type of shot with no backswing in which the puck is propelled by a quick flick of the wrists.

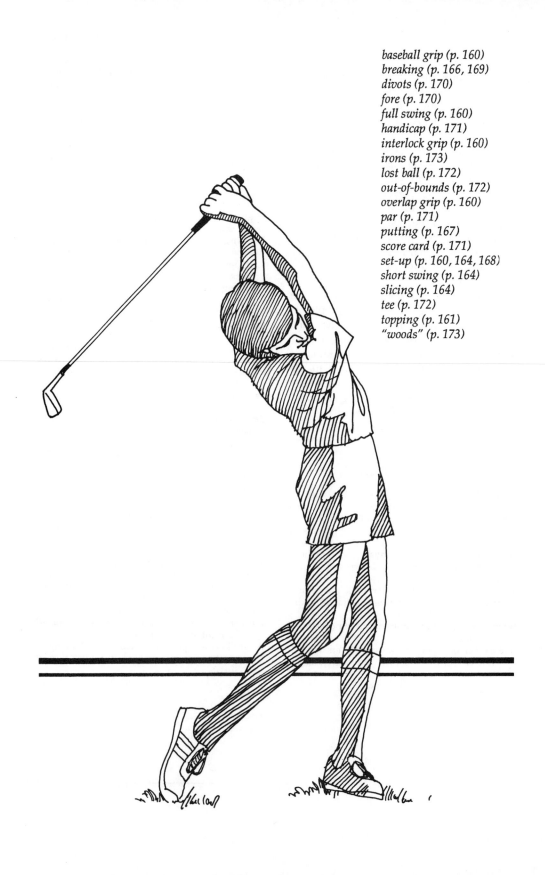

CHAPTER 12

Golf

JIM EWERS
University of Utah
Salt Lake City, UT

INTRODUCTION

Golf is a game that all individuals can play regardless of size, strength, age, or sex. It is simple enough for the unambitious to play with pleasure. If it is to be played well, however, a high degree of skill is demanded. The fascination that the game possesses for those who play it is equalled only by the indifference with which it is regarded by those who do not understand it. The truth is, the game is not as easy as it appears.

The material in this chapter is designed to assist the physical education teacher and students in a secondary school program golf unit. Information included in this chapter relates to:

- student outcomes from a golf instructional unit
- the fundamental skills of the full swing, the short approach shot, and putting
- correcting "common" errors in the swing and putting
- the courtesies of the game
- the basic rules of golf
- golf equipment
- golf terminology
- innovative ways to teach the game

What students should learn from a golf instructional unit in a secondary school program

- Although golf is one of the more expensive sport activities, it can be affordable for most students. The cost to play nine holes of golf, which takes approximately two hours, is about the same price as a movie ticket.
- Good used golf equipment can be purchased at very reasonable prices. Beginning golfers can enjoy the game and develop skills with three or four clubs, a few golf balls, and some tees.
- Students should know the number of golf courses in the area, the difficulty of each course, and the cost to play each of them. Golf courses are rated by experts for difficulty, based upon such variables as length, hazards, terrain, putting green surfaces, etc. This is called a "slope" rating and each course is rated by a numerical scale. The smaller the number, the less difficult the course. The most difficult courses may have a rating of 130 and higher. Beginning players should be encouraged to play on the easier courses if options are available in the area.
- The care and maintenance of the golf course is the responsibility of every player. This does not mean that players are expected to cut the grass or repair sprinkler heads. If the playing surfaces are to be kept in their best condition, every player must repair ball marks on the green and replace divots in the fairways and teeing areas. Carts and golf bags should be kept off the putting greens and teeing areas.
- Golf has some interesting and "different" traditions from most sports. These traditions are called "courtesies of the game." For example, it is discourteous to move or talk while one of your playing partners is hitting. Another courtesy is to try to play at the speed of the players in front of you. Students should learn the courtesies to other players before experiencing a round of golf.
- The golf ball is a dangerous object when in flight. Players must be aware of this danger and understand their responsibility for balls that they hit. Golf clubs are also potentially dangerous weapons and

can hurt someone very seriously. Players must be sure that there is sufficient space to swing their clubs at all times.

- Students should be able to execute the fundamental skills of the full swing, the short shot, and the putting stroke.
- Students should know the basic rules of the game.
- Golf has a unique language of its own. Students should know the more common terms of the game.

THE SKILLS OF THE GAME

The three basic skills/shots in golf are the full swing, the short swing (sometimes called the short approach shot), and putting.

THE FULL SWING

The full swing is an appropriate label for the shot because the player is attempting to combine distance with accuracy. The distance will vary according to the club selected, but the fundamentals of the full swing shot are basically the same with all clubs. One of the most difficult concepts to learn in the full swing is that you want to swing your 4 iron the same way you swing your 9 iron. The difference in distance between those two clubs should be approximately 50 yards, the 4 iron hitting the ball farther.

Grip

The grip is the first and most important concept. The hands are the only part of the body which comes in contact with the golf club. It is important, therefore, to have the hands positioned on the club so that they are not only comfortable but efficient. Although three grips are taught by most teaching professionals, they are basically the same grip with slight variations. These three grips are the overlap grip, the interlock grip, and the baseball grip. The variations in the three grips relate to the way your two hands contact each other on the club handle. With the baseball grip, all eight fingers are wrapped around the club handle, the index finger of one hand merely touching the little finger of the other hand (see Figure 1). The interlock grip is so named because the index finger of one hand interlocks with the little finger of the other hand; thus neither finger is actually in direct contact with the club (see Figure 2). The overlap grip gets its name because the little finger of one hand overlaps the index finger of the other hand (see Figure 3).

Set-up

The set-up position is the "ready position" of the body for swinging a golf club. It is important that the set-up permit easy freedom to move the entire body. The more

Figure 1. Baseball grip.

Figure 2. Interlock grip.

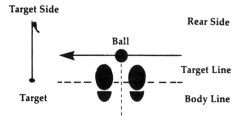

Target Side

Rear Side

Ball

Target Line

Target

Body Line

Diagram 1.

consistent the set-up, the more consistent the swing will become. The set-up is always taken as it relates to a target. The following steps are suggested for achieving an efficient set-up.

Step 1—Alignment. Establish a target (flag stick, tree, bush, etc.). Take two clubs (lines on a gym floor) and place them on the ground like railroad tracks (see Diagram 1). The ball is on one track (target line) and the feet are on the other track (body line). The feet, hips, and shoulders are parallel to the direction of the intended ball flight. This is called a square stance.

Step 2—Stance. The feet should be about shoulder width apart.

Step 3—Weight. The weight should be centered over the middle of both feet with the weight on the balls of the feet. (Hint: it should be easier to tap the heels than to tap the toes.)

Figure 3. Overlap grip.

Step 4—Posture. With the back straight, flex the upper body at the hips to about a 45 degree angle. The arms and hands should be relaxed and hanging freely from the shoulders. There should be a slight flex in the knees. (See Diagram 2.)

Step 5—Ball Position. The ball should be positioned in the stance just to the target side of center.

Diagram 2.

Full swing motion

The full swing is a continuous motion in which the body parts work sequentially. The parts are synchronized to produce the rhythmical and flowing motion. The various stages of the full swing are illustrated in Figure 4.

"COMMON" ERRORS, CAUSES, AND CORRECTIONS IN THE FULL SWING

Error. "Topping" the ball is hitting it above its center resulting in the ball rolling on the ground. Naturally, the ball does not travel far, and the loss of distance will vary according to the terrain (hard ground, long grass, uphill, downhill, etc.).

Cause. One of the major causes of "topping" the ball is straightening the target-side knee just before impact. Another is moving your head in front of the imaginary plane of the ball before impact, or moving your head forward through your downswing before making contact with the ball.

Correction. Don't rush your swing, especially your downswing. Be sure to complete your backswing before starting your downswing. Try to pause for one count at the top of your backswing before you start your downswing. Keep your head back of the ball through impact and your knees flexed.

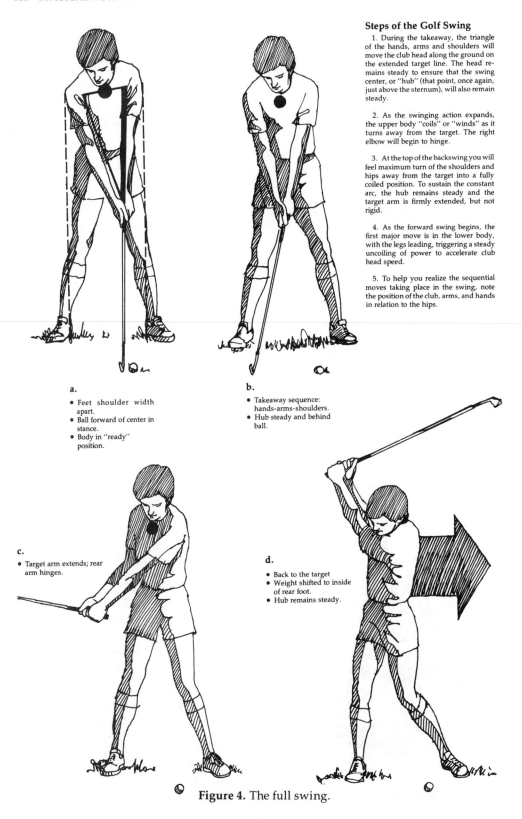

Steps of the Golf Swing

1. During the takeaway, the triangle of the hands, arms and shoulders will move the club head along the ground on the extended target line. The head remains steady to ensure that the swing center, or "hub" (that point, once again, just above the sternum), will also remain steady.

2. As the swinging action expands, the upper body "coils" or "winds" as it turns away from the target. The right elbow will begin to hinge.

3. At the top of the backswing you will feel maximum turn of the shoulders and hips away from the target into a fully coiled position. To sustain the constant arc, the hub remains steady and the target arm is firmly extended, but not rigid.

4. As the forward swing begins, the first major move is in the lower body, with the legs leading, triggering a steady uncoiling of power to accelerate club head speed.

5. To help you realize the sequential moves taking place in the swing, note the position of the club, arms, and hands in relation to the hips.

a.
- Feet shoulder width apart.
- Ball forward of center in stance.
- Body in "ready" position.

b.
- Takeaway sequence: hands-arms-shoulders.
- Hub steady and behind ball.

c.
- Target arm extends; rear arm hinges.

d.
- Back to the target
- Weight shifted to inside of rear foot.
- Hub remains steady.

Figure 4. The full swing.

6. At the moment of impact you should feel all body movement and energy directed toward the target. The hips will have begun to turn, and by now are well out of the way, permitting the arms and hands to swing freely, fully extending the club head out toward the target. Think of swinging through the ball not to the ball.

7. In the follow-through strive to maintain full extension of both arms until the diminishing momentum of club head speed carries them to a natural resting position.

8. At the completion of the swing, the shoulders and hips will have completed their rotation, shifting the majority of the weight to the target foot and forcing a natural lilt of the rear heel from the ground. The arms and hands should finish high.

Summary:

Think of the foregoing stages as one continuous movement governed by balance and timing that will maneuver the club head into position to strike the ball squarely and at its greatest speed.

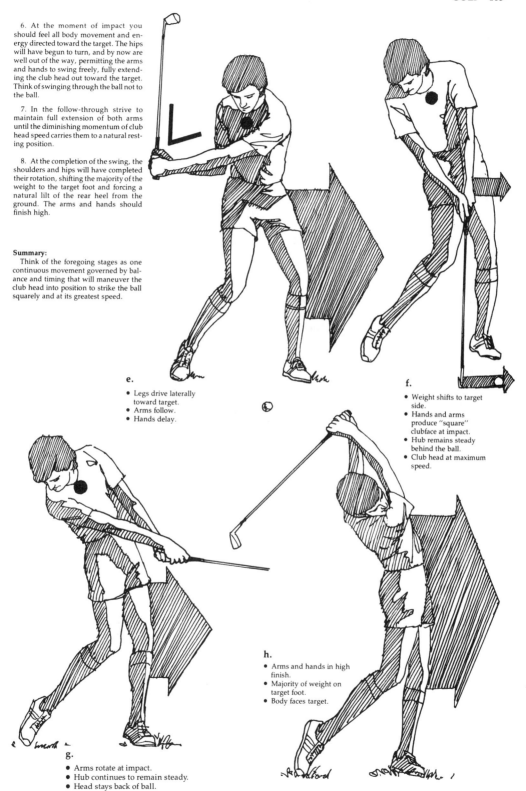

e.
- Legs drive laterally toward target.
- Arms follow.
- Hands delay.

f.
- Weight shifts to target side.
- Hands and arms produce "square" clubface at impact.
- Hub remains steady behind the ball.
- Club head at maximum speed.

g.
- Arms rotate at impact.
- Hub continues to remain steady.
- Head stays back of ball.

h.
- Arms and hands in high finish.
- Majority of weight on target foot.
- Body faces target.

Error. "Hitting behind the ball" causes grass or dirt to get between the ball and the club face. This results in a loss of distance. *Cause.* The downswing is initiated with your arms and hands with little assistance from your legs. Therefore, the bottom of your downswing is at a spot behind the ball. *Correction.* Emphasize a pause at the top of your backswing, and aggressively start your downswing with your hips and legs.

Error. "Slicing" is when the ball curves away from you. The right-handed golfer's shots curve from left to right, whereas the left-handed golfer's shots curve from right to left. *Cause.* Basically, there are two reasons your balls slice: because of a swing "plane" error or because of a club head problem. You might also have a combination of these two problems. Your swing plane is the path along which your club head travels. The club should be swung in a vertical plane traveling along the imaginary target line through the ball during impact. Most players who slice the ball let their club head get outside the imaginary target line prior to impact. As the club comes through the hitting area, the path of the club is from outside the target line to inside the line. The direction of the club face is also critical in determining the direction your ball will travel. You can have a perfect swing plane, but if your club head is open (facing away from your intended target line), your ball will still curve away from you. The distance the ball will curve depends on the degree your club head is open and/or the degree that your swing plane is off your imaginary target line. *Correction.* To keep your swing plane inside the imaginary target line as you initiate your backswing and on the target line through impact (1) push your club back, using your shoulders and arms as one unit in your take-a-way, keeping your club head inside the target line, (2) initiate the downswing with your hips and knees, and (3) be sure your head stays behind the imaginary plane of the ball through impact. To get your club head perpendicular to your intended target at impact (1) be sure your

grip is correct, (2) be sure your arms rotate on your take-a-way so that your club head turns approximately 90 degrees, and (3) release your club aggressively. Releasing your club means that your arm away from the target "rolls over" your target arm.

THE SHORT SWING

During a round of golf, the distances from the ball to the target continually vary. As a result, a full swing or distance swing is not always required. The short swing (sometimes referred to as the short approach swing) is primarily used when approaching the green when accuracy is the major objective. Most golfers refer to these shots as "half wedge shots," "pitch shots," "pitch and run shots," and "chip shots."

Grip

Most golfers use the same grip for the short swing shots as they use for full swing shots. If a player uses the overlap grip for full swing shots, that player will use the overlap grip for short swing shots. Regardless of grip preference, "choke down" on your club for this shot. This means that you place your hands on the club near the middle of the club handle. Grip your club lightly.

Set-up (see Figure 5)
1. Feet closer together.
2. Open your target-side foot about 20 degrees to the hole, and withdraw that foot about an inch from the imaginary line parallel to your target line. You are now in an open stance.
3. More weight on the target-side foot.
4. More bend at the waist.
5. Ball position will be near the center of your stance since your feet are closer together.
6. Hands, arms, and swing center slightly in front of the ball.

Short swing motion

To establish a feel for the short swing, imagine a clock as the one illustrated in Figure 6. The length of the backswing and follow-through will help determine the distance that the ball will go. As skill advances, varying the speed of the swing will also influence distance. Initially, concentrate on the techniques and vary the length of the swing with a constant speed: 7:00 to 5:00; 8:00 to 4:00; 9:00 to 3:00.

The swing is initiated and continued by swinging the arms and hands as a unit, back and through. The wrists should remain firm through the swing. There is very little motion in the lower body. This is primarily an arm and shoulder swing. Permit the lower body to respond naturally. Avoid being still and rigid in the lower body.

The purpose of this shot is to land the ball on the green and get it rolling to the hole, hopefully ending with the ball close to the pin. The technique which has been presented may be used with different clubs depending upon the distance, pin placement on the green, and the hazards between your ball and the green. Initially, the more lofted clubs (9, 8, 7) should be used for this shot. As your skill progresses, variations in the short swing can be learned.

Fundamentals of the short swing
1. Use an open stance. Your target-side foot should be withdrawn from the intended target line and turned toward the target approximately 20 degrees.
2. Keep weight on target-side foot. Approximately 70 percent of your weight should be on your target-side foot in your set-up position. The weight should remain there during the swing.
3. Choke down on your club. Place your hands on the club near the middle of the club handle.
4. Grip the club lightly.
5. Chip and pitch with your big muscles. The arms and shoulders, not the wrists and hands, should control your short shots.
6. Hit down and through the ball. Golf clubs are designed to loft the ball into the air at different degrees. You must understand that the only way you can hit your ball into the air is to hit down and through the ball. This is accomplished by keeping your weight on your target-

Figure 5. The short swing set-up position.

side foot, having your hands slightly ahead of your club head at impact, and keeping your wrists firm and your head steady.

7. Select the proper club to execute the proper shot. Assess all the variables that affect your shot: your lie, the distance of your shot, the contour of the green, your stance, and the hazards you have to negotiate.

"COMMON" ERRORS, CAUSES, AND CORRECTIONS IN THE SHORT SWING

Error. "Hinging" or "breaking" your wrists is one error in short swing shots. Players who break their wrists on the shot suffer from inconsistent distance, frequently sculling their shots, i.e., hitting the ball with the lower edge of the club, thus hitting the ball in a low trajectory and much farther than intended.

Cause. Trying to execute this shot with the small muscles in your wrist and fingers is the cause. Small muscles are inconsistent, especially under pressure.

Correction. Make a long-handled practice club. Cut off the end of the handle of a practice club. This leaves a hole since your golf club shaft is hollow. Insert a wooden dowel about 2 feet long or a broken club shaft about the same length into the end of your practice club. Grip the practice club by its original handle with the extension touching your ribs on your target-side. Take your set-up position to hit the short shot with the extended club. As you practice the basic short swing, the extended club will not permit you to "break" your wrists without the extended handle hitting your ribs. This drill forces you to keep your wrists firm and the back of your target-side hand pointing to the target.

Error. "Topping" your shot, or hitting the ball above its center, causes it to roll on the ground.

Cause. You want to watch your chip or pitch

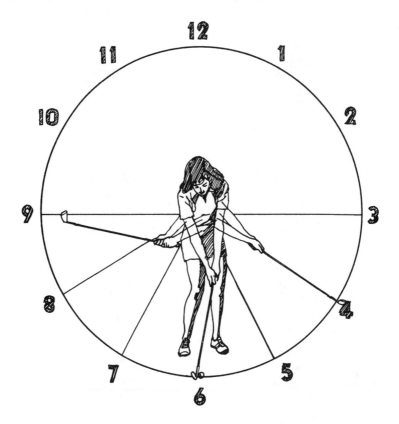

Figure 6. The short swing.

shot go into or near the hole. To do this, you move your head forward as you look up at the hole.

Correction. Ask your golfing partner to assist you by holding a golf score card or any piece of cardboard against the target-side of your head. Basically, this card is to obstruct your peripheral vision to your target, forcing you to concentrate on your stroke and not the results.

Error. Swinging across the imaginary target line will result in inconsistent direction. Sometimes your ball will go left of the target, and sometimes it will go right.

Cause. Most of the time the club face will close (the club face is turned to the inside of your target line) as you pull the club across the imaginary target line; thus the ball will go left of the target from a right-handed player. Occasionally, the ball will go in the opposite direction if you permit your club face to be open (your club face is turned to the outside of your target line) at impact.

Correction. Place two clubs in a parallel position on each side of the ball, forming a "track" 2 or 3 inches wider than the club head of your club. These two clubs should be pointing in the direction of your imaginary target line. Again, you may need assistance from a friend to watch your club to be sure it remains square to your target line and continues on the line in your follow-through. Practice the swing movement without hitting any balls, concentrating on keeping the club in the track and on the imaginary line to the target throughout the swing. Then practice hitting several golf balls using the track as an aid for establishing your stance, ball position, backswing path, and follow-through path.

PUTTING

Putting is the skill of rolling the ball on the putting green into a 4 and ¼ inch hole. A special club, aptly called a putter, is used for this purpose. The putter is significantly different from the other golf clubs. The club face has no loft, and it is usually the shortest club of a set. However, since there are no restrictions of the length of putters, some players are using longer putters and experiencing a lot of success with them.

Putting may be the most appealing segment of the game of golf. You do not need to possess the physical characteristics of strength, size, stamina, speed, quickness, or power to be an outstanding putter. As with the full swing and short swing shots, you need to develop good technique in putting, a "feel" for the putting stroke, a high level of concentration, and you need to be willing to practice.

Everyone who has played golf has searched for the best putting style and technique that will consistently "hole out" those 3 and 4 foot "pressure putts." Putting has been considered that segment of golf in which each individual is permitted the privilege to experiment with any putting style that works, that is, within the rules of the United States Golf Association. About the only rule that restricts putting styles is that both of your feet must be on one side of your imaginary putting line extended in both directions from the ball. Basically, this rule was instituted in 1965 to prohibit the croquet style of putting in which players were straddling the imaginary putting line.

Grip

The reverse overlap grip is still the most prominent grip used by the touring professional golfers. The reason it gets its name is because the index finger of the target-side hand overlaps the little finger of the other hand. This is the reverse of the overlap grip used for the full swing. In placing your hands on your putter for the reverse overlap grip, grasp the handle in your fingers, placing your thumbs directly on the top of the shaft. Your target-side hand will be above your hand away from the target (for the left-handed player, your right hand will be above your left, and the converse for the right-handed player). The index finger of your target-side hand will overlap the little finger of your other hand. (See Figure 7.)

The cross-handed grip is basically the opposite of the reverse overlap grip. For the right-handed player, the right hand will be above the left hand. This gripping technique complements the pendulum putting style because it tends to force a pulling motion with your target arm, thus reducing the chance of "breaking" your wrists.

Figure 7. The putting grip.

For those players using long putters (46 inches and longer), the hands are separated on the putter shaft. The target-side hand is placed on the end of the putter and "anchored" against the chest similar to a fulcrum. The hand away from the target is placed on the putter handle in a comfortable position with the arm extended. The arm away from the target serves as the force to propel the putter as a pendulum.

Regardless of the grip you use, do not "squeeze" the putter. Try to keep your hands and arms relaxed as you hold the putter.

Set-up

- After taking your selected putting grip, place the clubface behind the ball square to the intended target. The feet, shoulders, and hips should be parallel to your target line.
- Your feet should be about hip width apart with your weight evenly distributed on both feet.
- Your back should be relatively straight with a slight flexion at the knee and hip

joints. If you are using an extra long putter, your body would be in an erect, yet relaxed position.

- Your eyes should be positioned over or slightly behind the ball (see Figure 8).
- The ball should be positioned in your stance slightly closer to your target-side foot.

Putting stroke

The putting stroke is a pendulum motion, regardless of the style of putter and grip that you choose. The stroke is accomplished with arms and shoulders working as a unit (one-piece) back and through the ball. The club is a part of the unit. There is no hand or wrist action in the pendulum movement (see Figure 9). The tempo (speed) of your pendulum movement should be the same for your backswing and your forward swing. The length of your backswing will be the primary factor in determining the distance your ball will roll. On a level putting surface a good "rule of thumb" to help you determine the length of

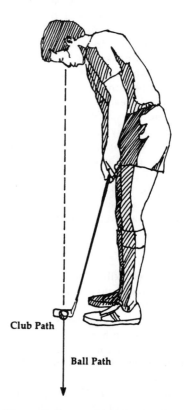

Club Path

Ball Path

Figure 8. Eye position for putting.

your backswing for putts up to approximately 8 feet in length is, "one inch per one foot." For example, you should take the putter back 3 inches for a 3 foot putt. Naturally, with longer putts your backswing will increase but not at the same proportion. There is a sensitivity or "feel" for the amount of force exerted in the longer putts. However, the fundamentals are still the same.

Fundamentals of putting
1. Strive for balance, stability, and relaxation. You want to feel comfortable and relaxed while in your putting stance.
2. Grip your putter lightly.
3. Make sure your eyes are over the ball.
4. Putt with your big muscles. Similar to the short swing technique, the muscles of your arms and shoulders should control the putting stroke. Take the wrists out of your putting stroke if you want to eliminate risks.
5. Keep your head steady and listen for the sound of the ball dropping into the cup.
6. Putt to a target. Regardless of the length of your putt and the contour of the green, identify a target before putting.
7. Keep your club head square to the target.
8. For solid putts, hit the ball on the "sweet spot" of your putter.
9. Accelerate through the ball. Continue your follow-through after you make contact with the ball.
10. Keep your tempo smooth and slow. The speed of your putter on your take-a-way should be the same as the speed of your putting stroke through the ball.

"COMMON" ERRORS, CAUSES, AND CORRECTIONS IN PUTTING

Error. "Hinging" or "breaking" your wrists results in inconsistent distance.
Cause. When you depend upon the small muscles in your wrists and fingers, they tend to be inconsistent under pressure.
Correction. Take a more upright stance, and let your arms hang in a relaxed position. Transfer the movements of your putter from your wrists to your arms. Keep your wrists

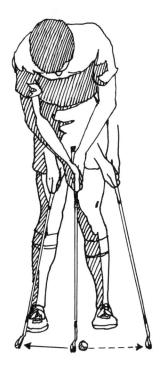

Figure 9. The putting stroke.

firm but not tense through the entire stroke.

Error. "Moving your head" results in inconsistent direction.

Cause. You want to watch your putt drop into the hole. None of us wants to miss seeing our outstanding putts. Also, to move your arms and shoulder without moving your head is unnatural.

Correction. Stand in front of a full-length mirror at home. Take your putting stance, and look at yourself in the mirror. Watch your upper body move while you concentrate on keeping your head steady. Transfer this movement pattern to the practice green. An additional tip to help you keep your head steady is to focus your eyes on the spot where you intend to hit the ball, and continue to watch the spot vacated by the ball. Listen for the ball dropping in the cup.

COURTESIES OF THE GAME

Golf has a recommended code of behavior for participants and an expectation of the players to help keep the golf courses in the best possible condition for other players. These behaviors and expectations are called courtesies of the game or golf etiquette. These courtesies are implemented to help everyone enjoy the game, to keep play moving on the course, to encourage safety, and to protect the course from unnecessary damages.

Examples of golf courtesies are:

1. When any player is preparing to hit, including players in your group as well as players within hearing distance of you, you are expected to remain silent and motionless. This also applies to spectators at golf tournaments.
2. If your group cannot keep up with the group playing in front of you and the group behind you is waiting to hit their shots, permit the group behind you to play through.
3. Help playing partners and opponents to find golf balls that are hit into hazards.
4. Keep your golf bag and cart off the teeing areas and greens.

5. Replace divots (pieces of turf) that are cut from the playing surface.
6. Repair ball marks on the green.
7. If you are required to hit a ball from a sand trap, rake the sand trap when you leave.
8. Be sure no one is in front of or behind you when you are swinging a golf club or hitting a ball.
9. A player should not hit until all players in front of him/her are safely out of his/her hitting distance.
10. A warning cry "fore" should be yelled if a ball is heading in the direction of other players. If you hear the word "fore," turn your back to the direction from which the yell was heard and cover your head with your hands and arms.

THE GAME OF GOLF

COURSES

Golf courses are composed of 9 or 18 holes and each course is different in appearance, length, terrain, and difficulty. A course has unique characteristics which reflect the design of different golf course architects. Just as an artist paints different pictures, an architect designs each hole with its own personality. The holes vary in the type of hazards or obstacles (water, sand, and trees), the length of the hole, the size of the green, and the contour of the playing surface. The courses may vary from flat to extremely rolling terrain. Some courses have very few trees and bushes while others are "cut out" of a forest of trees.

The fact that each hole on each golf course is different and each golf course has its own unique characteristics makes golf such a challenging sport. Diagram 3 is a drawing of a golf hole, with the respective parts of that hole identified.

SCORING

The objective in golf is to progress from the teeing area to the green and into the hole in the fewest number of strokes. The total number of strokes taken on the hole is recorded as a score for that hole. At the end

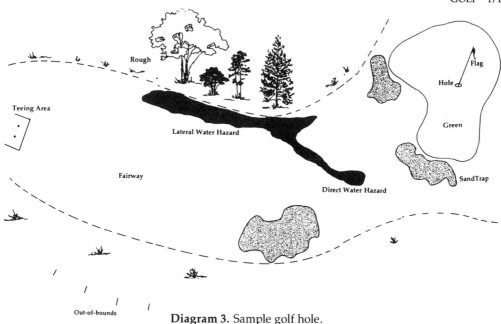

Diagram 3. Sample golf hole.

of the 9 or 18 holes, the scores for each hole are added for a total score for the round.

To make scoring easier a score card is provided at golf courses. A sample score card is illustrated in Diagram 4. Note the term *par* on the score card. Each hole has a designated par which is the established stroke standard for that hole. Par is determined by the length, the design, and the difficulty of a hole. Regardless of the length or difficulty of a hole, two strokes are allocated for putting. Generally, an 18 hole course is designed to have four par 3 holes, ten par 4 holes, and four par 5 holes.

Referring to the score card, par on the first 9 holes (called the front side) is 36 and par on the last 9 holes (called the back side) is also 36. Par for the entire course is 72.

The term *handicap* on the score care is merely a numerical rating of the respective 18 holes on the golf course. The handicap hole rated number 1 is considered to be the most difficult of the 18 holes on the golf course. In turn, the handicap hole number 18 is considered the easiest hole on the course. This rating is useful when players of unequal ability are competing against each other, utilizing some form of a handicapping system.

RULES

To give order and direction to the game of golf, rules were established. As in other sports, situations arise during play which may or may not invoke penalties. The rules

Yardage	510	326	137	365	342	160	490	362	382	3074	325	380	485	130	365	290	500	151	351	2975	6049
Handicap	1	13	17	7	11	15	3	9	5		12	6	4	18	8	14	2	16	10		
Par	5	4	3	4	4	3	5	4	4	36	4	4	5	3	4	4	5	3	4	36	72
Hole	1	2	3	4	5	6	7	8	9	Front	10	11	12	13	14	15	16	17	18	Back	Total

Diagram 4. Sample score card.

of golf are established by the United States Golf Association (USGA), the ruling body of golf in the United States. The rules govern situations on golf courses which are direct results of the actions of a player in attempting to hit the ball, end results of hitting the ball, or the conditions of the course over which the player has no control.

An understanding and knowledge of the rules help the players to make accurate decisions in situations which require an interpretation of the rules during the golf round. The most stringent penalty is disqualification and may occur in certain situations in competition. Most rule violations result in 1 or 2 penalty strokes (in stroke play competition) or loss of hole (in match play competition).

The rules of golf are intended to govern tournament competition. It is imperative that all players competing in a respective tournament play by the same rules. Tournament directors, club professionals, and tournament committees may make exceptions to the rules of golf because of playing conditions and/or the ability levels of the competitors.

Basic Rules That All Golfers Should Know

1. When starting a hole, you are permitted to place the ball on a tee (a wooden or plastic peg designed to hold the ball off the ground) within an imaginary rectangle formed between the two tee markers and a two club-length distance behind the markers. Your feet may be placed outside the rectangle as long as your ball is within the imaginary boundaries of the rectangle area. The penalty for hitting your ball from outside the designated area is as follows: In stroke play, you must count the stroke hit from outside the designated area and put another ball in play, hitting your second shot. In match play, your opponent has the option of requiring you to play from your first tee shot or hit a second ball from the tee.

2. When a ball comes to rest out of bounds (boundaries are marked with white stakes or boundary fences), the penalty, in both stroke and match play, is loss of distance and one stoke.

3. A ball is declared lost when it comes to rest within the boundaries of the course and outside a hazard and is not found within a five-minute time limit.

4. When you hit a ball into a direct water hazard (water directly between you and the target, marked with yellow stakes), there are three options: (1) you may play the ball where it lies in the hazard without penalty, (2) you may drop the ball on a line anywhere back from the point where the ball crossed the margin of the hazard, keeping that spot between you and the hole with a one stroke penalty, or (3) you may go back and drop a ball at the point where the last ball was played with a one stroke penalty.

5. If you hit your ball into a lateral water hazard (marked with red stakes), there are four options: (1) you may play the ball from the hazard without penalty, (2) you may drop a ball two club lengths from the point where the ball crossed the margin of the hazard, penalty one stroke, (3) you may drop a ball within two club lengths on the opposite side of the hazard no closer to the hole than the point where the original ball last crossed the margin of the hazard, penalty one stroke, or (4) you may drop a ball as near as possible at the spot from which the last stroke from outside the hazard was played, penalty loss of distance and one stroke.

6. You may move your ball, without penalty, from man-made obstructions such as permanent benches, drinking fountains, and buildings on the course property. You are entitled to a free drop within one club length from your nearest spot of relief. Moveable obstructions such as ropes, hoses, and rakes may be moved without penalty.

7. You are entitled to a free drop within one club length from your nearest spot of relief if your ball comes to rest in ground under repair, casual water, a wrong putting green, or if it is embedded in its own pitch mark in your fairway.

8. If your ball comes to rest in a sand bunker, you are not permitted to touch the sand with your club until your

downswing through the ball. Penalty: in stroke play, two strokes; in match play, loss of hole.

9. If you putt your ball from the putting surface and it hits another player's ball that is also on the putting surface, you are assessed a two stroke penalty in stroke play and in match play, you have lost that hole.

Except for the highest level of competitive tournaments, there are no officials in golf. Players are expected to enforce the rules on themselves and, when they are in doubt, they check with their opponents. Therefore, it is important to learn the rules because they can assist you as well as penalize you.

EQUIPMENT

A set of golf clubs is composed of both "woods" and iron clubs. The term "woods" has been used for many years because the clubs that were designed to hit the ball the farthest had wooden club heads. The technology in club making has developed metal club heads which may have some advantages over the traditional wooden club heads. Therefore, the term "woods" has been expanded to the contradictory term, "metal woods." It is not uncommon to see players using a "mix" of metal woods and wood clubs as a part of their set of clubs. The maximum number of clubs which may be carried by a player is 14. However, this does not prevent a player from carrying fewer than 14 clubs.

The advanced or intermediate player may have a complete set of 14 clubs. The beginner may initially have a "starter" set which may have five clubs, including one metal wood (or wooden club), 5, 7, and 9 irons, and a putter. Once the beginning player feels comfortable using these clubs, additional clubs can be added to the set or a complete set may be purchased.

SELECTION OF EQUIPMENT

Two considerations in selecting golf clubs are the fit and the cost. The first and most important consideration is selecting a club which is appropriate for the player. Clubs may be purchased in different lengths and weights. The appropriate club for an individual depends on height, strength, and hand size. Using a club which is too heavy or light or too long or short is detrimental to developing good technique. Club fitting charts, available in most golf shops, help an individual select the appropriate length, weight, and grip size in golf clubs. Most golf professionals and teachers can lend assistance in fitting clubs, and their assistance is advised.

The second consideration in selecting clubs is cost. New clubs may be very expensive but the money invested may be well worth it. A set of clubs can last for many years. Used clubs may be purchased for much less and often are equally good for an individual to use. Used clubs may be purchased individually or as a complete set.

BALLS

If you watch television commercials regarding golf balls, it appears that every manufacturer of golf balls makes the best ball for you. The selling of golf balls is a very competitive business because golf balls are the primary "dispensable" item in the game of golf. If you play golf, you will lose golf balls, you will cut or damage the cover to the point where the ball is virtually unplayable, and you will want to try different kinds of golf balls. In the golf ball market today, the differences in the performance of the numerous golf balls can only be noticed by the elite amateur and professional golfers. As with golf clubs, your golf professional and teachers can be most helpful in selecting golf balls to suit your game.

SPECIAL TIPS FOR INSTRUCTION

- Golf does not have to be taught at golf courses. The basic fundamentals of the golf swing and the necessary knowledge about the game can be taught within most school facilities. A carpeted room or hallway provides an excellent facility to teach the fundamentals of putting. A conventional classroom is perfect for teaching the basic rules of the game and the courtesies critical to the courses and other players. A gymnasium is ideal for teaching the fundamentals of the swing. Special golf balls have been designed to be used indoors. Hitting mats are available from golf stores which can be used indoors as well as outdoors. These mats look like a piece of astroturf (plastic grass).

- If the school property has an outdoor space the size of a football or soccer field, that is sufficient space to teach the fundamentals of the full swing and the short shot, and to play some interesting golf "lead-up" games. The only adaptation necessary to hit golf balls within a limited space is the type of golf ball used. Naturally, the regulation golf ball could not be used in this limited space. Golf manufacturers have developed practice balls that can be used indoors and outdoors without any danger of damaging personal property. The balls are made of plastic, foam, and other light weight synthetic materials. Local golf professionals and/or golf retailers are familiar with these types of golf balls.

- Teaching competency is the most critical variable in determining the activities included in a program. An option to consider when including golf in the physical education program is to approach a local professional golf association (PGA) teaching professional to assist with teaching some of the more complex segments of an instructional unit.

- Most teachers, regardless of subject being taught, are more effective when their class size is small. It may take some innovative scheduling or team teaching to keep class sizes small enough to teach golf effectively.

- The basic skills and knowledges of golf can be taught with one golf club, a putter, some tees, and practice golf balls for each student in a class. "Clubs for Kids" programs are in existence in many cities throughout the country. This program is a part of the PGA's effort to assist Junior Golf. Basically, the program consists of golfers in a community donating used clubs to the coordinator (a local PGA teaching professional) of the program, who, in turn, cuts down the length of the shaft to fit smaller players and installs a new grip on each club. These clubs are available, free of charge, for instructional programs to help develop young players. In addition, used golf clubs are frequently available at golf pro shops (located at most golf courses) and at reasonable prices. "Experienced" (used) golf balls are also readily available in most communities. Retrieving lost golf balls from lakes and wooded areas has developed into a rather lucrative business for some people. These balls are available at discount prices.

- Drills and lead-up games are imperative to keep students interested in the game of golf. It is easy to become discouraged when trying to learn the skills of golf. When students experience only limited success in a sport skill they get "bored" easily. Contests, target games, and other innovative approaches add to the basic instructional process in learning the full swing, the short shot, and putting.

- One of the most confusing elements in teaching the skills of golf is determining what teaching aids can assist students and what teaching aids are merely "gimmicks" attempting to "rip-off" the golf consumer. The number and variety of teaching aids for golf is unbelievable. There are aids to assist with teaching the proper grip, the proper alignment, proper swing plan, proper club "release" motion, proper shoulder and arm movements, proper leg movements, proper head position, proper wrist position, and any other "proper" movement in the skills of golf. Some of the instructional aids are terrific and are used by many of the touring professional players. The problem facing the physical education teacher is which teaching aids are the most effective for the money spent. Some aids are merely concepts and can be reproduced with little or no expenditure. Most Professional Golf Association teaching professionals are familiar with the teaching aids and can provide their expertise in selecting those aids that can contribute most to instructional programs.

- Another difficult task for the teacher is to know the equipment. Golf equipment is like the automobile industry. There are about as many "makes" and "models" of golf clubs as there are automobiles. For example, one golf club manufacturer produces more than 50 models of putters. The technology of golf clubs and golf balls has made it virtually impossible for even the full time PGA teaching professional to know the advantages of these different technologies. How can the teacher of physical education be expected to know the benefits of the different golf clubs and balls? This is an area where the golf professional can contribute as a resource person to the school's golf instructional unit.

• Patience may be the most important virtue when teaching and learning the skills of golf. It has been said, if you don't want to be humbled, then don't play the game of golf. It is important for golf instructors to inform students of the difficulty of learning the skills of this game.

• Good teachers of any sport must understand the importance of "time on task" and the way students learn sport skills. Students can watch, study, and listen but if they are to learn the skills of swinging a golf club, they must swing the golf club over and over. Practice is the most important variable to improving sport skill performance. However, it is important that practice time involves using the proper techniques.

TERMINOLOGY

Address (set up). Preparation to swing the club by taking a stance and placing the club behind the ball.

Apron. Short grass surrounding the green.

Birdie. One stroke less than par.

Bogie. One stroke more than par.

Casual Water. Water on the course not intended to be a hazard.

Divot. Turf removed from the ground while hitting.

Dogleg. Sharp bend or curve in the fairway.

Double Bogie. Two strokes more than par.

Eagle. Two strokes less than par.

Fairway. The short grass between the tee area and the green.

Fore. A warning to individuals in the direction of play that the ball is heading.

Green (putting surface). The very closely mowed area on each hole where the cup is located.

Handicap. A system of compensation based upon the player's past performance to enable players of different abilities to compete with each other. Also, a numerical rating of the respective golf holes on a golf course from most difficult to easiest.

Hazard. Encompasses several specific obstructions designed as challenges to the golfers. These include natural features such as sand and grass bunkers, permanent water (lakes, streams, ponds), trees, bushes, rocks, and grass areas that are not mowed (generally called "rough").

Honor. Order of teeing off (lowest score on preceding hole).

Match Play. Golf competition in which each hole is a separate contest. The winner of the match is the player who has won the most holes in the competition.

Out-of-Bounds. Area that is not part of the golf course.

Par. Standard score set for a hole.

Provisional Ball. A second ball hit when the first ball is thought to be lost or out-of-bounds.

Rough. The long grass parallel to the fairway.

Round. Completing play of 18 holes of golf.

Stroke Play. Golf competition in which the winner is determined by the total number of strokes for the round or rounds.

Tee. A peg (usually wooden) on which the ball may be placed on the teeing area.

Teeing Area. Area from which you begin each hole, usually a level surface with grass mowed short.

Unplayable Lie. A position of the ball from which it may be difficult to hit.

REFERENCES

Ewers, James R. *Golf.* Glenview, IL: Scott, Foresman and Company, 1989.

National Golf Foundation. *Golf Instructor's Guide.* North Palm Beach, FL: National Golf Foundation, 1980.

National Golf Foundation. *Twelve Golf Lessons.* North Palm Beach, FL: National Golf Foundation, 1980.

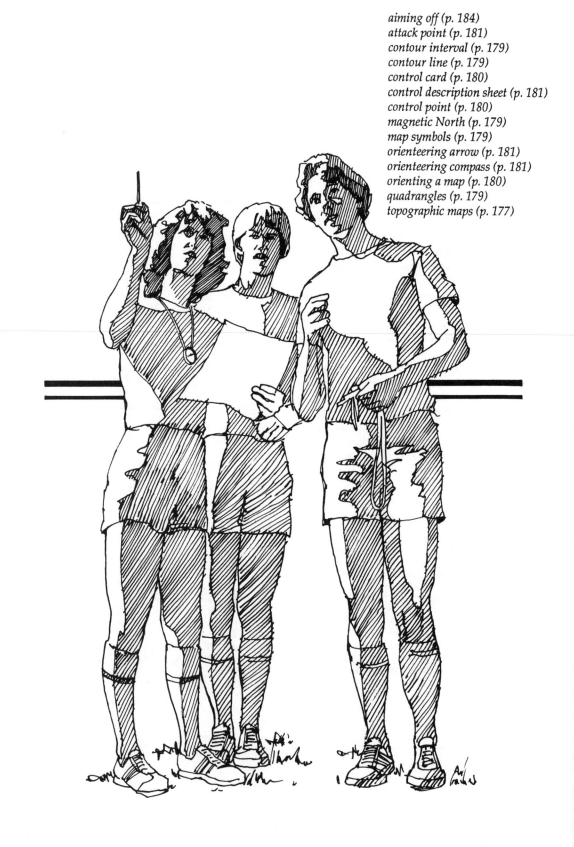

CHAPTER 13

Orienteering

DAVID J. HONCHALK
BERNARD SAMM, JR.
ARTHUR HUGGLESTONE
JOE HOWARD
Smith Environmental Education Center
Rockville, MD

INTRODUCTION

Orienteering offers the thrills and excitement of a track meet and a treasure hunt all rolled into one. Orienteering adds new purpose and interest to jogging. The jogger who takes up orienteering will find that he or she has substituted the highway fumes and noises for the forest sounds and smells and has replaced boredom with mental stimulation. The orienteerer must be mentally prepared to read a map, use a compass, and be physically able to run the course.

Orienteering is often called the thinking person's sport. The fastest runner going in the wrong direction cannot be a winner. Successful participants must solve a series of problems and make a number of choices before they can decide on the best course to take. Orienteering courses can be set up for novices, intermediate, and advanced competitors.

Orienteering probably began as a Swedish military exercise. A runner would be given a map with several destinations and a message to be delivered. Orienteering is considered a national sport in most Scandinavian countries and is a required sport for students. With the Scandinavian love of skiing, it is not surprising that orienteering began on skis almost as soon as it began on foot. Orienteering has increased in popularity and spread around the globe. Meets are now conducted on bicycles, in canoes, at night, on cross-country skis, and even underground. Orienteering may be a formal, sanctioned event, or it may be as informal as a family outing for the day with a map, compass, and picnic basket.

The first time runner will be content to complete the course with little regard for the time it takes. Later, as the runner becomes more skilled in using the compass, interpreting the map, and observing the geological features, more emphasis will be placed on the best route choice. With experience, speed and endurance will increase and confidence will be gained to tackle strange territory. The pleasure of going around a bend on an unfamiliar trail and discovering a landmark only seen on a map, or taking a cross-country shortcut and finding the trail just where expected is most satisfying. Conversely, it is all the more frustrating when the expected landmark does not appear. Initially, an uncomfortable feeling may be experienced. There are no road signs, no buildings, no buses, none of the aids unconsciously depended upon to aid with directions. However, a quick check of the map and compass can get the competitor anywhere.

EQUIPMENT

The best way to learn is by doing, but, before venturing afield, it would be wise to know how to use the equipment of orienteering. The best maps available are those specifically designed for orienteering. These maps cover a small area and are very detailed. Generally, they are topographic maps that have been enlarged and reworked by orienteering clubs. There are few of these maps at the present time and most of them cover park lands that have special features of particular interest to the orienteerer. Maps like these are only avail-

Match Column B with A.

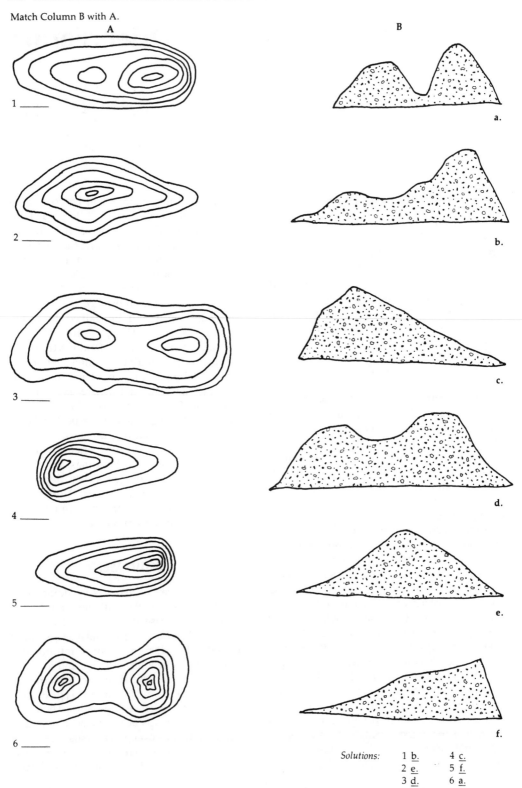

Diagram 1. Contour line exercise.

able where orienteering is a very active sport.

To contact local individuals who are active in the sport write to: Orienteering Services USA, Box 1604, Binghamton, NY 13904. They will forward free information about local orienteering groups. The U.S. Orienteering Federation, P.O. Box 1039, Ballwin, MO 63011, can send information about membership and local affiliations.

Most students, however, will have to be content with less detailed, but otherwise excellent topographical maps produced by the U.S. Geological Survey. These maps, called quadrangles or "quads," come in two sizes—15 minute maps and the more detailed 7½ minute maps. The 7½ minute quadrangle map covers an area bounded by 7½ minutes of longitude and 7½ minutes of latitude. The scale on this map is 1:24,000. This means that one inch on the map represents approximately one mile. Wilderness outfitters, sporting goods stores, or camping stores often sell these maps for local hiking areas.

If a quad cannot be located for a specific area, request a free topographical map index circular for that area's state, a free folder describing topographical maps, and a free topographical map symbol sheet from: National Cartographic Information Center, 507 National Center, Reston, VA 22092. When ordering the particular quadrangles, request a woodland copy. Mature forests are shown in green on these maps.

SYMBOLS

Once the quadrangle is received, study it and become familiar with the symbols. Buildings are shown in black; water is blue. If the map has been updated by aerial photography, all the recent changes are in a plum color. Contours of mountains and valleys are represented by brown lines. These lines indicate equal elevation which means that everything on that line is the same number of feet above sea level. The heavy brown lines have numbers written on them which makes it easier to determine the elevation for the other contour lines. The contour interval is the vertical distance between lines and may be anywhere from 10 to 80 feet depending upon the map being

used. The closer the lines, the steeper the slope; the farther apart, the flatter the land. If these swirling brown lines are closely examined, a pattern can be seen. The lines connect to form an irregular shape with one inside of another and another until the smallest shape is reached, representing the top of a mountain or hill. The contour line exercise should help test your ability to read symbols (see Diagram 1).

Study the maps you receive. Learn as much as possible about the area. Have fun planning different routes over the varied terrain. Even in a very familiar area, new things can be discovered.

SKILLS AND TECHNIQUES

In orienteering, use only the magnetic North as indicated on the lower margin of the map. If it differs from true or grid North, it will be seen as an arrow identified as "MN" off to either side of the true or grid North line which is identified by a star.

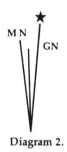

Diagram 2.

Find the magnetic arrow in the lower margin of the map and draw arrows that are parallel to the magnetic North arrow, approximately one inch apart and extending through the area of travel.

If the school or local club furnishes a photocopied section of a quadrangle, the parallel magnetic North arrows will probably extend the length of the map. If not, it is easy to put them there.

If a quadrangle is acquired that covers a nearby area, some informal orienteering may be attempted. Have a friend come along; tell a third person the starting point, destination, and the latest time expected to return. Be sure to check back with that person upon return.

Below is a list of equipment that you should have:

1. Map—most recent edition possible. There might be new buildings, roads, and even ponds, but the mountains and valleys won't change.
2. Compass—use a cord to tie it around the wrist or neck. Don't lose it or use it near iron or steel objects.
3. Wristwatch—make sure this is on the opposite hand from the one that will hold the compass.
4. Plastic whistle—use the whistle to signal for help in case there is an injury. Plastic is nonmagnetic and will not affect a compass.
5. Appropriate clothing—wear old clothes that will protect the orienteerer from thorns, poison ivy, or whatever the terrain and time of year have to offer. Shoes should be comfortable, support the feet, and give adequate traction when needed.

When at the starting point, mark it on the map as the center of a six mm triangle or with the letter "S." The first leg of the route should lead to an easily identified physical feature. The end of each leg should be identified on the map by a six mm circle. Use a red pen to mark the circles and to draw a single line connecting them. Fold the map so that it is just large enough for the landscape to be seen surrounding the direction of travel.

The next step, orienting the map, is an important one and will have to be repeated often. Turn the map around until the features on the map are in the same relative position as those on the land. If there is a hill to the left, then the hill should be to the left of the position on the map. If there are several recognizable features in sight, this can be easily done; otherwise use the compass. To orient the map using a compass, simply turn the map around until the magnetic North arrows on the map are pointing in the same direction as the magnetic needle on the compass. Directions on the map and on the ground will now match.

If heading northward, read the printing on the map. However, if the direction of travel is southward, the printing will be upside down. Every effort should be made to utilize the map for finding the control points. Reading the map means interpreting the contour lines and symbols that represent both natural and man-made structures such as hills and valleys, streams and lakes, churches and schools. The map should be held in front of the competitor. Turn the map around so that the starting point is closest and the first destination is farthest away. Turn around until the map is oriented. The competitor runner is now facing the direction of travel. Pick out features along the red line that mark the route from the starting position to the first destination. Look up and pick out a distant landmark that was seen on the map. As the already identified features are passed, put a thumb on the spot where currently standing with the thumbnail pointing toward the destination. Track of progress can always be kept with this procedure and exact location will be clear. This technique works well as long as the orienteerer is careful with the thumb and orientation of the map. When the thumb marks the point where the first circle was drawn, the first destination should have been attained.

COMPETITION

If participating in an orienteering meet, a control point would be at the center of the circle. The control point refers to a specific place and is not indicated by a dot. On land the control is indicated by a flag, a three-dimensional triangle, a painted stake, or a plastic gallon milk jug and is almost always red and white. The control is easily visible and is marked with a number or letter that corresponds to the one on the map for that specific location. In an orienteering meet, the competitor must prove arrival at each control point. Each competitor has a control card (see Diagram 3) often carried in a plastic envelope or bag along with the map. The card will be the document that proves how long it took to run the course and that each of the control points were located. The proof may be that each block on the card is marked with a different colored pen, a special punch that was tied to the control, or different code words that are written on the control.

Name		Course		No.	
		School or Club			
(Fold and tear along line)					
Name		Course		No.	
		School or Club			
Date		Compass			
		Hours	Min.		Sec.
Finish					
Start					
Time					
Penalty					
Place					
1	A	2	B	3	C	4	D	5	E
6	F	7	G	8	H	9	I	10	J
11	K	12	L	13	M	14	N	15	0

Diagram 3. Control card.

Each competitor may also be furnished with a control description sheet. This is a list of clues or short description sheet that will help to recognize the control point. If the map that is used is photocopied, the control description sheet is often put on the back. Table 1 is an example of a control description sheet (also see Diagram 4 for map).

When traveling from one control point to another, choose the fastest route. Often the most direct route will not be the fastest. If there is a hill in front of the next control point, the fastest route may be around instead of directly over the top. A good trail may be twice as fast as a rock strewn meadow, three times as fast as an open forest, and five times as fast as thick brush.

If there is no landmark close to a control point, use an orienteering compass to navigate from the nearest easily found landmark called an attack point. Draw a red line from the attack point to the control point. Put the compass on the map with the long side over the red line that extends from the attack point to the control point (see Diagram 5). Make sure that the direction of travel arrow is pointing in the direction parallel with the intended course. Hold the compass firmly to the map so that it will not slip as the compass housing is turned. Turn the compass housing around until the orienting arrow is parallel and points in the same direction as the North magnetic arrows on the map. Remove the compass from the map. Hold the compass level and in front with the direction of travel arrow pointing straight ahead. Turn around until the red or pointing end of the magnetic needle and the orienting arrow are pointing in the same direction. The direction of travel arrow is now pointing to the control point. (The most common mistake made by the beginner is to follow the magnetic nee-

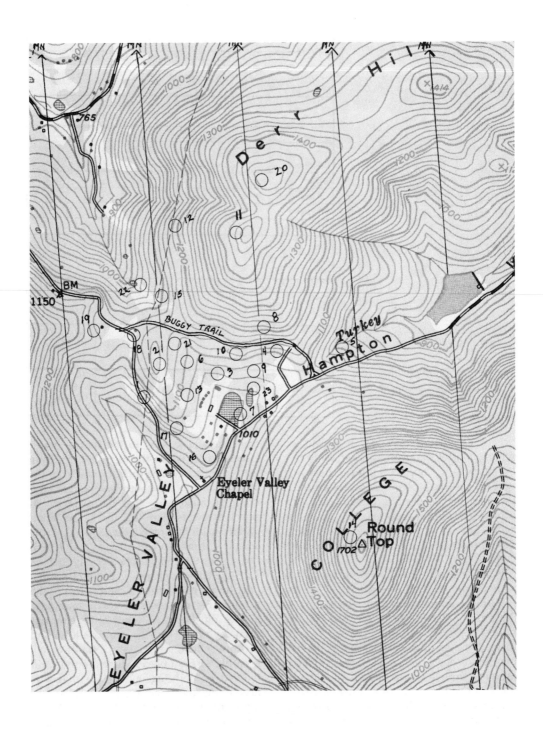

Diagram 4.

dle. Do not follow this needle unless you want to go north.)

Assuming that the control is not in sight, pick a distant object that is in line with the direction of travel and head out. If that object drops out of sight, use the compass again. Hold it level and in front, with the direction of travel arrow pointing straight ahead. Remember to turn around until the magnetic needle and the orienting arrow point in the same direction. Use the direction of travel arrow to pick out a precise spot in the distance and head out again. In a thick forest this process will have to be repeated often.

As long as the object or spot can be seen, the course is correct. If sight of the object is lost, and you keep on going without checking the compass, accuracy and time may be lost. A few extra seconds spent being careful with the map and compass work can save minutes of running and perhaps be

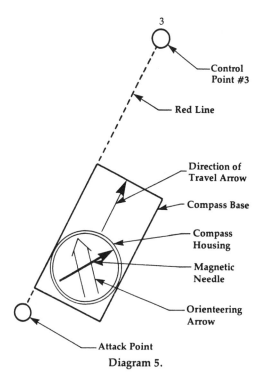

Diagram 5.

Table I. Summit Lake Orienteering Course

Control No.	Description
1	Intersection of road and cable right of way
2	Top of hill between path and road
3	Open pasture area/one tree
4	House ruins near buggy trail
5	Heavy woods/stream bed
6	Woods near game field
7	High ground between ponds
8	Rocky area north of buggy trail
9	Low, dense ground behind Summit Lake
10	Mid-point of buggy trail (down-hill side)
11	Hill top
12	Along power lines
13	White pines/behind girls' cabins
14	Long walk/mountain top
15	Look for the gate across cable right of way—go east
16	Behind boys' cabins/hill side
17	Maple tree
18	White cinder block shed
19	Stone foundation/west of road
20	Top of Derr Hill
21	Buggy trail/pasture edge
22	Near small pond/cabin
23	Small pond near Summit Lake

Note: There will be a penalty for being late. If you become completely lost and wish to drop out of the meet, head south to Hampton Valley Road. Road will be checked one hour after meet is over. Emergency phone number (301) 271-9810.

the difference between first and second place.

If you feel that the control point has been passed, stay on course. Check the map to see if there are any features that would indicate that the control point has indeed been passed. If there are none, or one is found that is not good enough to use as a new attack point, it is time to retrace the route. Use the compass to do this. Do not move the compass housing. Hold the compass in front, with the direction of travel arrow pointing straight ahead. Physically turn around until the red end of the magnetic needle and the orienting arrow are pointing in opposite direction. The direction of travel arrow is now pointing to the return route.

If a control point is located along a road, a cliff, a stream, or a trail, and the approach is from a position that is at right angles or broadside to that feature, try a technique called "aiming off." Instead of heading directly to the control point, aim enough to one side so that when the feature is reached, the other side should be turned to find the control.

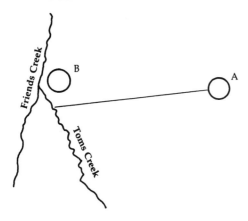

Diagram 6.

In Diagram 6, the participant at A decided to aim off to the left. When the stream is reached the orienteerer will know to turn to the right and continue until reaching the fork in the stream. If control point B is not in sight, the fork in the stream can be used as an attack point. If the orienteerer in Diagram 6 had not decided to aim off, a slight error in navigation could result in missing control point B. When the stream is reached, the orienteerer will not know whether to turn back or follow the stream to the left or right. Aim off and be sure.

The following exercises should help improve skill with the compass.

1. Find and face the following directions:
   a. 35°   c. 165°   e. 270°
   b. 90°   d. 180°   f. 345°
2. Place a penny or other small object by the feet.
   a. Take a bearing of 60°, walk 10 steps.
   b. Add 120°, walk 10 steps.
   c. Add 120°, walk 10 steps.
   d. Look down at the feet. They should be standing on top of the penny.
   e. Repeat the exercise with 20 steps.
   f. Repeat the exercise using the following three bearings at 20 paces:
       80°, 200°, 320°.
   g. Try f at 30 paces.

There are many kinds of orienteering meets and lots of tips and tricks to learn. Read as much as possible but, most important, get out and do it.

TERMINOLOGY

Aiming off. A technique that may be used when the target is located on a feature such as a river or ridge which is at right angles to the direction of travel. The orienteerer will aim off to one side of the target and be certain which way to turn when he/she reaches the feature.

Attack Point. An easy-to-find feature from which the orienteerer will carefully navigate.

Bearing. A direction of travel measured from North.

Contour Line. A line on a map representing an imaginary line on the ground that connects areas of equal elevation.

Control. An easily visible marker that can be seen from any angle and has a means of proving the visit.

Control Point. A specific location identified on the map by a 6 mm circle and a letter or a number; on the land it is identified by a control; on the control description sheet it is identified by a description of the feature.

Elevation. The height (vertical distance) above sea level.

Feature. A land form or structure that is identifiable on the map.

Legend. An illustrated description of symbols used on a map. It is most often located on the lower margin of the map.

Minute. A geographical unit of measure equal to 1/60th of a degree.

North Grid. The vertical grid used as a zero reference.

North Magnetic. The particular direction indicated by the needle of the compass.

North True. The direction of the North geographical pole.

Quadrangle. A topographic map produced by the U.S. Geological Survey.

Ravine. A depression larger than a gully and smaller than a canyon.

Topographic Map. A map that shows physical features in minute detail.

REFERENCES

Andresen, Steve. *The Orienteering Book.* Mountain View, CA: Andresen World, 1980.

Geary, Don. *Step in the Right Direction: a Basic Map and Compass Book.* Harrisburg, PA: Stackpole Books, 1980.

CHAPTER 14

Racquetball/ Handball

JOHN P. SMYTH
The Citadel
Charleston, SC

INTRODUCTION

Racquetball and handball are court games that can be learned with relative ease. As with other sports, performance can be progressively improved and enjoyed with planned practice and play.

Early forms of handball have been historically traced to the *thermae* of ancient Rome. The present American game can be traced back to the mid-1800s. Handball can be played on courts of one, three, and four walls by two, three, or four players. It requires only the playing surface, ball, and protective gloves. Protective glasses are required in youth competition and are strongly recommended for the safety of players of all ages. The goal of the game is for the players to alternately strike the ball with the hand causing it to strike the front wall and then bounce twice on the floor before the opponent can successfully return it to the front wall. The game is played to 21 points, with only the serving side or player eligible to score. Handball play is governed by the unified rules adopted by the AAU, YMCA, USHA, and the Jewish Welfare Board.

Racquetball is played on the same court as handball with essentially the same rules. The use of a paddle to replace the hand can be traced to Earl Riskey at the University of Michigan in the 1920s. Joe Sobek brought the strung racquet into the game nearly 20 years later. The International Racquetball Association and the United States Racquetball Association have promoted the sport and regulated competition since the early 1970s. Racquetball involves the same strategies and fitness requirements as handball, but the use of the backhand replaced the use of the nondominant hand. The backhand, the larger striking area, and the absence of direct contact between the ball and the hand are differences that might lead novice players to choose racquetball over handball.

The added weight and velocity of the racquet add a potential safety hazard to the game, however, and therefore great caution is required when playing a ball near a partner or opponent.

Handball and racquetball are good health fitness activities. The simple rules, short game duration, and enjoyable nature of the activities have made them one of the fastest growing American sports, with the promise of even greater popularity in the future.

Four-wall court facilities are rapidly expanding in number, but the building rate has not matched the growth in popularity. The use of one- and three-wall courts found in many parks and gyms has helped to provide modified opportunities to play handball and racquetball. The game can be fun for any age and any skill level. As with most games, the greatest enjoyment comes from participation with and against players of nearly equal ability.

Racquetball in the United States reached a market of eight and one-half million players in 1990. That year it was played by males at a 3:1 ratio to females and was more popular in the South and West than in the East and Central regions by a 2:1 ratio. Two-thirds of the players were between the ages of 17 and 35. Racquetball clubs enjoy extreme popularity as free standing enterprises and are even more utilized when paired with fitness centers involving aerobics, weight-training, and swimming.

SKILLS AND TECHNIQUES

BODY POSITION

The body position fundamentals of handball and racquetball follow the general rules for most racquet sports. The ready position is a balanced position with the feet spread shoulder width apart, the knees comfortably bent, the back straight, and the head held erect. When strokes are executed to the side of the body, the body should be turned perpendicular to the front wall, permitting leverage of the body to assist the primary movement of the striking arm and hand. Underhand and overhand strokes can be executed while facing the front wall by using the basic throwing positions with the legs functioning in opposition to the striking action.

HAND POSITION

The gloved hand is the striking implement in handball; therefore, it is important to cup the hand to contact the ball with the palm of the hand and permit it to roll off the closed fingers.

The grip in racquetball is the conventional handshake grip. The racquet is held with its face perpendicular to the floor with the grip extended toward the body. The dominant hand "shakes hands" with the grip. It is important to keep the palm of the hand parallel with the face of the racquet, by keeping the "V" formed by the thumb and index finger slightly to the left of the middle position, as the player looks down at the grip. It is equally important to lay the racquet grip across the palm diagonally from the heel of the palm to the base of the index finger, permitting the racquet to become an extension of the arm, as opposed to a segment that joins the arm at a right angle. The index finger should act as a "trigger finger" on the grip. Beginning players have difficulty in adjusting the grip during play; therefore, a slightly weaker forehand grip, involving the counterclockwise rotation of the right hand should be used to assume a position that is more suitable for the backhand. This modified grip is called the continental grip. It is employed by players who cannot or prefer not to switch grips by rotating the hand over the top of the grip to put the wrist behind the backhand stroke.

STRIKING POSITION

The ready position is the best position to assume in anticipating the shot of an opponent; it facilitates reactive movement in any direction with the least amount of wasted motion. The often overlooked ability of body position and anticipation is in use between the ready position and the striking position. The player must anticipate the speed, direction, and height of the ball to move to the most advantageous position.

Much of playing the bounce is learned through court experience; however, there are some fundamental considerations. Optimal court position is just behind the short service line, because of its potential for court coverage. A high bouncing or flying ball is difficult to strike on low trajectory without the return resulting in a high bounce. Also, forehand shots are generally easier for beginners to execute. Ideally then, the beginning player should seek to play the ball near center court from a low position and when possible with the forehand.

Since this position is not always possible the player must adjust court position while the opponent's shot is heading toward the front wall or as it rebounds. The feet should be slid or shuffled, rather than using a stride in which the legs are crossed. The last slide step should take the body into a position perpendicular to the front wall or the angle of the oncoming ball.

The arm and hand must be taken back in the back swing position in anticipation of the stroke. The knees permit adjustments in height corresponding to the height of the bounce. The high back swing arm position is assumed before the ball bounces on the floor. The hand and wrist are relaxed but cocked in a high back swing position to permit the hand or racquet to hit through the ball as the body weight is transferred from the back foot to the front. The elbow should be bent and held slightly away from the body in the back swing. The forward swing should combine hip and shoulder rotation with the weight shift and arm swing. The ball should be contacted at approximately three-fourths of an arm's length and the point of contact should be at a point even with the lead foot. The follow-through should be level with the swing and in the direction of the intended line of flight.

BASIC STROKES

Most of the basic strokes can be hit from the forehand, overhead, underhand, and, in racquetball, backhand positions. The game situation will dictate which shot is employed. The player's court position, the court position of the opponent, the speed of the ball, the court placement of the ball, the height of the ball, and a working knowledge of the opponent's strengths and weaknesses help determine proper shot selection.

THE SERVE

The ball is put into play by a serve. The server stands within the serving zone, drops the ball, and strikes it on the first bounce so that it contacts the front wall first and rebounds past the short service line, either before or after touching one of the side walls. The serve may be played from any of the hitting positions, but because of the power and accuracy, the forehand in racquetball and the dominant hand in handball are most frequently used.

The Drive or Power Serve

The drive serve is the most powerful of all serves. The serve is struck from a low bounce and contacted well below the knees. The path of the serve forms a "V." The rebound from the front wall carries the ball toward the backhand corner at a speed great enough so it will get to the corner but not sufficient for it to rebound from the back wall. Another desirable target is the side wall on the backhand or nondominant hand side just beyond the short service line; when this spot is hit near the floor line, the result is a short low bounce. The purpose of the shot is to take the receiver out of offensive position and permit a minimum amount of time to react to the placement. Speed is important, but speed without placement is often counterproductive, as the ball will rebound off the back wall in

good position for a high percentage offensive return by the receiver.

The server should select a spot on the front wall as a target for optimal trajectory and angle. The height of the target should be three feet or less, depending on the speed of the serve. The target is lowered as the server learns to generate more speed. The serving spot should be a stationary point in the service zone, to add consistency to the required angle to the deep corner. The server can mark a target area on the floor with tape, for practice and self-evaluation. The size and shape of the target will vary with ability level; for beginners a rectangular target measuring 3 feet by 10 feet should represent a suitable challenge. When the target area is hit at a 70% level of accuracy, the server can reduce the target area or increase the speed. The beginner should practice bouncing the ball to provide proper placement. If difficulty is encountered in making contact, the student should practice throwing the ball at a target, using an underhand motion. The throwing drill will emphasize proper weight shift from the back to front foot, and emphasize the need for hip and shoulder rotation.

The follow-through is a good indication of the direction of force, and the length of the follow-through indicates the extent of force at contact. The server should visualize a full follow-through extended toward the

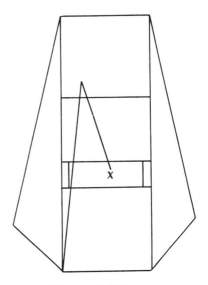

Diagram 1. Drive serve.

line of flight. Some players find that a step into the serving action aids in transfer of weight and increased momentum for the hand and arm.

The Cross-court Serve

The server should stand two feet away from the center of the court, on the same side as the target corner. From this off-center position, the server can strike the ball against the front wall at a point 3 or 4 feet away from the far side wall, causing the ball to carom at a sharp angle against the side wall and bounce deep into the diagonally opposite corner. The ball should strike the front wall about 3 to 5 feet above the floor with sufficient force to carry it near the back corner after one bounce. It should be noted that each additional wall the ball touches affects the spin and reduces the speed of the ball.

Accuracy is important in the cross-court serve to avoid a middle court set-up for the receiver. If the receiver errs by striking the side wall *first*, then the serve is lost. If the serve strikes three walls before striking the floor, the server has committed a fault and must make a second serve. A second fault causes the server to lose the serve, which is called side-out. The beginner can mark the front wall with an "X" to practice accurately placing the ball in the back corner, permitting the receiver the lowest percentage shot. The same serve can be hit high off the front

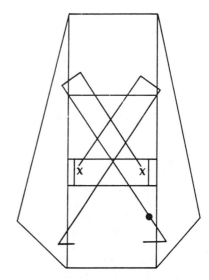

Diagram 3. Z serve from right or left side.

wall if it is struck with the proper amount of force to cause a high bounce in mid-court and then permitting it to die in the corner.

The "Z" Serve

The "Z" serve is a cross-court serve delivered at a sharper angle than usual, causing it to strike the floor and then the side wall deep in the corner. The impact on the third wall slows the speed of the ball and imparts a reverse spin, causing the ball to rebound nearly parallel with the back wall. The unusual spin causes beginning players some difficulty, but when the "Z" serve is used against skilled opponents it is imperative to cause the ball to strike the third wall near the back wall to prevent an easy return. The serve will bounce parallel to the back wall if it is struck hard and if it strikes the front wall near the corner. This serve needs more than the usual amount of practice to perfect. The server should be cautioned not to move too near the side wall to achieve the "Z" path of flight, because of the amount of court space which cannot be covered to prepare for the return shot.

The Lob Serve

The lob serve may be struck underhand or overhand. The height of the bounce should accommodate the striking position, that is, a shoulder high bounce for the overhand and a bounce below the waist for the

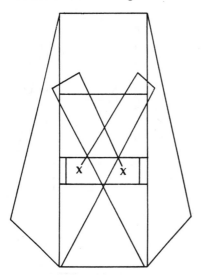

Diagram 2. Cross-court serve from right or left side.

underhand stroke. Because of the high bounce and the greater difficulty in achieving the desirable arc with the overhand, the underhand is more appropriate for the beginning player. The underhand serve should be struck with moderate speed to a point approximately three-fourths of the way up the front wall. The ball should arc near the ceiling and bounce near the side wall with the arc of the bounce ending near the back wall. If the ball brushes the side wall slightly the ball will tend to die in the back corner. The lob serve is easier to keep near the side wall if the server assumes a position near the wall and strikes the ball parallel to the side wall, but this approach leaves much of the court unprotected for the return shot. It is better if the serve can be struck from the off-center position, but the server must be careful not to select an angle so sharp as to cause the ball to strike the side wall early and rebound into center court for an easy return.

The lob serve can be used to vary the game pace and make a skilled opponent play a high bouncing ball or a corner dig shot. The beginner should practice the lob with a 3 foot by 6 foot target box in both back corners. The serve is executed with the same mechanics as the underhand throw. The overhand serve is not used in racquetball.

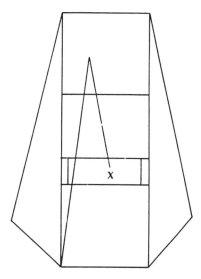

Diagram 5. Change-of-pace serve.

The Change-of-pace Serve

The change-of-pace serve is executed with mechanics similar to the lob serve. The path of the serve should follow that of the drive serve. The speed of the serve determines how high on the front wall the serve should hit, but the speed and point of aim should always be coordinated to permit the trajectory of the bounce to end in the corner. When the change-of-pace serve is executed properly the receiver does not know if it will carry to the back wall or fall just short of the wall. Experienced players refer to this strategic serve as a *half speed* or *garbage* serve, but these terms should not be negatively interpreted. The strategy, timing, and placement of a change-of-pace serve cause it to be frequently used at all skill levels. The primary advantage of this serve for the beginning player is that it emphasizes accurate placement rather than speed. The deemphasis of speed is particularly important, since beginning players tend to overhit shots rather than execute finesse shots.

Serving Fundamentals Review

Speed is limited by the ability of the player to use it accurately. It is the frequent mistake of beginners to overhit all strokes, including the serve.

Placement is determined by the strengths and weaknesses of both players. Most play-

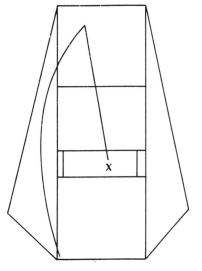

Diagram 4. Lob serve from off-center position.

ers are weaker on the backhand or non-dominant hand side. The opportunity to hit the ball low and end the rally diminishes in proportion to the distance from the front wall and the increased height of the bounce. The prime target of the serve is in the backhand corner close to the side wall. It is generally undesirable to hit the ball so hard that it bounces against the back wall and rebounds into mid-court. It is also undesirable to permit a serve to contact the side wall unless this contact is early and causes the ball to rebound toward the back diagonal corner, or is late enough to cause the ball to take only a very small bounce in the back court.

The serve must be struck on the first bounce. The stroke should be a total body activity much like throwing. If the serve strikes the floor, ceiling, or side wall first, it is a side-out. If a serve touches three walls in the air, carries to the back wall in the air, or fails to carry beyond the short service line, it is a fault. Two consecutive faults constitute a side-out.

GAME SHOTS

Many of the strokes made during a rally are executed with the same mechanics and placement as the serve. The greater difficulty of executing the service-type stroke during play lies in anticipating the speed and direction of the return. Beginning players have difficulty in visualizing the rebound from the side walls, and often find themselves following the ball too near the back wall to be able to play it off the rebound. Also, the beginning player frequently tends to think of the sport as a "my turn, your turn" game wherein the ball is hit to the opponent on the rebound, and the player moves to the side of the court after each stroke. This misconception should be contrasted with the competitive strategy of hitting the ball away from the opponent or low enough that the opponent cannot play it, after which the player should immediately return to center court position. Scoring is greatly enhanced by a varied repertoire of strokes and the ability to execute them in sequences that cause the opponent to move the greatest distance between strokes and to hit while moving.

The Kill Shot

The kill shot is a shot of high velocity and low trajectory. The name "kill" is derived from the fact that the rally is ended by a shot that hits so low on the wall that the opponent has no chance to play it before it bounces twice. An effective kill shot will hit the wall less than a foot above the floor. As the skill level improves this height from the floor will have to diminish if the shot is to be an effective kill shot. The probability of executing a kill shot with the necessary trajectory is related to the height of the shot preceding the kill. If a player attempts to kill a high bouncing ball at the height of its bounce, or to kill a shot from an overhand volley position, the probability of getting a low bounce from the rebound off the front wall is much less than it would be for playing a forehand rebound off the back wall at calf-height.

The low shot is ideally suited for a kill return. Thus, it is crucial to hit an effective kill shot, or the low ball resulting will be subject to a kill shot by the opponent. The kill shot may be hit against the front wall to rebound along the side wall. An even lower bounce results from contacting two walls with the kill shot. When two walls are contacted the angle of the bounce is very different when the side wall is contacted first from when it is contacted second. The angle and speed determine whether the ball will carry to the front wall after encountering the resistance of the side wall. Corner or "pinch" kill shots tend to rebound out to a center court position, and must carry a low trajectory to be effective.

The kill shot should be struck below the knees with a stroke parallel to the floor. The height of the shot is more important than the speed. The beginner should practice hitting consecutive kill shots in a rebound drill from the front court, emphasizing the bend of the knees, back knee near the floor, racquet face perpendicular to the floor, and the swing plane close to the floor. The goal can be adjusted by lowering the target line on the front wall or by raising the target number of consecutive hits.

The Passing Shot

The passing shot is a drive shot that is executed when the opponent is in the front

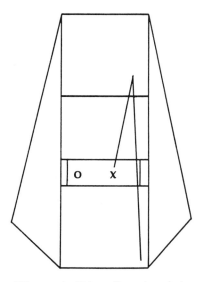

Diagram 6. Side wall passing shot.

court; the angle of the shot prevents the opponent from reaching the ball. The passing shot can be targeted down the side wall when the opponent is positioned near the side wall in the opposite half of the court. It is especially important to keep the side wall passing shot off the side wall to avoid an easy return for the opponent. The side wall passing shot should be struck hard enough to carry to the back wall, but not so hard that it rebounds back into play.

If the opponent is beside or in front of the player, then the ball can be angled off the front wall to strike the side wall adjacent to the opponent. The carom from the cross-court passing shot should travel to the opposite corner but not rebound from the back wall. If the opponent is near enough to the front wall, then the shot can be angled off the front wall with a carom directly to the back corner. It is important that this type of passing shot not hit the side wall and rebound out to the middle of the floor.

Passing shots should be struck from below the waist to produce a bounce that will fall short of the back wall. The shot is most effective when the opponent is near the front wall or a side wall. This side wall should be avoided unless the shot is intended to strike the side wall adjacent to the opponent while passing the opponent on the way to the diagonal back corner.

A good drill for practicing the side wall pass is to set up near the short service line, about 3 feet from the side wall, and hit consecutive drive shots between that position and the wall without rebounding the ball off the side or back walls. The drill should be practiced from both sides of the court. The cross-court passing shot is practiced with the drive serve drill. It is important for the player to remember that the opponent is generally more difficult to pass on the forehand or dominant side, so a greater angle may be required when passing on that side.

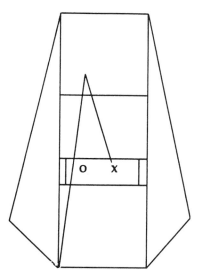

Diagram 7. Cross-court passing shot.

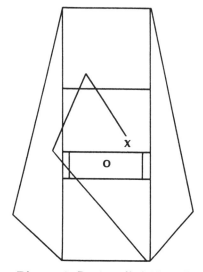

Diagram 8. Passing off of side wall.

The Drop Shot

The drop shot is a change-of-pace shot requiring great touch and finesse. The shot should be executed by playing the ball at a reduced speed into the corner producing a low, short bounce. The shot is most effective when the player is in the front court and the opponent is in the back court. It can be played from either side, and is more accurate when played at waist level or lower. The drop shot is best practiced in a consecutive volley drill from near the front court into the corner from 10 to 12 feet away from the front and side wall. Practice at this shot is important as a poor drop shot is almost invariably subject to a kill or passing shot by the opponent.

The Ceiling Shot

The ceiling shot is primarily a defensive shot. The shot should contact the ceiling about 2 or 3 feet from the front wall. In the front court variation, the front wall is hit first, then the ceiling is hit by the upward arc. The front court variation should not be used from the back court because of the difficulty of achieving the desirable depth of rebound. The ceiling shot can be struck overhand with more accuracy than can most of the other shots. The best target for the ceiling shot is along the side wall, deep into the back corner. Like most bad shots, the poor ceiling shot is subject to a high percentage return shot when it strikes the side wall. The ceiling shot can be practiced by using the overarm throwing drill to gain accuracy and confidence.

Stroke Variations

Most shots can be struck from a variety of positions and under a wide variety of conditions. Three of the more common stroke variations are the volley, back wall shot, and the fistball.

The *volley* is a stroke contacting the ball before it bounces. Hitting the ball on the fly this way requires quicker reflexes and often produces a higher contact point than is desirable, but it allows the player to maintain a front court position instead of retreating to play a ball from the bounce. The volley should be executed with a short, firm stroke for accuracy. The beginning player tends to hit too many volleys, especi-

ally from the overhand position. The volley should be used to maintain court position, or to force the opponent to react more quickly to returns that will require considerable court movement.

The back wall shot has much variety. Any ball which rebounds from the back wall before it is struck is a back wall shot. It is often more desirable to play the ball from the back wall than to play it off the front wall. The advantages of the wall shot are the reduced height of the bounce, reduced momentum of the ball, greater time to achieve court and body position, and the movement of the racquet or hand in the same direction as the ball. Beginning players often fail to realize that the ball will return to them from the back wall and, therefore, follow the ball too near the back wall to be able to take a full swing. The beginner should remember not to get closer to the back or side wall than one arm's length. Unlike a tennis ball, the ball will come back to center court, often with a more advantageous height of bounce.

In executing the handball strokes, the closed fist may be substituted for the open hand technique. The closed fist often results in a more powerful but less controlled shot. The novice player often prefers this stroke because of the reduced sensitivity of the fist to the impact of the ball.

SAFETY

Safety precautions should begin before the game ever starts. Warm-up exercises should be planned to stretch the legs, back, arms, and shoulders before stroking the ball. Handball players should wear padded gloves until the hands become accustomed to striking a hard rubber ball. If bone bruises occur, the player must permit sufficient time for recovery by resting. The feet should be protected by two pairs of socks to minimize friction caused by sliding in the shoe. Shoes should be light to accommodate the running, but the soles should be substantial to protect the feet from the constant pounding. The eyes should be protected by eyeguards. The guards are of great benefit in reducing accidental contact by the handball, racquetball, racquet, or other players. Players should not turn to face the shot behind them. The ability to see the ball with peripheral vision, paired with the skill of determining the opponent's position by the direction of the return, enables the player to face the front wall and reduces the danger of being hit in the eye by the ball.

One of the greatest dangers of both games is overswinging at the ball. When the player overswings there is less muscular control and a greater likelihood of striking a wall, another player, and even himself/herself. When there is the slightest chance of striking an opponent, a "hinder" should be called, and the point replayed.

STRATEGY

Court position is vitally important to developing and implementing a game strategy. The center court position, just behind the short service line, is considered best. It is important to hit shots which move the opponent away from the center court position. The opponent should be moved from front court to back court and back again, by hitting shots in combination.

The hitting position should be fundamentally the same for each shot. It is important to assume a stance facing the side wall, and to get the hand or racquet back in a striking position while bending the knees to bring body force into the low swinging action. Good strategy involves moving the opponent to prevent his/her having time to assume the correct hitting position, or forcing the opponent to hit while moving, the most difficult circumstance in which to execute an accurate placement.

The most effective shot selection strategy is to force the opponent to play his/her weakest stroke most often. Players can also affect tempo and shot control by playing high percentage shots from a good low bounce position. For instance, the time gained by permitting a high flying ball to pass by to the back wall will allow the player to be set up in good position to play the ball from a much lower position as it rebounds off the back wall. In the three-wall or one-wall game, the passing shot can be used more frequently without fear of bringing the ball back to center court, since there is no back wall rebound.

RACQUETBALL/HANDBALL RULES OF NECESSITY

The following rules are the primary ones necessary for the novice to effectively begin to enjoy the game of racquetball or handball.

1. **Points.** Points are scored only by the serving side, when it serves an ace or wins a volley.
2. **Game.** A game is won by the side first scoring 21 points.
3. **Match.** A match is won by the side first winning two games.
4. **Court.** See Diagram 9 for line designations.
5. **Order.** The player or side first winning the ball toss becomes the first server.
6. **Serving.** The server must serve from the service zone (see Diagram 9). The server must strike the ball on a bounce so that it hits the front wall first and on the rebound hits the floor in back of the short line, either with or without touching one of the side walls.

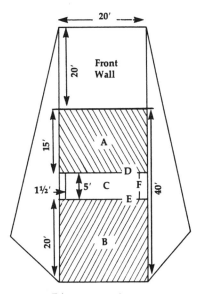

Diagram 9. The court.

A = Front Court
B = Back Court
C = Service Zone
D = Service Line
E = Short Service Line
F = Service Box

7. **Service Faults.** The following serves are faults, and two in succession result in a hand-out:
   a. *Foot Faults* —a foot fault results:
      (1) when the server leaves the service zone before the served ball passes the short line.
      (2) when the server's partner leaves the service zone before the ball passes the short line.
   b. *Short Serve* —a ball which rebounds before the short line.
   c. *Long Serve* —a ball which hits the back wall without bouncing.
   d. *Ceiling* —a serve which touches the ceiling.
   e. *Out* —any ball going out of the court.
   f. *Three-wall Serve* —any serve that hits two side walls on the fly.
8. **Avoidable Hinder.** Avoidable interference, not necessarily intentional, by one player with another's clear shot. The penalty is loss of serve or point.
9. **Unavoidable Hinder.** Unavoidable interference by one player with another's clear shot. This "dead ball" (unavoidable) hinder causes the point to be replayed.
10. **Volleys.** Each legal return after the serve is called a volley. Play during volleys must be according to the following rules:
    a. *One or Both Hands* —the ball must be hit with one or both hands. Switching hands to hit a ball is an out (racquetball only).
    b. *One Touch* —in attempting returns, the ball may be touched only once by the player on the returning side.

A violation of either (a) or (b) results in a hand-out or point.

EQUIPMENT

Clothing

The handball or racquetball player should wear comfortable and cool clothing. A short-sleeved shirt or blouse, gym shorts, cotton socks, and thick-soled gym shoes are best. The uniform should provide for easy movement and the absorption of perspiration. The shoes should be light, but of sufficient thickness to prevent blisters on the bottom of the foot.

Gloves

The racquetball player may select a glove for the racquet hand for the purposes of improved grip and protection. The racquetball glove should be thin and well-tailored for fit. If a wristband is used in conjunction with the glove, the player should find perspiration in the glove less of a problem.

The handball player must wear a glove on each hand. The handball glove is thicker than the racquetball glove for protection. Beginning players often choose a padded palm model to reduce bruising of the tissue of the palms.

Protective Glasses

Protective eyeguards are required for junior players and *strongly* recommended for adult players. While racquetball has the greater danger of racquet injuries, both sports generate sufficient ball speed to cause serious eye damage from impact directly on the eye or even on the side of the face beside the eye. Several types of eyeguards are on the market. All of these at least slightly reduce the player's ability to see, but the resulting protection may permit the player lifelong good vision that might otherwise be impaired by an errant shot.

Racquet

The racquetball racquet should be selected for grip size, grip material, overall length, head shape, overall weight, and construction material. The grip size relates to hand size, but generally a smaller grip is preferred to facilitate hand and wrist action in the stroke. The grip should provide for functional control even when heavy perspiration soaks the material. The overall length is generally from 17½ to 19 inches. Greater racquet length increases power, but reduces control. The weight of the racquet depends on the material used in the frame. Select a racquet that is heavy enough to generate power but light enought to be swung quickly. The plastic racquets are the lightest, followed closely by aluminum. Lightweight steel is of medium weight; the heaviest rackets are those of wood.

The ball manufacturing industries have greatly improved the quality of both handballs and racquetballs. A lighter-colored ball has largely replaced the traditional black ball in both games because of the black wall marks created by the black ball. Controversy has arisen concerning the two-hemisphere ball vs. the seamless ball, as to which has the liveliest bounce. Both models have had some difficulty with early breakage.

CONTEMPORARY TRENDS AND RESEARCH

Contemporary racquetball is a fast paced game which may belie its aerobic image. Several studies reveal an overwhelming majority of game rallies last 10 seconds or less. Power strokes and improved equipment enhance the scoring potential of today's players. Short bursts of effort and short bouts of rest ranging from a 1:1 to a 1:2 ratio intersperse to generate a competitive workout. Subtle differences in skill levels can produce one-sided scores and significantly reduce the fitness potential as the result of even shorter rallies.

Diagnostic coding of stroke patterns in winning and losing situations generate patterns of performance which can be beneficial in improving skills. Coding needs to be efficient and effective in stroke analysis and court coverage. Variations from the singles, cutthroat, and doubles format can produce skill or fitness specific results. A new approach in teaching the game focuses upon key points of instructional strategy rather than the traditional skill/stroke analysis. Skill instruction is included as a secondary focus supporting the "strategy commandment." The Personalized System of Instruction (PSI) sequential tasks approach has been effectively applied to racquetball at Ohio State and Kent State University. The use of practice tasks, flexible learning rate schedules, and peer tutoring distinguish this approach from other models. A working copy of teaching units complete with performance objectives and learning activities is necessary for effective implementation.

TERMINOLOGY

Ace. A legal serve not touched by the receiver.

Back Court. The portion of the court behind the short service line.

Backhand. Opposite of forehand side in racquetball.

Backswing. The preparatory movement to position the player for the down swing.

Back Wall Shot. Any shot made on a ball rebounding off the back wall.

Ceiling Shot. A shot which strikes the ceiling.

Center Court. The position directly behind the short line and between the side walls.

Crotch Ball. A ball which contacts the crack between two playing surfaces.

Cut-throat. A three-player game wherein the two receivers compete against the server.

Doubles. A four-player game wherein two-man teams compete.

Drive. A powerful stroke against the front wall between the knee and shoulder.

Fault. An infraction of the rules. Two service faults result in a side-out.

Fist Ball. Striking the ball with the fist in handball.

Front Court. The portion of the court in front of the short service line.

Game. The game is played to 21 points.

Hand-out. The loss of serve by one partner for his/her doubles team.

Hinder. An accidental or unavoidable interference with the opponent in the play.

Kill Shot. A low trajectory shot with no playable rebound.

Lob Shot. A high arching shot that bounces high to the back wall.

Long Serve. A serve that carries to the back wall on the fly.

Overhead. A shot struck at or above the shoulder level.

Passing Shot. A shot out of the reach of the opponent.

Rally. A series of shots by the players.

Service Box. The 5 foot × 1½ foot area at the side of the service zone where the nonserving doubles partner stands during the serve.

Service Line. The front line of the service zone.

Service Zone. That portion of the court between the service line and the short service line.

Short Ball. A serve landing in front of the short service line.

Short Service Line. The back line of the service zone.

Side-out. The loss of service to the opponent(s).

Singles. A game of one player versus one other player.

Straddle Ball. A ball passing through a player's legs.

Volley. Striking the ball on the fly, before it bounces.

CHAPTER 15

Self-Defense

KENNETH G. TILLMAN
Trenton State College
Trenton, NJ

INTRODUCTION

It is, unfortunately, possible to open a newspaper on any day and read about physical assaults, rapes, muggings, and other examples of personal violence. No community is immune and every person can be considered a potential victim. Self-defense becomes, therefore, a much-needed course. Violence is a fact of life in even the safest of communities. The goal of a self-defense course is not to create fear, but to develop self-defense skills that can be used if students are faced with a situation where their personal safety is jeopardized. More importantly, a level of confidence should be developed that will translate into mental preparedness to meet danger situations that may be confronted. Students must understand that physical skills alone have limited value. There is always the possibility that the attacker or attackers will have more strength and/or physical skills. The goal of psychological preparedness, therefore, becomes of prime importance in a self-defense class.

Students must know when to use the many defensive techniques available and be able to select the best maneuver for the danger situation that is encountered. They must also realize that there are situations when passivity rather than aggressiveness is the best defense. Gaining insight into the best approach to take in danger situations is an important outcome for students. Sometimes trickery, stalling for time, or immediate flight is a better alternative than using physical force.

There is a difference between skills learned in a self-defense class and the skills learned in most other physical education courses. In other courses, the goal is to develop skills that will be used on a regular basis, while in school and throughout life. Self-defense, on the other hand, must be approached from an entirely different perspective. The skills learned are to be used only in emergency situations when personal safety or the safety of another person is threatened.

Part of psychological preparedness is to gain confidence in one's ability to handle a dangerous situation. The physical skills that are learned in class give students a better understanding of the physical capabilities that they have. An emphasis in a self-defense class should be on increasing students' confidence through the realization that they do have the ability to defend themselves and can cope with dangerous situations. It is important to incorporate activities that will improve physical skills such as agility, balance, and body control. These attributes are an integral part of personal defense skills.

Techniques for defending oneself have been used as long as history has been recorded. Defensive techniques were necessary for survival in ancient times and were learned by children at an early age. This need decreased as civilization progressed into modern times. Unfortunately, physical danger continues to be a concern in even the most advanced societies and it is necessary to develop skills, both physical and mental, that can be used in times of danger. Practicing self-defense techniques develops physical skills and the mental alertness that is needed when threatened with violence by another individual or group of people.

Even with the advancement of civilization, violence continues to cause many problems throughout the world and this includes the highly technological cultures also. It is a teacher's responsibility in a self-defense class to inculcate in each student a respect for others and to encourage students to become involved in community activities and organizations that strive to decrease the amount of violence found in communities and in the world. An important principle of self-defense is for anyone, no matter how skilled, to do everything possible to avoid a situation in which violence may result. This is the first rule to follow. The second rule is to walk, or run(!), away from danger situations before they occur. This attitude of prevention must form the foundation for learning self-defense.

Why teach self-defense skills when it is possible to teach judo, karate, or some other martial art? There are basically two advantages. First, using a combination of techniques is better than being restricted to one style. The other reason is that an activity such as karate requires a much higher level of coordination, strength, and agility. It takes years of practice to become skilled in using karate self-defense techniques, and the high level of skill that is needed for success requires continual practice. Judo and karate are more than self-defense techniques. They are excellent sport activities that are fun to learn and provide enjoyable competition. The primary skills of self-defense are those that will disable an attacker. They are not used for fun.

CAUTIONS

It is important to introduce the self-defense unit by explaining the purpose of self-defense skills and emphasizing when it is legal to use physical force on another person. People have a right to defend themselves. Everyone should be able to live a life free from the fear that accompanies intimidation and physical abuse imposed by others. Self-defense techniques should not be used to violate the rights of others or to injure another person unless personal welfare or someone else's well-being is threatened.

Laws governing the actions people may take in defending themselves vary from state to state. In general terms, a victim must believe that bodily injury is about to occur and there must be apparent danger to the victim or another person. In these situations, all force and means that are considered necessary to prevent injury may be used. The same principles apply when saving a third party from death or injury. Deadly force may be used only if life is in danger and is not to be used in other situations such as when property is being damaged or stolen. Retaliation can be used only up to the point necessary to stop the attack. The intended victim is not permitted to use excessive force for defense or for punishment. Verbal abuse is not a legal cause for physical retaliation unless an act is threatened which justifies a defensive action.

It must be emphasized and re-emphasized that a person has the responsibility to avoid violence whenever possible. Legally, however, this does not mean that a person has to retreat before using aggressive defensive tactics if this is the best way to handle a dangerous situation. The following principles should be kept in mind:

● anticipate dangerous situations and use every possible measure to prevent them from occurring;
● defuse dangerous situations if at all possible;
● accept responsibility for a problem even if you may be in the right. Don't let your ego contribute to a dangerous happening;
● walk away from dangerous locations;
● run from danger rather than get into a situation where self-defense tactics are required;
● use self-defense tactics only as a last resort.

SAFETY

A number of safety guidelines should be emphasized when learning self-defense. These guidelines are to be followed at all times.

1. Tap for safety. Tapping is the universal signal to stop. It is not necessary to suffer extended periods of pain to become successful in executing self-defense techniques. Tap the mat, a partner, or

oneself to stop the action. It is imperative that participants stop instantly when the tapping signal is given. It will give confidence to try different skills if this safety procedure is explained during the first class period.

2. Proceed slowly when learning the techniques. The skill must be executed smoothly before entire movement can be controlled during practice. Increase speed after control is developed.

3. Learn how to fall properly. Skill in falling is crucial for learning self-defense techniques safely.

4. React properly to pressure. Go with the pressure whenever possible.

5. When starting a unit on self-defense, it should be emphasized that there must never be an attempt to injure a partner in practice sessions. Full scale self-defense maneuvers should be used only in danger situations.

6. Body blows and jabs should never be practiced at full force on a partner. Use dummies and other teaching aids when learning these techniques.

7. Class members should wear comfortable physical education clothing that permits easy movement and does not have buckles or other items that could cause injury when practicing self-defense techniques.

8. Do not wear jewelry or other accessories.

PHILOSOPHY OF PREPAREDNESS

The goal in a self-defense class is to do more than develop self-defense skills. Mental and psychological preparedness has an equally high priority. It is, therefore, important that activities such as reviewing of newspaper articles describing assaults, viewing pertinent videos, films, and TV shows, and class discussions emphasizing mental and psychological readiness be interspersed with skill development.

Self-defense is not the ability to use sheer strength to stop an attack. It is the ability to remain calm and choose the best alternative or combination of tactics. One of the best ways to accomplish this type of "coolness" and inner strength is for students to find out that their bodies are capable of performing at a much higher level than they realized was possible. It is, therefore, important to incorporate tumbling skills and weight-training principles into a self-defense class. It is appropriate to teach self-defense in conjunction with (or immediately following) a weight-training, tumbling, or gymnastics unit since there is a valuable correlation between the skills learned (see Chapters 22 and 24). Not only will the increased agility and strength from these other activities assist in executing self-defense tactics, but students will gain

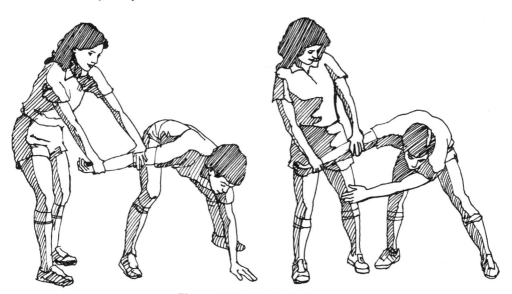

Figure 1. Tapping techniques.

insight into the physical potential that they have. This realization can result in a changed attitude and permit students to have confidence that they can be physically assertive if the need arises. Students must have confidence in their physical abilities. Learning to perform physical skills they didn't know they could do contributes significantly to a state of mental and emotional readiness.

Another factor that must be considered when learning self-defense is the inability many people have to injure another person even if they are being attacked. This is part of the mental preparedness that is an integral part of a self-defense course. Students, even the mild-mannered ones, who would never think of hurting another person must be willing to seriously injure someone when their safety is being threatened. It must be emphasized that the eye gouge must be deep and forceful, the knee kick disabling, and holds used to incapacitate an attacker. Use dummies and other teaching aids so full force can be practiced.

Every person has the right to live without having to change their lifestyle because of the possibility of being attacked. A good self-defense course destroys limitations rather than imposing restrictions, but it is still important for class members to discuss the common sense safety procedures that should be followed. Areas that should be included in this facet of a self-defense course include the following:

- Being alert to your surroundings;
- Knowing how to be safe in your home;
- Dangers when using a car;
- Walking in deserted areas;
- Getting acquainted with a new town or city;
- Traveling alone;
- Meeting strangers; and
- Importance of proper body carriage (projecting a confident, assertive demeanor will reduce the chance of being a victim).

LEARNING PROCEDURE

Work in pairs when learning self-defense skills. It is preferable to rotate partners during the course so that you experience size and strength differentials as well as have the opportunity to practice with a partner of the opposite sex. A partner should provide feedback to give an accurate evaluation of success in executing the skill being practiced. It is also important that partners give appropriate resistance so the student practicing the skill will get a realistic indication as to whether the execution would be successful or not. Start off with each partner practicing the self-defense move that is being learned. When both can complete the move properly, one will be the attacker and the other will use the self-defense technique. Then alternate roles. Start by going through the skills slowly and gradually increase speed until running through the maneuvers at full speed. Remember that all dangerous skills are acted out; they are never carried out with full force against a partner.

This chapter is arranged to cover the major categories of self-defense skills. After learning the proper stance and gaining a basic knowledge of the vulnerable body parts, begin practicing the basic skills found in each section of this chapter and learn skills in each category. It is best to learn one or two techniques in each area rather than covering all the techniques in one category before moving to the next. Many skills are easy to use. Start with these so participants will experience success and gain confidence to try more difficult moves. Continue to review even the most basic skills so they become an automatic reaction for each person when their partner attacks.

Drill all the self-defense procedures until each person performs the self-defense tactic smoothly and with confidence. When all have this foundation, learning will be enhanced by having two students develop a fight routine. Start by having each partner use two or three skills they have learned in class and design a routine which incorporates these skills. They should practice slowly at first and eventually go as close to full speed as possible. As more skills are learned, more should be incorporated into the routine. Naturally, most of the skills in the routine cannot be completed because they could cause an injury. The teacher can provide guidance so partners move to a different maneuver before there is a danger of injury. One maneuver should flow smoothly to the next one before there is pressure which could stop the routine or injure one of the participants. The constant repetition of moving from one skill to another develops competency with the skills and increases ability to use self-defense tactics as effective fighting tools.

STANCE

Students should be prepared to defend an attack from any position in which they find themselves. Regardless of position, balance is extremely important. This concept can be learned by practicing a well-balanced standing stance. The principle of maintaining a solid base that gives good stability and maximum protection from kicks and blows and also allows effective maneuverability should be explained. The feet should be about shoulder width apart with the knees slightly flexed, weight over the legs. This provides a firm base for exe-

Figure 2. Basic stance.

cuting the basic movements of self-defense. The arms should be in front of the body with the elbows flexed about 90 degrees and the hands slightly cupped. This position assists in blocking blows and puts the hands in position to rapidly retaliate. The feet may be slightly staggered with one foot in front of the other. A comfortable stance makes it possible to both defend and attack while maintaining good body balance. Any defensive stance should permit rapid movement and give the best possible protection to parts of the body that can be injured.

VULNERABLE BODY PARTS

There are specific body parts that are particularly vulnerable to attack. Students should become familiar with these body parts as jabs and blows can be used effectively in these areas. A high degree of skill is not needed, and a forceful jab or blow will disable an attacker, at least long enough to escape.

Figure 3 illustrates the parts of the body that are most vulnerable. Memorize each of these vital areas. A handout of this diagram showing the vulnerable parts of the body will assist students in developing an awareness of the vulnerable areas.

Although the body has numerous vital areas, there are seven principal targets that should be the first parts of the body to be struck since they are the most vulnerable. Students should practice striking these areas (using simulated targets) first and then expand their targets to include the other vulnerable areas. The seven principal targets (circled on Figure 3) are:

temple
eyes
under the nose
Adam's apple
testicles (males)
solar plexus
kneecap

Many different types of blows can be used effectively on these areas. The eyes are vulnerable to finger jabs or a forceful thumb gouge. The other areas can be struck in a variety of ways. Blows with the fist, heels of the hands, elbow, knee, and foot as well as a knife-like slash with the side of the hand can all be effective. (See the section on blows for additional information.) All blows must be used with full force in order to immobilize an attacker.

The 31 vulnerable parts of the body are:

1. temples
2. eyes
3. bridge and tip of nose
4. side of neck
5. under nose
6. chin
7. Adam's apple
8. collarbone
9. armpit
10. heart
11. solar plexus
12. under last rib
13. stomach
14. groin and testicles
15. inside edge of thigh
16. kneecaps
17. side of knee
18. shins
19. instep
20. ear
21. base of skull
22. back of neck
23. under shoulder blade
24. small of back
25. kidneys
26. elbows
27. tailbone
28. wrists
29. fingers
30. behind knees
31. Achilles tendon

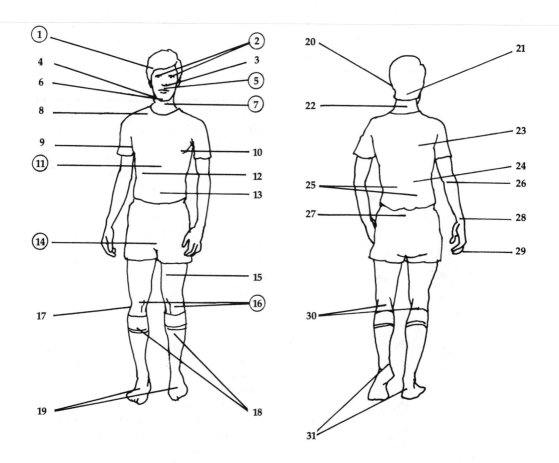

Figure 3. Vulnerable parts of the body and the seven principal targets (circled).

BLOWS AND KICKS

Side of hand

There are several different hand positions that should be learned. One of the most effective positions for delivering a blow is to hold the hand straight, with the fingers together and extended. Then strike a vulnerable area of the opponent's body with the fleshy outer edge of the hand. The temple, the bridge of the nose, under the nose, the Adam's apple, the side or back of the neck, and the stomach are good examples of body parts where this type of blow is effective.

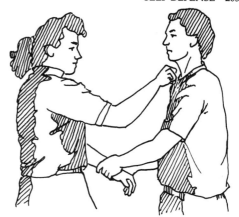

Figure 5. Closed fist blow.

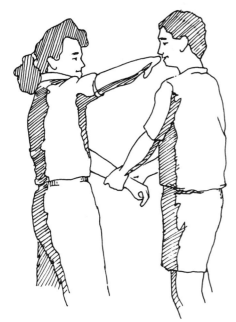

Figure 4. Side of hand blow.

Closed fist

A closed fist can also be used to make contact with vital areas. When delivering a blow with the fist, make contact with the second knuckles of the first and second fingers. It is also possible to extend the knuckle of the middle finger and use this weapon against unprotected body parts. Remember that the fist is used primarily on soft body parts of the opponent. If bony areas are hit there is a risk of breaking a bone or bones in the hand. A backhand motion is another way the fist can be used. This is a particularly good way to strike the face of an attacker.

Finger extension

Extending the fingers on the hand makes a good fingertip jab weapon. Poke an eye forcefully with a two-finger thrust. This should cause at least temporary blindness and extreme pain. This type of blow is primarily successful when used on an eye but it can also be used when striking the groin or solar plexus.

Heel of hand

The heel of the hand is one of the best weapons in a student's defensive arsenal. Smash the heel of the hand under the attacker's nose and attempt to drive the nose bone into the head. A strong blow can cause unconsciousness. An alternate point of attack is the chin.

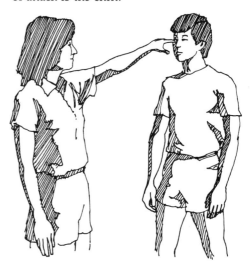

Figure 6. Finger extension jab.

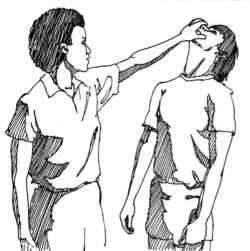

Figure 7. Heel of hand blow.

Elbow

The elbow is an exceptionally good defensive weapon. It can be used to drive into the solar plexus when grabbed from behind. Students should also be cognizant that they can use the elbow as a weapon when striking many of their attacker's vulnerable areas, particularly those on the head if they are within reach of the elbow.

Figure 8. Elbow blow.

Figure 9. Head butts, front and back.

Head

The head can be used effectively for delivering blows to an attacker whether held in a front or rear bear hug or if a hand is not free to deliver a blow. Either the front or back of the head can be used as a battering ram against the nose, preferably, or other parts of the attacker's face.

Front kick

Self-defense situations call for different types of kicks. One of the first kicks to learn is the front kick. This is a fast, short kick and is sometimes called a snap kick. The toe, if protected with a shoe, or the ball of the foot is used. The kick is aimed at the shin or knee and a short, powerful kick is made. Quickness is of prime importance so that the attacker cannot grab the foot or step out of range. The groin can also be kicked by using the instep when making a front kick.

Side kick

The side kick is made by quickly turning sideways and driving the heel or the side of the foot into the knee or shin of the assailant. All kicks must be fast, concise movements. On this kick, the knee of the kicking leg is driven to the body as the side turn is made and the leg is vigorously extended to fire the heel or side of the foot toward the attacker's knee or shin.

Heel kick

The heel kick should be practiced to strike an attacker who makes a surprise attack from behind. The leg is driven straight into the groin, knee, or shin. Con-tact is made with the heel. Again, action must be swift so the leg is not grabbed. The kick must be carefully timed to be used either when breaking away from an attacker or stopping an assailant's charge from behind.

Figure 11. Side kick

Figure 10. Front kick.

Figure 12. Heel kick to the groin.

Figure 14a. Heel smash

Figure 13. Knee kick to head.

Knee kicks

The knee kick is another effective self-defense tool. It is used when facing and in close contact with an attacker. A gap should be created between the victim and his/her attacker. Drive the knee sharply to the groin area. There will usually be room to use the knee kick because most attackers will be using their arms to try to control the arms and upper body. It may be necessary to force the hips away to have enough room to use the knee.

If the assailant is bent down or the victim is able to deliver a blow to the back of the head to put the attacker's face within knee range, a vigorous knee kick to the face can abruptly stop the attack. Attempt to drive down on the head at the same time that the knee is being kicked upward. This will increase the power of the blow and will prevent the head from being pulled out of range of the knee.

Heel smash

This technique can be used when an assailant is either in front or behind. Smash the heel down vigorously on the top of the

Figure 14b. Shin scrape.

instep. The sole of the foot can also be used, but it is not as effective. Another good technique is to turn the foot and scrape down the shin prior to smashing the instep.

Caution

All blows and kicks should be practiced on dummies, padded walls, pillows, or some other soft surface. Full force should never be used against a hard surface or an injury may occur. Before using dummies or pads, develop correct body position and balance and then work on speed of execution without any resistance. *Never practice these blows on a partner.*

Points of Emphasis

1. Always have a target for the blows.
2. Hit fast and hard to the targeted areas of your assailant.
3. Use full force.
4. Always protect your own body when delivering a blow.
5. Return to a good defensive position immediately after delivering a blow.
6. Remember that joints are good attack points.
7. Practice developing a mental picture of an assailant's vulnerable areas for the various blows and kicks.

FALLING

When a victim experiences a mugging or some other type of an assault, being knocked down is a common part of the experience. It is for this reason that it is important all students learn how to fall properly. This skill will reduce their chances of being injured when falling and therefore being unable to defend themselves. Just as importantly, being able to fall properly will minimize the advantage of the attacker because students will know how to maintain body control and recover rapidly to a defensive position. Also, being thrown to the ground will not cause them to panic, since they will have experienced the feeling before.

Students must be able to execute the forward, backward, shoulder, and forward dive rolls before practicing falls. Students should be able to perform the rolls competently before starting to learn the falls. It is also good to practice rolls as part of the warm-up before each class.

Always practice falling on thick mats to protect from injury and to give confidence when learning falls. Develop proper form by practicing each fall slowly and then speed up as proper technique is learned. Remember that a fall should not be broken by reaching out with the hand. The objective should be to spread the impact of falling over a larger surface of the body and to develop the ability to relax the body rather than stiffening it.

Side Fall

The side fall is a frequently used fall. It is an effective means of avoiding injury when thrown to the ground or floor. A good way to learn this fall is to start in a squatting position with one leg crossed in front of the other. The forward leg is moved forward and the arm on the falling side brought up in the air as balance is lost. When landing, distribute the force of the fall from the foot to the shoulder and slap the mat with the palm of the hand to break the fall. The arm should be extended and the fingers slightly spread. Emphasize that the head should be kept off the mat and slap the mat vigorously. After the side roll is mastered from a

Figure 15. Side fall from squat.

Figure 16. Side fall from feet.

squat, gradually start farther from the mat until you are capable of falling from a standing position. Then practice rolling to the stomach by bringing the bent leg over the straightened leg. Use this maneuver to move away from an opponent and come to the feet.

Figure 16 illustrates the side fall technique from the feet. Standing with the weight evenly distributed, kick the foot across the body and fall to the side. The right arm and leg are raised as the right buttock hits the mat; roll back to the shoulder and slap the mat with the right hand. The head stays off the mat at all times and the legs should be raised when the fall is completed.

Front Fall

Learn the front fall by beginning in a kneeling position on the mat. As the body falls, slap the mat with both hands slightly cupped. The force of the fall is absorbed with the hands and forearms. Keep the hands and forearms straight.

When the front fall can be performed from the knees without jarring the body, move to a standing position. Fall forward smoothly from a relaxed position and make contact with the mat simultaneously with hands and forearms. Keep the body straight when falling forward; only the hands, forearms, and toes should be in contact with the mat when the fall is finished. Do not hit the mat with bent wrists.

Figure 17. Front fall from knees.

Figure 18. Back fall from sitting position.

Back Fall

The back fall is learned by beginning in a sitting position. Have the back slightly rounded and the head tilted forward. Round the back and roll back with an easy motion as the arms and legs are raised. Slap the extended forearms and hands to the mat as the upper back hits the mat. As with other falls, keep the head from hitting the mat.

The next step is to begin the back fall from a squatting position. Roll onto the back while tucking in buttocks to avoid shock to the back. The movement after making contact with the mat with the buttocks is the same as when starting from a sitting position. Finish by slapping hands and forearms against the mat and keep chin tucked to chest. Legs should be raised in the air when finished.

BREAKING HOLDS

Sometimes the natural reaction is not the reaction that will allow one to break a hold. Analyze each technique to see how to get a mechanical advantage even if the attacker is bigger and stronger.

Wrist Release

The natural reaction when someone grabs the wrist is to pull back. This is exactly what the attacker wants the victim to do. The appropriate action is to drop the elbow forcefully and use a twisting action to exert force against the attacker's thumb.

The same action is used when the assailant has a hand on each of the wrists. Each wrist should be twisted toward the attack-

Figure 19a. Single wrist release.

Figure 19b. Double wrist release.

er's thumb. Immediately move to a good defensive stance or attack if the assailant is off-balance or in a position where they are vulnerable to a kick or hand blow.

Figure 20. Two-hand release.

Figure 21. Chop release for two-hand wrist grasp.

Two-hand Wrist Release

If an attacker grabs one wrist with both hands, release can be gained by grasping the fist of the grasped arm with a free hand and pulling it sharply upward while lowering the elbow of the held arm. Lower the body weight to give additional leverage and maintain a balanced position when the arm is freed.

Another release technique, when one of the wrists is controlled, is to deliver a blow to the attacker's throat, mouth, nose, or eyes, with the free hand. Use the extended hand position and expend all force possible to slash into the attacker with a chopping action. Repeat the blow rapidly if the attacker remains in a vulnerable position by maintaining hold of the wrist.

Bear Hug

Learn several different ways to break free from a bear hug. The bear hug prevents the victim from moving away from the attacker and limits the blows that can be used to overcome the attacker. It is therefore important to know how to break free from a bear hug.

Several techniques were covered in the section on kicks. The shin can be kicked with the toe or scraped with the side of the shoe. The groin can be kicked with the knee. One can also lean back and give a hand chop to the throat or a vigorous smash to the chin with the heel of the hand.

If the bear hug is from behind, kicks and blows are again effective. A kick to the shin, stomping on the instep, or stepping to the side and striking the groin with the hand are all effective methods. Grasping a finger and pulling back with all possible force and biting a hand or arm across the face should also be considered.

Two other techniques that can be used against the bear hug are to butt forcefully into the opponent's face and pinch tightly on the inside of the thigh.

Front Choke Hold with Two Hands

There are some important principles to emphasize when learning defenses against choke holds. If the attacker grabs the neck with both hands and begins choking, react rapidly. The first action to use to release the

Figure 22. Bear hug defenses.

grip is to clasp the hands and drive the arms up between the attacker's arms. This will release the grip. Immediately go on the offensive by smashing the hands over the bridge of the attacker's nose or use another striking or kicking movement to disable the attacker.

Another technique that can be used is to raise the arms above the head outside the attacker's arms, twist rapidly and turn away to apply pressure on the attacker's wrists. This will release the neck grasp and provide an opening for a counterattack or an escape maneuver if the attacker is momentarily off-balance.

Rear Choke Hold with Two Hands

The double arm twist described in the previous paragraph also works effectively to counter a rear choke hold. As soon as you turn and free yourself, look for an escape route or strike a vulnerable part of the attacker's body.

Figure 23. Front choke hold release action.

Rear Choke with Two Arms

When the throat is encircled from behind, be prepared to act rapidly. Tuck the chin into the chest to take pressure off the throat. Next, grasp the assailant's right elbow with the right hand as shown in Figure 24. The left hand grasps the attacker's right wrist. Lift on the elbow, push down on the wrist, and duck under the arm. Keep control of the arm if possible and pull it behind the attacker's body where it can be twisted or jerked upward to control the assailant. See also the flying mare throw.

Figure 24. Rear choke lift and duck release.

Special Defense Against a Male Attacker

A special technique that can be used against a male attacker is the testicle jerk. This is a technique to be used if threatened with physical violence. The procedure is to grab tightly around the top of the testicles, twist vigorously, squeeze, and jerk.

THROWS

Throws should not be considered a first line of defense. To throw someone, the victim must be close to that person. This leaves the victim vulnerable to blows, choke holds, and kicks. It is best to use a defensive tactic that will keep the victim out of range of the assailant. Throws require skill and an attacker can sometimes neutralize the skill with strength and brute force. Learn throws only after learning how to fall properly.

It is important to learn some basic throws since there will be times when a victim finds himself/herself in a position where a throw is the best and, perhaps only, defensive technique.

Throws are also good to practice since the victim learns to fall correctly and recover rapidly after being thrown. In many rough and tumble fights, throws to the ground will be used, and it is good to know how to react.

Hip Throw

Practice getting in the correct position before attempting this throw, which is used when the victim is close to the attacker. The victim should grasp the attacker's right arm with the left hand and slide the right arm around the waist. Simultaneously place the right foot next to the inside of the attacker's right foot. The victim then pivots on the right foot and steps back so that the attacker's body will be across the victim's hip. To initiate the throw, the victim bends the knees and then springs up. This will pull the attacker off the mat. The victim completes the throw by bringing the opponent forward over the victim's hip and follows to the mat.

Flying Mare

This is a technique to use when grabbed from the rear with a choke hold. The technique to use is as follows.

The victim should reach both hands up and hold as high as possible on the attacker's upper arm. Keep good balance with a low center of gravity. With the attacker's weight on the victim, an explosive forward and downward motion of the head should be used to bring the assailant over the vic-

Figure 26. Flying mare being executed.

tim's head and onto the mat. A vigorous downward motion should be used while the arm is pulled hard.

Using the flying mare will free the victim and provide an opportunity to escape or use one of the disabling techniques once the opponent is on the ground.

When practicing this throw, be sure the victim keeps control of the attacker's arm and helps the attacker land safely. Practice initially with a thick mat until both victim and attacker are under control from start to finish of the throw.

Back Trip Throw

Another situation that it is good to be prepared to handle is when the attacker's arms are around the waist. As with all moves, immediate action is important. The first movement should be forward to destroy the attacker's balance. It is important to maintain a position above the attacker if at all possible. Shift the hips quickly to the side; step the inside leg behind both legs of the attacker; push vigorously at the shoulders while simultaneously kicking the attacker's leg upward.

Figure 25. Hip throw.

This will drop the attacker to the ground with sufficient force to provide the victim with an opening to attack with a kick or blow.

ADVANCED SKILLS

The front and rear wrist breakers are not difficult to use in the practice situation, but they would be used primarily by people experienced with self-defense skills in an attack situation. In spite of this, they are good to include in a secondary school self-defense unit because they demonstrate how pressure can be used to gain a mechanical advantage and how a person can use self-defense skills to stop a larger and stronger antagonist. They are also good to learn so students will experience pain when pressure is exerted properly and will learn the importance of going with the pressure to prevent injury during practice.

Front Wrist Breaker

Grasp the assailant's right hand with your left (or the assailant's left hand with your right). Place your thumb on the center of the knuckles and grab the palm of the hand near the thumb with the fingers. Pull the attacker's hand to the inside so that the fingers point straight up. While turning the hand, place your right thumb on the knuckles next to the attacker's left thumb and grab the palm of the hand near the little finger with the fingers of your right hand.

Note that the fingers meet in the palm of the assailant's hand and that the little fingers are near the wrist. When the hands are in position, immediately drive the attacker's fingers straight up and push hard with your thumbs to cock the wrist as far as it will go.

Keep the wrist cocked and turn the palm of the attacker's hand to the outside. Keep pressure on the wrist as your body weight is shifted forward; pivot your hips toward the attacker's free arm and drop him/her to the ground with the pressure being placed on the wrist.

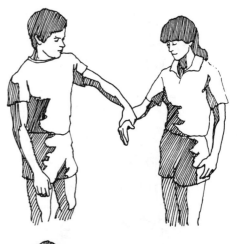

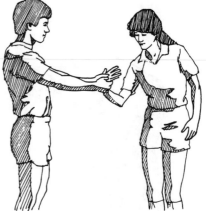

Figure 27. Hand position for front wrist breaker.

Figure 28. Wrist cocked.

There are many other more advanced skills that can be taught after students develop the ability to use the skills described in this chapter. Various types of advanced blocks, trips, throws, and holds will provide a continuing challenge.

Once students know the basic self-defense techniques, stage different types of danger situations and have students react by using the best self-defense skill or skills for each situation. They should continue to

Figure 29. Finish of front wrist breaker.

Rear Wrist Breaker

The rear wrist breaker technique has many similarities to the front wrist breaker. Reach across the attacker and grasp his/her right hand with your right hand or his/her left hand with your left hand. The thumb is again placed in the center of the knuckles and the little finger side of the hand is grasped with your fingers. The attacker's hand is then twisted to the outside and the wrist is cocked.

The other hand is then placed in a similar position with your thumb on the knuckles and your fingers clamped on the thumb side of the palm. Place the second hand in position as soon as possible. Turn the attacker's hand to the outside of his/her body; then move your body to a rear position. Point the fingers of the attacker straight up by putting pressure with the thumbs and pulling in vigorously with the fingers. This is a very painful hold. The attacker can be driven to the ground; control can be maintained by extending your arms and increasing the leverage being placed on the wrist. The correct leverage is being applied if the knuckles are being driven toward the elbow.

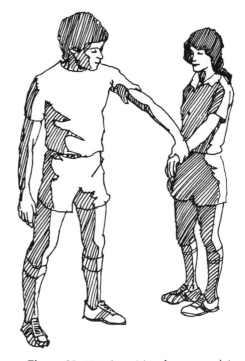

Figure 30. Hand position for rear wrist breaker.

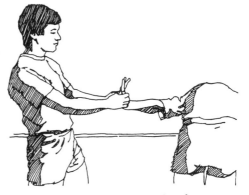

Figure 31. Rear wrist breaker.

practice the skills they have learned until they become automatic reactions to simulated attacks.

Throughout the course, the teacher should continue to emphasize that self-defense techniques are used only when absolutely necessary and that every measure must be used to avoid physical encounters. Blows, kicks, and other types of force are used only when such action is clearly indicated because personal safety is threatened or life is endangered.

REFERENCES

Bullard, Jim. *Looking Forward to Being Attacked: Self Defense for Every Woman.* New York: M. Evans, 1987.

Campbell, Sid. *Self-Defense for Wimps: The Art of Oneupmanship.* Oakland, CA: Gong Prods, 1989.

Clark, Robert. *Self Defense in Action.* North Pomfret, VT: Random Century, 1988.

Conway, Frank, and Hallander, Jane. *Kajukenbo: The Ultimate Self Defense System.* Burbank, CA: Unique Publications, 1988.

Cooper, Jeff. *Principles of Personal Defense.* Boulder, CO: Paladin Press, 1988.

Cramer, Lenox. *War with Empty Hands: Self-Defense Against Aggression.* Columbus, OH: Alpha Publishing Co., 1987.

Deser, Edwin. *Streetwise Self-Defense.* London, England: W. Foulsham & Company, 1989.

Eustace, Brian, and Mitchell, David. *Advanced Self Defense.* North Pomfret, VT: Random Century, 1988.

Fein, Judith. *Are You a Target? A Guide to Self-Protection & Personal Safety.* San Francisco, CA: Torrance Publishers, 1988.

Hess, Joseph C. *First Move: Street Self Defense.* Dubuque, IA: Kendall-Hunt, 1987.

Lavergne, Connie H. *Self-Defense.* Washington, DC: American Press, 1989.

Mroz, Raoph. *The Beginners Guide to Self-Protection: Your Options & Choices in Martial Arts & Firearms Training.* Sterling, MA: Iris Development, 1990.

Seabourne, Thomas G., and Herndon, Ernest. *Self Defense: A Body-Mind Approach.* Scottsdale, AZ: Gorsuch Scarisbrick, 1987.

Smith, Curtis, and DeBiaso, Richard A. *Buy Yourself a Minute: The Byam Method of Self-Defense.* Indiana, PA: Halldin Pub., 1989.

Smith, Susan E. *Fear or Freedom: A Woman's Options in Social Survival & Defense.* Racine, WI: Mother Courage Press, 1986.

Ventimiglia, Sebastian B., and Pesiri, Salina. *The Rape Defense Handbook for Women.* Plainview, NY: Jaz Publications, 1990.

Watson, John. *Save Your Hide! Tools for Self-Defense.* Boulder, CO: Paladin Press, 1987.

Weiss, Bernd W., and Weiss, Hilda O. *Beginning Self-Defense for Everybody.* Canoga Park, CA: Hiles & Hardin Pubs., 1988.

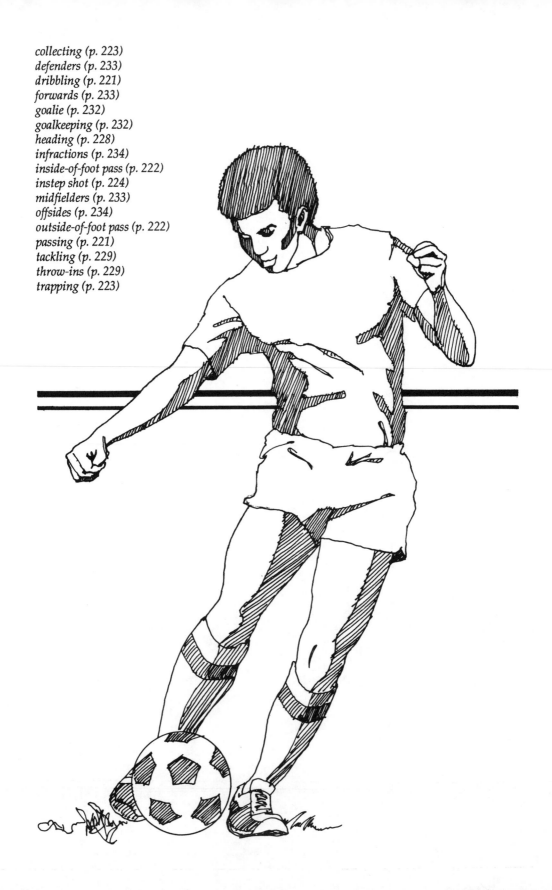

CHAPTER 16

Soccer

JOHN F. FELLENBAUM, JR.
Lincoln Junior High School and
Franklin and Marshall College
Lancaster, PA

INTRODUCTION

Soccer is the world's most popular sport. It is a simple, inexpensive, and safe activity which can be enjoyed by both boys and girls regardless of size or age. This team sport can be played leisurely at a slow deliberate pace as recreational soccer or at a very fast pace as professional or World Cup competition. At all levels eye-foot coordination is a basic part of the game since the ball is kicked up and down the field. Fitness components such as strength and endurance must also be developed along with agility, quick judgment, tactics, and strategy.

In earlier times fitness may have been stressed in playing soccer, but due to the number of players on a team, other skills remained undeveloped. For example, in Japan a game called Kemari was played where a leather-filled ball would be kicked from one end of a village to the other with as many as a few hundred players on a team. However, the modern version of soccer originated in England with the formation of Association Football, later shortened to "Assoc" which became the word "soccer." In 1863, the English Football Association was organized giving soccer unified rules for the first time. FIFA (Federation Internationale Football Association), established in 1904, has become the governing body of world soccer and under its leadership the USSF (United States Soccer Federation), founded in 1913, oversees soccer organizations in our country.

One of these organizations is the USYSA (United States Youth Soccer Association) which, since its formation in 1974, already represents over two million youth soccer players. Soccer is the fastest growing team sport in the United States.

SKILLS AND TECHNIQUES

DRIBBLING

Dribbling is the use of soft touches of the feet to control the ball on the ground without the help of a teammate. Three different types of dribbling are inside of the foot, outside of the foot, and with the sole of the foot.

With the inside of the foot, the ball is gently touched at the base of the greater toe and pushed along the ground with control. Using the outside of the foot, the ball is caressed at the base of the small toe. Using the sole of the foot, the ball can be rolled forward and backward and in a right and left direction. In soccer both feet should be used, the ball should be kept close to the feet, short strides should be taken, and the weight should be carried on the support foot.

Dribbling Exercises
1. Dribble in a restricted area, changing directions and speed.
2. Dribble around cones or pylons.
3. Dribble against a passive defender.
4. Dribble against an active defender.

Self-testing
Place six cones three yards apart and time how long it takes each student to weave around the cones and back again.

PASSING

Passing is the art of playing the ball from one player to another. It is the fastest way to advance the ball on the field and, therefore, is one of the most important skills to be developed.

Figure 1. Dribbling with the inside of the foot.

Figure 2. Dribbling with the outside of the foot.

To have success, proper coordination between the server and receiver is necessary. Timing of the pass, proper pace on the ball, and correct contact with the ball are essential elements in good passing.

Passing with the inside of the foot is the most accurate type of short pass. This is made with the inside of the foot just below the ankle bone between the big toe and the heel. Points to emphasize using the inside-of-the-foot pass:

- when striking the ball, lock the ankle with the toes pointed upward;
- concentrate on the ball;
- follow straight through the target with the kicking foot;
- contact the ball from the center to the top with the support foot pointed toward the target.

The outside-of-the-foot pass is done by striking the ball with the outside part of the instep. The ball is contacted on the outside part of the shoelaces with the support foot placed away from the ball to give the kicking leg room to properly kick the ball. This type of kicking motion comes from the knee and is a flicking action of the leg.

A player saves time with this pass since the lead foot can be used and it is not necessary to set up as for the inside of the foot. In soccer, which is a game of time and space, it is important to be able to use this type of pass. Points to emphasize using the outside-of-the-foot pass:

- keep the ankle locked and the toes pointed downward on the kicking foot;
- concentrate on the ball and follow through with the kicking foot to the target;
- strike the center to the top half of the ball to keep it low.

The instep pass which is executed with the hardest part of the foot is used for power in passing or shooting. It is generally utilized for long passes downfield or by defenders to get the ball out of danger in front of the goal. Points to emphasize with the instep pass are:

- concentrate on the ball;
- lock the ankle;
- follow through to the target;
- the support foot should be beside the ball 6-8" away and pointing toward the target.

Passing Exercises

1. Two players pass the ball back and forth down the field using the inside and outside of the foot.
2. Several players in a circle pass to each other and follow the pass.

Self-testing

1. Pass 10 times with each foot through two cones three yards apart from a distance of 10 to 15 yards.

COLLECTING

Trapping or "collecting" is the ability to control the ball on the ground or in the air and stop it close to the body before it is put into play. When a ball is not properly collected, possession can easily be lost and taken by the opponent.

One must be able to collect balls that are on the ground or in the air. With ground balls the sole of the foot, the inside of the foot, and the outside of the foot can be used. Air balls can be collected with various surfaces such as the inside and outside of the foot, the thighs, and the chest.

Ground Balls

The sole of the collecting foot is raised about four inches off the ground with the knee slightly bent. The toes are higher than the heel so the rolling ball is wedged in the "V" formed between the sole of the foot and the ground. The inside of the foot trap can be performed the same way as the inside of the foot pass except the foot is drawn back on contact to cushion the ball. The ankle, instead of being locked, should be relaxed for ball control. The outside of the foot trap is similar to the outside of the foot pass except the foot is relaxed to cushion the ball.

Air Balls

In the thigh trap, collecting is done by getting in the path of the ball and moving toward it. Just before the ball arrives, raise the thigh and make contact with the top of the thigh drawing it back and allowing the ball to drop to the ground.

With the chest trap, once again it is important to position the body in the path of the ball. Lean back with the chest and, on contact with the ball, relax the chest and

Figure 3. Inside-of-foot pass.

a. Put the balance foot ahead and away from the ball so that there is room to swing the kicking foot.

b. Point the toes of the kicking foot down and hold the ankle firm. Kick with the outside of the foot through the center of the ball.

c. Keep the eyes on the ball and follow through with the kicking foot.

Figure 4. Outside-of-foot pass.

straighten the body to bring the ball under control. Using the instep, get in the ball's path, relax the instep on contact, and draw the ball to the ground. Collecting air balls with the inside and outside of the foot is the same procedure as when collecting ground balls with the inside and outside of the foot.

Points to emphasize in collecting:
- body in path of the ball;
- relax body surface on contact;
- concentrate on ball;
- deaden balls on ground as quickly as possible.

Collecting Exercises
1. Two players pass the ball back and forth while practicing collecting.
2. In a circle, practice passing and collecting.
3. Two players stand 8 yards apart and throw the ball underhanded to practice collecting air balls.

Self-testing
One player throws the ball to a receiver who is awarded a point for each good trap.

SHOOTING

In today's game of "total" soccer, the objective is for all players to play both offense and defense. Fullbacks have opportunities to score goals and every player, except the goalkeeper, must learn to shoot with power and accuracy. Unless shooting is learned, one cannot be a complete player.

The most powerful type of shot in soccer is the instep shot. Contact is made on the hardest part of the foot at the shoelaces.

Shooting Exercises
1. Two lines, one from the left and one from the right, alternately dribble and shoot at goal from 15 to 18 yards.
2. Two or three players pass the ball between them down the field. One player takes a shot at goal from 15 to 18 yards.

Self-testing
Ten balls are placed on the ground in a semicircle about 15 yards from the goal and a shooter tries to score using first the right foot, then the left foot. Continue alternating feet until all balls have been kicked.

a. Bring the kicking foot back and keep the eyes on the ball.

b. Hold the ankle of the kicking foot firm and point the toes down so that the ball is hit by the top of the instep.

c. Kick through the center of the ball and follow through with the toes pointed down.

Figure 5. Instep pass.

d. Move the leg forward and meet the ball with the inside of the foot.

e. Move the foot back as contact is made to slow the ball down.

f. Bring the ball far back to control it and stop it dead.

Figure 6. Collecting low balls with the inside of the foot.

a. Meet the ball in midair with the thigh.

b. Let the ball land midway between the knee and the top of the thigh.

c. Withdraw the thigh on contact so that the ball drops to the ground.

Figure 7. Collecting high balls with the thigh.

d. Prepare to meet the ball with the center of the chest. Arch the body backward to cushion the ball.

e. Bend the knees to aid in cushioning the ball.

f. When contact is made, straighten the chest immediately so that the ball drops directly down.

Figure 8. Collecting high balls with the chest.

a. To prepare to kick the approaching ball face it and point the balance foot toward it.

b. Point the toes down and keep the ankle rigid, as in instep passing. Strike through the center of the ball. Put plenty of weight behind the shot by lifting the heel of the balance foot at the moment of impact.

Figure 9. Volley shot using the instep.

c. Prepare to kick the approaching ball by facing it and pointing the balance foot toward it.

d. Keeping the toes down and the ankle rigid, strike through the center of the ball.

e. Pivot on the balance foot in the direction the shot is to go. Put weight behind the shot by lifting the heel of the balance foot at the moment of impact.

Figure 10. Sideways volley shot using the instep.

HEADING

Heading is the ability to control, pass, or direct the ball with the head. A complete soccer player needs to perform heading skills to score a goal, collect the ball, pass to a teammate, or, as a defender, head the ball out of danger.

When heading from a stationary, or standing position, the feet should be placed shoulder width apart while bending at the knees and waist and arching the back. The chin should be toward the chest as the body is whipped forward striking the ball with the head. On contact, the chin is released

a. Keep the feet shoulder width apart. Bend the knees and arch the back from the hips.

b. Tuck the chin into the chest and whip the body forward so that the ball is hit with the forehead.

c. As contact is made, release the chin and follow through with the forehead.

Figure 11. Stationary heading.

a. Keep the eyes on the ball while jumping up to meet it. Slightly arch the back.

b. At the high point of the jump, meet the ball with the upper part of the forehead.

c. Follow through with the head and upper body in the direction the ball is to go.

Figure 12. Jump heading.

from the chest and the ball hit straight through to the goal.

In a jumping header, or jumping to head the ball, the skill is performed the same as in standing heading, only contact with the ball is made at the top of the jump. The take-off is usually on one foot and the head is snapped through the ball to the target. Points to emphasize in heading:

- Identify a contact point (i.e., the hairline).
- *You* hit the ball; do not let the ball hit you.
- Get in the path of the ball.
- Concentrate on the ball, keeping the eyes open and the mouth closed.
- Strike the top half of the ball to pass or shoot, and the bottom half to clear the ball out of danger.
- Begin to move the head when the ball is about 12 inches away and contact the ball on the forehead.

Heading Exercises
1. Practice heading to another player 8 yards away. Pass the ball back and forth across a circle of players.
2. Count the number of times the ball is headed without touching the ground.

Self-testing
Count the number of times a thrown ball can be accurately headed to a teammate's feet.

TACKLING

Tackling is the act of taking the ball away from the opponent. By making good tackles and winning the ball all over the field, a team is ensured of greater success. Points to emphasize on the front tackle:

- square up on the opponent;
- bend the knees and keep a low center of gravity;
- block the ball with the tackling foot;
- keep the weight on the support leg;
- push the ball through with the tackling foot.

Tackling Exercises
1. Two players stand 15 yards apart. One player passes to a teammate who traps and dribbles the ball while the first player makes the tackle.

2. Two players start in a tackling stance at a stationary ball and, on a given signal, each player tries to gain possession of the ball.

Self-testing
Play one against one in a small area (10 yards by 10 yards) for two minutes and whoever has possession of the ball for the longest time is the winner.

THROW-INS

A throw-in is the method used to put the ball into play from the sideline or touchline. For the standing throw-in, the player faces the field with two hands equidistant on the ball. The ball is thrown from back over the head with a follow-through and both feet in contact with the ground. A running throw-in is done the same as a standing throw-in except the thrower runs to gain distance on the throw.

Throw-in Exercises
1. Two players practice throws back and forth.
2. One player runs and the other player attempts to throw to the moving player's feet.

Self-testing
1. Mark five targets at various places on the field. Attempt one standing throw-in and one running throw-in at each target. Score two points for each direct hit and one for each near miss (within three feet).
2. Repeat the same exercise using a moving player as a target. A two-point throw will land just in front of his/her feet. A one-point throw may be up to four feet in front of the player.

a. Block ball with tackling foot.   **b.** Weight on non-tackling leg.

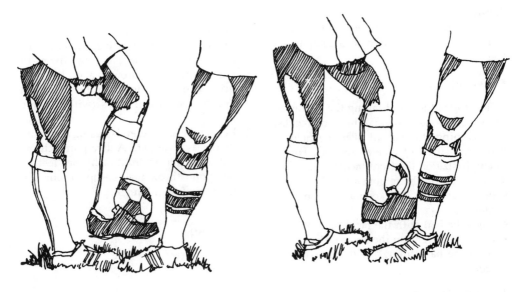

c. Knees are bent.   **d.** Push ball through with tackling foot.

Figure 13. Tackling techniques.

a. Use staggered stance with feet approximately 12 inches apart.

b. Lean trunk backward. Knees are bent.

c. Bend elbows with ball behind head.

d. Drive trunk forward and straighten arms.

e. Follow through to target.

Figure 14. Throw-in techniques.

GOALKEEPING

The goalkeeper is the only player on the field allowed to use the hands and, being the last line of defense, serves a very important function. The keeper not only tries to prevent goal-scoring by the opponents, but is also in a position to begin the team's attack with a quick outlet pass to an unguarded teammate. Because of their important team function, "goalies" must learn to use both feet and hands.

Catching Balls

When catching ground balls, the goalkeeper should: Face the ball with the body directly facing the line of flight. Bend at the waist allowing the arms to drop with the palms facing the ball and the fingers spread. Hands and elbows should be held close together. On contact with the ball, give with the hands and bring the ball up to the chest. The procedure for catching low air balls is the same as catching ground balls. With the high air balls, an attempt should be made to get the chest in back of the ball. Hands should be held close together with the fingers spread and the thumbs touching each other.

Figure 15. Positioning and grip.

SAFETY

Players can protect themselves from injury in soccer by keeping physically fit, by developing proper skills, and by using body protectors. Soccer is a vigorous game for which the body should be gradually conditioned. Provide a complete warmup every day before practice or playing a game. Take care of early season blisters and muscle pulls. Alternate tennis shoes with soccer shoes the first week to help prevent blisters. Kicking too hard at the beginning of the season should be discouraged as it often results in serious strains in the legs and groin.

Injury can be prevented by using shinguards and guards for glasses (the latter a "must" for the player who has to play with glasses). Shinguards are worn inside knee length socks.

Shoes are the most important part of the player's equipment. Regulation shoes are cleated with rubber to protect the player against slipping.

It is recommended that the goalie wear a distinguishing color to enable forwards to recognize him/her easily as they attack. The privileges of a goalie may result in dangerous maneuvers if he/she is not known during an aggressive play.

Students should be warned that they should never kick a ball that is above the hips and never head a ball that is below the head.

The playing fields or areas should be checked for holes and cleaned of dangerous objects such as rocks and glass.

RULES

The soccer field is rectangular (110-120 yards in length and 55-75 yards in width). (See Diagram 1.)

The official ball is made of leather or a synthetic material. It is 27-28" in circumference and weighs between 14 and 16 ounces.

A soccer team consists of eleven players, divided among the following positions:
Goalie—the person who defends the goal against scoring attempts. The goalie is the

only player who is allowed to touch the ball with his/her hands. This privilege is only allowed, however, when they are within the penalty area.

Defenders—field players whose task is to help defend the goal. They are frequently referred to as wings, the stopper, and the sweeper.

Midfielders—players who provide a link between the offense and the defense. They are frequently called on to assist both the defenders and the forwards and must be able to assume either role with equal skill. Midfielders are often referred to as half-backs.

Forwards—the scorers on the team. Often referred to as strikers or wings, they align themselves in positions to gain the advantage over the defense and score on the goal.

The game of soccer consists of two halves and is begun with a kickoff in the center of the field. Every player must be in his/her own half of the field and the initial kick must be forward and move at least one full revolution before being touched by another player. Kickoffs occur at the start of each half and after each goal. A goal may not be scored from the kickoff.

After the kickoff, play continues until the ball passes out-of-bounds, a penalty occurs,

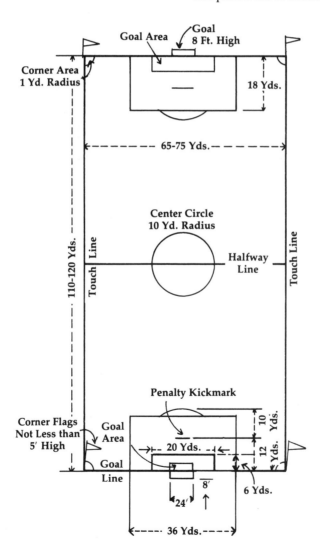

Diagram 1. Regulation soccer field.

or a goal is scored. A goal is worth one point and is credited only when the entire ball passes over the goal line and into the goal. A ball which is on or only partially over the goal line will not be considered a score. A goal will not count if an offensive player is offsides. Offsides occurs when an offensive player is nearer the opponent's goal line than the ball unless: the player is in his/her own half of the field; two defensive players are between the offensive player and the goal line; the ball was last played by the other team. One cannot be offsides on a corner kick, throw-in, or a goal kick. It is permissible to move into an offside position to receive a pass *if* one moves *after* the ball has been kicked.

If, during the course of play, the ball passes out-of-bounds on the sidelines, it is awarded to the team opposite that which last touched it. The team awarded possession will then restart play with a throw-in. If the ball passes out-of-bounds at the endlines, the game is restarted with either a goal kick or a corner kick depending on which team last touched the ball. If the offense last touched it, then a goal kick is awarded. If the defense last touched the ball, the game is restarted with a corner kick.

When, during the course of play, it becomes necessary for an official to stop play due to a rule infraction, either a minor or major infraction may be called. A minor rule infraction is penalized by awarding an indirect free kick to the team which was fouled. If the official views the infraction as a major penalty, a direct free kick may be awarded. A direct free kick, unlike an indirect free kick, may go directly into the goal without being touched by another player. If a major defensive infraction occurs within the penalty area, a penalty kick will be awarded. This is a free kick from the 12-yard line with no defenders except the goalie between the ball and the goal.

A player who is guilty of one of the following infractions will be cautioned by the referee:

1. joins the team after the kickoff and leaves or returns to the field of play without first reporting to the referee or linesman

2. persistently infringes on any of the rules of the game
3. argues with the referee
4. uses vulgar or profane language
5. is guilty of unsporting conduct.

In imposing a caution the referee will hold a yellow card over the offending player and will award an indirect free kick to the opposing team.

The referee shall eject from the game, without allowance for replacement, a player who:

1. is guilty of violent conduct or serious foul play
2. is abusive in gesture or language
3. persists in misconduct after having been cautioned (second yellow card).

In imposing an ejection, the referee will hold a red card over the offending player and will award either an indirect or a direct free kick, depending on the nature of the offense. The penalized player's team shall be required to play the remainder of the game shorthanded. In most leagues an ejected player will also be suspended from the next sanctioned league game.

For a further explanation of the rules of soccer and the judgment involved in assessing penalties, the reader is referred to the various soccer rulebooks, particularly the National Federation edition.

SOCCER TECHNIQUE

Soccer technique is best taught and practiced in three stages, fundamental, match related, and match condition. From simple to complex, fundamental instruction is introducing the technique without any pressure from an opponent and no limitations in time and space—basically, walking through the technique. Match related instruction provides experiences under conditions more closely related to the game. Introducing an opponent who applies pressure to the player attempting to execute the technique is an example. Match condition is the last stage of technical development. The player must now be able to execute under pressure from opponents, in limited time and space, while attempting to attack and score or defend and prevent a score. For example, playing 8 versus 8 on a full field with no goals, every successful chest collection will count as a goal scored.

General guidelines in teaching a particular technique are as follows:

- Introduce the technique
- Demonstrate the technique
- Briefly explain the key teaching points
- Organize into groups
- Practice
- Make corrections
- Confirm under match conditions

Tactical exercises are combined exercises that improve fitness, skill, and teamwork. They are among the most important factors in soccer teaching.

The use of restrictions or limitations is a valuable method of teaching tactical play. The following restrictions are suggested:

- Allow only one-touch passing
- Allow only two-touch passing
- Every third pass is wide
- Every third pass is back
- Players have to sprint into space after executing a pass

Small sided games, playing with fewer players than a regulation team, are important teaching vehicles for both skill development and enjoyment. These short sided games provide "economical training" while requiring application of techniques, tactics, and physical stamina.

TERMINOLOGY

Backs. Halfbacks and fullbacks.

Center Circle. A circle with a 10-yard radius at the center of the field.

Centerline. A line connecting the two sidelines at midfield, dividing the field into two equal parts.

Clear. A defensive play moving the ball away from scoring range.

Corner Kick. A direct free kick taken by the offensive team from within a one-yard arc at the corner of the field.

Direct Free Kick. An unobstructed place kick which may go directly into goal.

Dispossessing. Taking the ball away from an opponent. Tackling.

Dribble. The act of running with the ball under control using a series of pushes or taps of the feet.

Feed. To pass the ball to a teammate in position for a shot on goal.

Goal Area. A marked area immediately in front of the goal 24 yards wide and 6 yards deep.

Goal Kick. An indirect free kick taken by the defense after the ball has passed over the endline.

Goal Line (Endline). The boundary line marking the end of the field.

Head. To play the ball with the head.

Holding. To restrict an opponent's movement with the arms or hands.

Indirect Free Kick. An unobstructed place kick which must be touched by another player before it can enter the goal.

Instep. The inside portion of the foot from the toes to the ankle.

Interchanging. Offensive players moving out of regular positions to confuse the defense.

Offside. A player who is nearer the opponent's goal line than the ball at the moment the ball is played, except as provided by the rules.

Pass. To kick or head the ball to a teammate.

Penalty Area. A marked area in front of the goal, 44 yards wide and 18 yards deep.

Penalty Kick. A direct free kick taken by the offensive team in response to a foul occurring in the penalty area.

Save. To prevent the ball from entering the goal.

Striking. The act of kicking or contacting the ball.

Tackle. A maneuver used to cause an opponent to lose possession of the ball.

Throw-in. A method of restarting the game after the ball has gone out-of-bounds over the sideline.

Trap. A method of bringing the ball under a player's control.

CHAPTER 17

Softball

BECKY L. SISLEY
University of Oregon
Eugene, OR

INTRODUCTION

The game of softball is over one hundred years old. It has undergone numerous changes since its first appearance on Thanksgiving Day in 1887. George Hancock of Chicago is credited with originating the game. Hancock made the first ball out of a boxing glove and wrote the first set of rules, which were modified as the game spread throughout the United States and Canada. Some of softball's variations were known as Kitten Ball, Mush Ball, Fast Ball, Big Ball, and Diamond Ball.

It soon became apparent that there was a need to standardize the rules and equipment used for the game. The first set of unified softball rules was established in 1933. The Amateur Softball Association was created in 1934 and still remains the governing body for softball in the United States. This organization has done much to encourage expanded programs for participants of all ages and competitive interests. Leagues are sanctioned under the sponsorship of ASA as well as state, regional, and national tournaments.

The 12-inch slow pitch game emerged in the mid-1950s. This game permits a team to be successful without possessing a pitcher who is a fast-ball, strike-out artist. Rules require that the ball be pitched with an arc of anywhere from three to twelve feet. Slow pitch was first played primarily by older players, but this emphasis has changed. The fact that there are many hits and runs indicates that the game is filled with plenty of action.

The ASA has developed a broad youth program for both fast and slow pitch. Most local communities sponsor summer softball leagues on different competitive levels and for various ages. Coed teams are popular for school intramurals as well as for city league play. There are plenty of opportunities to enjoy the exciting and challenging game of softball.

SKILLS AND TECHNIQUES

The following basic skills are essential in playing softball: throwing, catching, fielding, batting, running. The first three are considered defensive skills while batting and baserunning are offensive skills.

THROWING

There are three basic ways of throwing: overhand, underhand, sidearm. Regardless of which type of throw is used, students should be taught to observe the following fundamentals:

1. Stand in a stride position with the foot opposite the throwing hand in front.
2. Grip the ball with the first and second fingers on top of the ball and with the thumb under the ball (three fingers may be used with a small hand). The ball rests only on the finger pads and is away from the palm of the hand.
3. On the wind-up, rotate the body by turning the glove side toward the direction of the throw. Keep the eyes on the target as the body weight is rotated onto the rear foot.
4. The elbow should lead the forward arm motion with the hand following.
5. As the throwing arm moves forward, let the body rotate forward so that the weight is transferred from the rear foot to the front foot.
6. Release the ball with the fingers pointing toward the target.

Figure 1. Overhead throwing pattern.

7. Follow through with the arm in the direction of the target.

Each of the throws differ in regard to the position of the palm of the hand as the ball is released. In the overhand throw the palm faces down; in the underhand throw the palm faces up; in the sidearm throw the palm faces the body.

Since the ball can be thrown farther with the overhand throw, it should be used by catchers and outfielders; however, all players can use this more easily controlled and accurate throw when they have sufficient time to make a play. The sidearm throw is generally used by infielders when they need to throw in a hurry. When tossing the ball a short distance to a teammate, an underhand throw should be used.

The overhand throw is one of the most used skills in softball. Figure 1 shows the body action of a skillful thrower. Notice that the rear leg is under the body, supporting the body weight, at the beginning of the movement pattern. The weight is transferred to the front foot as the body starts to rotate toward the target. It is important that the elbow of the throwing arm be held up and away from the body and that the arm is directed forward in a whip-like action. The wrist is snapped just as the ball is released. The greater the distance and the faster the movement of the arm, the greater the force that can be transferred to the ball.

The following activities can be used to evaluate ability in the overhand throw.

Throw to a Wall Target. Place a target consisting of three concentric circles on the wall. The center circle should measure two feet in diameter, the middle circle four feet, and the outer circle should be six feet in diameter. Students stand behind a line 40 feet from the wall for girls and 65 feet for boys and attempt to throw the ball to the center of the target. Score five points for hitting within the smallest circle, three points for hitting within the middle circle, and one point for hitting within the outer circle. Ten trials may be attempted. Score the total of all trials.

Velocity Throw. Players stand in the shortstop position, field a ground ball which is thrown by a teammate from home plate, and throw to first base. The ball must be picked up after it has crossed a line between second and third base.

Throw for Distance. Measure the distance the ball can be thrown in the air. Make sure that a proper warm-up is provided before students throw as hard as possible.

CATCHING AND FIELDING

A large part of catching and fielding is being in a "ready" position, able to move quickly to react to a hit. In this position the body is crouched with the knees and hips flexed. The feet should be comfortably apart in a parallel position. The hands should rest on the knees, or the arms should hang loosely toward the ground as the pitcher begins the delivery. The eyes should focus on the pitcher. As the ball is pitched, the weight is evenly distributed on the balls of the feet, the body leans forward, and the arms are slightly raised, putting the body in a complete state of alertness. This is particularly true for outfielders. Infielders usually keep their gloves close to the ground as they anticipate the hit.

Fielding Ground Balls

Learning how to properly field ground balls requires much practice. Figure 2 shows the position for fielding a ground

Figure 2. Fielding a ground ball.

ball. The following cues will help describe the mechanics of this skill.

1. The eyes need to watch the batter's swing and remain in contact with the ball throughout the fielding action.
2. The body is moved to center behind the ball.
3. The feet should be in a stride position with the knees bent and the glove side foot forward.
4. The body should be bent at the waist with the hips low to the ground.
5. The arms should be outstretched, and the fingers pointed downward with the little fingers together. Contact should be made with the ball opposite the glove side foot.
6. The arms should "give" as the ball is caught.

The following drills can be done to develop ground ball fielding ability:

1. **Wall rebound fielding**—Player throws a rubber ball or tennis ball against a wall and reacts to the rebound off the wall to field the ball. The ball can be thrown slightly to the right or to the left so that the player will have to move to get behind the ball when fielding.
2. **Fielding thrown balls**—Divide the group into pairs. One partner throws ground balls to the right and left of the other. Have the balls thrown softly at first and then thrown harder as fielding ability improves.
3. **Fielding hit balls**—Have a batter hit ground balls to be fielded. See if ten balls in a row can be successfully fielded and returned to a catcher.

Fielding Fly Balls

When catching fly balls players should position themselves so that the ball is caught on the throwing side of the body in front of the throwing shoulder. These cues can be used to emphasize the mechanics of catching a fly ball:

1. Hustle to where the ball is to be caught.
2. Get the body behind the ball and move forward to catch.
3. Have the arms outstretched and make the catch with two hands at head height. Hands are held with thumbs together and fingers pointed upward.

4. The catching motion blends into the backswing for the throw as the body weight shifts onto the throwing side leg.
5. Grasp the ball securely before throwing and make sure the body weight is balanced.

Players must learn to get a quick start when fielding fly balls and also to call for the ball if more than one player is likely to try to make the catch. It is best to clearly and loudly yell "mine" or "I have it."

The following drills will help to improve skill in fielding fly balls.

1. **Catching thrown balls**—Each student stands about 20 feet from a partner. Have the partner throw the ball so that it can be caught with a forward, backward, or sideward movement of the body.
2. **Turn and catch**—Player stands approximately 10 feet from a partner with the back turned. Have the partner toss the ball high into the air and yell "turn" as they do so. When the partner yells "turn," player must locate the ball, move into position, and make the catch before the ball hits the ground.
3. **Catch thrown balls**—Player stands 5 feet from a partner who will be the thrower. Player runs toward the thrower, tosses him or her a ball, then circles away. The thrower should toss the ball high into the air as if throwing a long forward pass. Player runs out and away, keeping an eye on the ball, moves into position and makes the catch.

PITCHING

Another major defensive skill in softball is pitching. The pitcher must know how to grip the ball, release the ball, control the pitch, pitch the ball so that it hits the corners of the plate, and be ready to field a batted ball. The style of pitching will vary depending on whether fast or slow pitch ball is being played. The pitching rules describe what makes a pitch legal. The mechanics presented here will be for fast pitch. Rule differences which relate to slow pitch are discussed later in the chapter.

The pitcher should assume a starting position with the ball held in both hands in front of the body and with both feet touching the pitcher's plate. One step toward the batter is taken as the ball is released. A second step is necessary to follow through to regain balance and get the body in a good fielding position. The quicker the arm and hand are moving at the time of release, the faster the ball can be thrown. The pitching motion can be divided into three distinct phases: the backswing, the forward swing and release, the follow-through.

Backswing

The pitching arm should swing backward as far as possible. Ideally, the hand should come up higher than the shoulder. The shoulders and hips rotate toward third base (left-handed pitchers toward first base) while the wrist is cocked. Throughout this motion the weight should be placed on the back foot.

Forward Swing and Release

The weight should begin to shift forward as a step forward on the foot opposite the pitching arm is taken. The shoulders and hips rotate back to their original position so that they face the batter. As the pitching hand swings past the thigh the wrist snaps forward and the hand releases the ball.

Follow-through

The pitching arm continues up and across the body while the rest of the body continues to face the batter in the ready position so that the ball can be fielded if necessary.

A good pitcher must practice many hours to develop speed and control. The following drills may be of help:

1. **Wall target pitching**—Place a target the size of a normal strike zone on the wall. Boys take their pitching stance 46 feet from the wall while girls stand 40 feet from the wall. Practice pitching to the target using a legal pitching motion.
2. **Four corners**—For this drill pitching may be done to a catcher or a wall target. Pitchers practice throwing at the extreme corners of the normal strike zone for the purpose of developing control and accuracy. Since it is important to concentrate on the catcher's target, the pitcher should learn to wait off the mound until the catcher is ready. Once the catcher is in

position, the pitcher steps on the mound and begins the motion.
3. **Calling balls and strikes**—Each player pitches a designated number of innings to a catcher who is calling balls and strikes. This drill permits different count situations and game-like pressure to be experienced.

BATTING

Batting is a striking activity that involves hitting one moving object with another. The most important factor in hitting a ball is to provide force with the bat. A firm grip is necessary to transfer power and to control the bat. In batting, practices and drills are essential for developing timing, a level swing, and a "batting eye." It is seldom that two players will use identical batting techniques.

The following fundamentals lead to good batting skills (instructions are written for a right-handed batter):

1. Students should use a bat which feels comfortable to swing and is easy to control, to make sure that the weight and

Figure 3. Batting stance.

length of the bat and the size of the grip in relation to the size of the hands are right, and to avoid the tendency to use a bat that is too heavy or too long.

2. While waiting for the pitcher to deliver the ball, the bat should be held with a firm but relaxed grip. Hands are together at the neck of the bat. The arm closest to the pitcher should be extended parallel to the ground. The bat should be held back and off the right shoulder (see Figure 3).

3. The batter stands in a comfortable position facing the home plate. The head is turned toward the pitcher so that the oncoming ball is being viewed directly. Emphasize the importance of watching the ball as it is released by the pitcher and stepping into the swing with the left foot.

4. The bat should be swung forward in a smooth motion to make contact with the ball in front of home plate. (*Note:* There is a tendency for the inexperienced batter to jerk the bat forward then backward and then forward again.)

5. The swing finishes with a follow-through past the left hip.

6. The feet should provide a solid base of support with the back foot planted.

As progress is made in the ability to bat and as skill becomes more refined these cues for efficient performance should be emphasized: swing the bat level, have the arms straight and snap the wrists at the point of contact, keep the body level during the swing (no dipping), keep the step toward the pitcher short and consistent, and keep the head position still.

There are a number of ways to work on batting skill. Some suggestions are below.

Mirror Swing. Batters stand in front of a mirror and take a normal swing. Stress concentration on the mechanics of a good swing. The bat can also be swung while a partner evaluates form. Be sure the evaluator maintains a safe distance between himself/herself and the batter.

Toss Ball. Stand about 10 feet from a net, fence, or other impact-absorbing surface. A partner kneels in a facing position so that he/she is opposite the rear foot and well out

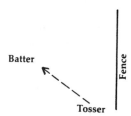

Diagram 1. The toss ball drill.

of swinging range. When in position, the partner tosses the ball to the strike zone (see Diagram 1). Batter executes a normal swing at the ball. It will be helpful to concentrate on one element of the swing at a time.

Batting Tee Hitting. Hitting a stationary ball placed at a variety of heights can be practiced with the use of a batting tee. Batters should practice hitting line drives in all directions as well as distance hitting to all fields. This is also a good opportunity for other players to practice fielding. It is best to have a catcher nearby to retrieve the balls thrown in from the field. It is also possible to work independently with a batting tee by hitting into a screen or backstop.

BUNTING

Fast pitch rules allow the batter to bunt the ball. A bunt is a legally hit ball, not swung at, but purposely met with the bat and tapped slowly within the infield. In most cases the bunt is used to advance a baserunner from one base to the next while the batter is put out. This is called a sacrifice bunt. Some batters can have such accurate placement on a bunt that they can beat the ball to first and thus get a base hit. In addition to the sacrifice bunt and the bunt for a hit, there are the drag bunt and swinging bunt. Foot placement varies with the type of bunt being executed.

Bunting is an intermediate level skill that can add to the strategy used in the game. When performing a sacrifice bunt, the bat should be held parallel to the ground at shoulder level in front of the body with the arms slightly extended. The batter can pivot into this position with the feet square to the pitcher when the pitcher starts the arm action. Figure 4 illustrates the batting stance for the bunt. If the ball is low, the knees should be bent so that the bat is kept level. It is good advice to bunt only pitches which are within the strike zone. Diagram 2 shows the best area in which to place a bunt.

Figure 4. Bunting stance.

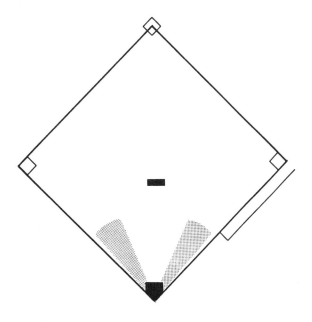

Diagram 2. Bunt placement.

BASERUNNING

Running speed and the ability to use sound offensive judgment are essential qualities of a good baserunner. Quickly getting out of the batter's box is very important. A common fault made by batters upon hitting the ball is waiting to see where the ball goes before running. To correct this fault concentrate on finishing the swing and practicing the push-off start toward first base. The batter should run out every hit because a field error could occur and he/she may reach first base safely. The following suggestions will help improve baserunning:

1. Keep an eye on the ball and advance additional bases whenever possible, e.g., when four balls are called on the batter, on a wild throwback from catcher to pitcher, on a wild pitch, and on any poorly thrown ball.
2. Avoid wide turns when rounding the bases.
3. Run on any hit ball when there are two outs.
4. Lead off after each pitch and advance if possible (differs in slow-pitch).
5. When running out an infield hit stay within the running lane in foul territory, which is designated by a white line to the right side of the baseline about midway between home and first base.
6. Run along the foul territory side of the line from third base to home to avoid being hit by a fairly batted ball.
7. Know the number of outs, innings, score, and count on the batter.
8. Avoid interfering with a player or the ball while it is being fielded.
9. Listen to and watch the base coaches for assistance.

To work on baserunning skills the following drills can be practiced:

1. **Getting out of the box**—Batter practices taking a swing at an imaginary pitch then dropping the bat, getting quickly out of the box, and running straight through first base.
2. **Around the bases**—Player runs all the way around the bases making narrow turns and touching the inside corner of each base. Have someone time running speed with a stopwatch.
3. **Stealing a base**—Practice leaving the base when the ball leaves the pitcher's hand and advancing to the next base before the catcher can make the play.

SAFETY

There is much that can be done to ensure that the game of softball is played under safe conditions and that precautions are taken to prevent injury. Proper equipment which complies with the rules is mandatory. The catcher's mask and chest protector should fit properly. The catcher must be wearing this equipment when a batter is involved in practice situations as well as in game play. Bats should have grips which help to prevent them from slipping out of the batter's hands. Check to be sure that all aluminum bats are of single unit construction. An aluminum bat with a handle that is separate from the barrel is dangerous because these elements can separate from one another on impact. There must always be a place to put equipment when it is not being used so that it is not a hazard during game play or practice.

The softball diamond should be located where there are no protruding hazards such as goalposts, telephone poles, or sprinkler heads. The surface must be smooth. Rules state there must be 25 feet of unobstructed area beyond each foul line and behind home plate, and that the pitcher's plate must be securely fastened.

It is each player's responsibility to warm up properly in order to avoid potential injury to muscles, joints, and tendons. Warm-up drills which include stretching, easy throwing, and running are an essential part of any softball class or team practice. When drills are performed it is important to have groups working in the same direction and with adequate space. It is also important to be alert to the direction of the sun, which can be very blinding at certain times of the day.

Everyone must do his/her part to ensure their own safety and that of fellow players. Always keep an eye on the ball to be aware of what play is developing and so that the appropriate reaction can be given. Players must be alert for the actions of teammates and opponents to avoid unnecessary collisions and injuries. Remember, safe play means fun play for all.

SCORING, RULES, AND ETIQUETTE

THE GAME

A game of softball is played between two teams of nine players (fast pitch) or ten players (slow pitch) on a softball diamond. Diagram 3 shows the layout for a softball diamond and placement of the defensive team. The extra player in slow pitch usually plays in a short field position. The object of the game is to score more runs than the opponent in a regulation game, which consists of seven innings. An inning is that part of a game within which the teams alternate on offense (up to bat) and defense (in the field) and in which there are three outs for each team. A run is scored each time a baserunner crosses home plate having legally touched all bases before the third out of an inning is made. The home

team takes the field first. For class and intramural games the team first in the field can be determined by the toss of a coin.

Fast Pitch and Slow Pitch Rule Differences

There are several major rule differences between fast pitch and slow pitch. Most of these differences relate to pitching regulations. Listed below are some of the most important rules which differ.
1. In slow pitch the ball shall be released at a moderate speed and must have an arc of at least three feet and go no higher than 12 feet from the ground.
2. The pitching distance for men's and women's slow pitch is 46 feet, while the fast pitch distance is 46 feet for men and 40 feet for women.
3. At the beginning of the pitch the slow pitch pitcher need only have one foot in contact with the pitcher's plate while in fast pitch both feet must touch the plate.
4. Slow pitch does not allow any base stealing and the baserunner may not leave the base until the ball crosses home plate or has been hit by the batter. In fast pitch

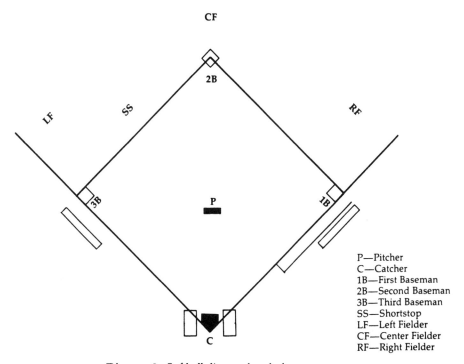

Diagram 3. Softball diamond and players.

P—Pitcher
C—Catcher
1B—First Baseman
2B—Second Baseman
3B—Third Baseman
SS—Shortstop
LF—Left Fielder
CF—Center Fielder
RF—Right Fielder

the baserunner can take a lead-off when the ball leaves the pitcher's hand.

5. While bunting is a major part of fast pitch, the batter is out in slow pitch if he/she chops downward on the ball or attempts to bunt the pitch.

6. In slow pitch if a swing is made and a third strike missed, the batter is out whether the catcher catches the ball or not. In fast pitch, if the catcher drops the third strike the batter may run to first base with the liability to be put out if there are less than two outs and the base is unoccupied. If there are two outs, he/she may run whether or not the base is occupied.

7. If a batter hits a foul ball with a two strike count in slow pitch, the batter is out.

Pitching Rules

A few of the major rules are listed below.

1. The pitcher must take a stance on the pitcher's plate and present the ball in front of the body before beginning the delivery.

2. The ball must be thrown with an underhand motion and the wrist can be no farther away from the body than the elbow when the wrist passes below the hip.

3. The pitcher's delivery motion may not involve more than one arm rotation, or include a change of forward motion or rocker motion where both hands return to the ball.

4. The pitch is completed when one step is taken toward the batter as the ball is released. In slow pitch a step is not required.

Batting Rules

Listed below are some of the basic rules for batting.

1. If the batter swings at a pitched ball and misses, a strike is called.

2. If the batter gets three strikes, he/she is called out. The batter is awarded first base if he/she gets four balls.

3. A foul ball is called if a hit ball lands outside the lines defining the playing field.

4. The batter may reach first base by one of the following methods: by hitting the ball in fair territory and getting to first before the ball; by being hit with a pitched ball; by getting a walk when four "balls" have been thrown by the pitcher; by an error by a fielder; by the catcher or catcher's equipment interfering with him/her.

5. The batter is out under these conditions: when a fielder catches his/her fly ball; when a third strike is caught by the catcher, or on a third strike when first base is occupied and there are less than two outs; when a bunt goes foul on a third strike; when the batted ball is thrown to first before he/she arrives; when an "infield fly" is hit, if first and second bases are occupied and there are less than two outs; when he/she interferes with players attempting to make a put-out; when batting out of order; when hitting the ball while standing out of the batter's box.

Baserunning Rules

The batter becomes a baserunner as soon as he/she hits the ball in fair territory. Here are some important rules which govern baserunning:

1. A baserunner may leave the base as soon as the ball leaves the pitcher's hand (fast pitch).

2. A baserunner is out if he/she interferes with a player fielding a batted ball.

3. A baserunner must run the bases in order and may not leave the imaginary three-foot base path in order to avoid being tagged out.

4. A baserunner is out if touched with the ball while off a base.

5. A baserunner may attempt to advance a base after a legally caught fly ball (fair or foul) is first touched.

6. Two baserunners may not occupy the same base.

ETIQUETTE

Good sportsmanship helps to make the game of softball fun to play. There are many things teammates can do to display good sportsmanship. It is important to respect the umpires and to graciously accept their decisions. Be sure to give positive encouragement to teammates and acknowledge the good plays of opponents. Pick up the catcher's mask at the beginning of the inning. Remove the bat from home plate area when up to bat. Make every attempt to avoid unnecessary collisions. As a baserunner or as a fielder learn how to execute skills in a safe manner which will help to prevent injuries. Congratulate the opposite team after the game. Play hard and be a good sport.

STRATEGY

The game of softball becomes more challenging as basic skills improve and attention is turned to offensive and defensive tactics. Probably one of the most important elements of strategy is to place the players in the field in the positions which best match their defensive skills.

In intermediate and advanced level play, much strategy is used in determining the order in which the players will bat. The game situation takes into account the number of outs, location of baserunners, and the score of the game. The inning as well as the specific skills of fielders and batters determine the particular strategy to be employed.

Many of the elements of strategy used in baseball can be applied to softball. The following hints on strategy which relate to defensive play, batting, and baserunning will be helpful as softball playing ability is developed.

DEFENSIVE PLAY

Defensive strategy results largely from anticipation, i.e., knowing what to do with the ball when it comes. Keep these hints in mind when concentrating on the defensive elements of the game.

1. Recognize that the primary task is to field the ball first and then to make an accurate throw. Player should get behind the ball and use two hands when fielding.
2. Before the ball is pitched, each player should know the play to be made. Mental preparation is important.
3. Always play for one sure out.
4. Teammates should talk to each other to build strong team unity. Remind each

other of the number of outs, where the batter hit the last time up to bat, and give positive encouragement to the pitcher.
5. Players should know the defensive skills of their teammates, especially those playing nearby. They should practice sharing responsibilities such as covering a base or backing up a play. (To back up a play means to be positioned behind a player who is fielding a hit or thrown ball so as to be in position to get the ball if it is missed by the first fielder.)
6. A baseman should not stand on base unless involved in a play, because the positioning could block a baserunner.
7. Players should learn how to cover a base properly for a tag play or a force out.
8. Outfielders should know their responsibilities for backing up hit balls and thrown balls. They must effectively communicate with other fielders to avoid collisions. The basic rule is to throw the ball one base ahead of the runner on fly balls and two bases ahead on ground balls.
9. Fielders should hold up the throw if it will be too late to make a play. Having good judgment about when not to throw is just as important as knowing where to throw.
10. The pitcher should concentrate on the target given by the catcher. It is best to work on getting the ball over the plate rather than trying to strike out opponents.
11. Fielders must be ready to anticipate the play and react to the action of the offense. Intermediate level strategy may involve bunting and stealing.
12. In more advanced play the pitcher will attempt to pitch to each batter's weakness and the fielders will adjust their positions depending on the batter's strengths and the game situation.

BATTING STRATEGY

Some elements of batting can be practiced by performing drills; however, the real test of offensive power is how well a player can produce in a game. Here are some suggestions which can help batters achieve more success:

1. Once in the batter's box, be ready, but relaxed, and concentrate on the pitcher.
2. A batter's primary task is to hit the ball. Be ready to swing at every pitch. Hold up the swing if the ball is not in the strike zone. Know the strike zone.
3. It is best not to swing when there is a three-ball and no-strike count.
4. Be prepared to bunt the ball if there is a runner on first base with one or no outs.
5. If a skillful batter, survey the defensive positioning of opponents to see an open space where a bunt or hit may be placed.

BASERUNNING STRATEGY

Aggressive baserunning is an exciting part of softball. Although the baserunner may not leave the base prior to the ball leaving the pitcher's hand, which is legal in baseball, there are many offensive tactics which challenge each baserunner's ability. A good baserunner is aggressive and confident. Below are some suggestions for developing baserunning skills.

1. Runners must touch each base in order. Remember that second and third base cannot be overrun.
2. Runners should take a lead-off with each pitch and be ready to advance a base if the ball gets away from the catcher.
3. Runners should always know the number of outs and the running options involved. If there are two outs, run with the hit. On a fly ball hit to the outfield if there is one or no outs, stay near the base, and return to the base after the ball is caught. Run to the next base after the ball is caught if time permits. A runner on third should stay on the base and run home after the catch. On ground balls with one or no outs, advance to the next base with the hit.
4. Runners should always try to avoid an unnecessary collision with defensive players covering a base.
5. Runners on first base in the early part of the game should be told to try to steal second base to determine the throwing ability and alertness of the catcher.

6. On a bunt play, runner must be sure the ball is hit to the ground before advancing to the next base.
7. In more advanced level play, when coaches are used to guide the offensive strategy, the runner must be ready to follow the signals of the coaches who might call for a steal, hit-and-run, or squeeze play.

The offensive and defensive strategy employed in slow pitch is somewhat different from that described above because of rule variations. The pitching method contributes to more hits and more baserunners; however, some of the more advanced aspects of batting and baserunning tactics related to stealing and bunting cannot be used in slow pitch. Both games create a challenge to the players as the players attempt to apply strategy to beat their opponents within the spirit and requirements of the rules.

EQUIPMENT

The quality of softball equipment used and its care can have a definite effect on skill performance. Experience has shown that it is best to buy equipment which is made by a well-known manufacturer and which meets the official standards specified by the rules. Equipment will last longer if it is of good quality.

Balls

There are numerous brands and kinds of softballs. Those which meet ASA approval are so marked and have "official softball" stamped on them. The cover of the ball is made of tanned horse or cowhide. Balls with a whiter cover are designed for both day and night use. These often have a slicker surface. Restricted flight balls have red seams. These balls are used for the slow pitch game. It is important that balls be kept dry. Once they become wet and dry out, they get heavier and could cause injury to the throwing arm. It is good to have rubber-covered balls for poor weather.

Bats

Bats come in various shapes and sizes. In recent years there has been more use of aluminum bats because they last longer than wooden bats. Bats which meet rule specifications are marked "official softball" by the manufacturer. It is good to have a variety of bats.

Gloves

One key to success in playing softball is to have a top quality glove. Rules allow only the catcher and first baseman to use mitts. Purchase a glove which has a good pocket and one that can be easily manipulated in the hand. Glove oil may be used to loosen up the leather of a new glove. Saddle soap can be used to clean dirt from the leather. Let a wet glove dry naturally; then oil it and use saddle soap on it. It is helpful to store a ball in the glove with a band to hold it in place to create and retain the shape of the pocket. Treat a glove with care and it will last a long time.

Catcher's equipment

Acquiring the appropriate catcher's gear is a must. The mask needs to be adjustable so that it can snugly fit the head. There are both lightweight wire masks and heavier bar-style models. Chest protectors can be purchased in different models and sizes. Here again, it is necessary that the protector fit properly. For fast-pitch softball, it may be advisable for the catcher to wear shinguards. These should be securely fastened and fit the length of the lower leg. When equipment is properly cared for and stored in the appropriate manner, it will last longer.

Uniforms

Sharp-looking uniforms can add spice to any team. The better the quality of the uniform, the longer it will last. Long-sleeved undershirts are an essential part of the uniform in cooler weather. Sun visors or hats may be a necessity. Sliding pads can help to prevent abrasions, especially if players are wearing shorts. Cleated shoes help to ensure good footing for baserunning and fielding. Both rubber and metal cleats are available. Take pride in a uniform and care for equipment.

TERMINOLOGY

Advance. To run from one base to the next.
Backing Up. A fielder moving behind another fielder to stop the ball if an error occurs.
Bag. A base.
Ball. A pitch which is not within the strike zone of a batter.
Batter's Box. The area on either side of home plate where the batter must stand when batting.
Battery. The pitcher and the catcher.
Bunt. A legally hit ball, not swung at, but purposely tapped with the bat and directed near the foul lines in the infield.
Cleanup. The fourth hitter in the batting order.
Diamond. The area formed by the four bases (the entire playing field is also considered the diamond).
Double Play. Defensive action which results in two outs.
Error. A defensive misplay.
Fair Ball. A batted ball which is touched or stops between the foul lines in the infield or which first lands between the foul lines beyond the bases.
Force Out. A put-out on a baserunner who was forced to advance due to the batter becoming a baserunner.
Foul Ball. A ball hit outside of fair territory.
Full Count. Three balls and two strikes on the batter.
Infield Fly. A fair hit ball within the infield area which can be easily caught by an infielder. With one or no outs and with runners on first and second or all three bases, the infield fly rule is in effect.
Inning. That portion of a game within which the teams alternate on offense and defense and in which there are three outs for each team.
Lead-off. A quick move off the base by a runner once the ball leaves the pitcher's hand (fast pitch).
On Deck. The next batter to come to bat.
Pitcher's Plate. The rubber form, two feet by six inches, from which the pitcher must pitch.
Sacrifice. A batted ball which intentionally advances the runner, but results in the batter being put out.
Shut Out. A game in which one team does not score.
Squeeze. To advance a runner home from third base on a bunt.
Steal. To advance from one base to the next from the time the ball leaves the pitcher's hand until he/she is ready to pitch again.
Strike Zone. That area above home plate between the batter's knees and armpits (fast pitch) when the batter is in his/her normal batting stance. The batter's highest shoulder is the top of the area for slow pitch.
Wild Pitch. A pitched ball which is so high, so low, or so wide that the catcher has no chance of controlling it.

CHAPTER 18

Swimming

RALPH L. JOHNSON
Indiana University of Pennsylvania
Indiana, PA

INTRODUCTION

VALUES OF SWIMMING AND DIVING

The development of skills in swimming and diving has the potential to open new horizons to secondary school students, leading them into the vast world of aquatic recreation, instruction, competition, and a degree of wellness that can enhance and extend human life.

Since vacations and summer camp experience are often centered around aquatic activities, good swimming skills are essential to fun. Swimming also provides access to the exciting recreational activities of skin and scuba diving, water skiing, sailing, canoeing, windsurfing, and parasailing.

For those students who develop their swimming skills to more proficient levels the opportunity exists to obtain certification as a lifeguard, swimming instructor, or perhaps as an instructor capable of working with the disabled and other special population groups. Certification can lead to aquatic jobs as a lifeguard, swimming instructor or facility manager.

Some students will be able to elevate their skills and abilities to even higher levels in competitive aquatic sports. Many schools provide competition for young men and women in swimming, diving, water polo, and synchronized swimming. These sports can provide recognition for participants and their school and can provide a sense of pride for the entire community. Outstanding athletes also enjoy the possibility of earning college scholarships.

Swimming is a form of life insurance since it is a fitness activity that enhances individual wellness. Four workouts a week for 30-45 minutes can improve circulation and respiration and lower cholesterol, triglycerides, and blood sugar. Five to six workouts a week can significantly reduce fat tissue and increase muscle mass. And few activities offer so much benefit in a low impact aerobic workout. Skill in swimming, along with some knowledge of water safety, can provide an increased measure of aquatic safety in a community.

CONFIDENCE AND ADJUSTMENT SKILLS

Entering the Water

For beginners, the safest way to enter shallow water is to sit down at pool side with their legs in the water and ease in or use the pool ladder. At no time should beginners be allowed to dive or jump into the pool at the shallow end. When diving and jumping entries are taught, all instruction must take place in the deep end in at least 9 feet of water.

To ease in, the students should sit on the side or coping with their legs in the water. Have them place both hands on the deck at one side of their body. Their weight should be transferred to their hands while they turn 180 degrees and then slowly lower themselves into the pool while maintaining their hold on the side of the pool.

Control of Breathing

The first adjustment skill for beginners should be breath holding. Inhale through the mouth, hold the breath and when exhaling, do so by exhaling through the mouth or nose and mouth. After several successful attempts at breath holding with face in the water while holding on to the pool side, bobbing can be introduced.

Bobbing is a breathing skill practiced in chest deep water. Take a breath, flex at the knees and slowly submerge below the surface. Exhale slowly through the mouth and then return to a standing position. Practice this technique until the skill can be repeated 20 times consecutively in a comfortable manner.

FLOATING

Floating means achieving balance in the water without movement. It does not mean that students can lie on their back with their toes out of the water. Floating can be done in the prone position, rolled up in a ball (tuck float), arms and legs down (jellyfish), in a semi-vertical position, or face up. Students do not have to be able to float to be a good swimmer, but it helps them to be confident knowing they can rest in the water without effort. Almost everyone can float, face down in the jellyfish position. Students should be taught to recover to a standing position by tucking their legs underneath them, while pressing down with hands before lifting their head.

The forward position can be experimented with, having the knowledge of breath holding and position recovery. To float on the back, stand low in the water (up to the chin), lay the head back gently, and lean back until the feet leave the bottom. Keep the shoulders back, chest up, and arms in a "Y" position in the water overhead while holding the breath. Holding the breath is essential to floating.

FORWARD GLIDE

The next step is to practice two skills previously learned: taking a breath and putting the face in the water, while stretching out with the face submerged. This skill should also be practiced by pushing against a pool wall, beginning from a standing position and back to the wall. One foot should be placed against the wall, while the arms are extended in front of the body prior to pushing off. Recovery to a standing position is the same as recovering from a floating position.

BACK GLIDE

Begin this skill as if it were a back float. The arms should be kept at the sides while pushing off from the bottom or the wall. When movement stops, reach forward with the arms and the face forward in the water. When the feet are under the body the swimmer should be able to stand up.

KICKING AND FINNING

Movement while on the back can be sustained in a back glide with an easy up and down movement of the feet. The knees and ankles should be relaxed and the upward movement of the feet strong enough to break the surface. The body position is flat in the water. Propulsion from the hands and arms is accomplished by pushing water toward the feet. The arms begin at the sides with the elbows bent and the hands up close to the body, fingers pointing toward the feet. With the fingers pointed outward, the arms reach out and push down to the sides. The arms then pause for a short rest at the sides. This arm movement is called finning (see Figure 1).

SCULLING

A more advanced form of hand-arm propulsion is called sculling. In this skill, instead of sliding the hands close to the body, the arms are held straight along the sides. The hands are turned over so that the thumbs are toward the bottom; then the hands are pushed out slightly away from the body so that the thumbs face upward and pull back to the sides. During this action, the wrists are extended and firm, fingers are held together so that the hand is flat, and the elbows are relaxed. Sculling is stronger than finning because there is no recovery, only a quick turning of the hands.

With finning or sculling while kicking on the back, a lot of distance can be covered. These skills are easy to master and will create confidence in students, who know they can resort to them in an emergency.

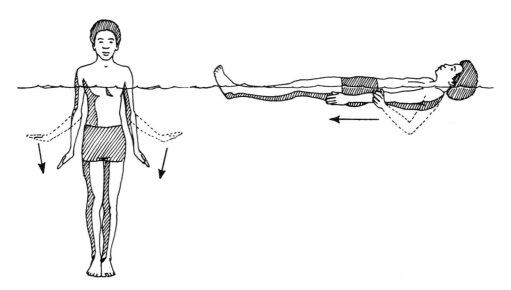

Figure 1. Finning.

ELEMENTARY BACKSTROKE

The elementary backstroke is an excellent progression step from finning and sculling. It is a stroke performed on the back that features an extended glide and is referred to as a resting stroke. The arms and legs move at the same time, below the water's surface. Strokes should be long and easy, and usually there is no special breathing technique to learn, as the face is out of the water at all times. Nonbuoyant swimmers, however, can be taught to hold their breath for a short period of time in the glide, which will help to maximize the distance achieved.

Arms

The arms are recovered close to the body and move up to the shoulders, are extended out and pulled just under the surface back to the sides. The pull may be done with the forearms fairly close to the body, or by straightening the arms a little over the head while sweeping out and down. The initial movement of the arms begins with the hands close to the body moving up in a slow and easy recovery. The recovery is followed by a strong push or sweep toward the feet, and the resulting glide is held until the legs begin to sink.

Kick

When learning the kick, students glide on their back and bend their knees, dropping the feet below the knees. There should be no turning out (pointing the knees to the sides), though the knees should be three or four inches apart and parallel to each other. The hips must be kept up to avoid a sitting position. The soles of the feet are pressed back and a little to the side in a circling motion that causes the knees to spread apart a little more. Students should continue pressing with the feet as the legs are straightened and brought together. Emphasize holding the glide at the finish of each stroke.

Arms and legs bend and move easily in their first actions; then both are pushed back simultaneously in the direction of the feet, and finish together. As the strokes improve, students start the arm recovery slightly before the leg recovery, then push at the same time with both arms and legs into the glide. Figure 2 illustrates the movement pattern and sequence of the elementary backstroke.

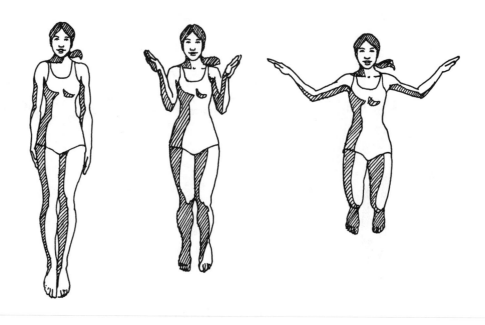

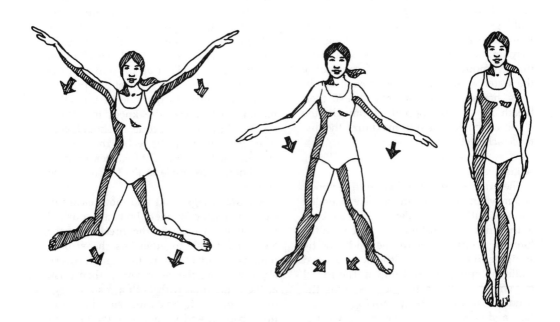

Figure 2. The elementary backstroke.

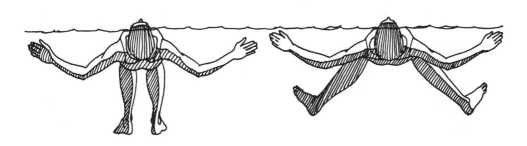

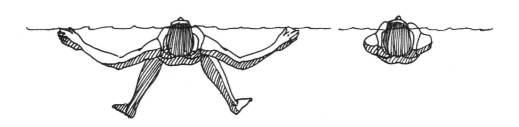

Figure 2. (Continued).

INTERMEDIATE SWIMMING

Intermediate swimmers should learn to perform five basic strokes reasonably well: the elementary backstroke, backstroke, crawl stroke, breast stroke, and sidestroke. Swimmers will feel confident in deep water and should be able to swim longer distances after learning these strokes.

BACKSTROKE (BACK CRAWL)

The simplest of the intermediate strokes is the backstroke, sometimes called back crawl. It is similar to the crawl stroke, but performed while lying on the back. The body position is flat on the water, and the legs move up and down in a flutter kick. Arms alternate in pulling the water from overhead to the sides of the body and are recovered over the water to their starting position, beyond the head. Figure 3 shows the sequence of movements involved in the backstroke.

Kick

The legs move up and down past each other so that there is about 12 inches between the foot breaking the surface and the one below. In the movement of each leg, the knees bend a little to finish the downward movement of the foot, then straighten up on the way back to the surface. The feet are relaxed on the down kick and extended on the upward kick. This extension of each foot is mostly a passive action as it occurs due to pressure on the instep. The knees should not break the surface; the hips should stay as close to the surface as possible throughout. Kick timing is steady and continuous, with more force in the upward direction than the downward.

Arms

The arms move in opposition to each other; one pushes water from the overhead position to the side while the other recovers above the water to return to the overhead position. The recovery arm is placed overhead on the water with the little finger contacting the water first (palm turned outward). The arm drops beneath the surface as the hand presses back to begin a push.

The arm should drop underwater 8-12 inches and then begin moving strongly. Ideally the elbow bends to about 90 degrees as the hand pushes past the shoulder. The forearm then moves rapidly to a finish at the side with the arm straight. A slight body roll occurs toward the side of the pushing arm. This will make the push stronger and help the recovering arm clear the water on the other side. The recovery is an easy lift of the whole arm, straight but not tense, up and back. It drops easily into the water again in line with the shoulder and behind the head.

Arm actions are continuous, one arm always exactly opposite the other. Attention to this oppositional timing, that is, never letting one arm begin to "catch up" with the other, creates a cross-balance of power from one arm to the other and makes a smooth backstroke. The rapidity of kicking depends upon the individual swimmer. Most swimmers average about three kicks per arm push.

CRAWL STROKE

The crawl or American crawl, sometimes called the freestyle, is the fastest of all strokes. It utilizes a flutter kick, an alternating arm movement, and a rotary style of breathing with the body in a prone position.

Arms

The hand of one arm enters the water in a line with the shoulder while pressing down underwater. The elbow bends slightly as the hand pushes water down the center of the body toward the feet. As the hand passes under the body, it will finish pushing at the thigh. At this point, the shoulder and elbow lift while the arm is recovered out of the water and the hand is placed in front of the shoulder. During the recovery, the elbow is lifted fairly high, the forearm relaxed, and the hand hangs down underneath. The arm recovery should be as relaxed as possible, not tense and tight. Hands are firm and straight during the push underwater (not "cupped") and completely relaxed on the recovery.

One arm is pushed underwater while the other is recovered over the water. Timing is

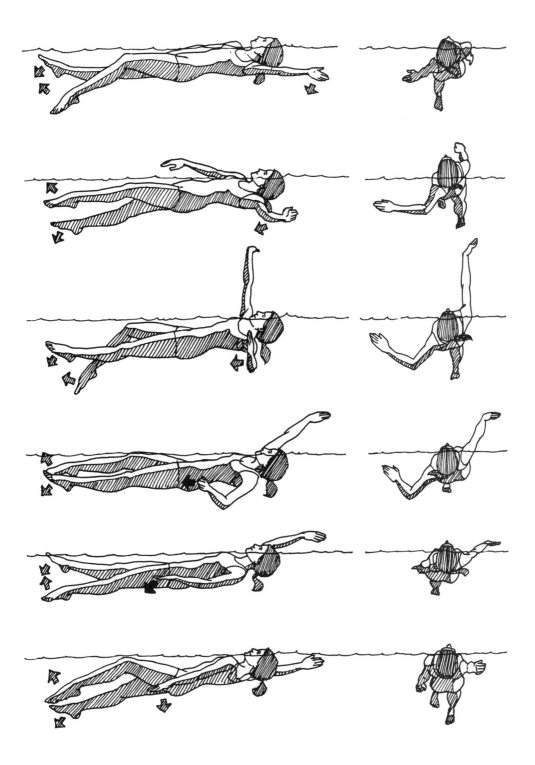

Figure 3. The back crawl stroke.

best if one arm is exactly opposite the other in a continuous alternating motion, just as in the backstroke. One arm pushing helps the other to recover. An easy body roll toward the shoulder that is underwater helps in the strength and balance of the stroke.

Breathing and arms

When breathing, the head is turned to one side with the chin up a little as the arm on the breathing side is recovered. The inhalation is quick, through the mouth. The head is then turned back into the water and air is exhaled from the mouth. Keep the head up slightly so the water contacts the head at the hairline.

Kick

The kicking movement is a total leg action all the way from the hips in an up-and-down flutter kick. The knees bend downward slightly at the start of the kick and straighten on the upbeat. The ankles remain relaxed all the time and will flex slightly because of the water pressure against them. The heels should just break the surface of the water on the up kick. This steady alternating kick is best at about three kicks per arm cycle, but there is no rule. See Figure 4 for the sequence of movements involved in the front crawl.

BREAST STROKE

The breast stroke is also a resting stroke. Swimmers move in a prone position, alternating arm pulls with leg kicks, and hold a glide at the end of each whole stroke.

Arms

From a front lying position with arms forward in the water and face in the water, the hands press in a sideward and downward direction. Before the arms reach halfway to the sides (still in a forward "Y" position), the head is lifted and a breath is taken; the elbows drop down, and the hands move forward together from under the chin. Then the head is returned face down to the water, the arms straighten out and are held together for the glide. Air is exhaled during the glide and during the first part of the pull.

Legs

The legs begin straight and together at the beginning. The kick pattern is similar to the elementary backstroke. First, the knees bend with the legs slightly apart. Do not allow the knees to "turn out." The knees are pointed down to the bottom and the heels brought up to the body. The recovery is a slow easy action. The feet and ankles are relaxed to this point, then make a quick movement to a flatfoot position (dorsal flexion). They immediately press slightly outward and backward in a small moving circle, straightening and stretching the knees together at the finish while pointing the toes. The first part of the kick is a recovery; the second part is a power or propulsive phase. The timing of the kick is ONE—bending knees followed by picking up the feet; TWO—press around and back and together.

Coordination

When the hands start pressing, the legs begin to recover at the same time. Legs press around and back as the arms reach into the extended position. The glide should be held until the legs begin to sink before starting the next stroke (see Figure 5).

Tips

Some refinements should be made as the swimmer progresses in learning the breast stroke. The palms of the hands press back as soon as possible within the arm stroke, not sideward. The elbows are held in a slightly bent position during the hand press and should be under the shoulders. Inhalation of air should be completed toward the end of the arm pull, but before the forward reach. The timing of the kick in relation to the arms should give a feeling of kicking into the stretched position of the whole body.

In the kick, the action of the ankles is extremely important. The feet must be flat, pushing into extension throughout the power phase of the kick, ending with the toes pointed.

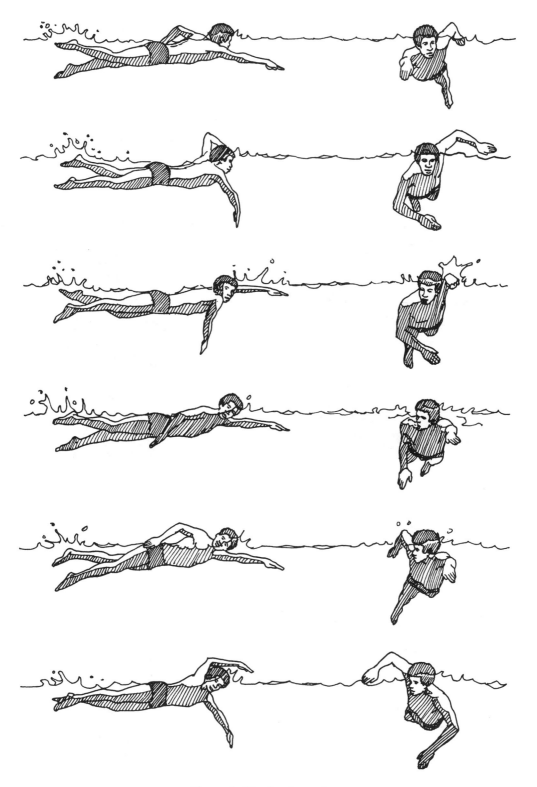

Figure 4. The front crawl.

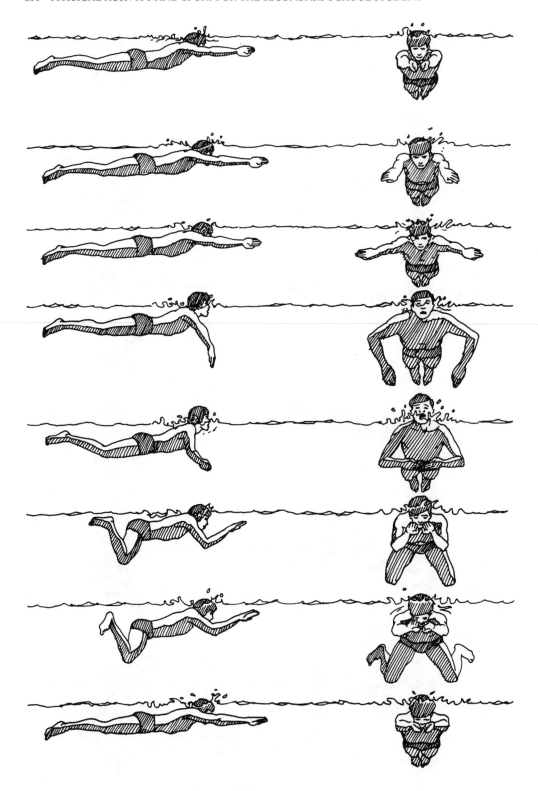

Figure 5. The breast stroke.

SIDESTROKE

Along with the breast stroke, sidestroke is one of the oldest swimming strokes. It is extremely useful as a resting stroke, for strengthening the kick for treading water, for lifeguard carries, and for synchronized swimming.

The starting position is on the side with legs extended and together. The arm on the lower side reaches straight overhead on the surface, and the other extends straight along the side of the body. The head lies on the water so that one ear is underwater and is turned slightly toward the back so that the face is clear. The body should remain on the side and in a straight line throughout the stroke.

Legs

The kick provides the propulsive power in this stroke, as in the breast stroke. The arms contribute, but more to balance than to power, and the coordination of the two is important.

From the extended position, the knees bend together, pulling up into a semi-tuck position. The top leg is extended forward and the bottom leg backward simultaneously, keeping both just under the surface. This is done in a sweeping, rounded action while keeping the lower foot pointed, and the upper foot flat (dorsal flexion) at the start of the push. Both feet are pointed at the completion of the kick. The strong circular sweep is parallel to the surface in a scissor action (hence called a scissors kick) and finishes as the legs meet together in an extended position. The timing of the kick is: ONE—easy tucking up of legs together; TWO—reach up-out-around in one big motion to complete the kick in the extended position; THREE—hold the legs extended until the glide is complete.

Arms

The upper arm, which is stretched overhead, pulls parallel to the surface toward the body, pushing the water toward the feet. Then it bends and returns overhead to full extension. At the same time, the arm at the side is recovered close to the body to a position in front of the face, then pushes out and down to return to the side. The coordination of the arms is similar to a paddle, one and then the other, each pushing in turn toward the feet and then holding at extension for the glide.

First, the swimmer should pull parallel to the surface with the overhead arm. While the knees are tucked, the upper arm is recovered as the lower arm begins extending beyond the head. The propulsive phase of the kick occurs as the upper arm pushes back to the side. This means that the arms and the legs finish in the glide position at the same time and then return to the starting position. (See Figure 6.)

BASIC ENTRIES

Jumping and diving safely into the water are important aquatic skills.

JUMPING

Jumping is an easy way to enter the water but should not be attempted unless the water is at least 5 feet deep. If not deep enough, use a pool ladder or ease in over the side. If starting above water where the bottom can just be touched, step off the side, reaching out with one foot, and keep the head erect so the eyes can look straight ahead. The feet should be brought together quickly, while the arms are held close to the sides. Remember to hold the breath. While entering the water, anticipate the feet touching the bottom. Knees should be relaxed a little, as if jumping down from a bench on land. This may allow the head to go underwater entirely; then knees should be straightened to permit a standing position. Lean forward after touching the bottom, and push forward with the arms extended in front of the body. This is called "leveling off" and means that in shoulder-deep water, it is easy to jump in and proceed to swim.

It is important to jump into deep water. Jumping into waist-deep water or less means that swimmers may land too hard. Impact with the bottom may severely injure the ankles, knees, or back. Jumping into water over the head is safer. The bottom can still be reached, and a push off to the top can still be attained in water that is slightly over the head. In water several feet over the

Figure 6. The sidestroke.

head, a breast stroke can be used after downward momentum has been lost to assist students in returning to the surface.

DIVING

Diving, or getting into the water head first, is an important skill used for gaining more distance when swimming for speed and for going deeper into the water. Beginning diving should be taught from pool side in water that is at least 9 feet deep and only after students have learned to swim well.

Learning to dive begins with a sequence of elementary dives learned close to the water at pool side. This sequence includes diving from a prone position, a sitting position, one knee, and finally a standing dive. (See Figure 7 and Figure 8.)

Remember that there are some factors that can inhibit the learning of diving skills. These factors include:
1. Moving head first down in the vertical plane is not natural. Leading with the head is characteristic of a few skills in sport activities, such as football, soccer, swimming, and gymnastics.
2. There may be a fear of landing flat and suffering pain and embarrassment.
3. There is a possibility of getting water in the nose and sinuses.
4. There is a fear of running out of air during descent and then struggling to return to the surface with little air.

Figure 7. A beginning dive.

Prior to attempting a first dive, students must be reminded of two important facts about diving. First, all dives must be attempted with the arms extended over the head for protection, and second, a person's head position helps determine the angle of the body upon entry into the water.

To minimize the fear of height, the possibility of landing flat, or descending too deep, the diving sequence of skills should begin with students starting their first dive as close to the water as possible. The teacher should first describe each dive, then demonstrate, and then have students do each dive. The progression should begin with a prone dive and move through the following sequence, concluding with a standing dive from pool side.
1. **Prone dive.** This entry requires assistance from the teacher. Students lie down on the deck with their head toward the pool. If the deck has a coarse surface, you may want to have them lie on a towel or an old piece of vinyl-covered wrestling mat. Stand behind the students one at a time. Have them pull the body out over the water, move their arms to an extended, protective position over the head, then take a breath and hold it. Next they should tuck their chin on the chest, pike at the hips, and slide over the side of the pool, down the wall until they are completely submerged. To return to the surface they should arch their back and neck, then press their hands toward the bottom, and swim breast stroke until they reach the surface. Have them practice the prone dive repeatedly until they become comfortable with it.
2. **Sitting dive.** This dive moves the students a little higher above the water surface. The dive begins with students sitting on the coping with their feet on the lip of the gutter or feet held flat against the wall in a pool with roll-out gutters. Arms are extended above the head and the head should begin in the neutral position (chin level and looking straight ahead). Take a breath, hold it, bend at the waist while tucking the chin on the chest, and dive down along the pool wall. Extend the legs to a straight position and return to the surface as with the

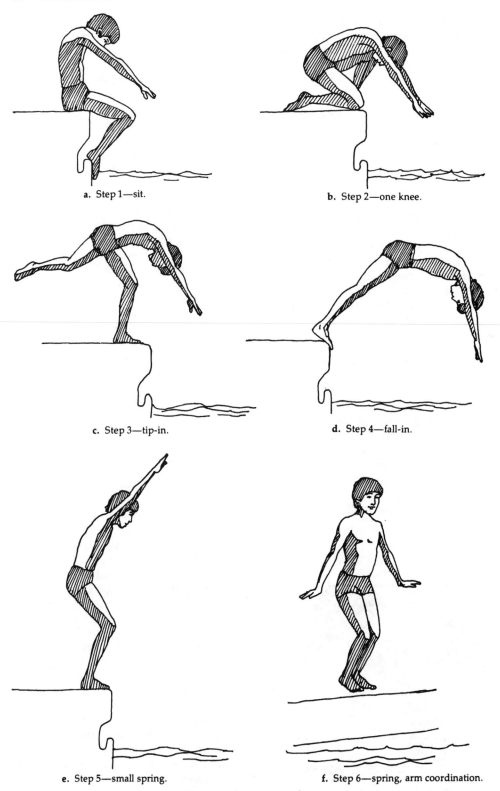

a. Step 1—sit.

b. Step 2—one knee.

c. Step 3—tip-in.

d. Step 4—fall-in.

e. Step 5—small spring.

f. Step 6—spring, arm coordination.

Figure 8. Learning to dive.

prone dive. Practice the sitting dive repeatedly until students are comfortable with the dive.

3. **Kneeling dive.** The kneeling dive is taught next in order to increase height above the water. It is also a dive that allows the teacher to introduce students to the concept of springing into the air. This dive position begins with students kneeling on one knee (back leg) while the front leg is forward, bent at the knee, foot flat with the toes curled over the coping in an effort to prevent slipping. The arms are held in an extended position above the head, the back is straight, and head is held in the neutral position. The dive begins by pressing down on the front foot, while leaning forward slightly. The back leg is not used to propel the body upward, acting only as a stabilizer to provide balance. As the body moves upward the feet lose contact with the wall; the chin should be brought down slowly toward the chest while the hips pike. Movement of the chin down and the piking action of the hips will transfer momentum downward allowing the body to enter the water at an angle of approximately 90°. The body should be fully extended in a straight position upon entry. Practice the kneeling dive repeatedly until students have achieved mastery of it.

4. **Standing dive.** This is the final dive in the sequence of diving from the deck. The standing dive begins by having students assume a normal, relaxed, standing position at pool side. Toes should be curled over the side to prevent slipping while the arms are extended over the head and the head is held in the neutral position (looking straight ahead). Next, bend slightly at the knees, take a breath, lean forward slightly, and straighten the legs up to full extension off the toes. Once off the wall the chin should be brought down slowly toward the chest while the hips move into a pike position. This will start the body down at an angle close to 90°. The legs will move up into the air as the diver descends toward the water. The body should be held in a straight position until completely sub-

merged. As soon as the descent rate slows down the diver should return to the surface with the same technique used in the prone dive.

Remember to hold the breath while entering. If water enters the nose, students should exhale. Pressure may be felt in the sinuses and ears as the body goes deeper in the water. This is a normal occurrence as one goes below the surface of water. Exhaling while underwater will help relieve the pressure. If actual pain is felt pinch nostrils and try to exhale through the nose while returning to the surface.

TREADING WATER

This skill is necessary to be able to remain at the surface in water that is over the head. (See Figure 9.)

Arms

A flat scull is done with the hands, that is, with the hands flat and fingers together. The hands should move back and forth to the front and to the side, turning over at each change of direction so that the palms always push against the water. The hands are kept slanted so that a downward force occurs slightly at the same time. As in all sculling, the movements should be continu-

Figure 9. Treading water.

ous, and constant pressure should be felt against the palms of the hands.

Legs

A breast stroke kick or scissors kick provides maximum downward force to keep the swimmer on the surface. See the description of these kicks in the sections on breast stroke and sidestroke leg actions.

When learning treading, experiment with the hand scull in shallow water. Then remove the feet off the bottom one at a time and support the body with sculling alone. Then move to shoulder deep water and finally to deep water.

INCREASING STUDENT LEARNING POTENTIAL

Swimming instruction can be a stressful experience for students who have not spent a great deal of time around the aquatic environment, students with coordination problems and those who are beginners. It is helpful for teachers to recognize and understand that there are a number of significant differences with which a student must cope when learning skills in the water as compared with learning skills on land. Factors which inhibit learning in water include the following:

1. *Sensitivity to water pressure.* Some beginners will display an uneasiness when standing in chest deep water, characterized by labored breathing and an increase in respirations. Students will normally adjust to water pressure discomfort naturally in a short period of time.
2. *Balance.* In the early stages of learning basic skills such as floating and gliding, some students will experience difficulty in regaining their balance when attempting to stand up. Suggest to them before attempting a prone glide or a face down floating position that they tuck their legs under their body and then press down with both legs. The tuck should occur simultaneously while pushing down with their hands prior to lifting their face from the water.
3. *Vision.* Vision is distorted and images are blurred when the eyes are open.

Moderate levels of chloramines (.3-.9 ppm) will irritate the eyes of students. These visual changes and discomforts slow the learning process but will eventually be accepted as a normal part of the environment. Encourage students to open their eyes occasionally when swimming in a prone position to prevent injury that may occur from swimming into a wall or another person. Unless there are medical reasons to the contrary, prohibit the use of goggles. Severe damage to the eyes can occur if students swim underwater at depths greater than 4 feet, as external water pressure will cause squeeze. There is no way to equalize this pressure in the goggles as there is when wearing a face mask.

4. *Hearing.* Most swimming skills require a horizontal body position, which allows the outer ears to fill with water, disrupting communication between teacher and student.
5. *Breathing.* The simple act of breathing can be one of the most frustrating and difficult skills to master for the beginner. Unlike breathing on land, which can be accomplished at any time, swimmers face drastic changes. In order to get enough air to satisfy the body's demand, inhalation must occur through the mouth and exhalation should occur through the nose, or mouth and nose. In addition, breathing often times must be coordinated with an arm stroke in a rhythmical fashion, as with the American crawl stroke. Beginners soon learn that they sometimes cannot get air when they need it and often times inhalations are accompanied by water, causing the student to choke.
6. *Buoyancy.* The ability to float enhances learning and increases student confidence in ability to master swimming and aquatic skills. Those students who are negatively buoyant are at a slight disadvantage. As a result the teacher might eliminate water orientation skills such as the turtle and jellyfish floats for nonbuoyant students.
7. *Body position.* Adjusting to movement of

the body in a horizontal position is a unique experience in swimming that requires some time. The teacher must recognize that beginners have adapted to their land environment using an upright posture. With few exceptions, all external stimuli in swimming are interpreted from the horizontal position. Adaptation to this change in orientation will take place gradually and can be accelerated by increasing the number and length of student practice sessions.

8. *Propulsion.* Also unique to swimming is a change in the primary source of propulsion. On land, students move using their legs to walk or run. In swimming, the arms serve as the primary source of propulsion.

9. *Resistance.* Since the medium of water is more dense than air, resistance to movement is quickly noticed. Resistance, along with unrefined swimming skill and water temperature below 82 degrees F, can cause fatigue and may have some bearing on the length of class time.

10. *Fear.* Fear and embarrassment are also factors that can significantly hinder the learning process. Some students will come to class with fears, real or perceived, based on personal experience or the experiences of others. In addition, the embarrassment of learning to swim as a teenager can be an inhibiting factor.

These ten factors are important considerations in planning a strategy for effective teaching. Analysis of the factors shows that the beginning learner will be placed in an environment where there is some amount of sensory deprivation, as significant changes occur in vision, hearing, breathing, and sense of touch. When these sensory changes are combined with fear and the principles of buoyance, resistance, and propulsion, the swimming pool becomes a truly unique and different world. These extreme differences indicate a need for careful lesson planning and for the teacher to be sensitive and patient while psychological adjustments are made by the student. Consideration of these differences also points to the need for the teacher to select the simplest and most expedient method of skill instruction, which is usually the "whole method."

REFERENCES

American Red Cross. *Basic Water Safety.* Washington, DC: American Red Cross, 1988.

American Red Cross. *Swimming and Aquatics Safety.* Washington, DC: American Red Cross, 1981.

Gabrielsen, M. Alexander. *Diving Injuries.* Fort Lauderdale, FL: Nova University Press, 1990.

Johnson, Ralph L. *YMCA Pool Operations Manual.* Champaign, IL: Human Kinetics, 1989.

Maglischo, Ernest W. *Swimming Faster.* Palo Alto, CA: Mayfield Publishing Co., 1982.

YMCA of the USA. *Aquatics for Special Populations.* Champaign, IL: Human Kinetics, 1987.

YMCA of the USA. *YMCA Progressive Swimming—Instructors Guide.* Champaign, IL: Human Kinetics, 1986.

CHAPTER 19

Team Handball

MICHAEL D. CAVANAUGH
United States Team Handball Federation
Colorado Springs, CO

INTRODUCTION

Team handball is a new sport emerging on the American scene and one that involves continuous play, high scoring, body contact, and graceful, skilled movements by the players. It is a permanent Olympic event for both men and women. The game has been described as ice hockey without the ice and sticks, and as water polo without the water. It also combines skills, rules, and strategy that are common to basketball and soccer. Yet, in spite of what appears to be a blend of many different sports, team handball retains a unique nature that makes it attractive to players and spectators of all ages.

In Europe, where team handball began, the game is referred to only as "handball." However, for most of the United States the name "handball" brings to mind a game using a little black ball played within a small enclosed, four-walled room. Thus, in the United States, we use the name team handball to distinguish a game involving 14 players, including two goalies, who, on a court larger than a basketball court, attempt to score by throwing a ball into a goal.

Germany, Czechoslovakia, and Denmark claim responsibility for the development of games that closely resemble team handball. The game originally was played during the early 1900s, on a large outdoor soccer field, and involved as many as 22 players (11 per team) at one time. Gradually, modern team handball evolved into its present-day accepted form of 7 players per side, predominantly played on an indoor court, the size of which resembles a court somewhat larger than a basketball court. In 1946 the International Handball Federation (IHF) was formed and the rules of team handball were formalized. Today there are over 100 nations affiliated with the IHF. The United States Team Handball Federation (USTHF) was formed in 1959, marking the beginning of modern team handball in the United States.

In 1972, team handball for men was included in the Munich Olympic Games. Four years later in 1976, the Montreal Olympic Games saw the addition of women's team handball. The U.S. Men's National Team qualified and competed in both the 1972 and 1976 Olympic Games. Team handball is now a permanent Olympic event for both men and women. In 1984 and in 1988 the United States qualified both a men's and women's team in the Olympic Games. While the United States has yet to win an Olympic Games medal, qualification for the Olympic Games is a reflection of this sport's potential because only twelve men's teams and eight women's qualify to compete in the Olympic Games tournament.

There are ongoing team handball programs at numerous high schools, junior high schools, and elementary schools throughout the United States, to include active programs in the Police Athletic Leagues and in the Boys and Girls Clubs of America. Our success in future Olympic competition will depend upon the success and exposure team handball will enjoy through these various grassroot programs.

While on offense, the idea of team handball is to throw a ball past a defense and a goalie, into a goal. While on defense, the idea is to defend one's own goal from the attack of the opponent. There are markings on the court that restrict play in the goal area and therefore influence offensive and defensive movement. Offensively, the ball is moved primarily by passing, though a player is allowed to dribble freely, run three steps with the ball, and may hold the ball for three seconds. While defensive "checking" and the use of the body to obstruct an opponent are permitted, there are rules restricting contact and unnecessary rough play, making the game sensible and safe for players of all ages.

BASIC RULES

Diagrams 1 and 2 are examples of a team handball court. Diagram 1 supplies the measurements of the court, while Diagram 2 shows the names of the various lines on the court. It is important to note in Diagram 2 that the area enclosed by the 6-meter line, or goal area line, has been shaded. Only the goalie is allowed to stand inside the goal area. However, both offensive and defensive players have "air space rights"

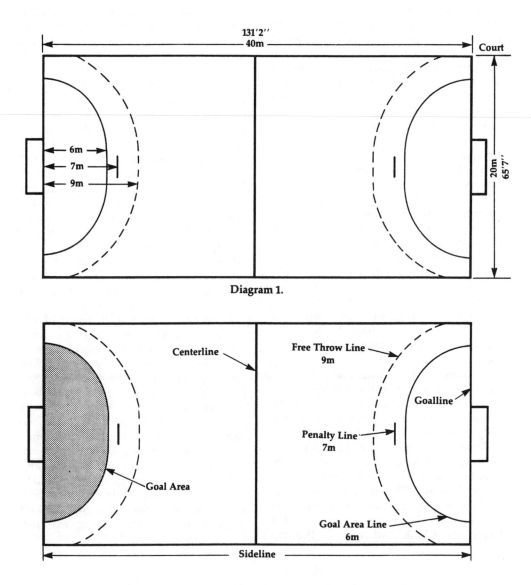

Diagram 1.

Diagram 2.

Goal

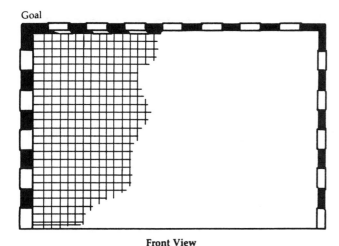 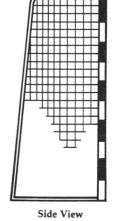

Front View   **Side View**

Diagram 3. Regulation goal.

inside the goal area. While trying to throw the ball into the goal, offensive players may jump into the goal area, as long as their take-off was from outside the goal area, and they release the ball before landing in the goal area. Likewise, the defensive player may jump into the goal area in an attempt to block a shot on goal, but may not touch the ball while in contact with the goal area. Once play is completed in the goal area, players entering must exit by the shortest possible route. The goal area is usually referred to as the circle or circle area. The 9-meter line, or free throw line, is used when minor penalties are given in the game. The 7-meter line, or penalty line, is used when major penalties are given. It is important to note that a team handball court can be adapted to a smaller area other than the regulation 20 x 40 meters, but that the width of the court is more important than the length.

Diagram 3 is an example of a regulation goal. Goals are 2 x 3 meters in measurement, painted in contrasting colors, and provided with a net. They are usually made of wood or metal tubing.

Ball

The ball used in team handball looks like a small soccer ball. Men use a ball that weighs 15 to 17 ounces and measures nearly 24 inches in circumference. Women and youth use a ball that is lighter (12 to 14 ounces) and smaller (nearly 22 inches in circumference). There is an even smaller ball

used for elementary children in a game called mini-handball. While common playground balls may be used to play team handball, the size and dribbling nature of a rubber bladder, leather-covered regulation team handball is recommended for play.

Duration of the Game

There are no time-outs in team handball. Men and women play two 30-minute halves with a 10-minute intermission. For tournaments and for youth teams, playing time is often modified to meet the needs of participants.

Players

Internationally, a team is allowed a total of twelve members. A playing team consists of seven players, six court players, and one goalie; there are five substitute players

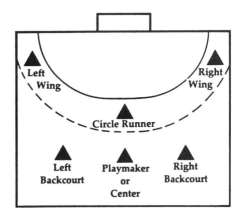

Diagram 4.

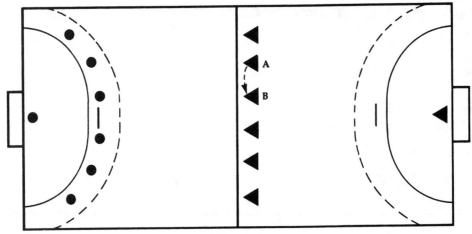

Diagram 5.

who may enter the game at any time from an area called the substitution area, located on either side of the center line in front of the officials' (timekeeper and scorekeeper) table. Diagram 4 illustrates a commonly-used offensive formation with the names of each position played.

It is helpful if both the right wing and right backcourt throw with the left hand, and if both left wing and left backcourt throw with the right hand, so that they may have the best possible throwing angle on the goal.

Starting the Game

Diagram 5 shows the formation used to begin a game. A coin flip determines who will first have possession of the ball. The game starts with the official's whistle and throw-on. A throw-on consists of a simple pass to a teammate at the centerline. This procedure is repeated after each goal is scored. Diagram 5 shows a throw-on; A starts the game with a pass to B.

Goal Area

The area inside the 6-meter line is called the goal area. Only the goalie is allowed to

stand inside this area. If, while scoring a goal, the offensive player steps inside the goal area or steps on any part of the 6-meter line, the goal does not count and a goal area violation occurs. The player may, however, land within the goal area after a dive shot as long as the take-off occurred outside of the goal area. If the defense likewise steps in the goal area or on the 6-meter line and gains an advantage by doing so, a penalty throw is awarded. A ball or player is not considered to be in the goal area if they are in the air.

Playing the Ball

Players may dribble the ball, and there is not a limit to the amount of dribbles to be taken. However, double dribbling, or touching the ball with two hands while dribbling, is not allowed and if this occurs the opponents are given a free throw. It should be noted that while dribbling is permitted it should be discouraged among new players. This is because team handball is a passing game and dribbling slows the tempo and should be used only when necessary. Players may not play the ball with their legs

	MAY	MAY	MAY	MUST
Player receives the ball.	Take 3 steps.	Dribble (as many times as desired).	Take 3 more steps.	Pass or shoot within 3 secs.

Diagram 6.

below the knee. Diving on the floor for a loose ball is not allowed. Diagram 6 depicts the possible sequence of movement a player may take upon gaining control of a ball.

Contact with the Opponent

Players are allowed to use their bodies to obstruct an opponent with or without the ball. A player is not allowed to use the arms or legs to push, hold, trip, or hit an opponent in any manner. Proper checking techniques will be covered in elements of defense. It is important to note that offensive players are not allowed to charge into a defensive player who is in proper position. In instances of an offensive or defensive violation to these contact rules, a free throw is awarded.

Throw-in

If a ball goes out-of-bounds on the sideline a throw-in is taken. The defense must be three meters away from where the ball is passed in-bounds. The player taking the throw-in stands near the spot where the ball went out-of-bounds and throws the ball into play with one or two hands with one or both feet on the ground.

A throw-in is also awarded when any defensive player (excluding the goalie) is the last one to touch the ball as it goes out-of-bounds over his/her own goalline. The ball is awarded to the offensive team, and the throw-in is executed in the manner shown in Diagram 7. Player A executes the throw-in by passing to any other team member, in this case player B.

Goal Throw

A goal throw occurs when a goalie deflects a ball over the goalline. The goalie puts the ball back into play by throwing it from the goal area into the playing area.

Penalties

When minor rule violations occur, a free throw is awarded. The free throw is taken from the place where the violation occurred and without the intervention of the referee. The defense must remain three meters away from the player taking a free throw. The thrower may pass to any teammate within three seconds while maintaining one foot in contact with the court. The thrower may score directly from a free throw. The majority of minor fouls or common fouls occur in the area between the goal area line (6-meter line) and the free throw line (9-meter line). When this occurs the free throw is taken from the free throw line at a spot directly opposite from where the violation occurred, as in Diagram 8.

A penalty throw is awarded for more serious or major violations of the rules. Penalty throws are usually awarded when an offensive player is in a good shooting position and has an almost sure chance of scoring when fouled. To distinguish between whether the foul that occurred should be given a penalty throw or a free throw the referee must carefully consider the position of the offensive player, that is, whether a clear scoring position had been established and whether the foul took that scoring

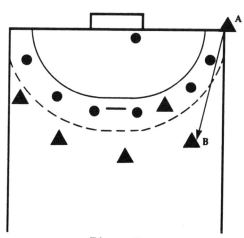

Diagram 7.

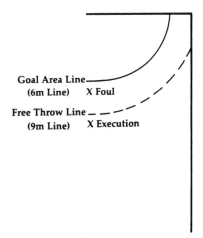

Goal Area Line
(6m Line)   X Foul

Free Throw Line
(9m Line)   X Execution

Diagram 8.

chance away. If, during a shooting drive by an offensive player, a minor foul occurs, which does not interfere with the advantage the shooter may be gaining, the referee will let play continue.

To execute the penalty throw, one foot must remain in contact with the court behind the 7-meter line until the ball is released. All other players must stand behind the 9-meter line when the penalty throw is taken. The penalty throw may be taken by any player on the team that is fouled. Internationally, penalty throws result in a goal nearly 80% of the time.

Suspension

If a player is involved in repeated personal fouls the referee will interrupt play and by displaying a yellow card to the responsible player will be issuing a warning to that player. If that player or any other player becomes involved with unsportsmanlike conduct, unnecessary rough play, or continued intentional fouls, the referee will issue a 2-minute suspension from the game. If a player receives a third 2-minute suspension or is involved in an unusually serious rule violation or in "dangerous play" he/she will be disqualified from the game. When a player receives a 2-minute penalty the team must play "short" (suspended player on the bench), until the penalty time has been served.

The preceding pages include information concerning the basic rules of team handball. To ensure a complete and thorough understanding of the rules, you are urged to obtain an official copy of the team handball rulebook issued to the USTHF by the IHF.

Referees

Two referees are used in team handball. They control the game solely by whistle and hand signals. The referees rarely touch a ball, as players retrieve balls to be put back into play. The referee has a very difficult task because of the fast pace of the game and the body contact that is allowed. While holding, pushing, and hitting are technical violations and result in free throws, individuals do not carry a limit to the number of these violations they can commit. However, repeated intentional violations or dangerous play can lead to a 2-minute suspension. A certain level of contact, holding, hand checking, and pushing occurs throughout the game and will not draw the referee's whistle depending on the level of the play and experience of the teams involved, and the degree of the violations occurring. Referees are charged with the control of the game and safety of the players, and must enforce the rules to allow both players and the game to develop.

SKILLS

PASSING AND CATCHING

Team handball is primarily a passing game. A variety of passes can be used effectively depending on the game situation. The primary pass is the shoulder pass with either an overhand or sidearm delivery. Bounce passes, wrist passes, lob passes, and shovel passes are all effective team handball passes. Timing, accuracy, and deception are all elements of a good pass. To catch a team handball, two hands are used to both secure possession and cushion the arrival of the ball. To ensure proper handling of the ball it should be caught away from the body. Dribbling is a necessary skill but should not be emphasized in play. Players should practice dribbling at full running speed to simulate fast break situations. Normal offensive movements require infrequent dribbling but during fast breaks the dribbling skill becomes very important.

Types of Passing Drills

1. Partner Passing—Two lines face one another at varying distances. Overhand, sidearm, jump passes, and bounce passes are attempted between partners. Accuracy is critical.

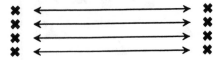

2. Line Passing—Two lines face to the center. Passes can be varied as in partner passing only now passers move forward

to receive the ball and pass while moving. Passers completing their pass move to the end of the opposite line or backpedal to the end of their original line.

3. Pairs Passing—Gradually introduce game conditions passing while running the length of the court.

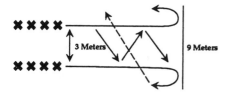

4. Position Passing—Exhaust all possible passes between positions—continuous passing. Advanced level may have players circulating between positions in organized or random fashion.

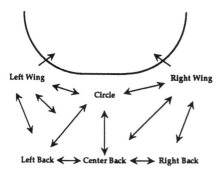

Figure 1. The overhand set shot.

SHOOTING

The basic concept of the game is to throw or shoot the ball into the goal. The most effective shots are taken while moving toward the goal. To become an effective shooter one must develop a quick release, accuracy with the corners of the goal, and the ability to know when to shoot. By knowing when to shoot, a player will know not to shoot with a defender directly in front of him/her when he/she is too far away, or at an extreme angle from the goal. Remember that the defensive opponent

Figure 2. The sidearm set shot.

Figure 3. The jump shot.

Figure 4. The circle, dive, or fall shot.

must first be beaten (out of position) and then one must also beat the goalie. The true essence of the game is a shooter waiting until the last possible second, reading the goalie's position, before taking the shot; the goalie must then react to the shot that has been taken.

Set Shot

Form for a set shot is similar to a baseball throw. It may be taken overhand or side-arm; it is bounced or shot directly at the goal. (See Figures 1 and 2.)

Jump Shot

In this shot the player attempts to jump in the air and throw over the defensive players. The ball is thrown while in the air and usually involves the use of three full steps to execute. Jump shooters land on the same leg from which they initiated the jump. (See Figure 3.)

Circle, Dive, or Fall Shot

This is a specialty shot usually taken from the 6-meter line. Upon receiving the ball the player attempts to dive or fall into the circle (goal area) and shoots while in the air. Upon completing the shot, players normally break their fall with their hands and a chest slide or by a modified shoulder roll. (See Figure 4.)

Wing Shot

Taken from the wing position this specialty shot is actually a combination jump shot and dive shot. Because of the extreme angle that the wing player is in in relation to the goal, an attempt must be made to jump into the goal area and improve the shooting angle. Recovery for the wing shooter is similar to the recovery for the dive shot.

Penalty Shot

Taken at the 7-meter mark, this specialty shot is actually a combination set shot and dive shot.

SHOOTING DRILLS

1. Set Shot—One line shooting, one line feeding. Change lines so that players pass and shoot from both lines. Variation—add a passive defense player at the free-throw line. Shoot from behind the 9-meter line in practice.

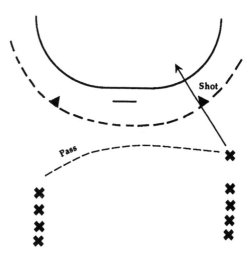

2. Jump Shot—Similar to the set shot drill. Variation—players can cross in the middle with the passer going first, shooter going behind passer—shot should be taken from the middle.

3. Circle, Dive, or Fall Shot—Pass from the back court position to the circle runner position. Circle runner catches the ball, turns to the goal, and falls or dives while taking the shot.

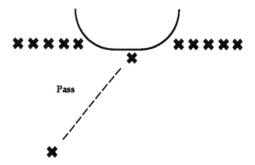

4. Wing Shots—Low angle shots taken while jumping into the goal area following a pass from the back court.

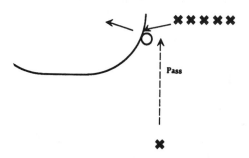

Pass

PRINCIPLES OF OFFENSE

OFFENSIVE STRATEGY—FAST BREAK

Offensive attack is generated by a strong defense. This is because the defense is in a position to steal a pass, block a shot, or take advantage of an offensive mistake to initiate a fast break attack before a defense can develop. If the fast break is successful, the eventual shooter should face the goalie from close range uncontested by a defensive player. The goalie is a major factor in the fast break attack as not only must a shot be blocked in order to gain possession of the ball, but then the ball must be quickly recovered before an accurate pass can be made to breaking players. Wing players are usually the faster players on the court and they are also usually the players who lead the fast break.

If the initial fast break does not result in a score, team strategy then shifts to the remaining players following the initial break. These trailing players constitute a secondary wave of attack, and they attempt to attack the defense before they fully recover to their organized defensive positions.

OFFENSIVE STRATEGY—ORGANIZED ATTACK

If the primary and secondary fast breaks do not yield a clear shot, the offensive team assumes their basic positions and begins a systematic attack. Movement and play can be organized around complex team plays, 2- and 3-player combination patterns, or to an individual's free attack. A team handball organized attack resembles a basketball offense in that it incorporates a variety of screens or blocks and pick and roll, give and go movements (see Diagram 9a and 9b).

A good, organized offensive attack comes from coordinated movements between backcourt, circle, and wing players. Cou-

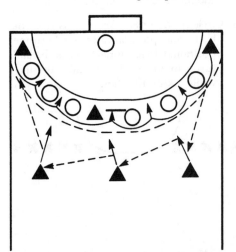

a. 3:3 Attack-wing switch. Wings exchange positions randomly looking for an opening in the defense for a pass and shot.

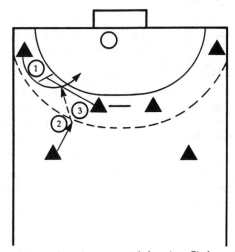

b. 2:4 Attack-circle runner pick for wing. Circle runner picks ①. Left backcourt attacks ② while left wing cuts off circle runner pick, and looks for pass from left backcourt for a shot.

Diagram 9. Offensive strategy.

pled with this coordinated movement, the team must have quick, accurate passing. Passing enables the offense to force the defense to shift into imbalance and thus create openings. The key elements in offensive attack are passing, movement (with and without the ball), and patience. It is interesting to note that effective wing and circle play serves to take defensive pressure off backcourt players and permits them, in turn, to become more effective in attack. Likewise, effective backcourt play serves to open up offensive play for the wings and circle player. A balanced scoring attack is the ideal situation in team handball.

ELEMENTS OF OFFENSE

1. Players should always be in motion before they receive any ball.
2. After receiving the ball, a player should attempt to get into a scoring threat position to draw the defense and to attract the goalie's attention.
3. It is essential that each player passing the ball to a teammate do so in such a manner as to not slow the player in motion to receive the pass—these "lead passes" provide a further advantage to the attacking player. Properly executed, this has a cumulative effect for the offensive team and ultimately places a player in a clear shooting position by moving the ball more quickly than the defense can adjust to the ball movement, player movement, and scoring threat.
4. An attacking player should attempt to draw two defensive players. Properly executed lead passes, offensive attacks, and drawing defensive players effectively yields a 2-on-1 opportunity for an offensive player. Often if initiated by one wing the opposite wing results in the open shot.
5. Team handball is a PASSING game. While dribbling is allowed and should be practiced (especially for fast breaks), it generally slows the movement in the organized phase of an offensive attack.
6. Players should avoid being "tied up" or fouled by the defense to the point where the referees must stop play with a whistle and award a free throw. Keep the ball moving by passing to get the defense out of position. Constant whistles by the referees to award free throws for common fouls are an indication that the defense is doing a good job in stopping the offensive attack.
7. Common sense dictates that a team should substitute while on offense only.
8. It is important to try to spread the defense from wing to wing and therefore the offensive team should maintain position balance on the court.
9. While set plays can be relied upon for offensive structure, each player must be encouraged to take the initiative to be a scoring threat by developing one-on-one offensive moves. Individual improvisation and simple combinations (picks, screens, crosses, pick and rolls, give and goes) are more effective than set team plays to take advantage of scoring opportunities.
10. Pace—at the highest level of international play, teams will quickly shift from one speed of passes to a much faster passing and moving sequence. This change in pace catches the defense out of position when a quicker attack is initiated.

PRINCIPLES OF DEFENSE

The basis for a good offense begins with a good defense: the defense in transition becomes a fast breaking offense. Therefore, the first responsibility of a defensive team is to stop the fast break before becoming organized into their defensive formation. The defensive team must remember that they are basically defending the 6-meter or goal area line. Therefore, they should be careful not to let an offensive player get between them and the 6-meter line unnoticed. If they must leave the 6-meter to check against a jump or set shooter they need not venture beyond the 9-meter line, depending upon the shooting ability of the opponent. Once the check has been completed the defensive player must immediately return to the 6-meter line to once again fill the area left open by the checking movement.

Figure 5. Three defensive movements.

Individual defense is played on the balls of the feet with the knees slightly bent. Hands and arms are held at the sides in such a manner as to block possible set or jump shots and block any passes to an offensive circle runner. Individuals shift laterally along the 6-meter line to balance any attack of the offensive players. Defensive players should always assume responsibility for one offensive player and be ready to help the players on their sides with their offensive opponent. It is easiest to think of team handball defense as being a zone defense until an offensive player with the ball threatens to shoot. Once a player is in a threatening shooting position, defense becomes one-on-one and contact should be made.

Proper checking technique is vital to playing good defense and to the safety of all players. Remember, unnecessary rough play may and should always result in a 2-minute suspension. On the other hand, a too passive defense will allow offensive players to penetrate their line and score easily. It is important when checking another player that you impress the referee that you are using your body to obstruct an opponent and reaching for the ball with a free hand.

Figure 5 depicts three defensive movements. A defensive player blocking a jump shot using both arms and a slight jump to counter the offensive player's jump is demonstrated in a. In b, a classic body check of an offensive player who may be in a set shooting position is shown; note that both players remain on the floor. Checking a jump shooter is shown in c; note that while the offensive player has jumped higher, the defensive player can counter this advantage by controlling the shooting arm. To control the offensive circle runner the defense usually relies on hand checking (to know the circle runner's position, while watching the ball) and then by blocking any attempt to pass the ball to the circle runner by using their arms or body to deny position or the ball. While checking is a part of team handball, for beginning players it is suggested that strict basketball defense be played. Gradually, as experience is gained, hand checking can be introduced and finally lim-

ited arm and body checking can be added.

The 6-0 is the basic defensive formation. Diagram 10 illustrates the positions of the defensive players and the paths of their checking and shifting responsibilities.

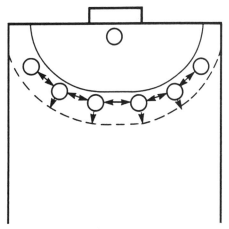

Diagram 10.

Remember, team handball defense is a basic combination zone that becomes player to player as the situation requires.

Defensive players talk to one another repeatedly to assure that each player knows his/her responsibility and to keep close watch on the ever-changing position of the offensive circle runner. Defensive players shift along the goal area line as the strength of the offensive team shifts.

Each defensive player must actively assume and announce responsibility for an offensive player. Defensive players should not exchange positions in providing defensive coverage. As the offensive team shifts positions in their movement, the defensive players just shift player responsibility. Team defense is a series of shifting, helping out, and recovery of position for the next threat.

Playing defense in team handball requires full effort by each individual. Once control of the ball is obtained and the defensive team goes on offense, the team can pace their attack and dictate the intensity of play and in doing so, recover from the effort expended on defense.

ELEMENTS OF DEFENSE

1. All defensive players should shift with the general direction of the ball. The defense focuses their strength on the location of the ball.
2. The defense should always strive to have 1½ defenders on the ball. This requires movement and adjustment of responsibilities as the ball moves.
3. The defense should immediately identify an offensive opponent's shooting arm and "overplay" this shooting arm to make shot selection more difficult.
4. The defensive players should maintain a constant stream of "chatter" between one another so that defensive responsibilities can be announced and shifted with offensive player and ball movement.
5. If offensive players are attempting to move or cut for better positioning, it is important for the defense to either deny this position or obstruct the movement of the player so as to disrupt the timing of the offense.
6. Players should not waste energy by attacking/checking an offensive player who is not in a threatening position.
7. Proper defensive checking position involves having one hand attempting to control the offensive player's shooting arm and having the other arm placed at the hip opposite the shooting arm of the offensive player. This assures good defensive positioning of the body.
8. It is better to switch offensive opponents than for the defense to switch their own positions.
9. The defense should always anticipate passing lanes and shooting "windows" and be ready to block the ball at all times.
10. Transition from defense to offense is a key element in a successful fast break attack and speed is of the essence.

GOALIE

The goalie has a major function on both offense and defense. On offense the goalie will initiate the fast break, while on defense the goalie's prime function is to block shots.

Quickness, both in thought and physical reaction, and courage are two major components needed to play the goal successfully. Figure 6 shows three common positions of a goalie. In a, the goalie is in the ready position. In b, the goalie is blocking a low shot to the corner, while in c, the goalie is blocking a shot to the high corner.

Several rules apply to the goalie only. The goalies may touch the ball with any part of their bodies and can move about the goal area without restriction. However, the goalie cannot leave the goal area with the ball under control. While a goalie can enter the playing area to obtain a ball he/she cannot reenter the goal area with the ball under control. While in the playing area with the ball in possession, goalies must observe step, dribbling, and 3-second rules as they apply to court players. A court player cannot throw a ball to his/her own goalie standing in the goal area; this violation results in a penalty throw.

If a goalie deflects a ball over the goalline the goalie puts the ball back into play by a goal throw. To execute a goal throw the goalie throws the ball from the goal area into the playing area. If a goalie deflects the ball out-of-bounds across the sideline, the opponents put the ball back into play by a throw-in.

Diagram 11 indicates when a shot becomes a goal.

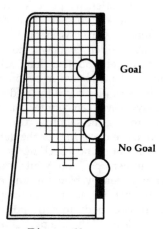

Diagram 11.

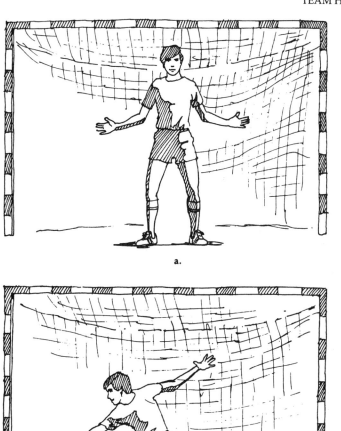

a.

b.

c.

Figure 6.

GOALIE DRILLS

1. Perceptual Clues—Offensive players form a single file line, each with a ball. They successfully throw set or jump shots at the goal according to the following sequences:
   - A. low left, low right, low left, low right, etc.
   - B. high left, high right, high left, high right, etc.
   - C. low left, high right, low left, high right, etc.
   - D. low right, high left, low right, high left, etc.

   This allows goalies the advantage of knowing where the next shot is coming from, reading the perceptual cues of that shot, and providing the movement element drill necessary to develop proper technique.

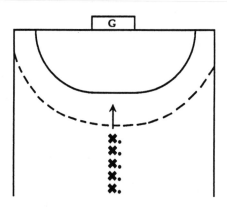

2. Wing Shots—Shooters stand on either the 6-meter or 9-meter line and alternate their shots from wing to wing working toward the center or they may shoot in sequence.

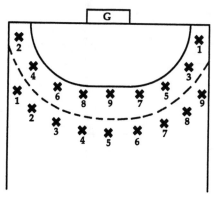

3. Fast Breaks and Passing/Shot Blocking—Players A and C start by passing a ball each to their respective goalies. A and C then sprint the length of the court as in a fast break for an outlet pass from their goalie. Upon receipt of the pass, player A attempts to score on goalie #2 and player C attempts to score on goalie #1. Once these blocks are completed the next players in line pass a ball to their goalie and sprint for a fast break. Players exchange lines and maintain dribbling and step rule integrity before shooting.

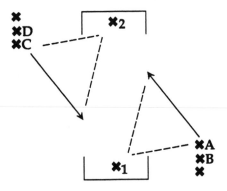

TIPS FOR BEGINNING PLAY

1. Court may be modified to suit available area indoors or out; width is more important than length. Regulation goals, net, and balls are recommended, but can also be modified to include available equipment.
2. Do not allow body contact for beginning players.
3. As team handball is a passing game, discourage dribbling for beginning players. A leadup game of keep-away with no dribbling allowed is ideal for beginners.
4. Do not allow defensive players to pressure the offense. As offensive skills are acquired, allow hand checking, limited contact, and finally arm and body checking.
5. Have every player touch the ball at least once before a shot is attempted each time on offense.

6. It is recommended to substitute only when on offense.
7. Referees should be verbal with beginning players, as well as giving the whistle and hand signals.
8. Beginning players have a tendency to shoot at the middle of the goal, right where the goalie stands! Put targets in the high and low corners of the goal for players to shoot at in practice and warmup situations.
9. Beginning players should be instructed to shout "corner," prior to shooting, as a supplementary reminder of where to shoot.
10. A gym mat draped over the front of a goal will leave only the high and low corners exposed for beginning players in practice situations.
11. Have everyone play the goal for an allotted time to gain an appreciation of the difficulty in playing the position.

TERMINOLOGY

Attack. A team attacks when they are in possession of the ball.

Centerline. Divides the court in the center; game begins at the centerline.

Charging. An offensive player runs into or over a stationary defensive player who is in proper position.

Checking. Obstructing an opponent from taking a shot or establishing position on offense by using the arms and body.

Circle. Area described by the 6-meter line, referred to as the goal area.

Free Throw. Play continues after a minor rule violation; opponents maintain 3 meters from the player taking the free throw.

Free Throw Line. Dashed line at 9 meters used for taking free throws following minor fouls that occur between the 6- and 9-meter lines. Ball is put into play at a point on the free throw line directly opposite from the foul, while the defense must remain 3 meters from the ball.

Goal Area Line. 6-meter line or circle.

Goal Throw. Throw taken by goalie from goal area after the goalie deflects the ball over the goalline out-of-bounds.

Penalty Line. A line one meter in length, 7 meters from the center of the goal. Penalty throws are taken from this line.

Referee's Throw. When players from both teams infringe the rules at the same time or gain simultaneous possession of a loose ball, or the ball hits an obstruction or the ceiling over the field of play the referee executes a referee's throw. Two players attempt to tap or gain control of a ball that is thrown in the air between them. This is very similar to a jump ball in basketball.

Substitution Area. Substitutes must enter and leave the game from an area 4.5 meters on either side of the centerline. This designated area is located between the substitution bench and the timekeeper.

Throw-in. When a ball goes out-of-bounds across the sideline, it is put back into play from the spot where it went out-of-bounds.

Throw-on. The throw-on is taken after the referee's whistle and is a pass to a teammate at the centerline to start the game and after each scored goal.

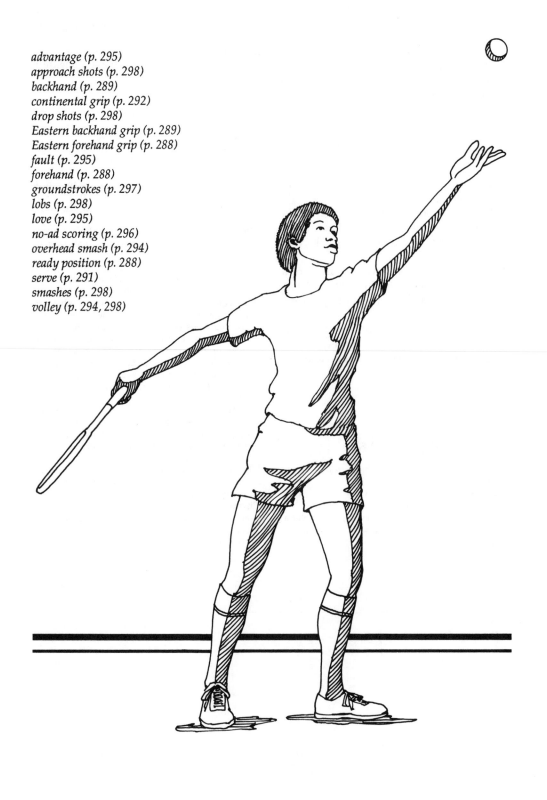

CHAPTER 20

Tennis

RON WOODS
United States Tennis Association
Princeton, NJ
and
JIM BROWN
McNeese State University
Lake Charles, LA

INTRODUCTION

Tennis can be fun to play, relatively inexpensive, good for general health, an individual or team sport, and one that can be played for a lifetime. It can be an activity for an afternoon of family recreation or a sport played competitively for hundreds of thousands of dollars in prize money.

Tennis is a physically demanding game at most levels of play. It requires a wide range of physical skills and mental alertness and can be a difficult game for some people to learn. People do not have to be great athletes to learn the game, but an organized progression of learning the skills of the game is important to ensure early success.

Several key ideas will help the novice player achieve early success in the game. First, players should choke up on the racket in the early learning phases to put the racket hand closer to the point of ball impact. Second, starting players should play close to the net so that it becomes less of a barrier. Third, beginning players should be encouraged to strive for accuracy and control rather than power.

Dramatic changes have occurred in the game of tennis over the last 25 years. There is much more variety in the style of play, significant increase in televised tennis, and technological advances that have produced space-age materials for rackets, balls, strings, and the tennis court itself.

Perhaps no change has been as significant as the movement from a game that was played primarily in the private clubs, often by the privileged class. Today tennis is played at public facilities throughout the country by players as young as eight and by others who are still young at eighty. More than twenty million Americans enjoy the game; worldwide, tennis is played in more countries than any other sport with the exception of soccer.

The United States Tennis Association, as the governing body for tennis, offers a complete range of programs starting in the public schools, junior team tennis, tournament play for novice players, and progressing upward to league play and tournaments for ranking for the more serious player.

SKILLS AND TECHNIQUES

CONTROL OF THE BALL

Height—Because tennis is a net game, the first challenge is to get the ball over the net. "Opening" the face of the racket at the moment of impact will direct the ball upward. Conversely, if the ball continually goes too high, simply "close" the racket face a bit more at contact.

Direction—Control of side-to-side direction is the key to placing the ball in different parts of the court in order to move the opponent around. Players must contact the ball with the racket strings facing the direction they want the ball to travel.

Depth—In order to take advantage of the entire court in moving the opponent, players must learn to hit the ball both deep and short. The depth of the shot can be adjusted by hitting higher to send the ball deep or lower to have it land short. More advanced players apply varying degrees of spin to the ball in order to control the depth.

Power—The speed of the ball is affected by the size of the swing and the speed of the racket throughout the swing. A short swing will produce little speed, but will help control the shot. In the early learning stages, players will get better results in consistency by keeping the swing relatively short and moving the racket through the stroke at a moderate pace.

THE READY POSITION

The ready position is the stance to be assumed while waiting for return shots. Hold the racket out in front of the body with the racket pointing toward the opponent or slightly toward the backhand side (a righthander's left side). Use the nonracket hand to support the racket at the throat or on the shaft (the parts between the head and the handle or grip). The racket should be far enough in front of you so that your weight is slightly forward. This position will force you to put your weight on your toes instead of your heels, a position that should help you react faster to any shot (see Figure 1).

FOREHAND

The Eastern forehand grip is used by most players for this shot. Shake hands with the base of the racket so that your palm is slightly behind the racket handle, the wrist is a little to the right of the top of the handle, and the "V" formed by the thumb and index finger is above, but slightly toward the back part of the grip (see Figure 2).

As soon as you know the ball is going to your forehand side, begin the backswing. The backswing is made by turning the shoulders and bringing the racket back either in a straight line parallel to the court or in an elliptical motion to a position where the racket is a bit lower than waist high and pointing to the wall or fence behind your baseline (see Figure 3).

As the ball comes to the forehand, move into a position so that the left shoulder

Figure 1. In the ready position, the weight is forward, the racket points to the opponent, and the knees are flexed.

Figure 2. The Eastern forehand grip. As the player looks down on the racket, the wrist is slightly to the right of the top of the handle.

Figure 3. Turning your side to the net and taking the racket back to the fence for the forehand backswing.

Figure 4. Making contact with the ball for the forehand.

points to the ball and the feet form a line approximately parallel to the sideline. Push off with the foot farther away from the net and transfer your weight forward as you begin to swing at the ball.

Swing in a slightly upward motion. This upward and forward action of the racket permits a hit with a little topspin, which is good for control and for making the ball bounce forward on the other side. Make contact with the ball at a point even with your front foot. Keep your wrist firmly in place throughout the stroke (see Figure 4), by squeezing the grip at contact.

Follow through in the direction of the intended flight of the ball, and high over the net (see Figure 5).

BACKHAND

There are two acceptable ways to hold the racket for a backhand shot (one that a right-hander hits on the left side of the body). The most common grip is the Eastern backhand, in which the right-hander's wrist should be to the left of the top of the racket handle as you look down on the racket (see

Figure 5. The forehand follow-through.

Figure 6). In this grip the inside part of the thumb is in contact with the back, flat part of the racket handle. The thumb may be extended or bent to provide support. The two-handed backhand is used at all levels of the game. It provides more support, but it may be difficult to reach some shots, and the racket is hard to manipulate on shots aimed directly at the body. There are players who use two forehand grips to attain a two-handed backhand, while others change to an Eastern backhand with the strong hand and add a forehand grip with the other.

However you decide to hold the racket, start taking it back as soon as you see the ball coming. Use the nonracket hand to cradle the racket along the shaft and to help turn the racket as you change to the backhand grip. Take the racket back to a position pointing to the fence at about waist height (see Figure 7).

Turn before you hit so that your shoulder is pointing in the direction you want the ball to go. Bend your knees slightly, and take a small step forward with the foot closest to the net.

Swing in a motion approximately parallel to the court. Keep your wrist firmly in place as you swing. Make contact with the ball before it gets even with your front foot (see Figure 8). Follow through out toward the net in the direction of the intended ball flight and high over the net (see Figure 9).

Groundstroke Tests

Most skill tests are based on the number of successful attempts in hitting balls into a target area. This type of test can be used with any stroke in tennis. Here are some examples:

1. **Drop and Hit.** Standing at the baseline near the center mark, drop and put into play as many balls as you can out of ten attempts. Shots that fall into the forecourt area count for one point; shots landing in the singles backcourt count for two points.
2. **Toss to Forehand.** Standing at the baseline near the center mark, return as many balls as you can out of ten balls thrown underhand on one bounce to your forehand. Shots into the forecourt

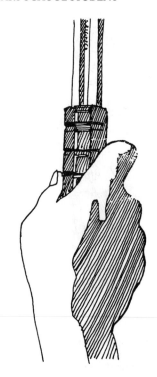

Figure 6. The Eastern backhand.

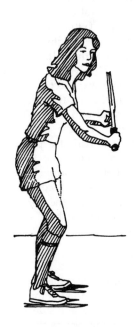

Figure 7. Taking the racket back so that it points to a wall or fence behind you for the backhand.

Figure 8. Making contact with the ball for the backhand.

Figure 9. The backhand follow-through.

count one point; shots into the backcourt count two points.

3. **Toss to Backhand.** Same as the previous drill, except that balls are tossed on one bounce, waist high to the backhand.

4. **Wall Test.** Standing behind a line 25 feet from a rebound wall, drop the ball and put it into play. Continue hitting groundstrokes against the wall for 30 seconds. Every shot must be hit from behind the line, but shots do not have to be played on one bounce. If a shot does not come back behind the line, the player can retrieve the ball and return to the starting position before hitting the next shot. Each hit during the 30 seconds counts for one point.

BEGINNER'S SERVE

The serve is used to begin a point and must be delivered from behind the baseline. The racket arm motion is similar to that used in throwing a ball. Beginners should hold the racket with the Eastern forehand grip described earlier and start with the racket behind the back or head.

Stand at about a 45° angle to the baseline with your weight on the foot away from the net (see Figure 10).

Toss the ball a little higher than you can reach and about a foot in front of you. Try

Figure 10. Starting the beginner's serve with the racket up and back, and the ball out in front.

Figure 11. Extending the arm upward to hit for the beginner's serve.

Figure 12. The follow-through for the beginner's serve.

to lift the ball without spin so that when you swing at it your arm will be fully extended. Remember to reach high to hit (see Figure 11). Follow through out toward the net, across the front of your body, and down on the other side (see Figure 12).

Toss the ball a bit higher than you can reach. Reach high to hit and make contact in front of your body so that your weight will move forward with the swing. The foot that started out away from the net should move forward and touch down inside the baseline after you have hit the ball. This happens almost naturally to keep your balance after you have reached up and forward to hit. Follow through out, across, and down to the other side, in that order (see Figure 13).

Beginner's Serving Test

Standing at the baseline, start with the racket in the back scratch position and attempt to serve ten balls into the service court diagonally opposite from where you are positioned. Count one point for each ball that lands in the proper service court. Use the beginner's serving motion and try only for accuracy, not power.

INTERMEDIATE AND ADVANCED SERVE

Players with advanced serves usually hold the racket with a continental grip. Some even move their wrists a bit toward the backhand side of the grip. These grips enable the server to hit with control, pace, and spin, while the Eastern forehand grip is mainly for beginners.

Stand at an angle to the baseline described for beginners, but begin motion with the ball near the strings out in front of your body about chest high. Drop the racket in a pendulum motion by the side of your leg and at the same time drop the tossing hand prior to the toss. The arms should work together in unison. Down together and up together. As the racket arm swings back, the knuckles of your hand should point up to the sky. Next, the racket arm bends naturally and then straightens during the forward swing toward contact with the ball.

a.

b.

c.

d.

Figure 13. Intermediates and advanced players begin the serve with both hands in front. They then go down together and up together. Extend your arm to a hit, and follow through, out, across, and down.

Intermediate/Advanced Serving Test

Draw a line across the service court four feet from and parallel to the service line. Standing behind the baseline and using the full swing motion, attempt to serve ten balls into the proper court. Shots that land in front of the line drawn count one point; shots hitting between the four-foot line and the service line count two points.

VOLLEY

A volley is a shot hit before the ball bounces. It is usually hit from a spot in the forecourt. Beginners will be more comfortable holding a forehand grip for forehand volleys and a backhand grip for backhand volleys. The advantage is comfort in hitting; the disadvantage is that there may not be enough time to change grips between shots. Intermediate and advanced players use the continental grip. They sacrifice comfort in order not to have to change grips from the forehand to the backhand. The other fundamentals are the same.

Take a short backswing. There is not enough time for a big one. Block or punch the ball in front of and to the side of where you are on the court. Since you will not have time for a big backswing to provide power, it is important to make contact in front so that moving your body weight forward will help make up for the power loss. Step forward if you have time. If you are right-handed, step in the direction you want to hit with your left foot on forehand volleys. Step forward with the right foot on backhand volleys. If you do not have time to take a step, turn your shoulders before reaching forward to hit. Keep your eyes level with the ball. If it goes low, get down with it. Finally, try to hit the ball while it is rising. If you let it drop, you will have to volley up and hit a defensive shot.

Volley Test

Standing approximately ten feet from the net, attempt to return as many balls as you can out of ten shots fed from the baseline. The feeder should mix forehand and backhand shots. Volleys that fall into the forecourt count one point, and shots that hit the backcourt area count two points.

OVERHEAD SMASH

Beginners seldom hit overhead smashes, but when they do they usually hold an Eastern forehand grip. As with the serve, this grip allows for control but does not provide controlled power. Intermediates and advanced players hold a continental grip for control and power. Take lots of steps to prepare for a smash. If you get set too soon, you may misjudge the ball and be in a poor position to hit. As you get ready to hit, your feet should be staggered so that the right foot is back and the left foot forward. Again, this position allows you to shift your weight forward as you swing. Take an abbreviated backswing. Bring the racket straight up in front of your body to a position behind your head. A full wind-up does not give you as much control as this short one will. Keep the ball in front of you as you swing and reach high to hit. Your arm should be fully extended as you hit (see Figure 14).

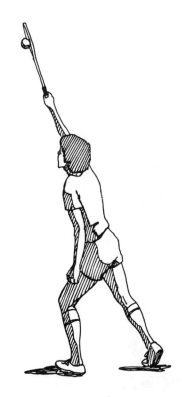

Figure 14. Shift your weight forward and reach high to hit the overhead smash.

SAFETY

Since there is no body contact in tennis, there is less of a chance for injury than in some other sports. There are, however, ways to get hurt and ways to avoid injuries. In practice, stepping on balls scattered around the court or getting hit by stray tennis balls is always a problem. Clearing the court of extra balls and being alert can reduce the possibility of getting hurt that way.

Blisters, sprains, strains, cramps, shin splints, and tennis elbow are the most common injuries. Gradually increasing the amount of playing time and using the correct grip size can cut down on blisters. Sprains are difficult to prevent, but playing within your capabilities and working to improve flexibility may help. Stretching and other warmup activities can prevent pulled muscles. Good conditioning and maintaining a proper balance of potassium, sodium, and water might help you avoid getting cramps. Shin splints can be caused by running on hard surfaces, poor conditioning, and poor running techniques, so correcting those problems might help solve the shin splint problem. Proper hitting technique, strong muscles, and using the right racket can reduce the possibility of getting tennis elbow.

RULES

STARTING THE GAME

The players or teams spin a racket or flip a coin to decide who serves first. The winner of the spin or flip can choose to serve first, receive first, to begin the match on either side, or to let the opponent make the choice.

The first serve is made from behind the right side of the baseline between the center service mark and the singles sideline. The serve for the second point is made from behind the left side of the baseline, and the server continues alternately serving from the right and left sides of the baseline until the first game is completed.

The serve is a "fault" if the server steps on or beyond the baseline before the ball is hit or if the ball does not go over the net and into the service court diagonally opposite the server. If the first serve is a fault, the server gets another chance. If the second serve is a fault, the server loses the point.

The serve is a "let" if the ball touches the top of the net and goes into the proper service court or if the receiver is not ready. If a serve is a let, that serve is repeated.

The players alternate serving complete games. After the first game, the server becomes the receiver and the receiver of the first game becomes the server. Change ends of the court (with a 90-second rest) when the total number of games in a set equals an odd number.

A player loses a point if:
- the ball bounces twice before it is hit;
- the server serves two faults in a row;
- a ball is returned so that it hits outside the boundary lines (balls that hit lines are good);
- a ball does not go over the net;
- a player touches the net while the ball is in play;
- the ball is hit by a player reaching over the net (unless the wind or spin has carried the ball back across the net);
- a player throws the racket and hits the ball.

In doubles, the players on each team take turns serving. The order of serving can be changed at the end of each set. The receivers take turns receiving the serve in each game. The order of receiving must be decided at the beginning of each set and maintained until that set is completed.

SCORING

The server's score is always given first. The first point won by a player is 15; the second is 30; the third is 40; the fourth is game unless the score is tied. Each player has zero points or "love" at the start of the game. If the score is tied at 40-40, the score is deuce and the game continues until one player gets ahead by two points. After the score is deuce, the player who wins the next point has the "advantage." The score can be called "ad in" if the server is winning and "ad out" if the receiver is ahead. "My ad" and "your ad" are also common expressions. If the player who has the advantage wins the next point, that game is over. If not, the score goes back to deuce.

No-ad scoring is simpler and sometimes used to shorten matches. Instead of calling the points love, 15, 30, 40, and game, the points are called 0, 1, 2, 3, and 4. The first player to win four points wins the game. When the score is tied at 3-3, the player who wins the next point wins that game. At 3-3, the receiver chooses the side from which he/she will return the serve.

In both regular scoring and no-ad scoring, play continues until a player wins at least six games and is ahead by at least two games (for example, 6-0, 6-2, 6-4). When that happens, a set has been completed. If the score is tied at 5-5, the players continue to play until one goes ahead by two games (for example, 7-5, 8-6, 9-7). A match usually consists of two out of three sets.

In most matches and tournaments, "tie breakers" are used when the score is 6-6 in a set. There are two widely used tie breakers, one consisting of the best of nine points and the other the best of twelve points. Both systems are rather complicated, but details can be obtained by writing the United States Tennis Association, 707 Alexander Road, Princeton, NJ 08540.

THE COURT

A tennis court is 78 feet long and 27 feet wide for singles play. A doubles court is 78 by 36. The net is 3 feet at the center and 3 feet, 6 inches at the net posts. Lines should be two inches wide. A diagram of a singles and doubles court is shown in Diagram 1.

ON-COURT RULES

1. If you have any doubt as to whether a ball is out or good, you must give your opponent the benefit of the doubt and play the ball as good. You should *not* play a let.
2. It is your obligation to call all balls on your side, to help your opponent make calls when the opponent requests it, and to *call against yourself* (with the exception of a first service) any ball that you clearly see out on your opponent's side of the net.
3. Any "out" or "let" call must be made instantaneously (i.e., made before either an opponent has hit the return or the return has gone out of play), otherwise the ball continues in play.
4. Do not enlist the aid of spectators in making line calls.

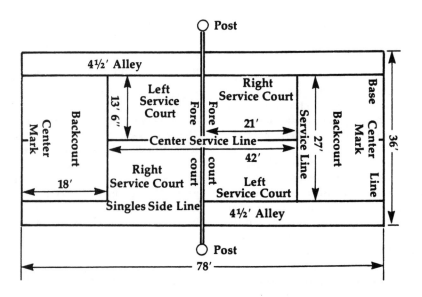

Diagram 1. Diagram and dimensions of tennis court.

5. If you call a ball out and then realize it was good, you should correct your call.
6. To avoid controversy over the score the server should announce the set score (e.g., 5-4) before starting a game and the game score (e.g., 30-40) prior to serving each point.
7. If players cannot agree on the score, they may go back to the last score on which there was agreement and resume play from that point, or they may spin a racket.
8. Foot faults are not allowed. If an opponent persists in foot faulting after being warned not to do so, the referee should be informed.
9. Do not stall, sulk, complain, or practice gamesmanship.
10. Wait until the players on another court have completed a point before retrieving or returning a ball.

CODE OF CONDUCT

1. Once you have entered a tournament, honor your commitment to play. Exceptions should occur only in cases of serious illness, injury, or personal emergency.
2. From the beginning of the match, play must be continuous. Attempts to stall or to extend rest periods for the purpose of recovering from a loss of physical condition (such as cramps or shortness of breath) are clearly illegal.
3. Intentional distractions that interfere with your opponent's concentration or effort to play the ball are against the rules.
4. Spectators, including parents, friends, and coaches, are welcome to watch and enjoy matches. Their role, however, is clearly restricted to that of passive observer with no involvement of any kind during the match.
5. Players are expected to put forth a full and honest effort regardless of the score or expected outcome.
6. Players are expected to maintain full control over their emotions and the resulting behavior throughout the match. If you begin to lose your composure during play, try the following:

- Take several deep breaths, exhale as slowly as possible and feel your muscles relax.
- Concentrate on your own game and behavior while ignoring distractions from your opponent or surroundings.
- Be your own best friend—enjoy your good shots and forget the poor ones.

SINGLES STRATEGY

THE SERVE

1. Stand near the center of the baseline to serve.
2. Do not waste energy and time trying to serve aces (serves which the receiver cannot touch with the racket).
3. Place serves to your opponents' weakest sides or to an open area in the service court.
4. Serve directly at players who take big backswings on their groundstrokes.
5. Do not follow your serve to the net unless your serve is very good and unless you can volley well.
6. Use more spin and less pace on second serves.
7. Use a variety of serves during a match.

Returning Serves

1. Stand so that you are in the middle of the two extreme sides to which the ball can be served (usually on or behind the baseline one to two steps from where the baseline and singles sideline meet).
2. Move in a step or two on second serves.
3. Learn to anticipate your opponent's second serves.
4. Return fast serves with a short backswing and a blocking motion. Do not try to return a hard serve with a hard return.
5. Return the ball deep to the corners when possible.

GROUNDSTROKES

1. Stand on or just behind the center of the baseline between groundstrokes. As soon as you hit one shot, move back to that position unless you are in the forecourt.
2. Hit most groundstrokes cross-court, deeply to the backcourt, and high over

the net. That will make your opponent run to hit shots and to stay in his/her backcourt. It will also give you more distance with which to work.

3. Hit to open spots on the court when you can.
4. Do not try to put shots away from a position behind your baseline.
5. Keep the ball low and wide on passing shots against a net player.
6. Use your best stroke on all set-ups, even if you have to run around the ball to hit it.

APPROACH SHOTS

1. Use approach shots on balls that bounce near or inside the service court.
2. Take a shorter backswing on approach shots.
3. Use a backspin on most approach shots.
4. Hit most approaches down the line to which you are closest.
5. Do not try to win the point with an approach shot. Set your opponent up; then win with a volley.

VOLLEYS

1. Play volleys from a position about ten feet from the net near the center of the court.
2. Move closer to the net following a good volley.
3. Volley to the open part of the court.
4. When you volley a low shot, volley it deep and down the middle of the court.
5. When you volley a high shot, volley at an angle and go for a winner.
6. Cover the open court on your side after you hit a volley.
7. Get set to hit volleys. Do not hit on the run unless you have to.

LOBS

1. When you run wide to retrieve a deep shot, lob cross-court.
2. Make defensive lobs go deep and high into your opponent's court.
3. Use lobs more often when the other player has to look into the sun.
4. Follow offensive lobs to the net.

SMASHES

1. Change the direction of two smashes in a row.
2. Try to put smashes away when you are close to the net.
3. Do not attempt put-aways from the backcourt area.
4. Hit smashes flat (without spin) when you are near the net. Use some spin when hitting smashes farther from the net.

DROP SHOTS

1. Do not try drop shots from the baseline, when the wind is at your back, or against players who can run fast.
2. Use drop shots when your opponent expects you to hit a deep shot.

DOUBLES STRATEGY

1. Stand about halfway between the center mark and the doubles sideline to serve (see Diagram 2).
2. Serve to the backhand or to the open part of the service court.
3. Let the strongest server begin serving each set.
4. Receive the serve at a point where the baseline meets the singles sideline (see Diagram 2).
5. If the server stays back after the serve, return the ball deep and cross-court.
6. If the server comes to the net following a serve, return the ball short and cross-court.
7. If the server's partner plays too close to the net, try lobbing.
8. Occasionally try to pass the server's partner at the net to prevent poaching.
9. When your partner is receiving the serve, stand either even with him or her on the baseline or move up to the middle of the service line on your side of the court (see Diagram 2).
10. When your partner is serving, stand about eight to ten feet from the net and two steps inside the singles sideline toward the center of the court (see Diagram 2).
11. If your partner has to move off to the side of the court to retrieve a shot, shift

in that direction to cover the open court.

12. When your partner is serving, protect your side of the court, take weak shots down the middle, and smash any lobs hit to your side.

13. When you are playing at the net and a lob goes over your head, cross to the other side and fall back to cover the open court while your partner retrieves the lob.

14. When volleying, hit for the open part of the court or at the closest opponent if you are in an offensive position.

15. Volley to the opponent farther away from you if you are hitting a defensive volley.

16. When both opponents are at the net and you are on the baseline, hit most shots low and down the middle.

17. Hit most smashes down the middle of the court.

18. Play with a partner you like and can get along with on and off the court.

19. Talk to your partner during the match.

20. Let the player with the strongest backhand play the left side of the court when receiving serves.

GENERAL STRATEGY

1. Change tactics if you are losing.
2. Hit toward a general target area instead of going for lines and corners.

3. Play the ball instead of your opponent, especially in pressure situations.

4. Do not try risky shots on points you cannot afford to lose.

5. Learn what percentage shots are and use them during a match.

6. Concentrate on winning the first point of every game and the first game of every set.

7. Try to be consistent rather than powerful. Most points are lost with poor shots, not won by great ones.

8. Do not fight power with power.

9. Start getting ready for the next shot as soon as you have hit the last one.

10. Find out what your opponent's weakest shot is and take advantage of that weakness.

EQUIPMENT

RACKETS

Prior to 1967, all commercially produced rackets were made of wood. Wood absorbs shock and vibration well but is not very strong. Today's choices include metal, fiberglass, graphite, boron, ceramic, and composites of these and other high tech materials. The way these materials are combined determines the racket's stiffness, vibration dampening abilities, and playing characteristics. Since many of these materials are expensive, the price of rackets has steadily increased.

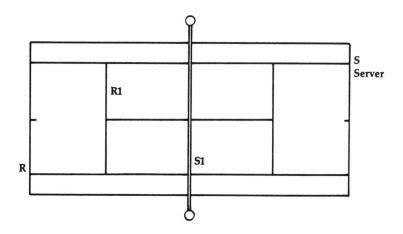

Diagram 2. Positions for starting a point in doubles. The receiver's partner (R1) may want to begin the point on the baseline instead of on the service line.

The use of these new materials has enabled rackets to become stiffer. Stiffer frames generate more power, result in a more uniform ball response, and have a larger sweetspot. However, a stiffer frame also transmits more shock to a player's arm than a more flexible frame.

The availability of stronger and more flexible materials allowed manufacturers to vary the size and shape of rackets without increasing their weight. Currently, there are three sizes of rackets from which to choose: traditional (up to 84 sq. in.), midsize (85-104 sq. in.), and oversize (105 sq. in. and up). Oversize rackets are often a good choice for beginners because they generate more power, have a larger sweetspot, and are more resistant to twisting. The midsize racket is the most popular size sold. Intermediate players often find that these rackets provide more control and are more comfortable than the oversize rackets while providing more power than the traditional size rackets.

Manufacturers are now focusing on the structural design of rackets. The first wide body rackets were stiffer and returned more energy to the ball at the cost of control and comfort. Manufacturers are now offering a variety of cross sections to create different combinations of flexibility, control, and power.

Rackets usually come in standard grip sizes of 4⅜, 4½, and 4⅝ inches. To determine the proper grip size, measure the playing hand from the tip of the ring finger to the second long line that crosses the center of the palm. Choose the largest grip that can be comfortably held because a larger grip makes it easier to control racket twist and results in less shock to your arm.

The weight of rackets varies from 10 to 13 ounces. Heavier frames vibrate less, have a larger sweetspot, and generate more power. However, if there is too much weight in the head, it will be harder to swing. Experimentation is necessary to find the right balance of weight and maneuverability for a player's game.

Strings

Racket strings are made either from synthetics or from the muscular layers of beef intestine. Natural gut provides the greatest playability; however, most recreational and intermediate players use synthetics. Synthetics cost less, have increased durability, and tolerate humid weather better.

String thickness (called the gauge) is a major factor in achieving a balance between playability and durability. Thicker strings (16, 16L, and 17 gauges) are more durable while thinner strings (15 and 15L) offer greater feel.

Each racket has a range of string tensions recommended by the manufacturer. The rule of thumb for racket tension is "loose for power, tight for control." If you want a larger, livelier sweetspot, need more power from your racket, or have a problem with tennis elbow, have it strung at the lower end of the recommended range. Experienced players who already hit with sufficient pace often find that the higher end of the range gives them added ball control.

Playing style also influences the choice of string tension. Baseliners often prefer looser strings to get more depth and pace, while serve and volley players often prefer tighter strings for more control. A certified racket stringer can evaluate your needs and help you choose the best string and tension for your game and level of experience.

BALLS

Manufacturers of tennis balls send samples of their balls to the U.S. Tennis Association for testing. Those balls which pass the tests say "USTA Approved" on their cans. Heavy duty balls have more nylon woven into the wool felt covers and are more durable for hard courts than regular duty balls.

TERMINOLOGY

Ace. A serve which the receiver cannot touch with the racket.

Ad-in. The score when the player serving has won the point after the score was deuce.

Ad-out. The score when the player receiving the serve has won the point after the score was deuce.

Alley. The lane or area on each side of the singles court. The alleys can be used for all shots after the serve in doubles.

Approach Shot. A shot which the hitter follows to the net. It is usually hit from the forecourt area.

Backcourt. The part of the court between the service line and the baseline.

Baseline. The boundary line at the back of the court that runs parallel to the net.

Chip. A groundstroke hit with a short backswing, with backspin on the ball, and one that usually falls into the opponent's forecourt.

Choke up. To hold the racket at a point away from the base of the grip.

Chop. A shot hit with backspin to any part of the court.

Continental Grip. A way to hold the racket so that the player does not have to change grips between the forehand and backhand. Holding the racket so that one edge points down, the wrist is directly over the top of the racket handle.

Cross-court. A shot hit diagonally from one corner of the court to the opposite corner.

Deuce. A tie score at 40-40 and each tie after that in the same game.

Double Fault. When the server does not hit either of his or her two attempts into the proper court.

Drive. A groundstroke hit with power deeply into the opponent's backcourt.

Fault. When the server does not serve the ball into the proper court.

Flat. A shot hit with little or no spin.

Follow-through. That part of the swinging motion after the ball has been hit.

Groundstroke. A shot which is hit after the ball has bounced.

Half Volley. A shot hit immediately after the ball has bounced on the court.

Let. A serve that hits the top of the net and bounces in the proper service court. Let also means that a point should be replayed for a number of reasons.

Lob. A high, arching shot.

Love. A word used meaning zero points.

Match. A contest between two players, two doubles teams, or two teams representing schools, clubs, or other groups.

No-ad. A scoring system in which the first player to win four points wins a game. The score is counted 1—2—3—4, instead of 15—30—40—game.

Passing Shot. A groundstroke hit out of the reach of an opponent at the net.

Percentage Shot. The safest, most effective shot hit in a particular situation.

Poach. Movement of a player at the net in front of his or her partner to hit a volley.

Pro Set. A match which is completed when one player or team has won at least eight games and is ahead by at least two games.

Rally. An exchange of shots.

Receiver. The player who returns the serve.

Service Line. The line that is parallel to and 21 feet from the net.

Set. That apart of a match when one player or team has won at least six games and is ahead by at least two games. The set may continue until one player is ahead by two games, or a tie breaker may be played when each player has won six times.

Sideline. The boundary line that runs from the net to the baseline. The singles sidelines are closer to the center of the court than the doubles sidelines.

Tie Breaker. A method of completing a set when both players or team have won six games. Nine-point (best of nine) and twelve-point (best of twelve) tie breakers are the most commonly used.

Topspin. The spin put on a ball by a racket when the ball spins or rolls forward like a car wheel going forward.

Umpire. The official for a singles or doubles match.

Volley. A shot hit before the ball bounces on the court.

REFERENCES

Gould, Dick. *Tennis, Anyone?* Palo Alto, CA: National Press Books, 1985.

Tabak, Lawrence. *Teaching Tennis—The USTA Way.* Dubuque, IA: Wm. C. Brown Publishers, 1991.

USTA. *USTA Schools Program Tennis Curriculum.* Princeton, NJ: USTA Publications Department, 1990.

Van der Meer, Dennis. *Dennis Van der Meer's Complete Book of Tennis.* Hilton Head, SC: Van der Meer Tennis Center, 1986.

CHAPTER 21

Track and Field

LEROY T. WALKER
*Atlanta Committee for the
Olympic Games
Atlanta, GA*
and
SUZI D'ANNOLFO
*West Hartford Public Schools
West Hartford, CT*

INTRODUCTION

"Citius, Altius, Fortius"
Swifter, Higher, Stronger
Olympic Motto

The first Olympic Games took place in 776 B.C. in Ancient Greece. Male athletes participated in running events and throwing of the discus and javelin. Winners were awarded an olive wreath. Women participated in their own festival, the Herea, which was held once every five years and featured a 100-foot race.

With the emergence of the Romans, the Olympic Games withered and eventually became a farce in 66 A.D. In 394 A.D., after 291 Olympic Games, Emperor Theodosius of Rome, a Christian opposed to pagan spectacles, formally abolished the Olympic Games.

The Modern Olympic Games were revived in 1896 by Baron de Coubertin, who authored the Olympic creed, "The important thing in the Olympic Games is not winning but taking part. The essential thing in life is not conquering but fighting well." His plan was simple: Amateur athletes from all nations would gather every four years and compete in various sports. The champions of the First Olympiad received a gold medal and an olive branch.

Baron de Coubertin wished the Modern Games to be similar to the Ancient Games where the exclusion of women, as in the past, was a basic ingredient. Against the wishes of Baron de Coubertin, women's track and field was initially included in the Olympic Games of 1928. The events included the 100 meters, high jump, discus, 400-meter relay, and 800-meter run. In 1932, the 80-meter hurdles and javelin were added, but the 800-meter run was deleted because it was "too strenuous" for women. The 800-meter run was not reinstated until 1960. While the 3,000, 5,000, and 10,000-meter races are collegiate events for women, the 1500-meter race was the longest event for women in the 1980 Olympic Games. During the 1984 Olympic Games in Los Angeles we saw the birth of the women's marathon.

SKILLS AND TECHNIQUES

THE START

Success in sprinting events depends upon natural speed as well as reaction time. An efficient start can make the difference in any sprint event. The fundamentals of the start involve three commands: (1) runners take your marks; (2) set; (3) go (the gun).

Runners Take Your Marks (See Figure 1a)
The runner should stand in front of the blocks with the left foot about 12 to 18 inches behind the starting line and the right foot slightly behind the heel of the left foot. The right knee should be lowered to the ground next to the left foot; toes should be in contact with the ground. Do not have toes of shoe bent on track. Place feet on

a. Take your mark.

b. Set.

c. Go.

Figure 1. The start.

pedals of starting block so that only the sole of the shoe touches the track. From this position, place the hands behind the starting line; the inside of the left elbow barely touches the left knee. The hands are spread shoulder width apart with the thumb and index finger placed behind the starting line and the remaining fingers bunched in back of the index finger. The fingers and thumb form a supporting arch. Body weight should be to the rear.

Set (See Figure 1b)

The runner shifts his/her weight forward over the hands. The hips are raised to shoulder height as the back leg is parallel with the ground. The eyes are focused 8 to 10 yards ahead. Concentrate on the sound of the gun.

Go (See Figure 1c)

React as quickly as possible to the sound of the gun. The rear leg and opposite arm explode forward as the other arm drives to the rear to hip height. The front leg drives off the block into full extension. The body angle is low and forward for about 10 to 15 yards. Emphasize force against the pedals of the block. Continue to drive the arms vigorously to aid in balance and power. Once a natural upright running position is achieved, elongate your strides.

Drills

1. One on one, coach and athlete with the coach analyzing the start from the front, back, side, watches the position of the head, legs, shoulders, and arms.
2. To self-analyze foot placement and stride length, the starter uses chalk on feet on synthetic track and works on the start, then by looking at his/her tracks, analyzes foot placement and stride length for efficiency.

SPRINTS

Sprinting consists of two basic principles: stride length; stride frequency or rate of stride. Sprinting ranges from the short sprint (100 meters) to the long sprint (400 meters).

There are three basic parts of effective sprinting: the start; efficient running form;

the finish. Each of these basic parts of the total sprint effort has essential demands which the sprinter must execute.

Sprinting form is a very individual matter because of different body builds; however fundamental running movements can be described in general terms of correct foot placement, arm action, shoulder and head angles, body alignment, and leg and knee action.

Foot Placement

Emphasize the toes pointing straight ahead as opposed to in or out. To illustrate the importance of this, have the runner stand toeing out, and make a mark on the track; now have the runner rock back on the heels, rotate the toes straight ahead, and mark the track. The runner will see a difference of 1-4 inches between the marks. Efficient running saves steps.

Arm Action

Arms are used for balance. As the right leg strides forward, the left arm comes forward, while the right arm moves back. The sequence is reversed when the left leg strides forward. Maintain a constant angle of the lower arm to the upper arm with thumbs up and the wrist and hand relaxed. The arm moves, driving the elbow forward and back, never passing higher than the armpit on the forward swing and never further back than 6 inches beyond the hips. Arms never cross the midline of the body.

Shoulders

The shoulders should be relaxed. There should be little or no rotation.

Head

The head should be straight ahead with the eyes focusing on the finish line. The face should be relaxed with the jaw hanging loose.

Body Alignment

Have the runner raise up on the toes and lean forward just to where a loss of balance is not being maintained. This is the correct body lean. Forward lean is greatest when accelerating.

Leg Action—Knee Lift

Knees should come up close to parallel

and straight ahead (don't permit the knees to rotate out or in). The sprinter should run on the ball of the foot, using a pushing action to get drive against the surface of the track. Maintain stride length regardless of fatigue. Run relaxed. The faster the run, the longer the stride. The good sprinter spends less time on the ground during each stride, and has a slightly shorter stride. This action permits faster turnover (stride frequency). The greater power generated through the gluteal hamstring muscles makes the faster turnover possible. Recent training trends tend to encourage ballistic strength training of the hamstring muscle group to develop the fast turnover. When finishing the sprint race, run *through* and *lean* into the finish line.

Fundamental Drills

1. Arm pumping standing still, accelerating tempo—concentrate on angle and importance of arm action.
2. Foot placement—run on chalk lines or on a dirt track. Analyze foot placement for running efficiency.
3. Knee lifts—lean against the wall and do high knee lifts for improving leg reflex.
4. Do 40-yard sprints concentrating on high knee lift and drive from the track.
5. Quick knees—using the length of a football field, pump arms and knees as fast as possible for 5-10 yards; ease or slow to a stop and then repeat drill until length of football field is covered.

Sprinting Drills and Workouts

1. Practice relays working in groups of 5 at 100-meter intervals. Runners #1 and #5 are at the first station. Runner #1 runs a relay to Runner #2, Runner #2 to #3, Runner #3 to #4, Runner #4 to #5, Runner #5 to #1, and so on. Run relay continually over a given distance.
2. Roll-outs or Trains (see explanation in distance running training drills section).
3. Pole Progression or Ladders (see explanation in distance running training drills section).
4. Work from the blocks, accelerate 30 yards, and lean into the tape.
5. Run gradual downhills.
6. Run tall with proper body position.

Sprinting is a coordination of the start, proper running form and all its facets, as well as the finish. Each must be taught individually and built upon to develop proper running form to further efficiency of stride length and stride frequency.

SPRINT RELAY

The sprint relay is an event in itself. It involves four runners, each running approximately 100 meters. It is important for the four runners who make up a relay team to realize it is the relay *baton* which is getting timed around the track, not the sum of four runners. The relay team members must possess a positive, aggressive attitude toward this race. All four runners need to understand baton handling, border positions, stride speed, zone awareness, and the finish.

Handling the Baton

So that the runner knows how the baton should feel in the hand, have the runner pick up the baton naturally from the ground, using the fatty part of the hand.

The two basic methods of exchanging the baton are with the palm up (Figure 2) or with the palm down (Figure 3). Use the method that works best for the team.

In handling the baton, the following two facts should be remembered at all times: the baton is an extension of the arm (remember, the baton is being timed around the track, not the runners; by using the baton as an extension of the arm, many steps can be saved by the incoming and outgoing runners); the incoming runner should always *"look"* the baton into the next runner's hand (by keeping the eyes on the receiving hand of the next runner until the baton is placed firmly into the outgoing runner's hand—this will prevent any missed handoffs.)

Border Positions

The shortest distance around the track for the baton exchange in the sprint relay is right-left-right-left. Numbers 1 and 3 runners hold the baton in the right hands and numbers 2 and 4 runners hold the baton in the left hands. There is not a change of hands by any individual runner; the hand used to receive the baton is the same one

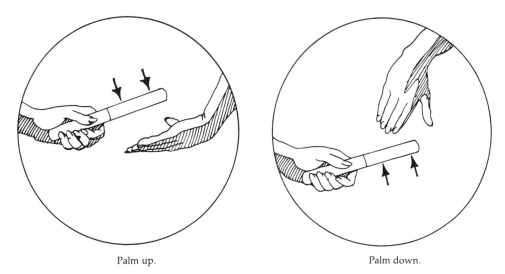

Palm up.   Palm down.

Figures 2 and 3. Exchanging the baton.

that a particular runner will use to hand off.

All four runners run borders of the lane (see Diagram 1). Numbers 1 and 3 runners run the curves, and thus, run the *inside* border of the lane, as this is the shortest distance around the track. Numbers 2 and 4 runners, who run the straightaways, run the *outside* border of the lane. Using border running, the baton is the only thing in the middle of the lane during the sprint relay.

Stride Speed (Acceleration and Transition)

The incoming and outgoing runners must adjust their speeds so that a smooth baton exchange takes place. The incoming runner must keep up a consistent pace when approaching the outgoing runner. At the same time, the outgoing runner must develop the stride transition from a standstill to near maximum speed so that the baton exchange does not interrupt the running (stride) pattern of either the incoming or outgoing runner.

The outgoing runner must select a point behind the rear border of the zone, which will serve as a handicap line for the incoming runner. If this handicap is accurately determined and there is no anticipation by the outgoing runner of his/her teammate striking the checkmarks, both runners should arrive at the critical zone approximately one meter apart with both traveling at nearly top speed.

Placement of the handicap mark will be determined by the speed of the incoming runner and the starting ability of the outgoing teammate. A final decision in this matter can be arrived at only through trial and error. The outgoing runner may start with 18 to 20 feet as a point behind his/her standing position and increase or decrease the distance depending upon the two previously mentioned factors. The final decisions can be reached only after practicing the exchange at full speed. The distance of the handicap mark from the rear border is increased or decreased in a relationship to the point before or after the pass or point where the contact is made. The handicap mark should not be changed if either runner demonstrates a faulty movement. The runners should not attempt to adjust their speed in order to make the pass work. The changes should be made in the handicap-

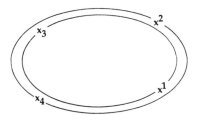

Diagram 1.

ping. Each runner should keep all factors of the pass consistent as the check mark is adjusted.

A word of caution. Once the check marks have been established, continuous practice of passing techniques may be achieved by employing 35-meter, full-speed approach runs. A shorter approach run permits many more passes and requires shorter periods of rest between baton practice sessions.

Zone Awareness

Each relay zone is 22 yards long. The baton exchange must be made within these 22 yards. However, the outgoing runner may begin a running pattern 11 yards before the official passing zone. This area is known as the international zone. The baton exchange should be made as close to the critical zone as possible (see Diagram 2).

Selection of Personnel

Selecting the four fastest runners won't always produce the fastest relay team; rather, it is how well the four runners work *together*. Some will have a natural feel for the baton exchange. The following general points should be kept in mind when selecting and placing relay personnel: #1 Runner—best starter—holds baton well in a good start—good curve runner—only involved in one handoff; #2 Runner—good straightaway runner—good competitor—handles baton twice; #3 Runner—good curve runner—handles baton twice; #4 Runner—reliable—can hold a lead or come from behind—knows the importance of running *through* the finish line.

Remember to incorporate the most workable combinations of runners and treat the sprint relay as a separate event.

Drills

1. Two students position themselves in border positions in a lane. #1 stands on the inside border; #2 stands on the outside border. $|_1\ ^2|$ In a stationary position, practice handoffs with two people. The #1 runner uses a verbal command, e.g., "Red," to alert the #2 runner to position the hand for the baton exchange.

2. Repeat the above drill using four runners. $|_1^3\ _2^4|$ Runners 1, 2, and 3 use verbal commands to alert the next runner to position the hand for the baton exchange.

3. In a stationary position, all four runners synchronize arm pumping action; then begin the baton handoff from the #1 runner, using a verbal cue.

4. Repeat the above drill but jog around the track in close formation.

5. All four runners position themselves in their zones around the track. Jog through a complete relay concentrating on running borders, using the baton as an extension of the arm, and looking the baton into the next runner's hand.

6. Set up in relay zones and jog through a complete relay concentrating on the baton exchange being made within the passing zone. The incoming runner should give a verbal signal, "Go," for the outgoing runner to begin the stride and a second verbal signal, "Red," to prepare the runner for the baton exchange. As the skills of the relay members improve with practice, verbal exchanges should be eliminated. Both the incoming and outgoing runners should concentrate on watching the critical zone (see Diagram 2). As the

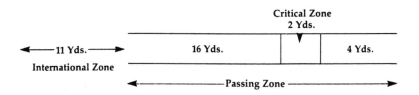

Diagram 2.

outgoing runner approaches the critical zone while running on his/her border approximately two strides from the beginning of the critical zone, the arm is extended back with palm up (or down). When the hand is steady, the incoming runner presses the baton into the hand.

7. Repeat the above with increased speed until a smooth baton exchange is achieved within the passing zone.
8. Practice in all lanes so that runners will be familiar with zones and runners' positions in relationship to their own.
9. Practice with people on either side of the lane to emphasize the importance of concentration and focus to the relay team.
10. Practice sprint drills with a baton.

Hints

The teacher/coach can minimize errors by observing the relay personnel from all angles. From the *front* and *back* angles observe:

1. border positions;
2. baton exposure (make sure the baton is the only thing in the middle of the lane);
3. body alignment (make sure the runner is running straight ahead; watch for body rotation);
4. position of incoming and outgoing runners;
5. hand position at exchange (the outgoing runner must keep a steady hand as the incoming runner plants the baton firmly in his/her hand);
6. *front* angle (the eyes of the incoming runner should be on the baton as it extends into the outgoing runner's hand. The teacher should not be able to see the whites of the incoming runner's eyes);

From the *side* angle observe:

1. the stride acceleration and deceleration of the runners;
2. extension of the arm on the baton exchange;
3. timing of the exchange;
4. body position.

HURDLES

Hurdling is a sprint event with seven or more obstacles. The hurdle race ranges from 80 to 400 meters. Regardless of a hurdler's build, the following three objectives apply to all hurdlers: to raise the center of mass as little as possible; to spend as little time in the air as possible; to return to the ground in a position to continue running as quickly as possible. Remember, it's speed along the ground that counts, not speed in the air!

Determine a Lead Leg

Using a low training hurdle, attempt to go over one hurdle to see which leg leads naturally. If there is no preference, use the left leg as it will serve as a definite advantage when running hurdles on the curve in the longer races.

Beginner's Drills

1. Walk over a low hurdle; straddle it to see that the body fits over it.
2. Walk tall, on the toes with the knees high. This will permit the hurdler to improve posture and by doing so naturally raise the center of mass; when the hurdle needs to be cleared, the movement will be accomplished with greater ease.
3. Wall drills (place tape on the wall, hurdle height.) The following drills work on specific segments of the complete hurdling skill:

   Lead Leg—the hurdler thrusts the lead leg toward the wall with the heel of the lead leg placed above the line. Emphasis should be on speed and aggressiveness (see Figure 4a).

   Arm Action—add arm action to the above drill. The arms are kept fairly close to the body and involve a quick movement. The drive or lead arm is opposite the lead leg. The lead arm is brought slightly across the body as the lead leg is thrust forward. As the hurdler clears the hurdle (tape on wall), the lead arm exerts a quick movement as if opening a door. Keep the shoulders square as not to cause rotation of the body.

   Trail Leg—place your hands on the wall for support. Draw the trail leg up with the knee driving up toward the chest, ahead of the thigh. The toes should be up to avoid hitting the hurdle on the follow-through (see Figures 4b and c).

Trail Leg Drills (work on side of hurdle)

Step in *front* of the hurdle with the lead leg (see Figures 4d and e). Then drive the trail leg up toward the chest and snap it down. Progression of this series of trail leg drills is:

1. walk tall with the knees high—exaggerate a marching motion over the side of the three hurdles;
2. add arm action over the side of the three hurdles;
3. jog over the side of the three hurdles;
4. run over the side of the three hurdles;
5. gradually add more hurdles as the hurdler progresses.

Lead Leg Drills (work on side of the hurdle)

1. With the lead leg, kick out and step past the side of the hurdle. Emphasize aggressiveness and speed (see Figures 4f and g).
2. Add the arm action.
3. Add more hurdles as the hurdler progresses.

Body Lean

When running over low hurdles, there is little or no body lean. Adjustments are made according to the length of the hurdler's legs.

Complete Hurdle Action

After working on the breakdown segments of the hurdling event, the student is

a. b. c.

d. e. f. g.

Figure 4.

now ready to attempt the complete hurdle action. Set up three hurdles at the correct racing distance on the track. Emphasize three steps between hurdles. The body *midline* should be in the middle of the hurdle so that the lead leg is to the right or left of the middle of the hurdle. This keeps the hurdler well within his/her own lane and avoids possible contact with the hurdler on either side. Emphasize acceleration and aggressiveness in the hurdle action. Add additional hurdles as the hurdler progresses.

Hints

1. Work on the start and getting to the first hurdle in control.
2. Snap the lead leg down and emphasize a quick step down with the trail leg to avoid floating or gliding over the hurdle.
3. Keep the shoulders square to avoid upper body rotation.
4. Throughout the hurdle race, focus attention on the top of the next hurdle.
5. Do flexibility exercises to increase the efficiency of the trail leg.
6. Remember that hurdling is a sprint event.

DISTANCE RUNNING

Distance running ranges from 800 meters to the marathon. In track and field classes, the 800-meter run (twice around the track) and the 1500-meter run (3¾ times around the track) are generally included.

All distance running programs are based on adapting to graduated stress on the body. Runners should start by building a broad base through slow intervals with short recovery periods and great quantities of running at much slower than racing pace. Distance runners should run relaxed, concentrating on a steady, even-paced rhythm.

The basic essentials of efficient running involve:

1. *Foot Placement*—the feet should be pointing straight ahead, not in or out. The sequence of the foot striking action is "Ball (outer edge), Heel, Ball."
2. *Arm Action*—the arms play a balancing role in running. The arms should be kept at about a 90° angle with the thumbs up. As the arms move forward and back in opposition, they should never pass higher than the chest on the forward move and never further back than the hip. The arms should never cross the midline of the body.
3. *Body Alignment*—once running speed is achieved, the body angle tends toward the perpendicular. The body is held almost erect with the shoulders and face relaxed. There should be little or no rotation in the upper body.
4. *Stride Length*—the slower the speed of the run, the shorter the stride. Conversely, the faster the run, the longer the stride. Longer strides require more energy. In distance running where economy of energy is important, runners should take *natural* strides.
5. *Breathing*—the runner should keep the jaw relaxed and breathe through the nose and mouth simultaneously.

Training Drills

1. Train work—runners form a line with the leader being responsible for the pace. At stipulated intervals, the last person in line sprints to the front and settles into a pace as the leader. The train continues until everyone has been a leader a specific number of times or until a specific distance is covered.
2. Variation of trains—see how many times each person can be the leader within a certain distance.
3. Ladders or pole progressions—(a) select a partner of equal ability and alternate running the following distances—100, 200, 300, 400, 500, 600, 700, 800, 900 meters and reverse beginning with 800 meters and working down to 100 meters (on reverse ladder, change directions). (b) same as "a" but select three other runners of equal ability and run in pairs. The pairs alternate distances with one pair doing a 100; as soon as they finish, the other pair runs it, etc. The rest time for alternating pairs is the distance just completed. (c) group all runners by ability (usually three groups) and run ladder distances one group at a time as fast as possible. This permits a greater recovery period.

4. Long sprints—group all runners by ability (3 groups). Run 400 meters, one group at a time. Repeat 5 times.

Hints

1. Although aware of other runners around, concentrate on maintaining individual rhythm.
2. Pumping the arms will take considerable stress off the legs and make running more efficient.
3. Run relaxed, maintaining stride length and stride frequency.

HIGH JUMP

The Fosbury Flop has quickly become the most popular form of high jumping and involves four major areas: approach; foot plant; take-off; bar clearance.

The high jump basically involves transfering horizontal velocity to vertical velocity. The essential movement is upward rather than forward. Speed and rhythm must be maintained throughout the entire technique.

Approach

The beginning point of the approach should be specifically determined and used every day. Using a tape measure, measure 10-14 feet from standard along the line of the jumping pit. From the selected point (approximately 12 feet), measure approximately 50 feet back from the point. This may vary a few feet depending on the number of strides.

The approach to the high jump follows a "J"-shaped curve involving 7-11 steps from the take-off (see Diagram 3). Three marks should be established by the high jumper: start; inside mark; foot plant; and take-off.

Approximately five steps from the start, the jumper should lean left as curving in begins, thus bringing the body almost parallel to the cross bar (see Figure 5). The jumper should initiate the curve of the approach with the right foot so that crossover steps on the curve do not have to be used. The next to the last step should be long to lower the center of gravity, and the arms should be gathering for the double arm lift.

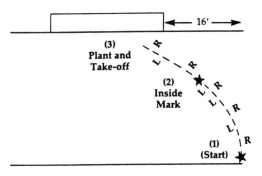

Diagram 3.

Foot Plant

Only one foot may be used for the flop take-off. Most righthanded people push off with the left foot. The left foot should be planted heel first between the near pole and the middle of the bar; the foot should be pointed toward the far pole. (See Diagram 4.)

Take-off

The take-off involves converting forward momentum to upward momentum. At the time of the take-off, the arms drive up to shoulder height and the bent lead knee (right) drives upward until it is parallel to the ground. This raises the center of mass and rotates the body so that the back is to the bar (see Figure 6).

Bar Clearance

The jumper arches the back to clear the bar, going over head first. The jumper should not reach out over the bar with the hands. As the torso clears, the knees and feet should be whipped up. When the hips are clear, it is often helpful to raise the arms, which in turn help to raise the feet. Again, maintain speed and rhythm throughout the entire technique (see Figure 7).

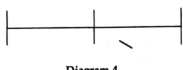

Diagram 4.

Figure 5. The high jump approach.

Figure 6. The high jump take-off.

Figure 7. Clearing the bar in the high jump.

Hints and Drills

1. Raising the center of mass as high as possible over the bar is the most important factor in the flop. Thus, the techniques of the approach, plant, and take-off should be practiced much more than the technique of bar clearance. (Work on leg and arm lift and bounding drills on the grass.)
2. If the jumper is hitting the bar on the way up (caused by reaching maximum height too soon, he/she is taking off too close to the bar).
3. Conversely, if the bar is being hit on the way down, the jumper is taking off too far from the bar.
4. To eliminate leaning into the bar, the jumper should press the inside shoulder up.

THE LONG AND TRIPLE JUMPS

The horizontal jumps—the long jump and triple jump—are quite similar to one another, yet the two are in some aspects quite different. Both have four phases: the approach run; the take-off; in-flight; the landing. However, the triple jump has three take-off phases, one each in the hop, step, and jump phases and also three in-flight phases.

The Approach

In both horizontal jumps, the approach run is most critical. A successful, well-executed jump cannot be done without a smooth, relaxed, and controlled approach run.

The approach run length varies from 100 to 140 feet (with an average of about 120 feet). The length of the approach run is influenced by the basic speed and quickness of the jumper. The speed of the approach run is usually about 75-80% of the full speed of the jumper with a gradual acceleration from the starting check mark. It is necessary to retain the speed until the take-off.

Most jumpers in their speedy, relaxed, controlled approach run tend to shorten the last three strides before take-off to avoid a stretching action for the board. The stretch action at the board will place the body weight too far behind the take-off foot. This will tend to act as a breaking force to the good forward speed and will also limit the lift from the take-off board.

Determining the check mark to guarantee successful striking of the take-off board requires special attention to detail. One check mark at the beginning of the approach is preferred so that the jumper can concentrate on the relaxed sprint effort. To achieve the end of using only one mark, six steps should be followed in determining the start of the approach run.

1. Measure on the track the number of feet from a take-off point which according to the speed of the jumper would be required for effective jumping. Mark that point on the track.
2. Beginning at the designated point, sprint with gradual acceleration toward the line which represents the take-off board. Do this approach a dozen or more times, with occasional rest periods to permit time for recovery. Check each approach run for relaxation and gradual acceleration at nearly full effort.
3. Mark the strike point near the edge of the runway nearest to the take-off line.
4. Draw a line where the cluster of marks are made. If the cluster is not in line with the board, measure the distance from the line to the imaginary board.
5. Move the tentative starting check mark forward or backward the same distance measured from the cluster of marks to the take-off board.
6. Measure the exact distance from the newly established check mark to the take-off point. This is now the distance which should be established on the runway.

The Take-off

The jumper must attempt to get sufficient height at take-off to allow time in the in-flight phase to execute leg extension. However, height alone is not enough. The action at take-off is a forward-upward lift.

Four essential points must be emphasized in executing the take-off:

1. The shorter last stride permits a slight bend of the take-off leg. A powerful extension of the bent leg provides a forward-upward lift from the take-off board.
2. The foot should strike the board firmly in a "flat foot" position. In this action, the heel lands first, but there is no attempt to execute a heel-ball-toe rock-up action.
3. The body weight should be directly over the board as the take-off foot strikes it but it should be very slightly in advance of the take-off foot as the jumper leaves the board.
4. The final thrust into the air results from running off the board.

The jumper should stride off the board in a sprint action. The body weight must be moved slightly forward with the head high and with the eyes focused on some imaginary spot high and beyond the pit. The chest should be elevated. The knee opposite the take-off leg is thrust forward and high as the arms move vigorously in a counterbalancing action.

Flight

The two styles most frequently used by jumpers are the hitch-kick (running-in-the-air) and the hang.

Hitch-kick (Running-in-the-air)

Running in the air (see Figure 8) is a reaction fight against the downward pull of gravity. There is no gain in the momentum, but the style does reduce the difficulty of holding the legs up and helps to bring the body to the correct position at the right time.

The running-in-the-air technique or hitch-kick requires:

1. Driving the knee of the free leg high as the take-off leg stretches down.
2. Stretching the free leg straight forward, down, and then bending it as it passes back under the body.
3. Snapping the take-off leg quickly forward in the same manner as the free leg was moved in the take-off action.
4. Bringing the heel of the leg which began the running action (free leg at take-off) adjacent to the heel of the take-off leg,

Figure 8. The hitch-kick.

holding the head up with the eyes focused straight forward.

The arms must be kept high and moving as they do in sprinting action. The chest must be elevated. The upper body must be kept erect and the head high.

The Hang

The hang style (see Figure 9) is used mainly by jumpers with great lift. The hang style requires excellent timing. The flight action in the hang is as follows:

1. The free leg is stretched straight forward and then dropped beneath the body.
2. The take-off leg is thrust forward from the board to a position next to the free leg.
3. The arms drop back to the side.

4. The trunk is held erect, the head high, and the chest is lifted.
5. The legs whip forward and upward in a vigorous stretching action.
6. The arms press forward and downward in the landing position.

Landing

It is important that the jumper not bend the trunk toward the thigh until the last moment before the legs are extended for landing. When the jumper hits the pit, the chest should be thrust forward as the knees are flexed.

At the moment of contact with the landing surface, the feet must be extended as far as possible in front of the body. Arms are pressed forward and downward.

Figure 9. The hang.

The Triple Jump (see Figure 10)

There are some major differences between the long jump and the triple jump (hop, step, jump). In secondary schools, the long jumper will usually be expected to double in the triple jump. Therefore, the jumper must understand the basic differences in the performance of the long and triple jump. These differences must be carefully practiced after the approach, take-off, flight, and landing phases of the long jump have been thoroughly learned.

The developing jumper should carefully consider seven basic differences in the technique of the long and triple jumps:

1. The body lean at take-off is more pronounced in the triple jump.
2. The take-off (for the hop) is executed low with minimum elevation. The head up, and eyes focused forward, are common to both.
3. The body position and elevation changes in each flight of the triple jump in contrast to the single flight of the long jump. The changes in the triple jump are from a very slight forward lean at take-off in the hop to a nearly erect position in the jump. With each increase in height, careful attention must be given to sustaining the forward momentum.
4. The triple jumper must master a coordinated, synchronized bending and unbending of the knees in the three flights as compared to the single action of the long jump.
5. The distance factor in the triple jump is influenced by the execution of three distinct flights instead of one. The step flight is the one that most often requires lengthening. The complete pattern must be considered when adjusting any flight distance.
6. The stronger (best) jumping leg should be used in the third phase of the jump. Arrange the three phases to place the jumper in position for a strong final jump.
7. The triple jumper must establish a pattern of distance for each phase of the jump. The established ratio for the phases will provide a measuring rod to determine which phase is inadequate.

SHOT PUT

A good shot put performance demands an appropriate blend of speed and quickness, a high degree of explosive power, great strength, good height, and motivation. Effective shot putting involves a simple and natural movement coupled with a coordinated drive of the legs and thrust of the back with arm delivery.

The logical order of progression in practice of the shot put should be: developing the proper grip; developing the correct stance and making the delivery; practicing the glide across the circle; integrating the putting technique.

The Grip

The shot is held in the hand so that it presses against the base of the fingers reducing tension and permitting the full range of the fingers in the snap release. The fingers may be placed together or slightly spread. The shot may be gripped by placing the first three fingers together and using the small finger and thumb to hold it in position. The wide finger spread is recommended for putters with small hands. The spread should not be exaggerated to the point that the fingers cannot be used to give impetus to the shot. Beginners should carry the shot lower down in the palm of the hand until greater strength is developed.

The Delivery

Early practice of the delivery should be done in a correct stance at the front of the circle. The delivery is a sequence of coordinated movements from the foot to the tip of the fingers.

The right foot is placed in the middle of the circle at approximately a 45° angle to the flight of the shot. The knee is slightly flexed with the body weight over the right leg, which is well under the body. The center of gravity is far enough over the right leg for maximum drive (see Figure 11a). The right leg is vigorously extended to begin the force which moves up the leg, to the hips, to the trunk, and to the arm for the final delivery with a snap of the wrist (see Figure 11b-d).

Figure 10. The triple jump.

Figure 11. The shot put delivery.

The left leg serves as a brace against which the force is exerted. The foot of the left leg is against the toe board. The right foot remains on the surface and continues to deliver power in the delivery.

The Glide

The glide is used to travel from the rear of the circle to the correct position for delivery. The glide begins by standing at the rear of the circle with the back to the direction of the put. The glide must begin with the athlete in good balance.

From the erect, relaxed, balanced position at the rear of the circle, the athlete lowers the head and shoulders by flexing the hips to a position in which the back is nearly horizontal. The eyes are focused on a spot directly behind the circle; the right knee is bent to a point which will give the greatest lifting power, and rocks forward until the weight is over the ball of the right foot (see Figure 12a).

Momentum is generated by moving the weight of the body toward the toe board. Additional momentum is gained by driving off the right leg and ball of the foot as the left leg engages in a piston-like motion. The piston-like motion is achieved by first bringing the knee forward, then vigorously extending it straight back and down toward the toe board (see Figure 12b). The hips should remain low. The entire action should be made with the legs rather than with the upper body. The left leg, as indicated, lands against the toe board to the left center of the circle (see Figure 12c). At the end of the glide and turn in position for delivery, the stance should be the same as the one assumed at the front of the circle during

Figure 12. The glide for the shot put.

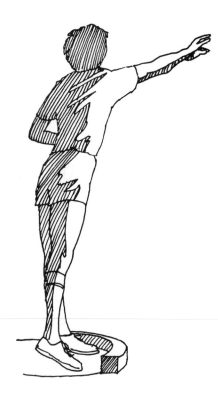

Figure 13. The shot put reverse.

earlier practice sessions without the glide (see Figures 11b-d).

The Reverse

The purpose of the reverse (see Figure 13) is to prevent a foul after completion of a powerful delivery. The reverse is completed by switching the feet. The rear foot replaces the front foot by placing the outer edge of the rear foot at the inner edge of the toe board. The body weight is shifted back after the landing, but not until all power is delivered.

DISCUS

The logical order of progression in learning how to throw the discus is: developing the proper grip; developing the correct stance and release; practicing the spin across the circle; integrating the throwing technique. Throwing the discus is a combination of balance, power, speed, control, and timing.

The Grip

The athlete places the discus in the non-throwing hand. Place the palm of the throwing hand on top of and in the middle of the discus. Only the first joints of each finger should come over the edge of the discus. The thumb is placed at the edge of the discus but does not come over the discus rim. The thumb in this position is pressed against the discus. Basically there are two ways that the fingers can be positioned on the discus: the fingers and thumbs are spread out; the index finger and middle finger are placed next to each other with the other two fingers and thumb spread out on the discus (see Figure 14).

Release from the Hand

Primarily the discus is released off of the index finger and the discus rotates in a clockwise manner.

Drill. Rolling the discus (using the lines on a football field or any lines on the gym floor). To do this the athlete takes 4-5 steps carrying the discus extended down at the side, swings, and releases the discus down the line. (The action is similar to a bowling movement.) The discus should travel in a straight line. This movement is essentially the same as a release from the throwing position in that it comes off the index finger last.

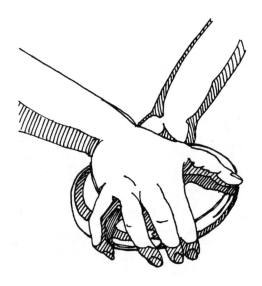

Figure 14. The discus grip.

Back of Ring

Both feet are at the back of the circle. The left foot is placed on the center line instead of having to straddle the line. Starting off in this position allows the athlete to use more of the circle and more of a circular motion, creating a greater velocity of the discus. (See Diagram 5 and Figure 15.)

Coaches should note that 70-80% of all mistakes in the circle occur in the back of the circle.

Power Position

Place the right foot on the middle of the circle. Rotate the foot so that the toe is pointing at about 10 o'clock. Weight is balanced on the flexed right leg. The left foot should land in the pocket. The toe of the left foot should be just about even with the right heel if not back a little, with the leg slightly flexed and relaxed. The feet are a little more than shoulder width apart (see Figure 16a). This is done so that when the

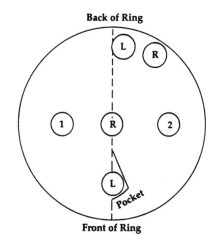

Back of Ring

Front of Ring

Diagram 5.

athlete rotates the hips, he/she will be open to the throwing area. The hips constitute the direction of the discus (see Figure 16b).

a.

b.

Figure 15.

Moving through the Circle

As the athlete moves through the circle, thought should be "slow, then fast with increasing speed," or just "quick." Be careful not to decelerate.

Spin

Always stay on the toes and rotate. The athlete must be active with the lower body and passive with the upper body.

1. Swing the right leg and foot around, keeping the leg ahead of the shoulders.
2. Relax muscles to get the right leg around, keeping the spread between the right leg and left leg on the first turn (pretend there is a bar between the two legs like a sprinter's running form—see Figures 17a and b): (a) legs and hips lead the movement to the key torqued position (see Figure 16a); (b) from the balance position, the body is accelerated across the ring by driving across the ring with the left leg.
3. The right foot is put down on the center of the circle. The right foot is turned upward prior to landing to ensure an early pivot and to keep the hips ahead of upper body for torque. (Stay on the toes and rotate.)
4. The hips must remain ahead of the shoulders and the discus, creating torque. (Torque: the difference between the hips and the shoulders which build up or make up an "X.") (See Figure 16a.)
5. Go into the power position. The upper body and discus are turned toward the right with the discus over the left heel (a torqued position).
6. Then release (see Figures 17c-e).

Finish

1. Finish in a 360° rotation, facing the front of the ring with the knees flexed and feet apart (see Figure 17f).
2. Replacing the left foot with the right foot and lowering the center of gravity completes the release.

a. b.

Figure 16. The power position for throwing the discus.

a.   b.   c.

d.   e.   f.

Figure 17. The discus spin.

CONDITIONING

Effective physical and mental conditioning provides a solid foundation for success in track and field performance. Three general areas make up physical conditioning: flexibility; strength; endurance.

FLEXIBILITY

Flexibility or stretching exercises should be done before and after daily activity. Flexibility exercises increase the blood supply to the muscles making them more pliable and resistant to injury. Begin with the head and work down to the feet, rotating each joint and *gradually* stretching each large muscle group.

All flexibility exercises should be gradual movements to the point of resistance (slight tightness) and then held at that point for a minimum of 10 seconds. This is known as *static stretching.* Avoid jerky, rapid movements during warming up and cooling down. Stretching exercises are based on principles of progression, from gentle to strenuous exercises, large muscle areas to smaller areas, back area before legs. Each exercise should not be rushed; go through the full range of motion. Focus on "feeling" the stretch of each muscle group. The importance of stretching during the cooling down period at the end of activity is to reduce the lactic acid level in the body and to avoid stiffness the following day.

STRENGTH

One of the major contributing factors in any sports performance is strength. Gains in strength are the result of three factors: the amount of stress or work that is applied to the muscle; the amount of time the muscle is under stress; the frequency (number of times) that stress is applied to the muscle. The muscle attempts to build up an immunity to stress or work by becoming stronger.

Weight-training is one of the most popular forms of strength-training. Three results can be achieved through weight-training: *increase in muscular strength* by performing a low number of repetitions with a high weight; increase in *muscular endurance* by using a lighter weight and increasing the number of repetitions; improvement in *power*—using a high weight and low repetition, the lifting movement is *explosive.* This result is a combination of force and speed and training for it is especially helpful when jumping or throwing.

Each activity in track and field involves different levels of strength. Some require more upper body strength (throwing) and some more lower body strength (jumping). However, overall strength-training will contribute to general sports performance.

ENDURANCE

Endurance can be increased by overloading the cardiovascular system (heart) by doing an activity longer than usual and raising the pulse level. Examples of endurance work would include distance running.

Each activity in track and field involves different levels of flexibility, strength, and endurance. Overall conditioning should be done by all students with specific additional conditioning for particular events.

MENTAL CONDITIONING

The track and field participant should practice blocking out what is occurring in the environment and learn to focus on the particular task or event at hand. He/she should learn to "listen" to the body and should practice visualizing each complete event prior to attempting it. At all times, "think positively and try to do your best."

SAFETY

The key to safety in track and field is to *look* before you move.
1. Before walking onto the track, *look* to see that you are not walking into the path of a runner or hurdler.
2. Before walking into the throwing area, *look* to see that someone isn't in the shot or discus circle.
3. Before going into the jumping area, *look* to see that you are not walking into the path of a jumper.

4. If preparing to throw an implement, *look* first to see that the area is clear. After throwing the discus or putting the shot, do not stay out in the field and throw the implements back to the next participant.

5. If walking during a recovery phase of a workout, move either to the outside lane or completely off the track.

6. If sprinting or being timed in the inside lanes and approaching someone either walking or jogging in the same lane, yell, "track," to signal that person to move to a middle or outside lane.

7. *Look* before walking between hurdles to be sure that the hurdler's run is not being interrupted.

8. Do not leave implements (shot, discus, hurdles, tape measures, or other obstacles) on the track or field where someone could trip on them.

CHAPTER 22

Tumbling

DIANE BONANNO
Rutgers University
New Brunswick, NJ
and
KATHLEEN FEIGLEY
Feigley's School of Gymnastics
South Plainfield, NJ

INTRODUCTION

Tumbling is a series of self-testing activities that offer the discovery and expansion of movement capabilities in a challenging and exciting setting. Unlike many other sports, tumbling is not only a competitive activity but a self-improvement activity as well. The goal of tumbling is to develop overall performance by increasing an individual's strength, flexibility, power, endurance, balance, agility, and coordination. This occurs through the use of prescribed exercises or skills, which range in difficulty from a basic balance like the front scale to a difficult twisting maneuver like a twisting back somersault.

Over the years a wide variety of skills and apparatus have been developed to assist the person in discovering and expanding movement capabilities. The basic forward roll, for instance, has at least 20 variations that can be used to add variety and challenge when learning a basic forward rotary movement. Tumbling offers something for everyone regardless of entry level. If patient and diligent when working through the progressions, many things can be accomplished that at first seemed impossible.

Media coverage of gymnastics in the Olympics has given a glimpse of what the sport is like at advanced levels, but what is not unattainable. Gymnastics covers a wide range of activities and is, in fact, several sports rolled into one. There is tumbling, vaulting, the balance beam, rings, unevens, evens, the horizontal bar, and the sidehorse, each of which requires special abilities. Regardless of the one that is chosen, recognize that a strong tumbling background is important.

Following is a progression which includes a description of the skill, spotting techniques, variations, and a self-analysis checklist. In order to facilitate learning and teaching each item has been written from the perspective of the performer. This ready-made program makes it possible to individualize the unit of instruction to ensure a safer and more productive educational atmosphere.

MOVEMENT SEQUENCES

The sole purpose of any tumbling routine is to provide the performer with an organized means of demonstrating control of the body while moving through space at varying speeds and different levels. A truly good routine will be composed of small units of activity which emphasize varying degrees of difficulty in the areas of flexibility, agility, power, strength, endurance, and balance. In combination, these smaller units, which are known as movement sequences, represent the totality of an individual's movement capabilities.

Like the sentences in a paragraph these movement sequences are composed of many separate elements. If the elements in the sequence, like the words in a sentence, are carefully chosen and placed in the proper order, they will permit the creator, or in this case the tumbler, to effectively communicate to the audience.

To be effective, each movement sequence in a routine should include at least four of the elements below:

- locomotor movements which can be performed
  1. forward, backward, or sideward
  2. at a high, medium, or low level
  3. fast, medium, or slow
  4. on different parts of the body
  5. along different pathways (straight, zigzagged, or curved)
- nonlocomotor movements (bending, stretching, twisting, curling, etc.) which can be performed
  1. rhythmically or arhythmically
  2. at a high, medium, or low level
  3. by a varying number of body parts
  4. symmetrically or asymmetrically
  5. at a fast, medium, or slow pace
- balances which can be performed
  1. at a high, medium, or low level
  2. using any number of points of contact with the floor
  3. in a symmetrical or asymmetrical position
  4. in different body positions (inverted, sideways, etc.)
  5. in different styles (angular, straight, rounded)
- flexibility movements which can be performed
  1. while moving or stationary
  2. in the air or in contact with the ground
  3. using different joints
- strength movements which can be performed to show strength of different body parts
  1. in a slow sustained manner or an explosive manner
  2. by moving slowly through the range of motion or by holding a specific position
- rotary movements which can be performed
  1. at a high, medium, or low level
  2. in different directions
  3. in contact with the floor or freely in the air
  4. at different speeds
- springing movements which can be performed
  1. at a high, medium, or low level
  2. from many different body parts
  3. in different directions

Three movement sequences, which are written in general terms, are presented here as an exercise. Think about each element that is listed. Next to each one, write a skill that you can do in order to accomplish that element. Practice the sequence as it is written. When you can move from one element to the next in the first sequence so that the movements are fluid, begin work on sequence number two and then three until you can perform them with equal success. When you have completed each sequence, write your own fourth sequence. Then connect all the sequences together so that you can move from sequence number one to sequence number four without stopping. When finished, you will have completed a tumbling routine. Then use the performance checklist.

Movement Sequence Number One

1. From a stand move slowly into a one-point balance
2. Do a rotary movement into a balanced position
3. Spring to a balanced position at a high level
4. Do a forward locomotor movement for at least three beats
5. Do a symmetrical jump
6. Do a rotary movement backward
7. Do a two-point balance at a medium level

Movement Sequence Number Two

1. Do a movement which demonstrates flexibility of some joint
2. Do an inverted balance position, hold for three beats, rock, or roll out
3. Spring, and do a one-half turn in the air
4. Do a rapid forward locomotor movement
5. Move sideways in an inverted position
6. Balance at a low level

Movement Sequence Number Three

1. Spin out of a low level pose into a high level pose
2. Do a rapid forward locomotor movement, changing types of movement at least twice
3. Do a movement onto the hands, with the feet momentarily leaving the ground

PERFORMANCE CHECKLIST

Ask your partner to watch your routine and evaluate your performance according to the guidelines provided below. Be sure they include comments for each category.

	Good	Fair	Needs Improvement
1. Were the movements creative?			
2. Were the movements performed with maximum amplitude (with greatest strength or height possible)?			
3. Were the movements controlled (performed without a wobble)?			
4. Was the sequence performed fully?			
5. Were the movements compatible (was it easy to go from one to the next; was extra movement needed)?			
6. Were the movements performed with proper posture and form?			

4. Do a half turn
5. Do a backward movement onto the hands with the feet momentarily leaving the ground
6. End in a movement which demonstrates flexibility of the legs
7. Move to a balance which demonstrates abdominal strength

Movement Sequence Number Four
1.
2.
3.
4.
5.
6.

TUMBLING SKILLS

FORWARD TUCK ROLL

Description

1. From a stand, squat, and place the hands on the mat, shoulder width apart approximately one arm's length from the feet.
2. Place the chin on the chest and elevate the hips.
3. Push off by extending the legs while placing weight on the hands.

4. As the hips come forward overhead use the arms to gently lower the shoulders back to the mat, keeping them rounded.
5. Remaining in a tight tuck, with the heels close to the buttocks, continue to land onto the feet.
6. Keep the hands reaching forward as though you were going into another roll so that you can stand up.

Spotting

A spotter can assist the beginner by placing a hand behind the performer's head to ensure that it is tucked.

Self-analysis

	Yes	No
1. Were the hands properly placed in front of the body?		
2. Did the hips elevate before moving forward?		
3. Was the head tucked?		
4. Did the arms lower the body to the floor with the shoulders making the first contact?		
5. Was the performer able to stand without having to touch the floor with the hands?		

Variations

1. Straddle to tuck
2. Lunge to tuck (the straight leg should be dragged across the floor until it meets the opposite leg which is now also extended)
3. Pike to tuck
4. Straddle to straddle (stay tightly compressed throughout the roll and use the hands in between the legs to return to the straddle stand)
5. Pike to pike

BACKWARD ROLL

Description

1. From a stand, squat and place the hands slightly above the shoulders with the palms facing the ceiling.
2. Rest the chin on the chest, with the forehead toward the knees; keep the elbows close to the body.
3. Remaining in a tight tuck, rock backward onto a rounded back (be sure not to open).
4. As soon as the palms contact the floor push against the floor while extending the elbows. (Remember to keep the elbows close to the body. If there is a problem with hand placement and elbows remaining tightly pressed toward body, the performer should practice rocking backward, checking to see if elbows are pointing to ceiling as hands contact mat.)
5. While pushing with the arms, quickly place the feet on the floor directly overhead (avoid shooting the feet into the air).
6. As soon as the feet are firmly on the floor and your head is free, immediately rise to a stand.

Spotting

1. Kneel at the performer's side.
2. The spotter should place the hand closest to the performer's back on the performer's near hip. As the roll begins and the hips start off the floor the other hand reaches around the performer's back to grasp the other hip.
3. To prevent any strain on the neck, the spotter should perform a lifting action of the hips as the hips rise above the shoulders and the body passes over the neck.

Self-analysis

	Yes	No
1. Was the body tightly tucked at the beginning of the skill?	_____	_____
2. Did the body remain tightly tucked throughout the skill?	_____	_____
3. Did the elbows remain close to the body throughout?	_____	_____
4. Did the arms push evenly after contact with the floor?	_____	_____

Variations

1. Tuck to tuck
2. Tuck to straddle
3. Tuck to straight leg (pike)
4. Straddle to straddle
5. Straddle to straight leg (pike)
6. Straight leg to straight leg (pike)
7. Tuck to knee scale
8. Tuck to front scale

HEADSTAND

Description

1. Start in a lunge position (see Figure 1), and place the hands and front knee on the floor. The hands should be placed under the shoulders in line with the knee.
2. Place the hairline on the mat so that it forms the top of an equilateral triangle which is made by the hands and head. Be sure you can see your hands.
3. Slide the straight leg forward until the hips are above the head then slowly, with control, lift the leg to a vertical position as the bent front leg begins to straighten and slowly joins the other leg in the vertical position. As you do this you will feel your weight shift from the hairline to the top of the head. Keep the neck straight throughout this movement.
4. Use the fingers and heels of the hands to maintain balance.

5. In case of overbalancing or as an alternate means of coming down, pull the chin toward the chest, bend at the hips, and pike the legs toward the face and continue rolling to a stand.

Spotting
1. Stand close to the performer facing his/her side.
2. Grasp the performer's leg as it hits the vertical position, thereby aiding in balancing.
3. If the performer chooses to roll out, the spotter should keep the legs in a vertical position until the performer can lower them in a controlled manner to a tight compression (verbally instruct them to maintain straight knee position to avoid injury).
4. If the performer chooses to return to original starting position by stepping down, the spotter must switch. Grasp from legs to hips to allow performer to regain balance.

Figure 1. The lunge position.

Self-analysis

	Yes	No
1. Did the hands and head form an equilateral triangle?	___	___
2. Were the hips placed directly above the head?	___	___
3. Did the neck remain straight throughout (or did a relaxed neck cause a roll-out or arch to occur)?	___	___
4. Did the legs lift in a controlled manner?	___	___
5. Was the performer's body absolutely straight at the top of the headstand or was there a pike or arch that pulled the headstand off balance?	___	___

Variations
1. Tripod to headstand, forward roll
2. Tip up headstand, forward roll
3. Kick up to headstand, forward roll
4. Kick up to headstand, to stag (pose), forward roll
5. Kick up to headstand, to double stag, forward roll
6. Straddle to headstand, forward roll
7. Drag-up headstand (start in a prone position and with the hands by the shoulders, drag the hips over the head; the legs should remain straight throughout), and without bending the legs bring them up over the hips.

HANDSTAND

Description
1. From a standing position step forward through a lunge position (the arms should remain overhead). (See Figure 1).
2. Bend forward at the waist while lifting the back leg and placing the hands on the floor approximately two feet ahead of the forward leg and shoulder width apart.
3. Gently push off the forward leg, while continuing to lift the back leg until the legs meet in a vertical position. The arms must remain perfectly straight throughout.

4. The head should be in a neutral position, not lifted or tucked, with the eyes focused on the floor between the hands. The back should be perfectly flat with no pike or arch.
5. To return to a stand the performer can split the legs and step back down to a lunge position or, bend the arms, tuck the head, and slowly, with control, lower the body to a forward roll with the legs remaining straight.

Spotting
1. The spotter should stand slightly back from where the performer will place the hands and slightly to the side. (It is better to be too far than too close to the performer as it is easier to move forward to compensate for the distance than back.)
2. As the performer kicks to a handstand the spotter reaches forward and grasps the performer's thigh with both hands to keep the performer from going over and to help support the performer's weight.
3. Under no circumstances should the performer's leg be pulled into a vertical position if he/she does not have enough leg lift.
4. If the performer chooses to step down, the spotter can shift the hand nearest the belly side of the performer to under the performer's stomach to help lower him/her down. If the performer chooses to roll out, the spotter should remain in contact with the performer's thigh, lifting up to support as much of the performer's weight as possible as the rollout occurs. (Remind the performer to roll slowly, tuck the head, and keep the knees straight.)

Self-analysis

	Yes	No
1. Did you begin in a perfect lunge?	___	___
2. Did you move your body toward the mat in a straight line position?	___	___
3. Did you lift your lead leg into place?	___	___
4. Did you maintain a straight body position while upside down?	___	___
5. Were you able to hold your balance at least three seconds without breaking form or moving hand position?	___	___

Variations
1. Handstand to stag pose
2. Handstand to double stag pose
3. Handstand snap down
4. Forward roll to a handstand
5. Headstand, pop into a handstand (draw knees to chest before popping legs upward)
6. Backward roll to immediate handstand (back extension)
7. Side handstand (half a cartwheel)
8. Handstand chest roll
9. Handstand to a split
10. Handstand pirouette
11. Press up handstand

CARTWHEEL

Description
1. This entire skill will be performed with the body traveling sideward along a straight line.
2. Perform a sideward lunge and place the closest hand on the floor arm's length from and in line with the bent front lunge leg. At the same time lift the straight rear leg overhead toward the ceiling.
3. As the bent front leg extends and pushes from the floor, the second hand should now make contact with the floor along the same straight line at a minimum of shoulder's width from the first hand; the body should now be in a straddled handstand.
4. Your momentum should continue to pass smoothly through the vertical position as the first leg over the head contacts the floor. The first hand down will now lift off the floor and straight over the head. Then the second hand will lift off over the head, and finally the pushing leg will land on the floor along the same straight line.
5. The entire wheeling action should have a 1,2,3,4 rhythm (hand, hand, foot, foot).

6. The elbows must remain straight throughout, and the head should remain in a neutral position, neither lifting upward nor with the chin in a tucked position.
7. The path of your cartwheel should be a very straight line and through a vertical position.

Spotting
1. The front of the spotter's body should be facing the performer's back and the spotter should be positioned with the feet in a stride position at the approximate spot where the performer's hands will make contact with the mat.
2. As the wheeling action begins, the spotter should place the hand closest to the performer on the hip of the lunge leg. As the performer's hand contacts the floor the spotter should place the second or hand farthest away on the performer's other hip which will now be leading.
3. The spotter may have to actually grasp and lift the hips to help the performer attain the vertical position and to support the weight in case the performer bends the elbows.
4. Instruct the performer to remain tight and to keep the legs straight throughout the skill to prevent the spotter from being kicked by bent legs.
5. Guide the performer through the skill until he/she is standing.

Self-analysis

	Yes	No
1. Did you start in a perfect lunge?	____	____
2. Did you stretch forward as you went to place your hands down?	____	____
3. Did you maintain a wide straddle throughout?	____	____
4. Did you maintain an even tempo throughout, i.e., hand, hand, foot, foot?	____	____

Variations
1. Cartwheel quarter turn at the end of the skill either in or out
2. One-handed cartwheel with the near arm
3. One-handed cartwheel with the far arm

4. Cartwheel, close the legs in a handstand position at the top of the cartwheel
5. Quarter turn at the start of the cartwheel
6. Dive cartwheel

BACK EXTENSION

Description
1. From a standing position, bend the knees and squat to a tuck position. The arms should move from a stretched overhead position to a bent position slightly above the shoulders with the palms facing the ceiling.
2. As in the backward roll, the chin should be toward the chest, the elbows close to the body, and the back should remain rounded to make the rolling action easier.
3. Begin to roll backward while remaining in a tight tuck. As the hands contact the floor, extend the elbows so that they are totally straight. At the same time open the hip angle and shoot the legs straight toward the ceiling to end in a handstand, split the legs, and step down to a stand. (If the timing is correct you will extend your body slightly before the vertical position is attained because the backward momentum will carry you right to the vertical by the end of your extension. The total opening action should have an explosive quality.)
4. Key timing and execution problems to look for: if you are short of the handstand or falling back toward the direction from which you started, then your push is premature; if you are over or beyond the handstand your push was too late and/or too slow; lifting your head as you open will cause an undesirable arch instead of a straight body handstand.

Spotting
1. Stand to the side of the performer near the spot where his/her hands will make contact with the floor.
2. Watch for the knees to contact the floor and immediately grasp the performer's closest thigh with both hands.

3. Exert your force upward to help the performer reach a balanced handstand position. Support the performer's weight in case the arms do not straighten quickly or completely.

4. Be aware that:
   • An *early push* by the performer may cause him/her to be falling toward the back. By grasping the thigh early you can pull the performer to a handstand or quickly instruct him/her to tuck the head and roll out as you lower him/her to the floor.
   • A *late push* would cause the performer to land in a push-up position. You can prevent this by picking the thigh up early and also by giving a verbal cue, e.g., "now," so that the performer learns to push as the hands contact the floor. If the performer has already passed the vertical position, quickly shift your hand that is on the front of the thigh to the performer's waist to break the fall and allow them to step down.

Self-analysis

	Yes	No
1. Was the body tightly tucked at the beginning of the skill?	____	____
2. Were the elbows held close to the body throughout?	____	____
3. Did the legs shoot upward as the hands made contact with the floor?	____	____
4. Did the legs shoot upward toward the ceiling (not toward the front or back wall)?	____	____
5. Did the legs and body straighten explosively?	____	____
6. Did the arms push evenly?	____	____

Variations
1. Tuck to extension and snap down
2. Tuck to extension, and walk out (one leg comes down at a time)
3. Tuck to extension, and roll out forward
4. Straddle to extension
5. Pike to extension
6. Tuck to extension to split
7. Tuck to extension to double leg shoot-through

ROUND-OFF
Description
1. A round-off begins in the same way a cartwheel does but builds much greater speed and the performer lands on two feet.
2. Start in a lunge position with the knee in front of the ankle so that your lower leg is at a 45 degree angle to the floor.
3. Hand placement is quite varied but in general the wider the hand placement the more power that can be exerted. The fingers of the first hand down should point toward your lunge leg, while the fingers of the second hand are facing the same direction as your back. Arms should remain next to the head throughout.
4. As the back leg drives over the hand and the front leg pushes powerfully from the floor, the hands are placed on the mat along a straight line, while the head is kept in a neutral position throughout.
5. The performer should push very hard off the lunge leg so it can meet with the other leg before the vertical position is attained. A pirouetting action or quarter-turn of the body occurs as the legs snap together. Quickly snapping the legs together will permit the trick to proceed at maximum speed.
6. As the feet contact the floor the arms should be continuing overhead and the body should now land facing the direction from which it came.
7. There are two very important methods of this last stage of round-off called the snap-down:
   • *Block under*—the feet are snapped down to the floor as close to the hands as possible so a backward momentum is continued so that a back handspring can follow the round-off (this action should not be done unless a spotter is standing behind you to stop your momentum or unless you are continuing to another skill such as a back handspring).
   • *Block out*—the feet are placed back away from hands so as to stop backward momentum and convert it to upward momentum. Blocking out would be used if the round-off were to be followed by a vertical jump or a somersault.

Spotting

1. The spotter should stand on the same side as the performer's lead leg and in the approximate spot where the performer will place the hands.
2. Grasp the performer's second arm down with your near arm and place your far arm in the performer's hip area to assist in landing.
3. As the performer's feet contact the floor switch your far arm to the performer's back to prevent over-rotation.
4. An advanced spotting technique for a powerful blocked under round-off would be to stand to the side and behind where the performer's feet will contact the floor. As the legs pass by, you must quickly reach in and grasp the performer's waist to prevent over-rotation. Your nearest hand should go on the performer's closest hip. Your second hand should reach around back to the opposite hip. Be sure you are standing on the same side as the performer's lead leg and do not step in until the legs have passed you.

Self-analysis

	Yes	No
1. Did the skill begin in a good lunge position?	____	____
2. Were the hands placed wide apart?	____	____
3. Were the hands placed in the proper pattern?	____	____
4. Did the arms remain next to the head throughout?	____	____
5. Did the back leg kick quickly upward?	____	____
6. Did the front leg extend and push off forcefully?	____	____
7. Did the legs meet before they reached the vertical?	____	____
8. Did the pirouette begin as the legs snapped together?	____	____
9. Did the hands push off the floor and continue overhead as the feet made contact with the floor?	____	____

Variations

1. Round-off, snap down
2. Round-off, walk out
3. Round-off, back extension
4. One-handed round-off

LEAD-UPS FOR LIMBERS AND WALKOVERS

BRIDGE KICK-OVER

Description

1. Start in a bridge position with the feet on a raised surface such as a folded mat.
2. Lift one leg toward the ceiling.
3. Begin to bridge the shoulders (move the shoulders beyond the fingers, away from the folded mat) and gently lift the support leg off the mat as the body moves toward a flat back handstand with the leg in a split position. The arms should remain very straight throughout.
4. While in a vertical position with the shoulders directly over the hands, rotate the hips toward the floor and bring the lead leg down as close to the hands as possible without letting the shoulders move from the position directly above the hands. Now lift the chest, head, and arms as the back leg lowers to a lunge position. (Allowing the shoulders to move forward during the last phase could cause the gymnast to collapse forward.)

Spotting

Spotter #1—(a) Stand to the side of the performer so that you are facing the direction to which he/she will be kicking (face the hands with your back to his/her feet). (b) Reach under the performer's body with the arm that is closest to his or her hip and grasp the waist. (c) Place the other hand on the hip that is closest to your body.

Spotter #2—(a) Stand to the side of the performer so that you are facing the direction to which he/she will be kicking (face the hands with your back to his/her feet). (b) Reach under the performer's body with the arm that is closest to his or her hip and grasp the waist. (c) Place the free hand under the performer's shoulder to stop the arms from collapsing during the skill. (d) As the performer kicks over lift the hips up and gently rotate forward.

BACK BEND

Description

1. Stand with the feet side by side and approximately shoulder width apart, with arms stretched toward ceiling, stomach in, and head facing forward.
2. Stretch the fingertips up and back as you begin to arch the upper back. The head should move back with the arms as you begin to look for the floor.
3. As you continue backward your lower back will arch. The knees and hips should not move forward but should remain directly over the base of support.
4. The hands should contact the floor with control permitting the shoulder to move to a proper bridge position. The hands should be shoulder width apart.
5. To return to a standing position rock the hips up and forward, taking care not to pike at the hips.
6. Push from the hands as you rock forward, keeping the head back between the arms.
7. Continue movement until you arrive back to the starting position.

Spotting

1. Stand to the side of the performer in a wide stable stance.
2. Place your far arm behind the performer so that your arm stretches across the small of his/her back and your hand grasps the waist.
3. The other arm should stretch across the front of the performer.
4. As the performer reaches backward, gently lower him/her to the mat and provide support in the bridge.
5. As the performer returns to a standing position, give gentle assistance as the back and hips move upward and forward.

Variations

1. A back limber could be performed following step "4" of "Description" by pushing off both feet simultaneously as the hips move up and back. As the body reaches a flat body handstand, pike at the hips and bring both feet to a standing position on the floor. Lift the chest, head, and arms to end in position "1" of "Description."

FORWARD LIMBER-OVER

Description

1. Begin as you did in the handstand. Upon reaching the vertical position, attempt to move your shoulders back toward the direction from which you came, so that your shoulders are now behind your wrists (this bridging action will permit a soft, controlled landing).
2. Continue your forward momentum as you arch your lower back and place the feet softly on the floor in a bridge position with the hands as close to the feet as possible without an extreme back arch. Ideally the feet will be placed side by side but as a beginner you may have to place the feet shoulder width apart. Your knees should be only slightly bent upon contact with the floor.
3. Your hips should continue to move upward and forward, with your head back. The arms remain next to the head as you rise to a stand (be sure to keep the head back until the hips are over your base of support).

Spotting

1. The spotter stands to the side of the performer's path of action and, as in the spot for the handstand, grasps the performer's nearest thigh.
2. As the performer safely reaches the vertical position the spotter's hand on the back of the leg slides down the body to the middle back, while the hand on the front of the thigh moves to grasp the performer's nearest upper arm (during this phase it will be necessary for the spotter to bend the knees or widen the stance to stay in contact with the performer).
3. Use the hand under the performer's back to assist in lifting the hips up and forward and the hand on the upper arm to assist with the forward lifting momentum and to keep the arms in line with the head. The hand on the upper arm can also be used to pull the performer's weight backward if over-rotation is occurring as the performer is returning to a standing position.
4. Another advanced method of spotting could be used after the performer is capable of attempting the skill with less

physical lifting and is ready for more assistance with the correct technique. This method would have the spotter kneeling next to the performer and placing the farthest hand on the performer's waist. The spotter would then assist the performer in feeling the correct shoulder action by gently pushing the performer's shoulders back toward the direction from which they came.

Self-analysis

	Yes	No
1. Did you begin in a perfect lunge?	___	___
2. Did you stretch for the mat with a straight body?	___	___
3. Did you move into a handstand position without an arch?	___	___
4. Did you rely on an upper back arch rather than a lower back arch?	___	___
5. When your feet landed did you push with your hands?	___	___
6. Did you watch your hands throughout the exercise?	___	___
7. Was your head the last body part to come up?	___	___

FRONT WALKOVER

Description

1. From a standing position, step forward through a lunge position, with the arms over the head. (It is best to step forward onto the leg on which you do the best side split.)
2. Bend forward at the waist while lifting the back leg and place the hands on the floor shoulder width apart approximately two feet ahead of the forward leg.
3. Gently push off the forward leg, while continuing to lift the back leg.
4. As the body moves toward a vertical position, keep the legs in a wide split and begin the shoulder bridging action as described in the limber-over, where your shoulders move back toward the direction from which you came. Your shoulders are now behind your wrist. Your elbows should remain very straight throughout the entire skill.

5. Continue the bridging action as you arch your back and place your lead leg on the floor as close to your hands as possible without an extreme arch, and with your knee only slightly bent.
6. As you rise to a stand, your second leg should be held in a horizontal position or above, the hips should line up over the support leg with the stomach pulled in; the arms should remain by your ears, and your head should remain back until your weight is over your base of support. Then focus directly forward.

Spotting

Spotting is the same as the technique for the forward limber-over.

Self-analysis

	Yes	No
1. Did the body begin in a good lunge position?	___	___
2. Were the hands placed approximately two feet ahead of the forward leg?	___	___
3. Were the hands shoulder width apart?	___	___
4. Did the front leg push off as the hands made contact with the floor?	___	___
5. Did a bridging action take place?	___	___
6. Was there a wide split throughout?	___	___
7. Did the elbows remain straight throughout?	___	___
8. Did the lead leg land on the floor close to the hands?	___	___
9. Was the trailing leg held in a horizontal position upon landing?	___	___
10. Did the head remain back until the weight was over the base of support?	___	___

Variations

1. Front scale, front walkover
2. Front walkover, forward roll
3. Front walkover, front walkover
4. Front walkover, split
5. Front walkover, handstand double stag, roll-out

FRONT HANDSPRING

Description

1. From a standing position, step forward to lunge with the knee ahead of the foot.
2. Bring the hands quickly to the floor without breaking the shoulder angle and with the back in a hollow position (shoulder blades spread, stomach in). The hands must contact the floor before the forward leg straightens; otherwise a diving action onto the hands will occur and this is not desirable in the front handspring.
3. As your hands are beginning to contact the floor you must already be anticipating pushing off the mat so you can push immediately upon contact. At the same time your back leg should be driving straight overhead and your forward leg should be extending and pushing powerfully from the floor.
4. Your legs should join before attaining the vertical position if you are performing a two-foot landing. If you are doing a one-foot landing you should feel almost a stopping action of the first leg before the vertical position is attained. (To avoid pressure on the lower back it is recommended that the beginner learn this skill by landing on one foot, or landing on a soft mat with the assistance of a spotter.)
5. The push-off should be before the vertical position is attained so that flight (a moment in the air without floor contact by the hands or feet) occurs after the push but before the feet land.
6. The landing should be such that the foot or feet are directly underneath the hips. The arms should remain stretched beside the head at all times. The head should remain back until the very end when a shift is made to a forward focus. (Never tuck the chin as this breaks the body line and cuts off rotation causing a sitting action at the end of the skill.)

Spotting

Spotting is the same as the technique for the forward limber-over.

Self-analysis

	Yes	No
1. Did the body begin in a good lunge position?	___	___
2. Did the hands come to the floor quickly		
a. without breaking the shoulder angle?	___	___
b. with the back in a hollow position?	___	___
c. before the forward leg straightened completely?	___	___
3. Did the straight leg whip upward and forward forcefully?	___	___
4. Did the legs join together before either reached the vertical position?	___	___
5. Did the push-off occur before the vertical position was attained?	___	___
6. Did the arms remain stretched alongside of the head throughout?	___	___
7. Did the head remain back until the landing?	___	___
8. Upon landing did the head shift forward (but not downward)?	___	___
9. Was there an extended air moment (time when the hands and feet are off the floor simultaneously)?	___	___

Variation

1. Handspring walk-out

BACK WALKOVER

Description

1. Start from a standing position on one leg (the support leg) with your other leg lifted off the floor (the lifted leg should be the leg on which you do your best split). The arms should be stretched over the head, the support leg straight, and stomach and back muscles pulled tight without any arch or sag.
2. As you begin to arch backward you should feel as though you're going up and back as opposed to straight down

and back. Start by lifting your free leg, slightly arching your back, lifting your arms up and back, as your head watches your fingertips stretch toward the floor. The support leg should remain straight throughout and the hips should remain over the support leg without moving forward.

3. The hands should contact the floor softly, shoulder width apart, and as close to the support foot as possible without an excessive lower back arch. See Figure 2.

4. As the hands contact the floor, the shoulders should be in a good bridge position so that the support leg can just gently and with control lift off the floor.

5. As you pass through the vertical position, your back should straighten as the shoulders are extended. The head should be in line with the straight arms, and the legs should be in a wide split.

6. Continue your movement through the vertical position as your hips tilt toward the floor and lead leg keeps stretching toward a spot on the floor approximately 1-2 feet from the hands. Land on one leg with the free leg held up as the arms, chest, and head lift as one unit to the vertical position.

Spotting

1. Stand to the side of the performer facing the performer's shoulder.

2. Reach across the small of the performer's back and grasp the performer's waist with your far arm.

3. The spotter on the lead leg side should place the hand under the performer's thigh.

4. As the performer reaches backward gently lower the hands to the mat.

5. Assist the lead leg as needed.

Self-analysis

	Yes	No
1. Was the body stretched throughout the skill?	___	___
2. Was the lead leg straight throughout the skill?	___	___
3. Were the shoulders in good bridge when the hands made contact with the floor?	___	___
4. Did the head stay even with the arms throughout?	___	___
5. Was a wide split maintained?	___	___
6. Did the hands land softly on the mat?	___	___
7. Was the skill performed smoothly?	___	___
8. Did the hands push off of the mat?	___	___

Variations

1. Back walkover to front scale
2. Back walkover to split
3. Back walkover to chest roll (stop in handstand and chest roll-out)
4. Back walkover to kneeling pose
5. Switch leg back walkover (lead leg stops when it is vertical to the floor; trailing leg bypasses lead leg and lands first)

Figure 2. The back walkover.

TINSICA

Description

1. Begin as in the front walkover, from a standing position stepping forward through a lunge with the arms overhead.
2. The chest and arms lower to the floor as the rear leg lifts.
3. The hands are placed on the mat one at a time in a split position. The first hand contact is made by the same side as the forward lunge leg. The second hand should be placed along a line straight ahead of the first hand down as far away from the first hand as possible. The fingers should be facing forward and the shoulder should be on a slight diagonal line.
4. As you reach the vertical position the back should be straight, legs split, and the shoulder extended.
5. At the vertical position your shoulders will twist slightly back toward a normal handstand position. Then your shoulders will bridge as your first foot stretches toward the floor and the lower back arches slightly to pass through a bridge position. The first hand down lifts off the floor, followed by the second hand lifting off the floor.
6. You will rise to a stand as in the front walkover by aligning the hips directly over the landing foot, while keeping your head back, and the arms stretched alongside the head. As you come to a stand your focus will move forward and the stomach muscles will be pulled inward to allow you to bring your second leg down with control.
7. The skill has the rhythm of a cartwheel (hand, hand, foot, foot) and the appearance of a walkover.

Spotting

Spotting is the same as the technique for the forward limber-over.

Self-analysis

	Yes	No
1. Was the skill done in a four-count rhythm (hand, hand, foot, foot)?	___	___
2. Did the body begin in a good lunge position?	___	___
3. Were the hands shoulder width apart?	___	___
4. Did the front leg push off as the hands made contact with the floor?	___	___
5. Did the bridging action take place?	___	___
6. Was there a wide split throughout?	___	___
7. Did the elbows remain straight throughout?	___	___
8. Did the lead leg land on the floor close to the hands?	___	___
9. Was the trailing leg held in a horizontal position upon landing?	___	___
10. Did the head remain back until the weight was over the base of support?	___	___

Variations

1. This skill may also be done beginning in a complete sideward position as described in the cartwheel and at the vertical position shifting the hips and shoulders to finish as with a forward walkover.
2. Tinsica right
3. From a front scale
4. To a front scale

BACK HANDSPRING (FLIP FLOP)

Description

1. You can begin the flip with your arms in a variety of positions (overhead, forward at horizontal, or by the sides of your body). The important factor is that you do not let your chest come forward as you begin. For our purposes we will start with the arms at the sides since having the arms overhead sometimes gives the feeling of a lack of momentum and the arms in a horizontal position creates a down-up wind-up which usually causes the chest to move forward.
2. Standing with the arms at the sides begin to fall backward from your feet without letting your chest or knees come forward.

3. As you begin to fall bend your knees slightly to give power for the push-off (see Figure 3). Every body part should be behind your base of support.

4. Next you will very quickly and powerfully extend the knees and push from your feet as your arms are thrown overhead.

5. You should contact the floor with your shoulders over the hands, and the legs not quite vertical (see Figure 4).

6. The last and final phase is called the "snap-down." From a slight tight arch with the shoulder blades pinched, move quickly to a hollow body position with the stomach in and the shoulder blades extended to a very broad position.

7. Where you snap your legs down to the mat will depend upon the trick that follows. As in the round-off if you wish to do a series of flip-flops you must "block under," i.e., bring the feet down very close to the hands to continue the backward momentum. If you plan to continue to a somersault or stop your momentum you must block out; put your feet far from the hands to convert your speed to an upward direction.

8. The verbal cues for the flip-flop are "Lean-Sit-Go!"

9. The verbal cues for the snap-down are "Arch-Hollow!"

Spotting

1. Stand or kneel to the side and slightly behind the performer so that you are facing his/her shoulder.

2. Place the far hand on the performer's back at the top of the hips.

3. Place the near hand under the performer's thigh.

4. As the performer begins the skill, gently lift and rotate the hips over.

5. Assist the thigh as necessary.

6. Be sure that the performer's hips are lifted high enough to allow him/her to place the hands down so that the shoulders are above them.

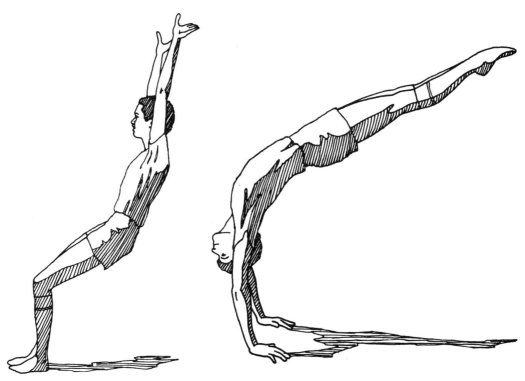

Figure 3. The fall for the back handspring.

Figure 4. Contact with the floor in the back handspring.

Self-analysis

	Yes	No
1. Did your body lean backward from the feet rather than the waist?	____	____
2. Did the chest and knees stay behind the base of support (ankles) during the initial phase?	____	____
3. Did the body extend rapidly and powerfully?	____	____
4. When the hands made contact with the mat		
a. were the shoulders over the hands?	____	____
b. were the legs almost at a vertical position?	____	____
c. was the head facing the mat?	____	____
5. Did the head stay even with the arms throughout?	____	____
6. During the snap-down did the body move to a "hollow" position?	____	____

Variations

1. Back handspring, back handspring
2. Back handspring, walk-out (one leg down at a time)
3. Round-off, back handspring

CONDITIONING

To meet the physical demands of tumbling and to be successful in learning new skills it is essential that the performer achieve a certain degree of strength and flexibility. Since it will be necessary to constantly support one's own weight while doing stunts like handstands and cartwheels, the minimum strength requirement would be the ability to support your own weight with your arms. Adequate strength not only permits the performer to perform the moves with control but ensures a greater degree of safety.

Flexibility, or range of motion of the joints, is another key component for safe and successful gymnastics. Flexibility not only protects the muscles from injury but is also essential for the performance of certain skills such as walkovers and splits.

In order to achieve the greatest degree of improvement, flexibility exercises should be performed daily and strength exercises performed a minimum of three times weekly. The exercises listed below are not warmup exercises but exercises that should be incorporated into a regular gymnastics conditioning program.

ARM AND SHOULDER STRENGTH

Pull-ups

From a straight hand on a bar with the hands in an overgrip, bend the arms and pull the body upward so that the chin is above the bar.

Lead-ups

1. Bent arm hang—have a partner lift you into a bent arm position and hold this position as long as possible—not to exceed one minute.
2. Modified pull-ups—perform pull-ups on uneven bars with the feet resting on a low bar if you are not strong enough to lift the body weight from a straight hang.

Push-ups

In a prone position with straight elbow support and the body totally straight, lower the body by bending the arms as close to the floor as possible; return to a straight elbow support.

Lead-ups

1. Assume the same prone position as above and remain balanced in that position for 15-30 seconds.
2. In a prone position as above, place the knees on the floor and lower and raise the body by bending the arms.

Variations

1. With the feet on a raised surface so that the hips are over the shoulders, bend the arms to touch the head to the floor and return to support.
2. While balanced in a headstand position, bend the legs slightly and push the arms straight to a handstand.

Dips

1. Stand between parallel bars or between two beams placed approximately shoulder width apart and raised to at least elbow level. Spotters should position

themselves behind the performer and assist at the hips to ensure that the performer does not fall.
2. Jump to a straight arm support.
3. Raise and lower the body by bending the elbows to a 90 degree angle.

Lead-ups
1. Bend and straighten the arms only slightly until your strength is adequate enough to support a full range of movement.
2. Jump up and down from the floor to a starting position (the performer can start with the bars low and eventually raise them to chest height).

ABDOMINAL STRENGTH

Sit-ups

The sit-up is one of the oldest yet most appropriate developers of abdominal strength.
1. Lie on the floor, with the hands clasped behind the head, the knees bent, and the feet flat on the floor.
2. Curl up starting with the head until the chest touches the thighs.
3. Curl down starting with the lower back to the starting position.

Lead-ups
1. Do sit-ups with a spotter holding your hands and assisting in raising and lowering during the sit-up.
·2. Do sit-ups with the hands overhead and use the momentum of the arms swinging forward to help lift the body.

Variations
1. Do sit-ups on a slant board with the head at a low portion of the incline board and the feet at a high portion.
2. V Sit-ups—with the hands behind the head and the legs straight, lift the head and chest at the same time as when lifting the legs to a V balance. (To increase difficulty of the V sit-up, raise the V and lower to an open position where the shoulders and legs come within inches of the floor but do not touch.)

L-Hold (see Figure 5)
1. Sit on the floor in a pike position.
2. Place the hands next to the legs near the top of the thigh with the fingers pointing forward.
3. Lift the legs and rear from the floor so that the entire body weight is supported on the hands.
4. Hold the position as long as possible.

Lead-up
1. Perform the exercise as above but raise and lower the legs only to a horizontal position.
2. Perform the leg lift with the spotter grasping under one thigh and helping to lift the legs and then, if possible, lower the legs alone.

Variation
1. Perform a leg lift in a straddle position so that when you lift the legs, your feet touch the bar on the outside of the hands.

Figure 5. The L-hold.

LEG STRENGTH AND POWER

Straddle/Pike Jumps

1. Alternate jumping into the air with the legs straddled on the first jump and the arms stretched sideward to touch the toes.
2. On the second jump, lift the leg straight forward to a 90 degree angle pike position with the arms forward.

Running

1. Running is still one of the best leg strength- and power-developing exercises. To increase leg strength and power it is best to do quick, short sprints, or alternate jogging with quick burst sprints.

SAFETY

Tumbling is an activity that permits a person to experiment and discover the outer limits of his/her movement capabilities. As such, those who participate in the sport often find themselves moving through space or performing in a way that is unfamiliar to them. While experiencing something for the first time can be exciting, it can also be risky unless we take the proper precautions.

Being cautious in tumbling means three things. First of all, it means being aware of the possible outcome of an activity. Second, it means being aware of the procedures that can be used to eliminate any negative outcomes associated with that activity, and third, it means being alert and practicing safety.

Familiarize yourself with the safety checklist that follows and resolve to practice it regularly.

BEFORE PERFORMANCE

Clothing Check

- Remove all jewelry, including rings and earrings when you perform.
- Be sure your hair is worn so that it does not block your vision or hamper your spotter's performance.
- Be sure to wear appropriate footwear. Heavy sneakers or shoes can be extremely dangerous to you and your spotter.
- Never have anything, e.g., gum or candy, in your mouth.
- Wear clothing that will allow you to perform freely.
- Wear clothing that is comfortable but not baggy. Baggy clothing makes it difficult to spot.
- Be sure your clothing is free of belts, buttons, rivets, or zippers.
- Eyeglasses should be secure.

Performance Area Check

- Be sure the area is sufficiently matted for the skill you are going to perform. As a general rule, the less familiar you are with the skill and/or the more difficult it is, the more matting you should have. Remember, a mat is not a substitute for a spotter and proper progressions.
- Check the matting to be sure that it is not slippery and that it is free of faults such as rips or gashes.
- If using more than one mat be sure they are securely fastened together.
- Check the landing surface to ensure that it can absorb the weight of a landing or fall. After years of use, mats lose their resiliency and landing on them is like landing on the floor.
- Be sure tumbling strips or individual mats are placed in such a way as to permit ample space between each area for traffic or spotter movement.
- Be sure that mats are located a sufficient distance from walls or other pieces of apparatus.
- Check the area to be sure it is free of equipment that is not in use or is inappropriate, e.g., scooters, balls, equipment carriers.
- Mats come in a variety of thicknesses and densities. Each has a particular purpose. When tumbling you should use at least a 2-inch mat. Before you begin, however, check with the instructor to see if a 4-8-inch mat is more appropriate. If a safety mat is recommended you must also check to see if a 2-inch landing mat is needed as well.
- Be sure the pathway you have chosen for your tumbling run does not cross anyone else's pathway.

Performer and Spotter Check

- Do not attempt a skill with a student spotter unless your instructor has given you permission to do so.
- Two spotters should be used at all times unless the use of two people interferes with the safe flow of movement.
- Be sure you have a thorough understanding of how to execute the skill.
- Determine whether you have the necessary prerequisites to safely perform the skill.
- Determine whether you are in the proper physical condition to safely execute the skill. Be sure your body is well-conditioned with regard to strength, flexibility, and muscular and cardiovascular endurance. Do not attempt a skill beyond your present physical ability.
- Be sure you understand the proper progression.
- Be sure your spotter knows what exercises you would like to try and that he/she knows how to spot the skill.
- Be sure your spotter is strong enough to spot a person of your size.
- Be sure you trust your spotter and that your spotter is confident in assisting you.

AT PERFORMANCE

Area Check

- Be sure the instructor is present in the gymnastic area.
- Be sure the instructor is aware of and has given you permission to attempt the skill you are about to perform.

Performer Check

- Warm up sufficiently.
- Stop and rest when you or your spotter become fatigued.
- Follow the progression step by step just as the instructor has outlined.
- Only attempt skills in which instruction has been given.

- Perform at your own level and not above, just because someone else is performing a skill.
- Always have competent supervision and sufficient spotting.
- Follow a skill through to its completion; never change your mind in the middle of a movement, because you could seriously hurt yourself as well as your spotter.
- Be sure your spotter knows exactly when you are ready to begin.
- Use gymnastics chalk to keep your hands dry so that you won't slip.

SCORING

The scoring system for gymnastics and tumbling has become quite elaborate, with competitors receiving credit not only for excellence of performance but also for originality and virtuosity. The highest possible score on each event is a 10.0. A woman can receive a maximum of 3.0 points for the difficulty of her routine, 0.5 for bonus points for original and risky moves, 2.5 for how well her routine is composed, and 4.0 for execution and virtuosity. A man receives 3.4 for difficulty, 1.6 for the value of his combinations, 4.4 for his manner of execution, and 0.6 bonus points for rare or original moves, and virtuosity.

In a national level competition there are four judges who make deductions as the gymnast performs such errors as form breaks and falls, lack of amplitude (which includes stretch of the body and height of each move), insufficient difficulty, and lack of originality. The scores of the high and low judge are dropped and the middle two scores are averaged to derive the gymnast's final score.

At the conclusion of the meet all the gymnasts' individual scores (4 for women and 6 for men) are added to determine what is called the gymnast's all-around score.

Volleyl

BARBARA L. VIERA
University of Delaware
Newark, DE

INTRODUCTION

The sport of volleyball was invented in the United States in 1895 by William G. Morgan while working in a YMCA in Holyoke, Massachusetts. Morgan needed a less strenuous game to meet the needs of some businessmen who would not play basketball. After experimenting with various balls, including the bladder of a basketball, Morgan decided no ball then available satisfied the needs of the new game, which he called mintonette. The Spalding Company eventually provided the first official ball, which was made of soft calfskin. In 1896 during a demonstration of mintonette in an old gymnasium at the School of Christian Workers (now Springfield College) a faculty member, Alfred T. Halstead, suggested that because the volleying action was such a characteristic of game play, the name of the activity should be changed to volleyball. Morgan accepted this change and the game of volleyball evolved to its present form.

Volleyball can be enjoyed by players of all ages. It is one of the few sports in the United States that has competitions in various age groups from elementary to the masters' level. It is also adaptable to many settings—from the informal to the highly competitive. Volleyball is the only team sport which has been professionally played on a coed basis. Although Morgan designed the game to be less arduous than basketball it has developed into a highly strenuous sport. When played by two teams, closely matched in ability, a best of five game match can last for as long as 2½ to 3 hours. During this time players are constantly moving, changing direction, jumping, and hitting the floor for defensive saves.

The addition of volleyball to the Olympics by the Japanese in 1964 helped increase its popularity. Volleyball is high on the list of participation sports in countries throughout the world. Over 25 countries currently list volleyball as their number one sport. The success of the United States teams during the 1984 Olympics in Los Angeles was a real boost for the growth and development of the sport in this country.

SKILLS AND TECHNIQUES

To be a successful volleyball competitor one must be able to perform the five basic skills of the game at an efficient level of control. These five basic skills are the forearm pass, the overhand pass or set, the serve, the spike or attack, and the block. The block is only essential when playing against a team with strong spiking. Other advanced skills including the dive, sprawl, and roll are only essential at higher levels of competition. The soft attack or dink is an excellent change of pace and can also be mastered at beginning levels of play.

FOREARM PASS

The forearm pass is used to receive the serve, to play any ball arriving low and with force, to receive spikes, and to play any ball below chest level. It is an extremely important skill because it is usually the first contact made by the team receiving the ball from the opponent. The skill is quite different from any that exist in other sports because the ball is contacted on the fleshy part of the forearms. The hands are gripped together and can be joined in a number of acceptable ways. The best posi-

a. Cupped hand grip with thumbs on top.   **b.** Interlocking hand grip with thumbs on top.

Figure 1. The volleyball grip.

tions are: placing one hand across the palm of the other, then cupping both hands so that the thumbs are together and facing up toward the ceiling (see Figure 1a). Options for more advanced players include: joining both hands by lightly interlocking the fingers with the thumbs side by side and on top (see Figure 1b), and making a fist with one hand and wrapping the second hand around the fist with thumbs on top, side by side and parallel.

It is important that the thumbs do not overlap, as this creates an uneven surface, causing an uncontrolled hit if the ball is accidently received on the hands. The elbows are rotated in, so that the widest portion of the forearm faces upward. The elbows may be bent or locked as the ball approaches but must be locked at contact. The ball is contacted between the wrists and the elbows. The arms should be held away from the body and parallel to the thighs. The back should be erect and leaning slightly forward. The knees are bent at approximately a 90° angle; the feet are

shoulder width apart and in a stride position with one foot forward, usually the right foot. The shoulders should face the intended direction of the pass. This position of the body in relation to the target is essential if the player is to successfully direct the pass. The player should always establish a set body position before contacting the ball, rather than passing the ball while still moving.

As the ball approaches, the player gets behind it so that the ball is played in front of the midline of the body and the player is in a low position. The player's eyes should be kept on the ball until it contacts the arms. The ball should be contacted low between the chest and the knees. As contact is made the knees are extended and the arms are raised slightly making a punching motion at the ball. It is the extension of the legs which is the most important action to apply force to the ball. At the same time the weight is transferred forward in the direction of the pass. The arms should not rise above shoulder level on the follow-through.

The three most common faults by beginners are too much arm swing, bending at the waist instead of the knees, and a transfer of weight away from the intended direction of the pass.

Figure 2 shows the forearm pass in a series of pictures. Check the following points of emphasis:
- the position of the body at contact;
- the point at which the ball contacts the arms;
- the locked elbows on contact;
- the transfer of weight from the back to the forward foot;
- the extension of the legs and arms;
- the height of the arms on the follow-through.

Players may not always be able to position themselves squarely behind an oncoming ball. In this situation the ball should be played outside the body and with one or two arm(s) or hand(s). If the ball is played with one arm, the hand should be held parallel to the floor so that contact is made

Figure 2. The forearm pass.

with the flat surface of the arm at the wrist. If the ball is contacted on the hand, the player should break the wrist to help direct the ball. If the ball is played to the left or right of the body with two arms the shoulder closest to the ball should be dropped or dipped, so that the platform made by the arms will direct the rebound back in the same direction from whence it came. If this is not done the direction of the ball will not change and it will continue in the same direction, past the player and out-of-bounds.

When any hard-driven ball is received it is referred to as a dig. A one-armed reception is also called a dig. The forearm pass is often referred to as an underhand pass or bump. Although these terms are used interchangeably, the forearm pass is the most descriptive term for the actual skill.

Players should have enough control over their passing to perform the following tasks:
- self pass the ball 15 consecutive times;
- pass the ball against the wall, to a height greater than 8 feet, 15 consecutive times;
- pass the ball with a partner 10 consecutive times;
- receive 5 out of 10 serves that come directly to the player by passing them to the target area with enough height so that they can easily be handled by the setter. The target area is the center one-third of the court and close to the net.

OVERHAND PASS OR SET

The overhand pass is the most accurate method of playing the ball. It is used to receive any ball chest high or higher and traveling slowly in a high arc. It is also used as the second contact by a team as it sets up its offense. When used in this manner, to deliver the ball to a spiker, the overhand pass is also referred to as a set.

In executing the overhand pass a player must first move into the correct position. As in the forearm pass it is extremely important that the player establish a set body position before playing the ball. When executing an overhead pass, the player's shoulders must be square to the desired

direction of the pass. Once in position the player should watch the ball closely until contact. The hands are raised to a position just in front of the forehead and the player continues to look at the ball through the window formed by the hands. The ball is contacted 6 to 8 inches above the forehead. The hands are cupped around the ball, on the sides of the ball more than directly behind it. The thumbs should be closer to each other than the first fingers. The contact points on the fingers are the upper two joints. The greatest force comes from the thumbs and the first two fingers of each hand but all fingers do contact the ball. The action of the set is a very quick catch-and-throw motion. The angle of the elbows should not decrease as the ball is contacted and the fingers should be firmly held throughout. The wrists are hyperextended and the hands and wrists are both relaxed.

The body should be in an upright position and leaning slightly forward, knees bent and back straight. The feet should be in an easy stride position with the foot closest to the net always forward. This helps prevent the ball from going over the net into the opponent's court, especially during a set.

On contact the wrists flick the ball forward as the elbows and knees extend and the weight is transferred toward the direction of the pass. The arms are fully extended on the follow-through and the hands point in the direction of the pass. The ball should be directed with good height.

Figure 3 shows the overhand pass in a series of pictures. Check the following points of emphasis:
- the position of the hands and arms before contact;
- the bent position of the knees and elbows before contact;
- the fully extended arms on the follow-through.

The player can increase the complexity of sets by varying the height and speed with which they are delivered to the spiker. At beginning levels of play a high set is recommended almost exclusively.

The set can also be sent backward over the player's own head to a teammate behind

Figure 3. The overhand pass.

the setter. This is called a back set. Everything is the same as in the front set until the point of contact. The player arches his/her back and pushes the ball straight up toward the ceiling, extending his/her arms and knees. The weight transfer will be back in the direction of the pass. The back set is very effective, as it often catches the opponents off guard.

All players should be more accurate when using the overhand pass than when using any other volleyball skill. The setter is the player who will set the spikers the greatest percentage of the time, and should be excellent in performing this skill. All other players must be able to set effectively when the setter cannot make the second contact.

Players should be able to complete the following tasks:

- overhand pass the ball successfully to themselves 20 times;
- overhand pass the ball consecutively against the wall 20 times to a height of 11 feet;
- complete 20 overhand passes while receiving a tossed ball from a partner with 10 tosses made to the passer's right and 10 made to the passer's left on an alternating basis.

It is very important when using drills with partners that the toss be accurate. When practicing the overhand pass the tosses must be in a high arc.

THE SERVE

The serve can be one of the most important skills of the game. If a team is lucky enough to win the first serve and is a good serving team it could get a good lead or even win the game before the opponents are able to serve. There are many varieties of serves that can be mastered and a server who has mastered more than one serve can be extremely effective. Beginners should concentrate on performing one serve until they have 90% consistency. That is, they are capable of making nine good serves in every ten attempts.

The easiest serve to master is the underhand serve. Many players feel that the underhand serve is not effective. This is not necessarily true. If it is the only serve a

player can perform with 90% consistency then the player should use this serve entirely until he/she masters other styles. The underhand serve is hit with less force and on a higher trajectory than the overhand or roundhouse serves, but if hit as a floater it can have a lot of "action" on it and be highly effective. The floater action is similar to that of a knuckleball pitch in baseball. Hit without spin, the ball reacts unpredictably to the air currents, either curving, dipping, or rising.

The underhand serve is hit with an open hand, the major point of contact being on the heel of the hand. The ball should be hit with a locked wrist. The body should be facing the net with the feet in a stride position and about shoulder width apart. The forward foot should be placed so that the toe is pointing in the direction of the serve. The foot on the opposite side of the serving hand should be the forward foot. The ball is held at waist level or lower in the nonhitting hand. The holding hand must release the ball before it is contacted or the serve is illegal. The hitting arm swings back as the weight is transferred onto the back foot. As the arm swings forward to contact the ball the weight is transferred onto the forward foot. The ball should be contacted in a low position and as the hand follows through the player moves forward onto the court into a position of readiness to receive the return.

For beginners it is not necessary to disguise the direction of the serve. The opponent who knows that there will be a serve to his/her position feels more pressure than one who does not expect the ball. This often causes a reception error.

The overhand floater is similar to the underhand serve as the player assumes the same initial position—body facing the net, feet in a shoulder width stride position, nonserving hand holding the ball, and eyes on the intended target. The holding hand begins with the ball at chest level or higher and tosses the ball in the air slightly in front of the shoulder of the hitting hand, and 2 to 3 feet higher than head height. The ball is contacted with an open hand, the heel of the hand again being the major area

Figure 4. The overhand floater serve.

of contact. The wrist is locked. There should be little to no follow-through. The hitting action is somewhat like a punching motion, and the ball is contacted on the center back. The server looks at the ball as soon as the serving motion begins, and should keep the eyes on the ball until contact. As the ball is tossed the weight is transferred onto the back foot. The striking arm is cocked back into a throwing position. As the arm swings forward toward contact it is extended, reaching full extension at contact. The entire action is similar to throwing a baseball. Once the ball is contacted the server moves onto the court and into his/her playing position.

Figure 4 shows the overhand floater serve in a series of pictures. Note the following points of emphasis:

- the position of the tossed ball in relation to the body;
- the cocked position of the arm before contact;
- the height of the ball above the shoulder at contact;
- the extension of the arm at contact;
- the server's concentration on the ball;
- the limited amount of follow-through of the arm.

Servers should have three priorities in serving. First, they must be consistent. They must be able to get the ball legally into the opponents' court on nearly every serve. Second, the server should be able to serve to any spot that might be advantageous to his/her team. Third, the server should try to "put something on" the ball, such as a spin or greater force. Servers should not try for the second priority until the first is met.

The most effective serves are directed to deep corners of the opponents' court, to the seams (the area between two opponents), or to a weak receiver. Once players have mastered the first two priorities above with one serve, they can begin working on another type of serve.

Each player should be able to complete the following tasks:

- serve 20 consecutive legal serves without a miss;
- serve to each of the court positions in order for two full rotations;

- serve to any court positions called out by the teacher on twelve consecutive serves.

The court positions in volleyball are illustrated in Diagram 1.

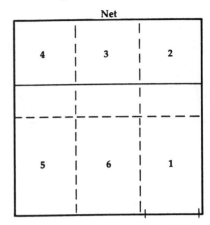

Diagram 1. The volleyball court divided into the six court areas.

THE ATTACK OR SPIKE

The spike is the most exciting skill of the game and at the same time one of the most difficult skills to perform. In making a spike the player must jump into the air and hit a moving object (the ball) over an obstacle (the net) into a bounded area (the court). This task is not easy. Timing is the most important element of the spike. Spiking can be done on a variety of sets. For discussion here only the high set will be considered. This set is 7-10 feet above the top of the net.

The approach for the spike begins at the attack line, 10 feet from the net. Moving toward the net can be accomplished with any number of steps but better volleyball players limit themselves to two or three. The spiker must wait until the ball is set by the setter before beginning the approach, in order to go to the spot where the ball will arrive. Once the spiker has reached the correct spot he/she brings both feet together by planting one heel first and closing with the other. The right foot should be planted first followed by the closing together with the left foot. Some spikers prefer to jump onto both feet simultaneously heels first.

All spiking is done with a two-foot take-off. Planting the heels changes forward momentum into upward momentum. As

Figure 5. The spiking sequence.

the heels are planted the arms swing down and back to about shoulder height; the knees are bent as deeply as they can go and get maximum thrust and control on the jump. As the spiker extends the knees to jump, the arms are swung forcibly forward and up. The swing of the arms is very important to increase height on the jump. The spiker concentrates on the ball as the jump is made. The hitting arm and hand are taken back behind the head into a throwing position.

At the highest point in the jump the spiker swings the arm forward to hit the ball. The arm action is the same as that used to throw a baseball. The ball is contacted with force, with an open hand. As soon as contact is made there is a snap of the wrist. The wrist snap is very important because it puts topspin on the ball, causing it to dip severely in flight. The hand should be open wide and fairly relaxed at contact. As with the serve, the heel of the hand is the most important hitting surface. The ball should be contacted two to six inches in front of the hitter's shoulder on the hitting side of the body. As the arm swing is made the nonhitting arm is dropped forcibly to the player's side. This gives the player greater reach. The ball should be contacted at the spiker's greatest reach. As contact is made with the heel of the hand, the hand is snapped forward over the top of the ball to impart a forward spin on the ball, thus directing it downward. It is extremely important that the jump is straight up and down. The planting of the heels effectively stops forward momentum so that no net foul is committed.

During the follow-through the player's hitting hand drops back to the player's side, and the spiker returning to the floor should land simultaneously on both feet. It is important that immediately after landing the spiker prepare for the next play.

Figure 5 demonstrates a spiking sequence. Look for the following points of emphasis:
- the plant of the heels, right and then left, and the two-foot take-off;
- the high back swing of the player's arms;
- the forward swing of both arms on the jump;
- the full extension of the arm on contact;
- the position of the ball in relation to the spiker's body (it is in front of the hitting arm's shoulder at contact);
- the snap of the wrist on contact;
- the landing of the spiker simultaneously on both feet.

Once the player has mastered the basic elements of the spike, the angle and direction of the spike should be practiced. The two main directions of the spike are cross-court and down-the-line. A cross-court spike is hit from the spiker to the opposite corner of the opponent's court (see Diagram 2). The down-the-line spike is hit along the sideline from the spiker to the corner of the opponent's court on the same side (see Diagram 3).

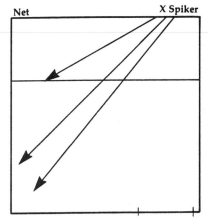

Diagram 2. Three different angles for cross-court spiking.

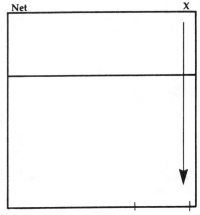

Diagram 3. Path traveled by a down-the-line spike.

Spikes are divided into two main categories: on-hand spikes and off-hand spikes. An on-hand spike is one in which the spiker's hitting arm is on the same side of the body as the approaching set. This occurs in the right forward position for a left-handed player and in the left forward position for a right-handed player. It is the spike that a player should be the best at executing. The ball does not cross in front of the player's body before it is hit. An off-hand spike is one in which the spiker's hitting arm is on the opposite side of the player's body from the approaching set. The ball must cross in front of the player before being hit. This style is employed when a left-handed player is in the left forward position, or a right-handed player is in the right forward position. The on-hand spike is the preferable spike for most players, but in any case, the spiker should always hit the ball with the dominant hand.

Players should be able to complete the following tasks:

- spike the ball against the wall at least ten times. To spike, a player stands 6 to 10 feet from a smooth wall, tosses up the ball, and spikes it onto the floor close to the wall. The ball rebounds from the floor and wall and is caught. The spiker then repeats the process.
- spike five out of ten high sets to the on-hand side into the opponent's court.
- spike five out of ten high sets to the off-hand side into the opponent's court.

THE DINK

Another form of attack is the dink. The dink is a change of pace play and can be used as an offensive move, to catch the opponents off guard, or as an alternative when a spike is not possible because of poor timing or a bad set. The dink is most effective when used as an offensive play.

The approach for the dink is exactly the same as the approach for the spike. In fact, this is essential to disguise the intent of the attacker. At the last minute the spiker holds back on a powerful swing, reaches as high as possible and with a soft fingertip touch from a position on the lower back of the ball, drops the ball over or by the block so

that it falls quickly to the floor. The dink must be high enough to clear the opposing block but low enough so that it hits the floor before the opponent's backcourt defensive players can move in to "dig it up." It is essential in dinking that the wrist be held straight to avoid the possibility of a carry.

There are two areas on the court most vulnerable to a dink: over the block and down the line but in front of the attack line, and by the block and to the center of the court but close to the net (see Diagram 4).

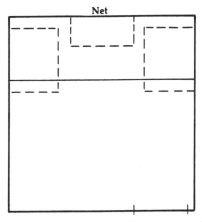

Diagram 4. The weak areas of the opponent for the dink. The left and right areas change depending on which side the dink originates. The center area is the same for both sides.

All players should be able to complete the following tasks:

- dink five out of ten sets so that they clear the block and land in front of the attack line;
- dink five out of ten sets by the block so they hit the floor near the net in the center of the court.

SERVE RECEPTION

Receiving the serve is extremely important. If a team cannot successfully receive the serve they will never gain the opportunity to serve and score themselves. Serve reception is a team effort.

The W-formation is the most common and most efficient formation for receiving the serve. In this formation five players are ready to receive and one player, the setter, avoids receiving under any circumstances

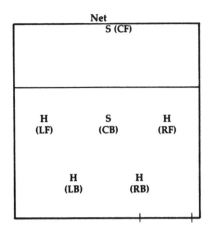

Diagram 5. The W-formation used for serve reception.

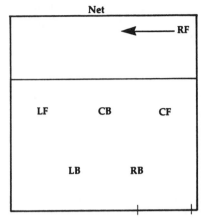

Diagram 6. W-formation when the RF is the setter. At ball contact by the server, the setter moves to the center of the court.

and "hides" at the net. Diagram 5 shows this formation using H's to indicate the spikers and S's to indicate the setters. No player should stand directly behind a teammate and all players must have a clear view of the opposing server. Each player on the court has certain responsibilities on serve reception. First, after the serve is hit, the players must determine who will receive it. The person receiving should call for the ball; then all the remaining players should turn and face the receiver. This action is called "opening up." Players should also help each other by calling bad serves out-of-bounds. The RF and RB work as a team calling the right sideline. If the ball is being played by one, the other player judges the ball's position and calls it out if necessary. The LF and LB call the left sideline. The LB and RB are a team for calling the end line. The CF and CB should alert their teammates if a serve is short, i.e., is going to fall in front of the attack line.

In the waiting position for serve reception all players should have their right foot forward in a slight stride. The setter standing near the net should not receive the serve under any circumstances. Any ball shoulder height or higher as it approaches the forward line should be received by a back row player. Any serve shoulder height or higher as it approaches a back row player should be allowed to go out-of-bounds. The setter should always face the left sideline with his/her right side toward the net.

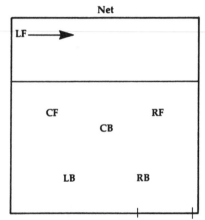

Diagram 7. W-formation when the LF is the setter. The CF must be ahead of the CB.

The sequence of action in receiving the serve should be as follows. The receiving player passes the ball to the setter at the net, who is facing the LF position. The setter then sets one of the two hitters, either forward to the LF or backward to the RF. As soon as the set is made the whole team moves into spike coverage.

When the team rotates the setter moves to the RF position. The setter must switch to the center of the court as soon as the ball is contacted on the serve. Diagram 6 shows the W-formation when the setter is the RF. The setter hides at the net and the CF moves toward the right sideline. The players who switch maintain their new positions until the next serve.

The next rotation finds the setter in the LF position. Diagram 7 shows the W-formation and the switch when the setter is in the LF position. Once the ball is contacted players may switch to any spot on the court. They should be careful, however, not to change positions with teammates until the ball has been served. When the setter switches to the center of the court the center forward stays near the sideline and plays as an outside forward.

SPIKE COVERAGE

The purpose of covering the spike is to be ready to play the ball if the ball comes right back at the spiker, usually falling behind him/her. Thus, the area behind the spiker is the one to be covered. Three players move to form a semi-circle around the spiker and the other two players move to fill the remaining spaces. All players must crouch low to have more time to react to the ball. Diagram 8 shows the movement of players when the LF is the spiker. Diagram 9 shows the movement of players when the RF is spiking. The center forward is customarily the setter and will only be called on to spike if there is a broken play.

THE BLOCK

The block is a team's first line of defense. The best way to stop an opponent's attack is to block it at the net and not allow the ball to come onto the blockers' side of the court. A single block is executed by one player. In a double block the center forward joins the outside forward on the side of the opponent's spike and they block together. The purpose of the block is to lessen the net area available to the spiker. A double block is of course more effective than a single block.

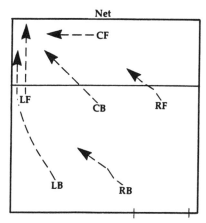

Diagram 8. Spike coverage for the LF spiker.

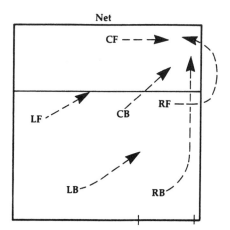

Diagram 9. Movement to spike coverage when the RF is spiking.

Figure 6. The position of the blocker in relationship to the spiker.

The ready position for a block is 6 to 12 inches from the net, with arms bent at the elbow so that the hands are at shoulder height and fairly close to the body. The blocker must concentrate on the opponent's play until the ball is set to the opposing spiker. Then the blocker stops watching the ball and concentrates on that spiker. The blocker gets into position so that one-half of the body overlaps one-half of the spiker's body on the side of the spiker's hitting arm (see Figure 6). The blocker attempts to put one hand on each side of the spiker's hand. The blocker times the block by jumping a split second after the spiker. The blocker reaches as high as possible over the top of the net and into the opponent's court. The shoulders are close to the ears. The body pikes slightly to prevent net fouls. The blocker's hand are wide open and turned so that the thumbs are up (see Figure 7). This positioning of the hands covers the maximum amount of space. When the ball contacts the blocker's hand the blocker snaps the wrists, causing the ball to drop quickly onto the opposing court. The blocker must quickly withdraw the hands so that no net foul will be committed in returning to the floor. After the block the player should be immediately ready for the next play.

Figure 8 illustrates the block sequentially. Look for the following points of emphasis:

- the starting position of the blocker;
- the position of the blocker's arms in relationship to the head;
- the wide position of the blocker's fingers;
- the penetration the blocker makes over the net;
- the piking position of the body.

When blocking in the outside position the blocker must be sure to turn the ball into the opponent's court. The hand closest to the sideline should be turned in, so that the ball will not rebound out-of-bounds after hitting the block. Successful blocking involves a great deal of practice emphasizing timing. Many beginning blockers have a tendency to rush the block, jump too soon, and miss the ball completely.

Players should be able to complete the following tasks:

- block three out of eight spikes off high sets;

- jump and reach so that both hands are completely over the top of the net;
- watch the spiker rather than the ball on every spike.

OFFENSE

With the basic skills of volleyball mastered, the offensive and defensive systems can be learned. The least complicated offensive system is the 4-2. Four players predominantly serve as spikers, and two as setters. The setters are directly opposite each other in the lineup, so that there is always one setter in the forward line. The setter in the forward line performs the setting task. The other setter plays as a defensive player in the back row until rotating to the forward line and becoming the working setter.

There are three different formations used on offense. They are serve reception, spike coverage, and free ball. In all of these formations the team is either receiving the ball from the opponent or playing it on their own side. Serve reception and spike coverage situations were covered in detail above.

FREE BALL

When the opposing team is unable to set up for a spike they will usually return the ball in a manner that makes it easy to handle. This is called a free ball. When it appears that the opponents are in trouble, immediately assume the free ball formation. The free ball formation is the same as the W-formation used for serve reception, except that the setter does not have to go to his/her correct rotational position and may remain in the center of the court. The team then proceeds as in serve reception, trying to get a three-hit combination pass, set, and spike.

a. The incorrect hand position on the block.

b. The correct thumbs up position. Note the wider area that it covers.

Figure 7.

Figure 8. The block.

DEFENSE

The best defensive system to use in beginning levels of play is the 2-1-3 defense. This defense is especially strong against a team with weak hitters, or one that dinks a good deal.

BASE DEFENSE

When the opponents are playing the ball the team should be waiting in a base defensive formation. As the opponents attempt to set up a spike, and the team sees that its first action will probably be a block, all three forwards place themselves at the net in a blocking position. The center back stays in the center of the court, and the other backs stay deep. Diagram 10 illustrates the proper team alignment during base defense. From the base defensive formation the team moves either into free ball formation if the opponents do not spike, or into position to block.

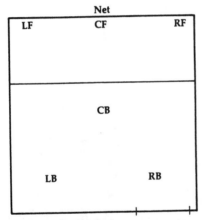

Diagram 10. Base defense when using the 2-1-3 defensive system.

THE BLOCK DEFENSE

In this defense two players form the block, one player plays close behind the block providing dink coverage, and the remaining three players remain deep to dig spikes. As soon as the team knows from which side the opponents will spike, the CF moves to that side to form a double block with the outside forward. The CF moves behind the block and gets into a low position. The remaining three players cover the rest of the court. The back on the same side

as the block plays close to the line, and is ready to dig a down-the-line spike. The forward, not involved in the block, moves off the net to the attack line, and is ready to dig sharply angled spikes, play dinks to the center of the court, and pick up any spikes which roll along the net and fall into the court. The back opposite the block plays in the power alley. This is the part of the court where most spikes are likely to come. This player lines up off the center forward's inside shoulder so that the player sees the spiker's hand and the ball. Diagrams 11 and 12 show the proper court positions for all players when the opposing right forward and left forward are spiking. The shaded area indicates the power alley. The area

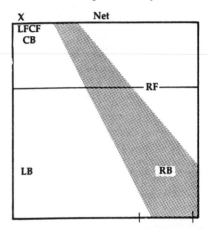

Diagram 11. The proper court coverage when using the 2–1–3 defense and the opposing right forward is spiking.

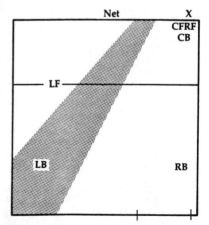

Diagram 12. The proper court coverage when using the 2–1–3 defense and the opposing left forward is spiking.

deep behind the block tends to be the weak area in this defense.

In the beginning levels of play few teams will spike from the CF position unless they are playing an international 4-2 offense where the setter sets from the RF position.

SAFETY

Volleyball is a relatively safe game to play. The only protective measure suggested is the use of knee pads. As in any sport, a sufficient warm-up before beginning activity is the best way to decrease muscle pulls. The legs and arms are used extensively, and should be thoroughly warmed up before play. The best way to prevent collisions on the court is to communicate with teammates at all times, calling for the ball immediately upon deciding to play it.

When practicing skills and running drills in a fairly small area with a medium to large size class it is suggested that a signal be established to stop activity in case a stray ball is in danger of rolling under a jumping player's feet. When this signal is given all activity should cease until the danger area has been corrected.

RULES

The court has several markings with which all players should be familiar. Diagram 13 shows a legal volleyball court and its markings.

The correct height of the net for women is 7' 4⅛" (2.24m), and for men 7' 11⅝" (2.43m). The court is 59' (18m) long and 29' 6" (9m) wide. The attack lines are 9' 10" (3m) from the net.

The game is started with a coin toss between the teams' captains. One captain calls the toss. The captain who wins the toss selects either to serve first or to play on the preferred side of the court. The other captain gets the remaining choice.

Matches consist of either best of three or best of five games. Each game is 15 points and the winning team must win by two points. The first serve alternates with each game. A second coin toss is made for the third game or fifth game which will decide a match.

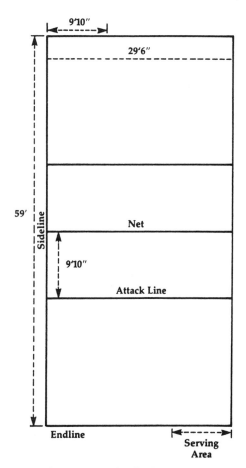

Diagram 13. A legal volleyball court with its markings and measurements.

A playing team is made up of six players. A squad can have no more than 12 players. Once the order of service is established for a game it cannot change until that game is completed. Players must be in their correct rotational position and on the court until the ball is contacted on any serve. At any other time in the game players may play anywhere on their court or off it provided they remain on their own side of the net.

There are several ball handling rules:
1. No player may hit the ball twice in a row unless the first contact is a block.
2. Each team may contact the ball three times on its side. If the first contact is a block it doesn't count as a hit, and three additional contacts are allowed.
3. Part of the ball must be on a team's side of the net before that team may spike;

but the team may block a ball attacked by the opposing spiker before it crosses the net.

4. Each contact must give the ball immediate impetus. The ball may not be held, thrown, or carried.

5. The ball may be contacted with any part of the body above and including the waist.

Players must be on the court during service (the line is part of the court). Players may step on or over the centerline, as long as part of the foot remains on or above that line. It is a fault if any other part of the body contacts the floor on the opponent's court.

The ball is put in play from the service area. It must go over the legal portion of the net (the part between the antennas) without touching it, and land within the boundaries of the opponent's court. The lines are considered in-bounds. The serve must be contacted with one hand or arm. It must be cleanly hit after it has been released or thrown from the hand or hands of the server.

A team only scores when serving. If the serving team faults, the receiving team gets to serve and no point is made. This action is called a side-out. Points are made by the serving team anytime the receiving team commits a fault. In some rules rally point scoring is used in the deciding game of the match. In rally point scoring every serve results in a point. The team that wins each rally receives a point whether it has served or received. The new scoring method makes the game even faster and more exciting.

A player may not touch the net at any time while the ball is in play. Any ball other than the serve which contacts the net is legal and remains in play. If a ball is hit into the net with force causing the net to hit a player, it is not a net fault. If two opposing players hit the net or cross the centerline simultaneously, it is a double fault, and the point is replayed. Only forwards may block. Backs may not spike from a position in front of the attack line. Players may leave the court in order to play the ball but the ball must pass over the legal portion of the net to be a good return.

EQUIPMENT

The best volleyball is made of leather with molded seams. It is softer to the touch and does not hurt the arms when played. A good volleyball will cost at least $25.00.

Net standards that fit into a sleeve in the floor are the safest. Nets which have a high tensile rope for the upper cable are easiest to use and store.

Players often prefer long sleeved shirts to help protect their arms when passing or digging.

TERMINOLOGY

Attack. The act of sending the ball to an opponent in a forceful manner. Often used synonymously with spike.

Attack Line. The line on the court which is 9' 10" (3m) from the centerline.

Back Set. A set in which the setter faces away from the intended direction of the ball and sets overhead to a waiting spiker.

Base Formation. The position of a team while their opponents play the ball and the team waits to decide their counter move.

Block. When a player jumps close to the net extending both arms over the top of the net with the hands in a wide position with fingers spread to prevent an opponent's spike from crossing the net.

Bump. The passing action in which the ball rebounds off the forearms and is directed to a teammate.

Centerline. The court marking directly under the net which divides the large court into two equal sides.

Cross-court Spike. A spike directed diagonally to the longest part of the opponent's court.

Dig. A one- or two-armed defensive save in which a player has difficulty getting to the ball and just passes it high so that a teammate can play it.

Dink. A soft off-speed change of pace play in which a spiker attempts to catch the opponents off guard. The ball is hit with the finger tips of one or two hands so that it just clears the block and drops quickly to the floor.

Double Fault. A play in which faults are committed by players on both teams at the same time. The point is replayed.

Down-the-line Spike. A spike directed along the sideline closest to the spiker.

Floater. A serve which is hit without spin causing it to move up, down, and/or side to side as it responds to air currents.

Free Ball. Any ball coming from the opponents which is not a spike or attack.

Heel of the Hand. The solid part of the hand which is close to the wrist.

Middle-in. A defensive formation in which the center back plays directly behind the block to cover against the dink.

Off-hand. A spike in which the ball must cross in front of the spiker's body before being contacted by the spiker's dominant hand. The set comes from the spiker's nondominant side.

On-hand. A spike in which the ball is set from the same side of the spiker's body as the dominant hand.

Opening up. The action of all players during serve reception who are not going to receive the serve. They all turn and face their teammate who is receiving and has indicated this by calling for the ball.

Overhand Pass. A pass in which the player plays the ball with open hands in a position 6 to 8 inches above the forehead.

Power Alley. That portion of the court where most spikes are aimed. It is the diagonal from the spiker's hand to the opposite corner of the opponent's court.

Seam. The space between two receivers during serve reception.

Serve. The act of putting the ball in play. The ball is hit from behind the end line and in the serving area so that it clears the net and enters the opponent's court.

Serving Area. The right one-third of the end line and behind or outside of the court. The place from which players serve.

Set. The placement of the ball to enable the spiker to attack it directing it into the opponent's court.

Side-out. When the serving team makes a fault and the receiving team gains the serve.

Spike. A ball which is hit with great force from a position higher than the top of the net so that it drops at a sharp angle to the opponents.

Target Area. The area to which the players pass the ball when receiving serve and/or another ball from the opponents. The setter is usually in the target area. In a 4-2 offense this area is the center one-third of the court close to the net.

Topspin. A ball which is hit by a player using a wrist snap which causes it to rotate away from the hitter resulting in a quick dropping action of the ball.

REFERENCES

Bertucci, B., & Hippolyte, R. (eds.) *Championship Volleyball Drills* (Vol. I). Champaign, IL: Leisure Press, 1984.

Bertucci, B., & Korgut, T. (eds.) *Championship Volleyball Drills* (Vol. II). Champaign, IL: Leisure Press, 1985

Fraser, S. D. *Strategies for Competitive Volleyball.* Champaign, IL: Leisure Press, 1988.

Gozansky, S. *Championship Volleyball Techniques and Drills.* West Nyack, NY: Parker, 1983.

Lucas, J. *Pass, Set, Crush Volleyball Illustrated.* Wenatchee, WA: Euclid Northwest Publications, 1985.

Neville, William J. *Coaching Volleyball Successfully.* Champaign, IL: Leisure Press, 1990.

Selinger, A., and Ackermann, Blount, J. *Arie Selinger's Power Volleyball.* New York: St. Martin's Press, 1986.

Stokes, Roberta, and Haley, Mick. *Volleyball Everyone.* Winston-Salem, NC: Hunter Textbooks Inc., 1984.

Viera, Barbara L., and Ferguson, B. J. *Volleyball—Steps to Success.* Champaign, IL: Leisure Press, 1989.

Viera, Barbara L., and Ferguson, B. J. *Teaching Volleyball—Steps to Success.* Champaign, IL: Leisure Press, 1989.

CHAPTER 24

Weight-Training

CLAIR W. JENNETT
San Jose State University
San Jose, CA

INTRODUCTION

Weight-training activities have been reported in many cultures from the beginning of recorded history. Ideas for increasing strength developed from the need for strength in all human activities. The need for strength continues today, and weight-training, as a means of strength improvement, continues to gain popularity. The many forms of weight-training allow persons of each age and gender to experience the benefits of added strength.

The current popularity has not always been accepted by all teachers and coaches who have often discouraged weight-training. Fears of skill loss, flexibility loss, or even power loss were reported in the non-scientific literature of the 1930s, 40s, and 50s. However, with the increasing scientific research of these decades, it soon became clear that the myths of the past were not supported and that weight-training was an important element in any conditioning or sport-training program. Today, a fitness or sport-training program without weight-training would be lacking. Well-established programs can be easily found in the fitness and sports literature. Four means of improving fitness or sports ability are improvement in skill, strategy, power, and strength. This chapter will focus on the latter two—the benefits of weight-training for improvement of strength and power.

The term weight-training is used in this chapter to define (describe) all exercise programs that are used to increase strength. Resistance-training, weight-lifting, strength exercises, and other terms are used. Each term has its advocates, but weight-training seems to be the most common term.

The types of exercises included under the heading of weight-training in this chapter are isokinetic exercises, isometric exercises, isotonic exercises, elastic cord resistance exercises, spring resistance exercises, and partner exercises. Each of these exercise forms is defined in the terminology section.

WHO SHOULD PARTICIPATE

Everyone should participate in weight-training. Few persons complete a day when they haven't wished for more strength to accomplish some task. Therefore, some reasons for participation in weight-training are: (1) Weight-training is used to build general strength. (2) Weight-training is an excellent recreational activity. Personal goals can be attained as well as socializing with friends. (3) Weight-training is used for competitive purposes. Olympic weight lifters, power lifters, and body builders use weight-training as the basic training for their events. (4) Weight-training is used in most sports by athletes to add strength and power to their sport activity. (5) Weight-training is used for rehabilitation after injury or surgery.

Some writers have suggested that weight-training programs can be used for weight gain or loss. This can happen (probably due to calorie intake), but the central focus of a weight-training program should be strength and power development rather than weight control.

Physical fitness has been a national concern for decades, and one of the primary components of fitness is strength. Weight-training is the best activity for strength improvement. Women, men, children, and older persons can all improve their fitness through weight-training.

BENEFITS OF WEIGHT-TRAINING

The chief benefit of a weight-training activity should be an increase in strength for the participant. A well-designed program of systematic, progressively planned activities will guarantee strength gains. The benefits other than strength have been documented by writers of fitness books and the list is quite long. A few of the benefits follow:

1. Feeling better
2. Body image and appearance
3. Better efficiency in work and play, e.g., lifting luggage, moving furniture, playing games and sports.
4. Better health
   a. Bone loss prevention
   b. Endurance for daily tasks
   c. Stress and tension release
5. Competition
   a. Self-testing
   b. Training with friends
   c. Comparing with previous year's records
6. Physical fitness changes
   a. Muscular endurance
   b. Body composition (percent of fat)
   c. Flexibility
   d. Speed of movement

None of these benefits is assured, but they can be accomplished with a well-designed program. The false conceptions that weight-training programs will result in muscle-boundness, bulky muscles for women, flexibility loss, speed of movement loss, coordination loss, etc., have been well refuted in the literature. Drugs and special diets are not necessary for benefits to accrue. Research concerning the deleterious effects of drugs used for strength enhancement is increasing each year, and a well-balanced diet, without supplements, is all that is needed for benefits to occur.

HOW TO START A WEIGHT-TRAINING PROGRAM

WHAT TO WEAR

Exercise wear for weight-training is the same as for other exercise and sport activity. Freedom of movement, sweat collection, and light weight are considerations. Cloth-ing that is too loose or too tight can cause some problems. The clothing should cover the body so that sweat is not a problem for persons using equipment after your use. Shirt (with sleeves), shorts, socks, and shoes should be required for safety and cleanliness. The shoes can be weight lifting shoes or game shoes (basketball or tennis). If competitive lifting is the objective, lifting shoes are recommended. A sports bra for women can be a helpful support, and a lifting belt for men and women can be especially helpful for handling heavy weights. Gloves can be helpful in protecting the hands during long workouts.

WHERE TO EXERCISE

Many private and public gyms are available for exercise programs for a fee. Selecting the gym for a personal program is a problem. The fee, of course, is one consideration; the cleanliness, the amount and type of equipment, the number of persons using the gym, and the location are all factors to consider in selecting a gym.

Home exercise is another consideration. Several equipment companies manufacture home equipment. If one wishes to buy equipment for the home, seeking the advice of a trusted expert is essential. The possibility of purchasing poorly designed equipment with little durability or flexibility is great. Therefore, expert advice is essential to the novice.

STARTING AN EXERCISE PROGRAM

It is important to understand what is to be accomplished through the conditioning program before a systematic program can be developed to achieve these ends. It is also important to understand how weight-training serves as an effective conditioning tool. The following qualities become highly developed through weight training.

1. Muscular power—the ability to do heavy workloads in very short periods of time. The clean is a commonly used measure of this quality.
2. Muscular strength—the ability to develop maximum force or tension in an exercise. This quality is usually measured by doing a one repetition maxi-

mum (1RM) for an exercise. The dead lift is an excellent example of total body muscular strength.

3. Muscular endurance—the ability to do an exercise, or series of exercises (circuit training), with below maximum weight, for a prolonged period of time. Various exercises can be done for repetitions with a percentage of the 1RM or a percentage of body weight.

Any or all types of resistance exercises —isometric, isotonic, isokinetic, elastic cord, spring, or partner exercises—can be used in weight-training programs. Each one of these types of exercises has positive and negative attributes. Selecting the exercise that meets the economic, time, developmental, and personal needs of the individual is a part of choosing an exercise program.

Isotonic exercises can be done concentrically or eccentrically. A concentric contraction is where the muscle shortens as it exerts force against the resistance. An eccentric contraction is where the muscle lengthens as it exerts force against the resistance. Resistance can be provided by adding weight, spring resistance, elastic cord resistance, or partner resistance. Many machines have been devised to vary the resistance in place, while freeweights usually require spotters to ensure safety. Therefore, machine devices are recommended for beginners.

Isokinetic exercises are similar to isotonic exercises that are done on a machine. The difference is that the movement is completed at a constant speed and allows for maximal contraction throughout the range of movement for the exercise. The speed of the movement remains constant even when the force is increased.

Isometric exercises are excellent rehabilitation exercises, because the exercises can be done with the amount of resistance supplied by the exerciser. No movement is made, but the exerciser simply exerts force against a fixed object at the maximum resistance he/she can exert.

Corbin and Linsey, in their book *Concepts of Physical Fitness with Laboratories*, present tables which evaluate the advantages and disadvantages of various weight-training exercises. These tables are helpful in making the selection of exercises for given individual needs.

WORKOUT PROGRAM

The elements of the workout are (1) the warm-up, (2) the exercise program, and (3) the cool-down.

WARM-UP

The warm-up should include walking, stepping, jumping, or running easily for 5-8 minutes. These activities can be alternated with mild stretching exercises. Each area of the body should be stretched and an increase of 15-25% in the resting pulse rate should result from the warm-up. When the warm-up is completed, the selected exercises begin.

EXERCISE PROGRAM

A total body exercise program should be planned. Exercises for each area of the body are then selected. The areas are:
1. Neck and spine
2. Shoulders and upper arms
3. Elbows and wrists
4. Abdominal
5. Hips and upper legs
6. Knees and ankles

Exercises for each of these body areas are found in the final section of this chapter. The exercises, in some cases, duplicate the muscle group to be exercised. Selection of the exercises for each individual, to meet the individual needs mentioned above, is the next step in starting a program. One or two exercises from each area are recommended for a circuit. A *circuit* is a group of exercises of 6-12 repetitions each. A circuit can be repeated or substitute exercises can be used on a second or third circuit. Changing the repetitions and the weight or resistance is another way of varying the circuit.

A progressive resistance exercise program should be used with each exercise. This means that to increase strength, the load on the muscle during exercise must be increased progressively. This added stress or *overload* will cause the muscle to adapt (hypertrophy) and become stronger. Overload can be accomplished by adding weight causing fewer repetitions or by increasing repetitions with less weight. Muscular endurance results from high repetition with low weight exercises and muscular strength results from low repetition with high weight exercises. If weight resistance can be added to the exercise, the number of repetitions suggested is between 6 and 12. If 8 repetitions can not be completed, weight should be removed. If more than 12 repetitions can be completed, weight should be added. Emphasis on results of speed, endurance, strength, or power can change the number of repetitions desired for overload.

In beginning a program, it is safer to begin with lighter weight—weights that are managed easily. Increase weight gradually as the exercises are learned and the repetitions increase. How the body feels is the best indicator as to the appropriateness of the program. Some general rules to follow are:

1. Have fun—work for experience and expression not for pain.
2. Change the routine—use different exercises for the same muscle groups for variance. Vary the repetitions and sets by changing the weights.
3. Work with another person—help each other, encourage each other, and spot each other.
4. Underwork is better than overwork—overwork should not be required for strength gains and may result in unneeded muscle soreness.
5. Be regular in workouts—work three or four times per week. Limit vacations (although a week or two off occasionally is motivating).
6. Complete exercises for all areas of the body—it is easy to leave out some areas and favor others.
7. Work on a circuit—8-10 exercises in a group. Vary the circuit.
8. Compete occasionally—compete with your established records, and compete with a friend in percentage gain for a month.
9. Keep a record of your workouts—record the repetitions, sets, and amount of weight lifted. Include your body weight and measure your body composition (percent of fat) every six months.
10. Record your resting pulse rate at each workout.
11. Don't work during sickness—missing one day occasionally will not have any long-term influence on strength.
12. Work safely—safety procedures in *Principles of Safety in Physical Education and Sport* (AAHPERD) are essential.

COOL-DOWN

Following the exercise program is the cool-down period. This time provides an additional opportunity for stretching as the pulse rate and body temperature return to normal. Walking and stretching for 5-8 minutes is a normal protocol for a cool-down.

BREATHING, SPOTTING, AND GRIP

It is very important that the weight-trainer have a good understanding of proper breathing, spotting, and gripping techniques before starting a program; consequently, it is fitting that these be discussed prior to getting into the actual program.

BREATHING

Proper breathing is one of the most important requirements in weight-training. Many weight trainers do not practice correct breathing techniques and limit performance. Here are some essentials:

1. If the exercise weights are light to medium, breathing can easily follow the pattern of out on exertion and in as the action returns the bar to the starting position.
2. The light to medium breathing technique keeps the internal body pressure at a comfortable exercise level.
3. The lifting of heavy weights, however, demands that the lifter stabilize the trunk to provide a firm foundation for the execution of the exercise. Therefore, the air is taken in prior to the lift and held during the exertion. However, a forceful exhalation does help in making close lifts, and also reduces the possibility of passing out.

SPOTTING

Spotting is a preventive safety measure. Many hazardous situations can be easily avoided by following proper training programs as well as sound spotting principles. Spotters are persons who stand by the lifter to provide assistance when needed. They may help position a heavy weight for the start of an exercise, or help remove it afterward. Their primary function, however, is to prevent injuries by controlling the weight in the event of a slip, or when the lifter cannot complete a lift. Some helpful principles of spotting are given below:

1. Follow intelligent training programs.
2. Properly use and inspect equipment.
3. Pay attention when spotting.
4. Use at least two spotters when working with extremely heavy weights.
5. Use appropriate lifting racks when lifting extremely heavy weights.

GRIPS

The grip depends primarily on the type of exercise or variation being done. Three major grips are used in weight-training: overhand, underhand, and mixed. These are shown in Figure 1.

WEIGHT-TRAINING EXERCISES

The following exercises are suggested exercises for each of six areas of the body: neck and spine; shoulders and upper arms; elbows and wrists; abdominal; hips and upper legs; and knees and ankles.

NECK AND SPINE

Neck Extension and Flexion
1. Exerciser takes a position on hands and knees and moves the head up and down.
2. Partner resists the movement with hands on the forehead and back of the head.
3. Don't hyperflex or hyperextend the neck and the partner must resist carefully.
4. Exerciser can be on a table with head extended over the end of the table.

Neck Abduction and Adduction
1. Exerciser takes a position on hands and knees and moves the head from side to side.
2. Partner resists the movement with hands on the sides of the head.
3. Partner must resist carefully.
4. Exerciser can be on a table with head extended over the end of the table.

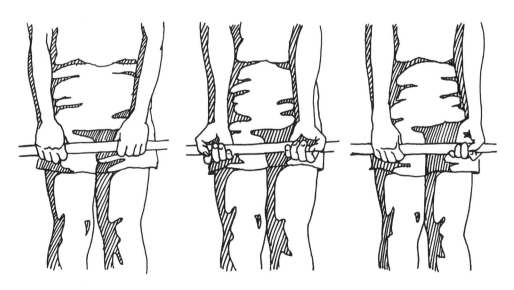

a. Overhand grip. **b.** Underhand grip. **c.** Mixed grip.

Figure 1. The grips.

Back Extension

1. Exerciser takes a prone (face down) position on the floor.
2. Exerciser lifts shoulders and toes one or two inches off the floor with his/her weight supported by the abdomen. Hold 5 to 10 seconds.
3. Don't hyperextend the back.

Abdominal Curls

1. Exerciser takes a supine (face up) position on the floor with knees bent as much as possible and the feet flat on the floor. Arms are folded across the chest.
2. Exerciser lifts the shoulders off the floor and returns to the floor.

Upper Back Extension

1. Exerciser takes a prone (face down) position on the floor.
2. Partner holds the legs down.
3. Exerciser lifts shoulders off the floor and returns to the floor.

SHOULDERS AND UPPER ARMS

Shoulder Shrugs

1. Exerciser takes a standing position and places dumbbells in each hand or a barbell is held at arms length in front of the body.
2. Exerciser lifts the weight by shrugging the shoulders upward and then down.

Bench Press

1. Exerciser takes a supine (face up) position on a bench with the barbell held with vertically extended arms. Feet are on the floor.
2. Exerciser lowers the barbell to the chest level and returns it to the extended arm position.
3. Don't touch the chest with the barbell. See Figure 2.

Dumbbell Flys

1. Exerciser takes a supine (face up) position on a bench with dumbbells in each hand and arms extended.
2. Exerciser lowers dumbbells to the side to bench level and returns them to the extended position.
3. Use light weights to begin.

Lateral Raise

1. Exerciser takes a standing or sitting position with dumbbells in each hand. Arms are extended at the sides.
2. Exerciser lifts dumbbells sideways to shoulder height and returns to the sides.

Front Raise

1. Exerciser takes a standing or sitting position with dumbbells in each hand. Arms are extended at the sides.
2. Exerciser lifts dumbbells forward to shoulder height or higher and returns to the sides.
3. Arms can lift together or alternately.

Seated Overhead Press

1. Exerciser takes a sitting position straddling the bench with the barbell resting on the shoulders.
2. Exerciser extends arms, lifting the barbell over the head and returning to the shoulders.
3. This can be done standing but with greater possibility of back strain.

Upright Rowing

1. Exerciser is standing and holds the barbell at arms length in front of the body. Hands are only 6 inches apart.
2. Exerciser lifts the bar toward the chin and returns the bar to arms length.

Bent Over Rowing

1. Exerciser takes a standing or sitting position and bends forward at the waist with dumbbells held in extended arms.
2. Exerciser raises arms sideways and returns.
3. Elbows can be bent.

Internal and External Rotation of Upper Arm

1. Exerciser takes supine (face up) position on the bench or floor. The arm is at the side, bent 90 degrees at the elbow.
2. Exerciser rotates the upper arm so that the hand moves inward or outward. Resistance is provided by a partner, elastic cord, or a dumbbell.
3. Lying on the side may provide more range to the movement.

a. The feet are flat on the floor.

b. The arms are fully extended when taking the barbell from the spotters.

Figure 2. Spotting for the bench press.

Pullovers

1. Exerciser takes a supine (face up) position on the floor or bench with the barbell held above the chest with extended arms. If on bench, feet on floor.
2. Exerciser lowers the barbell to the floor over the head. Arms can be bent at elbow during movement.
3. Use light weight when beginning. See Figure 3.

Lat Pulls

1. Exerciser hangs from a horizontal bar with the hands three to four feet apart.
2. Exerciser pulls the head above the bar with the head in front of the bar and lowers to hang. (Try to touch the shoulders to the bar.)
3. Variations as in the pull-up exercise can be used.
4. Lat bar pull-down devices are available with many models of machines.

ELBOWS AND WRISTS

Pull-Ups

1. Exerciser hangs from a horizontal bar.
2. Exerciser pulls the head above the bar and lowers to hang.
3. Variations with the feet on the floor can lighten the load. Lowering eccentrically can also be a strengthener.

Bar Dips

1. Exerciser supports with straight arms on parallel bars.
2. Exerciser lowers to bent elbow position and returns.
3. Variations with the feet on the floor can lighten the load. Lowering eccentrically, only, can also be a strengthener.
   See Figure 4 for dip on the Nautilus.

Push-Ups

1. Exerciser takes a prone (face down) position with elbows bent and hands flat on the floor under shoulders.
2. Exerciser pushes up by extension of the elbow.
3. Variation with the knee remaining on the floor lightens the load. Lowering eccentrically only can also be a strengthener.

Wrist Rolls

1. Exerciser takes a standing position and holds a weight tied to a round stick with a rope.
2. Exerciser rolls the rope around the stick with an overhand grip or an underhand grip.

Wrist Curls

1. Exerciser takes a sitting position with barbell held in an overgrip or undergrip with forearms resting on thighs.
2. Exerciser raises and lowers the barbell with only wrist movement.

Biceps Curls

1. Exerciser takes a standing position and holds the barbell at arms length in front of the body.
2. Exerciser lifts the bar by flexing the biceps (bending the elbow) and returns the bar to arms length.
3. Keep the body line straight without arching the back or swaying. See Figure 5.

Triceps Extensions

1. Exerciser takes supine (face up) position on the bench or the floor with the barbell held with extended arms. Feet are on the floor.
2. Exerciser bends elbows without changing the upperarm position and lowers the bar to the front of the face. Then he/she returns the bar to the extended position.
3. Use a light weight to begin.

ABDOMINAL

Abdominal Curls

(See Neck and Spine, above.)

Push-Ups

(See Shoulder and Upper Arms, above.)

Bent Knee Sit-Up

(Same as Abdominal Curls above, except the elbows touch the bent knees by curling further.)

Hanging Knee Raises

1. Exerciser hangs from a horizontal bar.
2. Exerciser raises knees as high as possible and returns to hang.

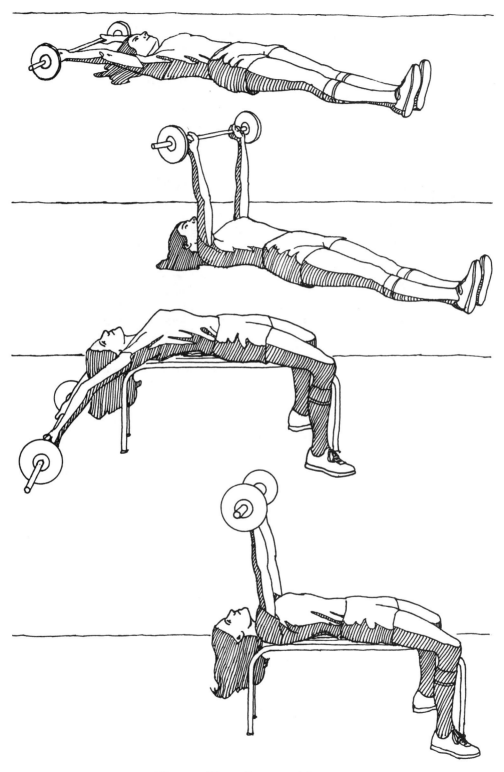

Figure 3. The pullover-straight arm.

a. Starting positions for the dip on the Nautilus multi-exercise machine.

b. Execution of the dip on the Nautilus multi-exercise machine.

Figure 4. The dip on the Nautilus.

Figure 5. The curl (regular).

Side Bends
1. Exerciser takes a standing position with a dumbbell in one hand.
2. Exerciser leans to one side, then to the other side.
3. Change the dumbbell to the other hand and repeat.

Twisting Curl-Up
1. Same as abdominal curls above, except the curling continues to move the shoulder toward the opposite knee (right shoulder toward left knee and left shoulder toward right knee).

Isometric Abdominals
1. Exerciser takes a standing position and draws the abdomen in and holds for 6 to 10 seconds.
2. Exerciser relaxes and repeats.

HIPS AND UPPER LEGS

Prone Flutter Kicks
1. Exerciser takes a prone (face down) position on the floor.
2. Exerciser moves the legs alternately up and down with the knee straight.

Supine Flutter Kicks
1. Exerciser takes a supine (face up) position on the floor.
2. Exerciser moves the legs up and down with the knee straight.

Side Leg Raises (Upper Leg)
1. Exerciser takes a side lying position.
2. Exerciser lifts the upper leg sideways and returns.
3. Partner can add resistance.

Side Leg Raises (Lower Leg)
1. Exerciser takes a side lying position with the upper leg separated and resting on the bench.
2. Exerciser lifts the lower leg sideways closing the legs together.
3. Partner can add resistance.

Side Leg Raises (Standing, using outer leg)
1. Exerciser stands with his/her side to wall, legs straddle (separated).
2. Exerciser moves leg near the wall, sideways, toward the leg away from the wall.

3. Partner can add resistance. Also, elastic cord or a spring, attached to the wall and ankle, can add resistance.
4. Turn to the other side for the opposite leg.

KNEES AND ANKLES

Squats
1. Exerciser takes a standing position with dumbbells in each hand. Feet shoulder width apart, and toes turned out slightly.
2. Exerciser squats one-half of a full squat. A bench can be used to end the squat, but don't bounce on the bench. Move down slowly and return faster.
3. The barbell can be used on the shoulders for this exercise if spotters or a rack are available.

Leg Presses
1. Exerciser can use a machine with a leg press device for the safest leg extension exercise.

Lunger
1. Exerciser takes a standing position and steps forward with dumbbells in each hand.
2. Exerciser bends the forward knee to 90 degrees and returns back to the stand. This is followed by stepping forward with the opposite leg.

Knee Curls
1. Exerciser can use a machine with a knee curl device. From a prone (face down) position, the lower leg is hooked under the resistance device. The knee is flexed moving the resistance.
2. This exercise can be done with a partner providing the resistance.

Heel Raises
1. Exerciser takes a standing position with dumbbells in each hand.
2. Exerciser raises the heels off the floor and returns.
3. Placing the toe up on a one-inch board increases the range of motion.
4. Using only one foot to do the work independently easily increases the load.

Knee Extensions

1. Exerciser can use a machine with a knee extension device. In a sitting position, with the knee bent to 90 degrees, the ankle is hooked under the resistance device. The knee is extended, moving the resistance.
2. This exercise can be done with a partner providing the resistance.

TERMINOLOGY

Aerobic Activity. Activities or exercises done at a rate in which the body is able to provide adequate oxygen to sustain the activity for a long period of time.

Body Composition. Generally refers to the percentage of total body weight that is fat.

Circuit. A series of exercises or exercise stations that have been placed in sequence.

Cool-down Period. A period of time after vigorous exercise when light exercise or walking is done to allow the body temperature and pulse rate to return to normal.

Concentric Contraction. Contraction where the muscle shortens as it exerts force against the resistance.

Eccentric Contraction. Contraction where the muscle lengthens as it exerts force against the resistance.

Elastic Cord Resistance Exercise. Resistance to a specified movement is provided by an elastic cord. (Surgical tubing of various sizes is often used.)

Isokinetic Resistance Exercises. Exercises done at a constant speed allowing for maximal contraction throughout the range of the movement. Usually requires a machine device.

Isometric Resistance Exercise. An exercise of muscle contraction against an immoveable resistance with no shortening or lengthening of the muscle (no movement of the body part). Strength gains are only at the specific joint angle of the exercise.

Isotonic Resistance Exercises. An exercise of muscle contraction against a moveable resistance with shortening or lengthening of the muscle through the range of the movement (can be eccentric or concentric contraction).

Muscular Endurance. The ability of a muscle to persist or repeat contraction; to continue contraction.

Muscular Strength. The ability of a muscle to supply contraction to the maximum. The number of pounds of force that can be exerted.

Overload. The stress adaption of the muscle; as the work of the muscle is increased, the muscle will adapt (hypertrophy, increase in size) to be able to do more work.

Partners. Another person to help, encourage, and spot exercises of a person.

Progressive Resistance Exercises. Overloading (adding to the weight, sets, and/or repetitions) exercises to the maximum load for 6 to 12 repetitions and three sets to improve muscular strength and endurance.

Range of Motion. Movement of a joint through the full limits of the joint movement.

Repetitions. The number of times an exercise is repeated in one set.

Resistance. The amount of weight or load that the muscle holds or moves. The resistance can be supplied by weight plates, springs, elastic cords, or a partner.

Sets. The number of times (bouts) 6 to 12 repetitions are done. A person could try to do 3 sets of 10 repetitions.

Spot/Spotting. To help, for safety reasons, a partner who is exercising.

Spring Resistance Exercises. Resistance to a specified movement is provided by a spring attached to a firm place.

Warm-up. Time before vigorous exercise when a person increases body temperature and pulse rate by easy running, stepping, walking, and/or stretching.

REFERENCES

Corbin, Charles B. and Ruth Lindsey. *Concepts of Physical Fitness with Laboratories*, 7th Ed. Dubuque, IA: Wm. C. Brown Publishers, 1991.

CHAPTER 25

Wrestling

DOUG PARKER
Springfield College (Retired)
Springfield, MA

SCHOLASTIC WRESTLING

Some people, by nature, are attracted to dual combative activities. It represents an exciting challenge to test one's strength, speed, skills, and endurance with another person in hand-to-hand combat. High school wrestling rules are designed to prevent injuries but provide students with an opportunity to create movement as well as execute techniques that have been used for thousands of years. A wrestler's spirit, mind, and body are engaged in combat with an opponent of equal weight. Time-outs and substitutions are not allowed. Balance and leverage are "key" factors in wrestling as well as other movement qualities such as timing, coordination, and flexibility. A wrestler gains considerable confidence from the proper execution of techniques, scoring points, and especially from the thrill of the *pin*.

Both girls and boys participate in wrestling at the secondary school level and receive instruction together in the physical education setting. However, girls should wrestle versus girls and boys versus boys.

Vision and learning impaired people as well as those with physical handicaps find wrestling an excellent sport to express themselves and develop in spirit, mind, and body.

In addition to scholastic wrestling, there are other forms of amateur wrestling. The most popular are International Freestyle and Greco-Roman as contested in the Olympic Games. Freestyle is similar to scholastic wrestling but in Freestyle more emphasis is placed on pins and near falls and not on control. Greco-Roman is scored the same as Freestyle but no holds are allowed below the waist.

Wrestling provides student-athletes with the rewarding experience of contributing to the team effort as well as the excitement of their own success. Practicing techniques presents a wrestler with the opportunity to teach and share with others as well as learn. Wrestlers learn to respect others through the adversity of challenging and hard fought matches. There is no professional, entertainment, or "pay for play" level in wrestling. Wrestlers may participate from Pee-wee through Jr. High, Sr. High Schools, and college to the International Olympic levels of competition.

High school wrestlers compete in the following weight classes:

103 lb., 112 lb., 119 lb., 125 lb., 130 lb., 135 lb., 140 lb., 145 lb., 152 lb., 160 lb., 171 lb., 189 lb., and 275 lb.

TEAM SCORING

A pin (fall) is the object of wrestling. A pin occurs when a wrestler's shoulders are held to the mat for two seconds, thus ending the match. Team points are scored as follows:

Pin	— 6 points
Default	— 6 points (wrestler cannot continue)
Forfeit	— 6 points (no opponent)
Technical fall	— 5 points (difference in match score reaches 15)
Note:	— when difference of 15 is reached, match is ended
Major Decision	— 4 points (difference of 8 points in score at conclusion of match)
Decision	— 3 points
Tie	— 2 points

MATCH SCORING

If neither wrestler is able to end the match by pinning the opponent, a match may be decided on points scored. Individual match points are:

Take Down	— 2 points (from neutral to control on the mat)
Escape	— 1 point (from controlled to neutral)
Reversal	— 2 points (from controlled to control)
Near Fall	— 2 points (opponent's shoulders held within 45 degrees or 4 inches from the mat for two seconds)
Near Fall	— 3 points (held for 5 seconds)

Figure 1, a. Starting the match.

Illegal holds, stalling, and other violations are penalized as follows:

First Penalty:	1 point
Second Penalty:	1 point
Third Penalty:	2 points
Fourth Penalty:	Disqualification

BASIC POSITIONS

A match is started with each wrestler's foot on a designated line and the wrestlers shake hands. The end of the match has the wrestlers in the same position, shaking hands, and the referee raises the hand of the winner. (See Figure 1, a and b.)

The starting position on the mat (referee's position) is shown in Figure 2. *Defensive* (D) wrestler's hands on mat in front of and knees behind two parallel lines 12" apart.

The *Offensive* (O) wrestler may start: On either side of defensive wrestler; arm around waist with palm on a naval, palm of other hand behind near elbow, head in mid-line of back, and one knee down on side.

Figure 1, b. End of match.

PRELIMINARY DRILLS AND ACTIVITIES

MAT DRILL WARM-UP

Run ("foot fire")—Run fast in place.
Sprawl or **Block**—Drop hands straight down to mat, throw legs back with feet spread and back arched.

Figure 2. Referee's starting position.

Recover—Knees to mat, shift weight back over feet, push off mat with hands to stance position, and continue to run.

Back—Squat, sit to mat, and roll to back.

Bridging—Heels to buttocks, arms to chest, lift body high and arch back, supported by toes and head.

Bridge Left/Right and Recover—Shoulder to mat, stepover, to knees and then to feet.

Cuddle Left/Right and Recover—On side (fetal position), raise and throw leg toward head to defensive starting position and then recover to neutral stance.

LEAD-UP GAMES

Turnover—D starts in prone position and tries to maintain that position—O has 10 seconds to turn D over.

Breakdown—Wrestlers start in referee's position. O has 10 seconds to momentarily move D to a prone position.

Go-Behind—Both wrestlers start in a neutral position with one knee on the mat. On whistle wrestlers have ten seconds to get behind and get control of opponent.

Sit-Throughs—Defensive position; bring right hand and arm in to body, raise right knee, move left foot to front right side, return, and repeat to opposite side. Continue for 30 seconds, 1 minute, or more for conditioning.

Spinning—O's chest on D's back push off left foot, throw right leg, and try to spin 180 degrees. Change directions and continue.

TAKEDOWNS

The takedown aspect of wrestling is fascinating because the many techniques and tactics required involve subtle deception to achieve set-ups as well as the timing, speed, agility, and coordination to move from one technique position to a more advantageous technique, which, ultimately, leads to control of the opponent on the mat.

Neutral Stance

Feet comfortably spread with weight centered on balls of feet, knees and hips flexed at 45 degree angle, head up, elbows in front of hips, and hands with palms facing in front of chin. (See Figure 3.)

Set-up

An act or movement which distracts opponent or makes him/her vulnerable for technique to be attempted.

Drop Step

When opponent is "set up" for a takedown attack, lower the hips, and take a long step toward opponent. Keep the hips low, chest-to-knee, elbows in, and head up. (See Figure 4.)

Figure 4. Drop step.

Tie-up (inside out)

Contact opponent to move him/her off balance and thus "set up" for a takedown. Move hands and arms into "praying position" then forward and out to opponent's neck, shoulders, arms, or wrists.

Figure 3. Neutral position. Shows square stance (right) and stride stance (left).

Collar and Bicep Tie-up

Hook left hand on back of opponent's head and simultaneously grip opponent's left bicep with right hand. Step to either side as you pull with left hand and push with right hand. (See Figure 5.)

Underhook Tie-up

Move your right hand under opponent's left arm and place your hand on top of the shoulder. Lift right elbow up to gain a control position. Put your head on the right side of opponent's head and circle in either direction for a takedown set-up.

Over and Under Tie-up

Put right arm under opponent's left arm and right hand on opponent's back. Put left arm over opponent's right arm above the elbow. Put left hand on chest. Note that opponent has the opportunity to take the same tie-up position.

Figure 5. Collar and biceps tie-up.

Snap Down

Use a collar and bicep tie-up. Pull opponent's head and arm down and to the side of "collar" hand as you step to the left with left foot. (See Figure 6.) If you are able to snap opponent down to hands and knees, put your chest on his/her back and spin behind to the left for control and the takedown.

Short Arm Drag

After a snap down, if opponent is on hands and knees but lifts head up to prevent a spin behind, move right hand from opponent's neck to inside right arm, pull the arm toward your right hip, and go behind to the left for a takedown.

Figure 6. Snap down (starting position).

Side Head Lock (from the knees)

After a snap down with opponent on hands and knees—if opponent lifts hands from mat, pull left elbow toward you with right hand, reach over opponent's right shoulder with your left arm, and "punch" left shoulder into opponent's head to turn opponent to the mat. Try to pin opponent with the head and arm hold. (See Figure 7.)

Figure 7. Side head lock (from knees).

Head Chancery (from the knees)

After a snap down, get opponent's head under one arm. Wrap arm (right) tightly around opponent's neck but be careful not to apply a choke hold. At the same time work other hand (left) under opponent's right arm and reach across opponent's back. Continue driving left arm behind opponent's back while forcing opponent's head down and in. When opponent goes to back, "walk" fingers of left hand out on mat to maintain balance in pinning position. (See Figure 8.)

Double Leg Tackle

Drop step with right foot between opponent's legs. Continue forward with right knee going to the mat. Hook hands behind opponent's knees and pull to your chest. Keep head up and into opponent's body. Step forward with left foot, lift opponent, and turn him/her to the right by pivoting on your right knee. (See Figure 9.)

Single Leg Tackle

The important thing is to get to the first position as shown. There are many ways to finish the takedown. (See Figure 10.)

Figure 9. Double leg tackle.

Figure 10. Single leg tackle (initial position).

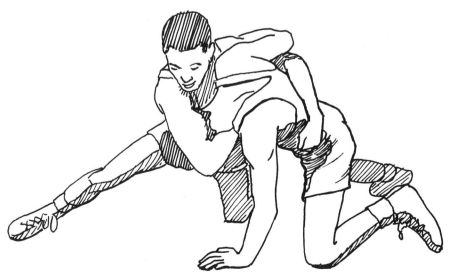

Figure 8. Head chancery.

a.   b.

Figure 11. Fireman's carry.

Fireman's Carry Takedown

From a collar and biceps tie-up, move your right hand to opponent's triceps. Step left foot between his/her legs and drop to right knee while turning a quarter turn right. Move your head under his/her left arm and pull his/her arm down with your right hand. At the same time, move your left hand from his/her neck to between legs and reach up the back. (See Figure 11a.) Drop your right hip to the mat. Pull down with your right hand on arm and throw his/her body up and to the side with your left arm. Pull your head out and up and reach across body with your left arm to hold right shoulder with your left hand. (See Figure 11, b.)

Arm Drag

Pull opponent's right wrist to your right hip with your left hand. At the same time, grasp right elbow with your right hand, let go of the wrist with your left hand, and pull the elbow to your right hip. Simultaneously, step forward with your right foot and put right shoulders together. Put right side of your head down on his/her back. Step left foot behind opponent and drop your right hip to mat outside opponent's right foot. Grasp right knee with your left arm and pull arm to the mat. Pull opponent's elbow to your hip and bring knee to your chest. (See Figure 12.)

Figure 12. Arm drag.

Figure 13. Duck under.

Duck Under

From a collar and bicep tie-up, step forward with your left foot outside opponent's right foot. Lift opponent's right arm and drop head under that right arm. Pull down with right hand on his/her neck. At the same time, drop to right knee and snap your head back against opponent's right arm. Grasp opponent's right knee with your left hand and pivot to the right on your right knee to get opponent down. (See Figure 13.)

Lateral Drop (from standing)

Work into over (left) and under (right) tie-up. Drive into opponent until he/she steps back with right foot. When opponent feels "set up" step forward with left foot, drop to left side, and turn opponent to left. Sit through with right leg to hold opponent in pinning position. (See Figure 14.)

Cross Face

Sprawl when opponent attempts a double leg tackle. Put right arm between your body and opponent's head. Hook hand on his/her triceps. "Chop" with right arm (straighten arm) and try to hook left ankle with your left hand. Bounce back to get hands off your legs and then spin left to go behind opponent and a control position. (See Figure 15.)

Whizzer

When you attempt to spin behind your opponent and he/she counters with a crawfish, overhook your right arm over the left arm, pull shoulder up with your right arm, look away from opponent, and put your right hip in under his/her left hip. Pull down with your right arm and thrust your hips into opponent by extending your legs.

Figure 14. Lateral drop (finish position).

Figure 15. Cross face.

Figure 16. Quarter Nelson.

Quarter Nelson

Put palm of right hand on back of opponent's head and push down. Move left hand over the right upper arm and hook hand on right wrist. Push with right hand on his/her head and lift left arm to turn opponent to his/her back. (See Figure 16.)

REVERSALS AND ESCAPES

There are four basic reversal and escape techniques: (1) roll, (2) switch, (3) sit out, and (4) stand up. The first objective of the wrestler in the defensive position is to establish a stable base and thus prevent the opponent from securing a breakdown. The next goal is to move with good balance and speed from the starting position to a roll, switch, sit out, or stand up and continue to move from one technique to another in "chain" fashion until a reversal or escape is achieved.

The roll usually results in a reversal and oftentimes near fall points. The switch is almost exclusively a reversal technique. The sit out may result in a reversal depending on the opponent's reaction but normally an escape is scored. The sit out is used as a good set up for a roll and occasionally provides a good opportunity to score a reversal with a switch. The stand up is almost exclusively an escape technique. A short, stocky, fast, and powerful wrestler has an advantage with the stand up. A tall wrestler with good leverage and balance may start a stand up and then change to a roll or switch, thus gaining a reversal and control. Generally, accepted strategy is to try to stand up if other techniques are not successful.

Side Roll

From the defensive position and feeling weight on right hand, grip opponent's right

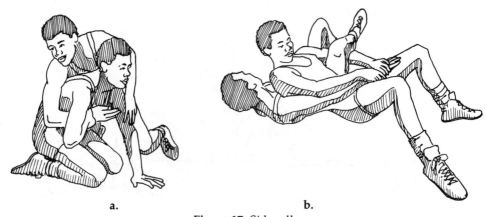

a.

b.

Figure 17. Side roll.

wrist while moving left hand and left knee left toward opponent, move right knee in toward left knee, move right elbow to mat near left hand, drop right hip to mat, and roll across hips. Move left hand inside opponent's right knee and pull knee to your chest while forcing opponent's wrist between legs. Move body perpendicularly to opponent and lift hips to apply weight to opponent's chest. (See Figure 17a and b.)

Switch

Defensive wrestler, feeling pull on the left arm, moves left hand to mat outside right hand, turns to right and raises right knee up as he/she puts right hand on right hip, sits through with left leg, puts right hand with palm up inside opponent's right thigh, grasps opponent's right arm with his/her left hand, and arches back to put weight on opponent's shoulder for breakdown to prone position. Defensive wrestler goes behind opponent for reversal and control. (See Figure 18a and b.)

Crawfish

The crawfish is used to gain control and prevent opponent from going behind. Turn toward opponent, raise knee, and bring arm back and up around opponent's body. (See Figure 19.)

Figure 19. Crawfish.

a.

Figure 18. Switch.

b.

Sit Out

From defensive position shift weight back into opponent while raising outside knee, grip opponent's right wrist with right hand and sit through with left leg to position 180 degrees in front of opponent, lift hips away, drop left shoulder to mat, pull opponent's wrist up toward chest, throw right leg to left toward head, put right hand on mat, and start a crawfish to prevent opponent from going behind. (See Figure 20a, b, and c.)

Stand Up Escape

From defensive position push off mat with hands, look up, grip opponent's right wrist with right hand, bring left elbow into hip, move left foot to mat where right hand was, rotate right knee out, move to standing position with hips low and back arched, step right foot forward to brace, put left hand on opponent's right hand and force opponent's right hand outside of right hip, turn to left, and crawfish with left arm as you step back with left leg pivoting on right foot. (See Figure 21a and b.)

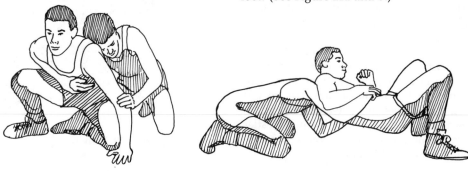

a. First position.   b. Second position.

c. Third position.

Figure 20. Sit out.

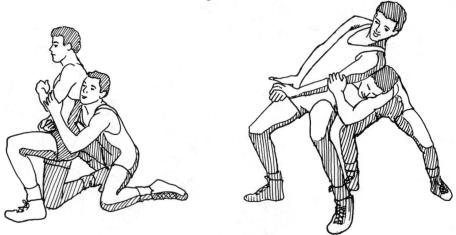

a. First position.   **Figure 21.** Stand up.   b. Second position.

BREAKDOWNS, RIDES, AND PINS

Breakdown techniques result in forcing the defensive wrestler to a prone position or at least a position on his/her side with hips on the mat and in a weak position from which to attempt a reversal or escape. Rides are positions that provide not only good control but also opportunities to score near falls and pins. The ultimate objective is to pin the opponent. The pin in wrestling is comparable to the "knockout" in boxing. Regardless of the score, as long as there are two seconds remaining in a high school match, a pin may occur.

Near Arm Breakdown

Hook left hand around front of opponent's left elbow and pull into opponent's body, force right or back knee forward under opponent's buttocks, pull opponent's body down with right arm. (See Figure 22.)

Far Arm Breakdown

Move left hand behind opponent's left arm and hook his/her right elbow, pull, and drive toward arm. (See Figure 23.)

Near Ankle Breakdown

Move behind opponent, move left hand to opponent's left instep, and lift his/her foot. (See Figure 24.)

Figure 22.
Near arm breakdown.

Figure 23.
Far arm breakdown.

Figure 24.
Near ankle breakdown.

Spiral Breakdown

Move right hand to inside opponent's right thigh close to knee and pry out, move left hand inside his/her left elbow with palm facing down, drive forearm forward, and circle clockwise. (See Figure 25.)

Half Nelson and Front Crotch

Move left hand behind and inside opponent's left arm to the back of head. Pry opponent to his/her side and place right arm between his/her legs with your right hand on the middle of opponent's back. Reach left arm as far around his/her neck as possible and place the hand between your chest and opponent's chest. (See Figure 26.)

Reverse Nelson and Front Crotch

When opponent is on his/her back put right arm under neck and place your hand on top of opponent's shoulder. Put left arm and hand in front crotch position and arch your body.

Wrist Bar and Half Nelson

With opponent broken down, move hands under his/her arms, grip high right

Figure 25. Spiral breakdown.

wrist with right hand, roll it back to chest, move left hand behind head, and pry opponent's head down and arm up. Move to left side, left arm should go all the way around his/her neck (you may grip his/her chin or put palm on own chest), turn opponent to back, extend right leg back with weight on right hip, put left foot on mat above his/her head with left knee under and lifting his/her head, lift head and arch back. (See Figure 27.)

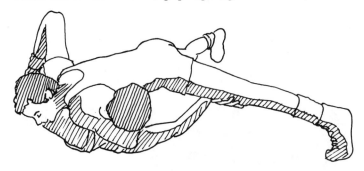

Figure 26.
Half Nelson and crotch.

Figure 27.
Wrist bar and
half Nelson.

Arm Bar and Half Nelson

Break opponent down with a near arm breakdown. Bring right hand up inside his/her right arm and put hand on back. Apply a Half Nelson with left hand, move to left side, place left arm as far round opponent's neck as possible ("sink" the Half Nelson). Circle on knees toward opponent's head to place in pinning position.

Front Cradle

If opponent turns toward you and raises the inside knee, reach over his/her head with your left arm (elbow behind head), reach behind his/her left knee with your right arm and lock hands. Put the top of your head in opponent's side and drive as you bring your arms together. Drive opponent to his/her back and then arch your body. (See Figure 28.)

Back Cradle

When opponent moves right foot to the side and uses leg as a brace, move your chest to his/her right shoulder and put your left arm around his/her neck (elbow at back of opponent's head). Move your right arm around right leg and lock your hands. Move to the right side and roll opponent back placing your left knee against right hip and push away. Put your forehead on opponent's temple and tighten arms.

Three-quarter Nelson

Start in a "Western Hook" ride position (slide right heel under opponent's left ankle to trap foot). Cup left hand on right ear and pull opponent's head down. Move right hand under body with your right shoulder well under opponent's chest and lock hands. Pull his/her head down to get right shoulder on the mat, then move on your knees to the left to get both of opponent's shoulders on the mat.

Crossbody Ride

From the offensive position hook your left leg in front and around opponent's left leg. Your body should be up and across opponent at a 45 degree angle to the front. Force left knee out to the side, keep left hip tight, and arch body with head up. This position provides control of opponent with legs and may set up pinning positions. (See Figure 29.)

Figure 28. Front cradle.

Figure 29. Crossbody ride.

Guillotine

From a crossbody ride position hook left arm inside opponent's right arm and pull it back. Grip right wrist with your right hand and put opponent's arm behind your head. Move left arm back and around opponent's head. Drop left hip to mat and lock hands around head. Place left foot behind right knee for a tight "Figure 4" scissors high on opponent's thigh.

Jacob's Ride

From a crossbody ride position, swing your body to the right to break opponent down to right hip. Reach back with your left arm and hook over his/her right arm. Put your left hand on opponent's back and force your left elbow down to the mat behind ear. Arch your body by lifting your left foot and look away.

Split Scissors

From a crossbody ride position, drive in to opponent to force him/her to sit back and brace with right leg. Lock your hands around his/her right knee and pull it in to your chest. Pull opponent back to a pinning position and put your left foot behind your right knee for a Figure 4 scissors held high on his/her thigh. Turn toward opponent's head.

Turk Ride

Similar to the crossbody ride. The difference is when opponent is on his/her back your body is on the opposite side.

SCRIMMAGE ACTIVITIES ("LIVE" WRESTLING)

1. *"Sharkbait" Takedowns*—Students/wrestlers are put in groups of four or five by weights. When a takeover is scored, the winner meets the next challenger. The most talented wrestler will score takedowns early but as endurance becomes a factor, the fresher challengers will have a better chance to score a takedown on the "sharkbait."
2. *Up-Down-Out*—Three wrestlers in each group by weights. Two wrestlers will start in the referee's starting position, one in the Defensive position and the other in the Offensive position. The third wrestler will be the referee. After each period of 20 or 30 seconds the wrestlers will rotate from Offensive (up) to Defensive (down) to referee (out).
3. *Short periods*—Starting in referee's position, wrestlers in pairs by weights, wrestle 20 seconds, 30 seconds, 45 seconds, or 1 minute periods. Increase the length of the periods as the students become more proficient.

TERMINOLOGY

Arm Bar. A lock on the arm of an opponent obtained by circling his/her arm with yours and holding your hand against his/her body.

Arm Drag. A quick pull on an opponent's arm, usually above the elbow, in an attempt to pull him/her to the mat.

Breakdown. The top wrestler forcing his/her opponent to the mat by taking away his/her supporting points.

Bridge. Elevating the body by use of the neck. Sometimes called a wrestler's bridge.

Crotch Hold. Holding an opponent by the upper leg near the crotch.

Drag. A pulling motion on the upper arm in an attempt to either pull the opponent to the mat or go behind him/her.

Drill. Working on a series of maneuvers.

Escape. An action by which the wrestler on the bottom breaks free of the top wrestler.

Fall. Occurs when a wrestler is held in contact with the mat for an "appreciable time" (two seconds in scholastic wrestling).

Half Nelson. A pinning hold that occurs when one arm is placed under an opponent's armpit and comes out over the top of his/her neck.

Helmet. Protective covering used to protect a wrestler's ears from being rubbed, thus eliminating the "cauliflower ear."

Hold. The technique of grasping an opponent. The grip on an arm or leg which will keep an opponent from moving.

Neutral Position. Both wrestlers are either standing or are locked in the same hold.

Pin. Occurs when both shoulders of a contestant are held to the mat.

Pinning Combination. The technique of securing a "hold" which will result in a pin or fall.

Referee's Position. The down position on the mat, in which the bottom wrestler is on his/her knees with the palms of the hands 12 inches from the knees. The offensive wrestler is on top with one knee up or both knees on the mat and one arm around the opponent's waist and his/her other hand at the bend of the elbow of the opponent.

Reversal. Occurs when the bottom wrestler maneuvers himself/herself to the top position, or the position of advantage.

Ride. An action in which the offensive wrestler effectively counters the moves of the defensive wrestler.

Sit-out. A maneuver in which the defensive wrestler assumes a sitting position to escape or reverse the opponent—the beginning of a chain maneuver.

Takedown. A situation where one wrestler gets the opponent down to the mat and gains control over him/her.

Tie-up. Obtaining a hold or grasping an opponent to work for a takedown.